Changing European Ac

CW00815758

European academics have been at the centre of ongoing higher education reforms, as changes in university governance and funding have led to changes in academic work and life. Discussing the academic profession and, most importantly, its increasing stratification across Europe, *Changing European Academics* explores the drivers of these changes as well as their current and expected results.

This comparative study of social stratification, work patterns and research productivity:

- Examines 11 national, higher education systems across Europe (Austria, Finland, Germany, Ireland, Italy, The Netherlands, Norway, Poland, Portugal, Switzerland and the United Kingdom)
- Provides a panoramic view of the European academic profession
- Confronts misconceptions of academic work and life with compelling results and detailed analyses
- Discusses new dilemmas inherent to the changing social and economic environments of higher education.

A thoughtful and comprehensive study of the changing academic profession in Europe, this book will be of interest to higher education practitioners, managers and policy makers, both in Europe and globally. *Changing European Academics* will benefit anyone whose work relates to changing academic institutions and changing academic careers.

Marek Kwiek is Director of the Center for Public Policy Studies and UNESCO Chair in Institutional Research and Higher Education Policy, University of Poznan, Poland.

The Society for Research into Higher Education (SRHE) is an independent and financially self-supporting international learned Society. It is concerned to advance understanding of higher education, especially through the insights, perspectives and knowledge offered by systematic research and scholarship.

The Society's primary role is to improve the quality of higher education through facilitating knowledge exchange, discourse and publication of research. SRHE members are worldwide and drawn from across all disciplines.

The Society has a wide set of aims and objectives. Amongst its many activities the Society:

• is a specialist publisher of higher education research, journals and books, amongst them Studies in Higher Education, Higher Education Quarterly, Research into Higher Education Abstracts and a long running monograph book series.

The Society also publishes a number of in-house guides and produces a specialist series "Issues in Postgraduate Education".

• funds and supports a large number of special interest networks for researchers and practitioners working in higher education from every discipline. These networks are open to all and offer a range of topical seminars, workshops and other events throughout the year ensuring the Society is in touch with all current research knowledge.

• runs the largest annual UK-based higher education research conference and parallel conference for postgraduate and newer researchers. This is attended by researchers from over 35 countries and showcases current research across every aspect of higher education.

SRHE *Society for Research into Higher Education*
Advancing knowledge Informing policy Enhancing practice

73 Collier Street
London N1 9BE
United Kingdom

T +44 (0)20 7427 2350
F srhe@srhe.ac.uk
  @srhe73

www.srhe.ac.uk

Director: Helen Perkins
Registered Charity No. 313850
Company No. 00868820
Limited by Guarantee
Registered office as above

Society for Research into Higher Education (SRHE) series

Series Editors:
Jennifer M. Case, University of Vermont, USA
Jeroen Huisman, University of Ghent, Belgium

This exciting new series aims to publish cutting edge research and discourse that reflects the rapidly changing world of higher education, examined in a global context. Encompassing topics of wide international relevance, the series includes every aspect of the international higher education research agenda, from strategic policy formulation and impact to pragmatic advice on best practice in the field.

Titles in the series:

Reconstructing Relationships in Higher Education
Celia Whitchurch and George Gordon

Possible Selves and Higher Education
New Interdisciplinary Insights
Edited by Holly Henderson, Jacqueline Stevenson and Ann-Marie Bathmaker

Enhancing the Freedom to Flourish in Higher Education
Participation, Equality and Capabilities
Talita Calitz

Student Plagiarism in Higher Education
Reflections on Teaching Practice
Diane Pecorari and Philip Shaw

Changing European Academics
A Comparative Study of Social Stratification, Work Patterns and Research Productivity
Marek Kwiek

For more information about this series, please visit: https://www.routledge.com/Research-into-Higher-Education/book-series/SRHE

Changing European Academics

A Comparative Study of Social Stratification, Work Patterns and Research Productivity

Marek Kwiek

For Simon,
a fantastic scholar, a generous colleague,
a role model in higher educationa and
a constant point of reference and source
of inspiration! Just unbeatable.
Thank you for everything!

Marek

Poznan, October 5, 2018

Routledge
Taylor & Francis Group
LONDON AND NEW YORK

First published 2019
by Routledge
2 Park Square, Milton Park, Abingdon, Oxon OX14 4RN

and by Routledge
711 Third Avenue, New York, NY 10017

Routledge is an imprint of the Taylor & Francis Group, an informa business

© 2019 Marek Kwiek

The right of Marek Kwiek to be identified as author of this work has been asserted by him in accordance with sections 77 and 78 of the Copyright, Designs and Patents Act 1988.

British Library Cataloguing-in-Publication Data
A catalogue record for this book is available from the British Library

Library of Congress Cataloging-in-Publication Data
A catalogue record has been requested for this book

ISBN: 978-0-8153-9647-5 (hbk)
ISBN: 978-0-8153-9648-2 (pbk)
ISBN: 978-1-351-18204-1 (ebk)

Typeset in Galliard
by codeMantra

MIX
Paper from responsible sources
FSC
www.fsc.org   FSC™ C013985

Printed in the United Kingdom
by Henry Ling Limited

Contents

Series editors' introduction

This series, co-published by the Society for Research into Higher Education and Routledge Books, aims to provide, in an accessible manner, cutting-edge scholarly thinking and inquiry that reflects the rapidly changing world of higher education, examined in a global context.

Encompassing topics of wide international relevance, the series includes every aspect of the international higher education research agenda, from strategic policy formulation and impact to pragmatic advice on best practice in the field. Each book in the series aims to meet at least one of the principal aims of the Society: to advance knowledge; to enhance practice; to inform policy.

Marek Kwiek's book focuses on the academic profession in 11 European higher education systems and deals with different forms of stratification in academic careers. Informed by theoretical insights from the sociology of science, data from the Changing Academic Profession survey are analysed to elucidate the contemporary nature of work in academia. Against the background of asserting that the profession in the Europe is highly stratified, the analyses show important differences between the higher education systems. The book offers significant food for thought for those embarking on an academic career, and also for institutional managers and national policy makers.

Jennifer M. Case
Jeroen Huisman

Introduction

Changing career structures,
award and recognition systems,
and work patterns

Toward a comprehensive cross-national comparative view of European academics

European academics have been at the very center of ongoing higher education reforms across the continent. Changes in university governance and funding, as widely reported (Musselin and Teixeira, 2014; Jongbloed and Lepori 2015; de Boer et al. 2017; Bleiklie, Enders, and Lepori 2017), have inevitably led to changes in academic work and life. Traditional theories of social stratification in science, penetrating as they are, appear to be only partially useful in analyzing the directions of ongoing changes as viewed from a cross-European empirical perspective. New academic realities seem to require a closer look at the micro-level data and, by extension, traditional theories. Today, academics are in the eye of the storm, and this book examines the drivers of the aforementioned changes and their current and expected results.

Only in the last decade has it become possible to study the academic profession—that is, academics' attitudes, behaviors, and perceptions, with the individual academic as a unit of analysis—from a quantitative comparative European perspective. A decade ago, it was difficult, if not impossible, to undertake a comprehensive cross-national examination of ongoing transformations. Most studies were single-nation, and most published research was country-specific, with individual chapters devoted to academics in the context of various aspects of changing university governance and funding.

This book provides a panoramic view of the academic profession—specifically, from the university sector—across Europe in 11 national systems (Austria, Finland, Germany, Ireland, Italy, the Netherlands, Norway, Poland, Portugal, Switzerland, and the United Kingdom). Until recently, gaining such a perspective was possible at only a very general level, and it was based predominantly on aggregated national higher education statistics. In contrast, this book adopts a quantitative approach based on 17,211 returned questionnaires that were distributed across Europe (and the accompanying qualitative background, which is based on 480 semi-structured in-depth interviews).

This book confronts misconceptions about academic work and life and provides compelling results of detailed analyses performed on large-scale primary empirical material. It asks traditional research questions that are rooted in new comparative empirical contexts, as well as entirely new questions that are pertinent to the changing conditions of academic work. It also confronts academics across Europe who are facing new dilemmas that are inherent in the changing social and economic environments of higher education. Academics from major European systems and beyond can view their own academic trajectories within the context of a larger, cross-national story.

Reputation-and-resource model of scientific careers

Research interest in social stratification in academic science was accelerated with Robert K. Merton's claim that science has an ethos and is organized by the four norms of universalism, communism (or communalism), disinterestedness, and organized skepticism. The four norms govern academic behaviors and form a theory of the normative structure of science (Merton 1973; Hermanowicz 2012). Academics follow the norms because 'like other institutions, the institution of science has developed an elaborate system for allocating rewards to those who variously live up to its norms' (Merton 1973: 297). Universalism is contrasted with particularism, which refers to factors such as age, race, gender, religion, and political or sexual orientation, which are said to be functionally irrelevant to institutional operation but are used in the evaluation of people and their work. Discussion of the extent to which science is governed by universalism, as well as by particularism, has been ongoing ever since Merton formulated this basic contrast. The norm of communism holds that knowledge must be shared, not kept secret, and this is where academic knowledge has often been contrasted with industry knowledge (especially before commercialization came to academe, modifying academic behaviors). The norm of disinterestedness holds that the motives and conduct of science should not be influenced by personal bias; neither personal gains nor issues related to prestige or money should be relevant. Finally, the norm of organized skepticism holds that scientific judgments are to be held until all necessary evidence is on hand to make evaluations of scholarship (Hermanowicz 2012: 211).

Merton developed a reputation-and-resource model of scientific careers starting with three premises: Resources in the scientific world are limited, scientific talent is difficult to observe directly, and the allocation of resources in science is governed by the norms of universalism and communism (DiPrete and Eirich 2006). In the process of accumulative advantage, exceptional research performance early in a young scientist's career attracts new resources, as well as rewards that facilitate continued high performance. Scientific resources are not simply rewards for past productivity; they are allocated to stimulate future productivity:

> With limited ability to evaluate the great mass of ongoing scientific work, and with limited ability to measure future productivity beforehand, the

scientific community favours those who have been most successful in the past, given their additional resources and attention.

(DiPrete and Eirich 2006: 281–282)

Three consequences of this mechanism are reported at the individual level: The gap in the rewards between a more able and less able scientist may grow over time; chance events may produce a relative advantage for scientists of identical talent, and this relative advantage may increase over time; and the so-called 'Matthew effect', according to which scientists with greater reputations may gain greater rewards from work of the same quantity and quality than scientists with lesser reputations, may result (DiPrete and Eirich 2006: 281–282).

In his theory of the normative structure of science, Merton pointed out that the institution of science has developed a reward system that is designed to give recognition and esteem to those scientists who have best fulfilled their roles:

On every side the scientist is reminded that it is his role to advance knowledge and his happiest fulfilment of that role, to advance knowledge greatly .... When the institution of science works efficiently ... recognition and esteem accrue to those who have best fulfilled their roles, to those who have made genuinely original contributions to the common stock of knowledge.

(Merton 1973: 293)

'Recognition for originality' in science is a 'socially validated testimony' to successfully fulfilling the requirements of the role of scientist (Merton 1973: 293). Academic rewards constitute academic recognition, which is centrally situated in the occupation of science and the lives and minds of scientists (Hermanowicz 2009: 12). Consequently, what is believed to motivate most scientists is 'the desire for peer recognition' (Cole and Cole 1973: 10).

Prestige, success, status, and recognition in academic science

In the last half century, Merton's institutional norms of science as a major mechanism governing higher education and academic research have been tested from various angles; however, they seem to have become systematically threatened within the last two decades or so.

The major attack on the traditional academic rules of conduct governed by the above overarching academic norms does not seem to be coming directly from outside the university sector: It seems to be coming from the inside, and only indirectly from the outside, powered by what has been termed 'academic capitalism' (Slaughter and Leslie 1997; Slaughter and Rhoades 2004), and specifically from the ever more widespread ideology of commercialism. While the impact of academic capitalism is much more powerful in American higher education, the implications of the growing policy emphasis on universities' 'third mission' across Europe should not be underestimated. In an American context, David R. Johnson (2017) explores qualitatively the 'conflict in academic science' between traditionalists and commercialists, and what emerges from this is a fractured profession that operates according to two contrasting academic ideologies: the traditional academic ideology, which reflects the Mertonian institutional norms of science, and the new ideology of commercialism. The focus of this book, which is driven by European data and their interpretation within the European context, will be on the former.

Knowledge produced in universities is increasingly converted into products or services that can be sold; this dramatically changes the nature of work in academic science and the social organization of higher education wherever the process is discernible. In the American case, this is at the elite research universities. As Johnson explains, American academic scientists are now exposed to two main reward systems, which are characterized by two different conceptions of the academic role and its corresponding occupational norms:

> Scholars once conceived of the scientific reward system as singular, referring to the *traditionalist*, or priority-recognition reward system, which mandates that scientists advance knowledge by sharing their discoveries with their scientific community through peer evaluation in exchange for recognition of priority in discovery. This honorary system of rewards now exists along-side a new *commercialist* reward system, which gives scientists a mandate to contribute to economic development through the dissemination of their discoveries in the market in exchange for profits. These are not simply different approaches to scientific work. They are career paths tied to competing visions of the role of the university in society that raise questions with broad implications.
>
> (Johnson 2017: 2, emphasis in the original)

Consequently, in the American elite university sector, the traditional role of universities exists alongside a new institutional role of science that emphasizes the creation of technologies that can be sold. Commercialism, which is defined by Johnson (2017) as a professional ideology that asserts that scientists should create technologies that control societal uncertainties, functions as a second competing reward system, and in academe, such systems 'engender intraprofessional conflict' (Johnson 2017: 3). What academics are supposed to do becomes increasingly unclear, especially as unequal rewards, as well as unequal conditions of work that are accompanied by the devaluing of commitment to traditional goals of science and higher education in the form of basic research, emerge in the system. In the specific American context, a new tension appears in the academic profession, which, in turn, becomes fractured.

However, in the specific European context that is studied in this book, the phenomenon of academic research commercialization is not equally widespread, although its importance as one of the items on the European Union's major policy agenda has been increasing systematically. Parallel processes affecting reward systems in European science can be explored in the context of the emergence of 'third stream' or 'third mission' activities. The commercialist–traditionalist divide explored in the case of the United States does not yet emerge as critically important to European universities. Although 'academic capitalism' has been studied in reference to a number of European systems, following the pioneering work of Sheila Slaughter, Larry L. Leslie, and Gary Rhoades, neither financial implications for individuals and institutions nor for the dominant academic norms (specifically, Merton's 'normative structure of science') seem to be as powerful in European as in North American universities (Cantwell 2016; Cantwell and Kauppinnen 2014).

Academic norms are of critical importance because they provide stability to the functioning of the academic profession. Academic norms demonstrate how academics should behave; they reflect common beliefs about how higher education systems and academic science systems should operate. However, in vertically stratified systems, they seem to be far more applicable to the upper and elite research-focused segments of national higher education systems than to the lower teaching-focused segments. While system segmentation grows, the appeal of the normative structure of science diminishes to the system as a whole. One of the consequences of this systemic segmentation and normative differentiation in this book is that we are focused entirely on the European *university* sector in terms of both theoretical underpinning and empirical data. Traditionally, common academic beliefs converge with common public beliefs to enable the institution of science to benefit from the power of public support, including the power of public subsidization. Finally, professional academic ideologies are formed by academic norms and are promoted in society, providing widely shared visions of how research universities should function. Moreover, professional academic ideologies define which academic roles are most highly valued and which are less valued or not valued at all, and they define success and professional status in science at the levels of individuals, institutions, and national systems.

Based on a traditional account of academic careers, research achievements mattered most, with all other achievements (in teaching, service, or administration) lagging far behind. The academic men and women are represented by their publications, as the traditional story goes:

> In a community of scholars, scholarly performance is the only legitimate claim to recognition ... the academic marketplace as a system rests on the assumption that the worth of the academic man can be measured by the quality of his published work.
>
> (Caplow and McGee 1958: 225)

In the specific European context explored in this book, publications are still key regardless of how much the so-called 'third mission activities' are being promoted internally and externally by the academic community and policy makers alike. Assessment of the research output of individual academics and their departments and institutions—compared with the research output of other individual academics in the same specialty, as well as their departments and institutions—is at the core of individual academic recognition and international university rankings (research-based being more informative and less subjective than reputation-based). As emphasized in the sociology of science, 'The working of a reward system in science testifies that the research role is the most highly valued. The heroes of science are acclaimed in their capacity as scientific investigators, seldom as teachers, administrators or referees and editors' (Merton 1973: 520). In other words, 'Contribution to scientific knowledge is the underpinning of the stratification system' (Cole and Cole 1973: 45). The various types of stratification discussed in this book will refer predominantly to research: the inequality in its production (Chapter 1), its links to high academic incomes (Chapter 2), its links to academic roles played within institutions (Chapter 3), its relationships with international collaboration (Chapter 4), the role of patterns of time investments in it and the role of patterns of orientation to it across academic generations (Chapter 5), and its role in enabling academics to climb up the academic ladder (Chapter 6). Research is the core issue in academic careers from the perspective of social stratification in academic science, and it is, therefore, the core of this book. For this particular reason, teaching and students are discussed only marginally.

In academic science, in a specific form of publications, prestige, success, status, and recognition are inseparable from research. Non-publishers or silent scientists do not traditionally belong to the academic community, even though they do work across European universities (see Chapter 5). No publications basically means no research, which, in turn, means no academic success and no academic recognition. Moreover, in the specific context of the increasing role of competitive research funding in most European systems, it also means no research funding. The existence of lower-ranked and, therefore, only indirectly competing reward systems in teaching, service, and administration may be explained as an institutional mechanism that allows higher education organizations to accommodate failures in the core mission of research. Recognition in research was traditionally found to maintain 'high motivation to advance knowledge, and high motivation resulted in the scientist's devoting more of his own time to research; this, in turn, resulted in the high-quality scientific performance, as judged by the researcher's closest professional colleagues' (Glaser 1964: 1012).

There are certainly 'comparative failures in science' (Glaser 1964) and, certainly, some scientists realize early in their careers that they will not be successful in achieving national or international recognition: They are prone to adopt their local colleagues as reference groups and to drop the national or international scientific elite as meaningful reference groups, spending their time teaching and doing administrative work instead. Put bluntly, 'Local prestige probably goes a long way to make up for failure to achieve national recognition' (Cole and Cole 1973: 260–261). In the context of this book, 'internationalists' in research differ sharply from 'locals' in research both in terms of reference groups for their research and their collaborators in research, with far-reaching consequences for access to prestige, status, and resources for further research, as shown in Chapter 4.

Thus, in the tradition of the sociology of science, recognition comes from scientific output rather than anything else inside or outside the science system (Cole and Cole 1967; Hermanowicz 2012; Johnson 2017). The reward system is designed to give recognition and esteem to the scientists who have best fulfilled their research roles with the use of an elaborate system for allocating rewards. Consequently, the reward system reinforces research activities, rather than any other academic activities, and few scientists are believed to continue to engage in research if they are not rewarded for it (Cole and Cole 1967). Consequently, in this traditional account, academics publish their work in exchange for scientific recognition. As Warren O. Hagstrom (1965: 168) stated in his theory of social control in science, and before the massive advent of lower-ranking journals, 'Recognition is given for information, and the scientist who contributes much information to his colleagues is rewarded by them with high prestige.' In this sense, only high-performance research leads to recognition in science, and reward systems function to identify research excellence:

> A substantial part of the efficient operation of science depends upon the way in which it allocates positions to individuals, divides up the rewards and prizes it offers for outstanding performance, and structures opportunities for those who hold the extraordinary talent .... In science, as in most other institutions, prestigious position, honorific awards, and peer recognition, as well as monetary rewards, combine to form an integrated reward structure. The pattern of stratification in science is determined in large measure by the way rewards are distributed among scientists and by the social mechanisms through which the reward system of science operates to identify excellence.
>
> (Cole and Cole 1973: 15)

The accumulative advantage hypothesis generalizes the 'Matthew effect' to include productivity and recognition: The process consists of two feedback loops in which recognition and resources are intervening variables (Allison and Stewart 1974). However, there is also the darker side of the accumulation of rewards: It is 'the accumulation of failures—the process of "accumulative disadvantage"' (Cole and Cole 1973: 146), leading to the stratification in science between the 'haves' and 'have-nots.' As scientific productivity is heavily influenced by the recognition of early work, the skewed distribution of productivity and the skewed distribution of subsequent rewards result not only in the rich getting richer but also in the poor getting (comparatively) poorer. The 'relative Matthew effect' occurs when both the rich and the poor get richer, 'but the rich get richer by a larger margin, creating a widening gap between themselves and the poor' (Rigney 2010: 8). In summary, the scientific community 'favors those who have been most successful in the past' (DiPrete and Eirich 2006: 282). Prestige in science is, in a way, a system of social control that celebrates 'heroes.' As William J. Goode argues in wider social rather than strictly academic contexts,

> To perform and be ranked at the highest levels ... demands both talent and dedication which only a few can muster. Such 'heroes' are given more prestige or admiration because both the level and type of performance are rare and evaluated highly within the relevant group. Most admirers recognize that such performances are possible for only a few people. The supply is and remains low.
>
> (Goode 1978: 67)

Science is highly stratified, the academic profession is highly stratified, and, like other professions, the latter is heavily status-based. While the intense research-related stratification of the academic profession—the major theme of this book—is not easily seen from the outside, it is enormously powerful inside. Science is dominated by 'a small, talented elite [and] [a]ll major forms of recognition—awards, prestigious appointments, and visibility—are monopolised by a small proportion of scientists' (Cole and Cole 1973: 254). The majority of scientists contribute little to scientific advancement, are low or very moderate publishers, and are still necessary to keep national higher education and science systems going, as we shall discuss in detail in Chapter 1. Prestige allocation in science makes some academics work much harder and some only moderately harder, while, on some, it exerts no pressure at all: The pressure or control through prestige allocation is 'fundamental in understanding why some people will try harder or not' (Goode 1978: 81). Certainly, this traditional elitist, exclusive, and hierarchical function of research in universities—differentiating and rank-ordering the academic profession (Marginson 2014)—has been strengthened in the era of new public management, as Marginson suggests, and it is merely one of six social functions of research, among which the balances and relations are constantly changing. However, as he argues, it has deep roots in academic cultures in elite research universities:

> The one unambiguous driver of career advancement in research universities is success at the highest level of research. 'Highest' means both the most prestigious and the most competitive level of performance, as in research grants, and academic publishing status is assigned on the basis of ranked performance .... A persistent pattern in intellectual fields is that a small number of people made a high proportion of the recognized major contributions.
>
> (Marginson 2014: 107)

In a sense, this book is about who gets what, why, and how in science—it is about its inherent inequality. Social stratification in science is not viewed as 'the patterning of inequality and its enduring consequences on the lives of those who experience it' (as is social stratification in general in sociological studies) and this book is not about 'how inequalities persist and endure—over lifetimes and between generations' (Bottero 2005). Stratification processes studied here are confined to the social institution of science; science being 'a communal social enterprise' (Cole and Cole 1973: 14).

Intraprofessional and extraprofessional status

Individual status within the academic community has traditionally been defined by original contributions to fundamental research. In the theory of professions (Abbott 1981; Abbott 1988; Carvalho 2017), which is useful for conceptualizing the organization and stratification of the academic profession, the most highly valued pursuits are 'professionally pure' pursuits—that is, those without nonprofessional considerations. Abbott (1981) draws a very useful distinction between the intraprofessional and extraprofessional status of professions, which explains the internal functioning of status conferment in European universities to outsiders. Intraprofessional status is a function of 'professional purity,' which is 'the ability to exclude nonprofessional issues or irrelevant professional issues from practice. Within a given profession, the highest status professionals are those who deal with issues predigested and predefined by a number of colleagues' (Abbott 1981: 823).

Over time, the academic profession, like all other professions, has developed an internal system of relative judgments of the purity or impurity of academic activities, with the resultant status hierarchy governing academic science. According to this hierarchy, purer considerations in science are more highly valued than less pure considerations; extraprofessional status (gained through nonprofessional channels of knowledge distribution) is less important in the academic world than intraprofessional status, which is traditionally gained through the visibility of research publications in the area of fundamental research. In the same vein, curiosity-driven research is more highly valued than application-driven research because, in the theoretical context of professional purity and impurity, leading to intraprofessional stratification in science, it is more professionally pure. Based on this account, visible science is transmitted through highly valued professional channels, such as top academic journals; much less visible science is transmitted through other channels (such as nonacademic journals, television, and social media). Most importantly, with the exception of humanities, parts of social science, and professional disciplines, scientific research is published primarily in English. As Marginson (2016c: 19) points out in his study of global stratification in higher education, 'Academic publications form a single world library. English-language science is the single global conversation: the claims of French, German and Russian have faded.'

In Merton's account of science and scientists and Abbott's account of professions and professionals, academic recognition comes exclusively from a single set of intraprofessional activities—that is, research activities converted into publications (as well as from their impact on the scientific community or from citations). All academic generations are being socialized to this widely accepted set of academic norms, and any deviance from this is being punished by the academic community.

Academic scientists need clear professional identities: They need to know how they should function to be among the top layers of the academic enterprise, should they choose to want this. In terms of their own academic careers, they need to know what is important, what is not important, and especially why this is the case. They also need to have clear images of a successful scientist and successful science, both in general terms and within their specific national contexts. The career stages of successful scientists need to be clearly defined in advance in terms of research achievements if the academic science enterprise is to continue successfully (see 'the Anna Karenina Principle' which links success to journal space, funds, reception and recognition in Bornmann and Marx 2012). Regarding promotion in the university sector, and especially within its upper layers, what matters and what does not matter need to be clearly stated, and this is exactly where ideologies of academic work and academic careers become useful. Stable professions tend to have clear definitions of high and low status and clear images of success and failure; therefore, they are not troubled by unnecessary tensions, feelings of undeserved inequality, or undue deprivation of access to opportunities, rewards, and resources. Status hierarchies in stable professions need to change slowly over time, if at all, especially as, in some of them, including the academic profession, careers are long term and clear guidance on how to function is needed throughout their lives. Intraprofessional conflicts about well-defined status and success do not serve the long-term goals of science. As Abbott stated, there is tension between what the public expects from professions and what professions expect from themselves:

> Intraprofessional status rests on the exclusion of nonprofessional issues or of professional issues irrelevant in a particular case …. In the pursuit of intraprofessional status, professions and professionals tend to withdraw from precisely those problems for which the public gives them status.
>
> (Abbott 1981: 819)

The changing stratification in science in the current massified higher education systems is related to the diversified external public and internal institutional expectations from the diversified academic profession. While (Abbott's) intraprofessional status rests on prestigious research results, prestigious research is increasingly publicly funded and is increasingly expected to be performed (by the public and by the university administration) only in the upper, elite layers of national systems. Consequently, the traditional rules of individual and institutional competition, academic recognition, and professional status seem to be ever more applicable to the upper university subsectors of national systems only. As evidenced by the European trend of strengthening national research councils as major bodies allocating research funding (with the European Research Council as a transnational manifestation of this trend)—with regard to academics and institutions, the minority garner the majority of competitive research funding.

The pertinence of academic profession studies

The academic profession across Europe is being exposed to similar external pressures despite national variations. The major global forces responsible for the actual changes in academic work and life, as well as those that prevail in international discourses, especially policy discourses on academic work and life, are as follows: economic globalization and its European responses (Europeanization), changing social and economic priorities in emergent generationally divided societies, intergenerational conflicts over the use of scarce public resources, changes in public services along the lines suggested in new public management, the increasing economic relevance of two major products of higher education systems: graduates and academic knowledge, and the transnationalization and internationalization of higher education policies combined with global policy convergence, especially through policies promoted by supranational institutions and organizations.

Simultaneously, the massification of higher education also means the massification of the academic profession, resulting in ongoing global struggles on the part of academics to maintain their traditionally stable (upper) middle-class social and economic status. Globally, huge numbers of students in national systems are accompanied by huge numbers of academics. As massification progresses, stratification follows. At the same time, as massification progresses, higher education research becomes a more attractive field that is gaining increasing scholarly and policy attention and mobilizing research funds (see Jung, Horta, and Yonezawa 2018; Kwiek 2013b). Massified and increasingly stratified higher education systems lead to a massified and increasingly stratified academic profession along dimensions such as institutional location within the system, access to human and material resources, productivity, and connections to global science networks. As Jürgen Enders noted,

> Privileges that were characteristic for members of the academic profession in an elite higher education system came increasingly under pressure in a massified and more diversifying system ... 'the gold standards' that were once characteristic for the few are not to be taken for granted for the many.
>
> (Enders 2006: 7)

Thus, the zero-sum logic of positional competition among universities derived from the high-participation system theory, which argues that there is little room at the top (Marginson 2016c), can be extended to include the level of individual scientists. Stratification guarantees competition and an endless struggle to move up the academic hierarchy at both the institutional and individual levels.

From a global perspective, higher education 'is no longer an elite enterprise, and this new reality has had dramatic implications for the academic profession' (Altbach et al. 2012: 4). However, new large-scale developments in university governance and funding lead to new challenges and require traditional stratification theories to be revisited. Tensions emerge between the traditional theories governing the social and academic imaginations and the reality on the ground, especially if examined through cross-national, large-scale empirical material.

To some extent, there is an element of 'business as usual' in the academic game; however, in many ways, European academics are facing harsh new realities that are not consistently understood across European systems. In some of these systems, changes are believed to be related to globalization; in others, to financial austerity or new public management; and, finally, in others, to the massification of higher education (Enders, de Boer, and Leišyté 2009; Enders and de Weert 2009a; Carvalho and Santiago 2015; Antonowicz 2016; Nixon 2017; Kwiek 2017c). New academic behaviors (how academics actually work) and new academic attitudes (what academics actually think about their work), combined with emergent teaching/research patterns across academic cohorts and emergent productivity patterns across genders and academic disciplines both intra-nationally and cross-nationally, call into question the traditional theories produced in (Martin Trow's) 'elite' systems. The academic profession is working in emergent 'high-participation systems' (Marginson 2016b; Cantwell, Marginson, and Smolentseva 2018; Cantwell, Pinheiro, and Kwiek 2018) across all European countries, including the 11 studied here.

This book attempts to show which elements of the theoretical tradition of higher education research may hold and which may need to be conceptually revisited. For instance, the book's findings clearly indicate that the performance stratification of the academic profession not only continues but also seems to intensify. Originally, the idea was formulated with reference to individual academics as follows:

> The scientific community is not the company of equals. It is sharply stratified; a small number of scientists contribute disproportionately to the advancement of science and receive a disproportionately large share of rewards and the resources needed for research.
>
> (Zuckerman 1988: 526)

For academics, the recognition of their work by the collectivity of competent peers is 'the only unambiguous demonstration that what they have done matters to science' (Zuckerman 1988: 526). In addition, as previously noted, recognition in science is converted into resources for further research. Highly recognized scientists (and their research institutions) are clearly more successful than less recognized scientists (and their less recognized research institutions) in obtaining resources for further research. The distribution of academic rewards, including research funding, is sharply graded. There is enormous inequality in research performance, accompanied by enormous inequality in recognition and rewards in science, and both are highly stratified. Both academics and institutions are also stratified, and the processes of stratification seem to have intensified rather than weakened in the last two decades.

Prime significance is given to symbolic recognition by colleagues rather than by any outside individual or collective body. Members of the scientific community are considered the only competent judges of the merits and significance of one's research. This is part of the socialization of young scientists into the academic profession: 'Differentials in recognition are not only fundamental to differential ranking in science but also provide the base from which scientists may acquire new facilities either in the form of resources for research or in increased influence' (Zuckerman 1970: 236). The viability of modern science depends on the existence of a substantial consensus on the quality of scientific work and the occupational status of academics, who are its producers; therefore, evaluations are constantly made. The current evaluations of academics that are conducted within their institutions and by funding bodies, as well as the evaluations of institutions in rankings (including their international rankings), are merely more sophisticated and data-driven, with growing importance given to bibliometrics and research assessment exercises in various forms for resource allocation (see Kulczycki, Korzeń, and Korytkowski 2017 on Poland). However, these are not new institutionally nor individually. The picture that is half a century old does not seem to differ much from the one presented in Chapter 1 on the inequality in academic knowledge production and the role of top research performers:

> Stratification and ranking are not, however, limited to individual investigators. Disciplines, publication in particular journals, types of research, organisations, and rewards are also ranked. Individual scientists can be located in each of these dimensions and their final rank is the sum or product of these evaluations of their research.
>
> (Zuckerman 1970: 237)

However, research—and even more so, publicly funded research—cannot be conducted across whole national systems, in all of their segments, and with equal intensity. Vertical differentiation, which expects different contributions to knowledge from academics representing diverse segments of the system, with upward mobility guaranteed, may be the only way to protect the academic profession from widespread dissatisfaction if not despair:

> Increased emphases on research will likely be accompanied by increased probabilities of dissatisfaction throughout the system of higher education. As research is more greatly stressed, by institutions as well as by individuals, career expectations rise, in accord with attempting to satisfy external reference groups that are consistent with fulfilling the institutional goals of academe. As expectations rise, the likelihood of satisfying them decreases.
>
> (Hermanowicz 2012: 238)

The attractiveness of academic careers is questioned for a number of interrelated reasons, and the stakes involved in the ongoing changes, including the overall functioning of the academic profession, are high. As discussed in the American context, which is applicable to the European one,

> On many objective criteria, chances of success in academia across many fields are low and, where won, are hard-fought: obtaining regular employment, obtaining tenure, obtaining promotion through standard ranks, publication, citation of work, competitive salary, and competitive salary growth. These basic rewards are also arguably more difficult to obtain across institutional types than in any other historical time in the profession.
>
> (Hermanowicz 2012: 238)

Inequality in academic knowledge production is combined with inequality in academic remuneration. New teaching-only or teaching-mostly segments of the academic profession emerge (in our sample, this is especially the case in the United Kingdom) with new tasks and new responsibilities, thereby contributing to the disintegration of traditional (research-focused) academic norms. There are new 'haves' and 'have-nots' in academia due to the growing role of competitive, project-based research funding distributed by new national research councils and other bodies with a similar function. Institutional governance structures change, and there is a growing cross-generational gap between younger and older academic cohorts: Increasingly, academic job portfolios differ cross-generationally, contributing to the redefinition of what academics do based on their age groups (see Chapter 5). The internationalization of research and international academic mobility change the traditional national prestige structures and exert a powerful influence on national research funding distribution.

A data-rich research context

Despite continuity at the level of ideas governing higher education research—the social stratification in science being a prime example—there has been a rupture in a single dimension: that of the available data, including self-produced primary data collected through international surveys. International comparative higher education has entered a 'data-rich' research context. Four decades ago, Paul L. Dressel and Lewis B. Mayhew analyzed the emergence of the academic profession and of higher education as a specific 'field of study,' and they complained that, with a few exceptions, 'The literature is virtually silent about how faculty members enter the profession, what kinds of people they are, how they proceed in their careers and how they succeed in their professional tasks' (Dressel and Mayhew 1974: 89). Similarly, three decades ago, Burton R. Clark opened his exploration of 'The Academic Life' by stressing that

> relatively little is known about what goes on in the profession's many quarters. What is the quality of the workaday life for its varied members? How do they conceive of themselves and their lives? What, if anything, holds them together?
>
> (Clark 1987a: xxi)

Since the 1990s, both from single-nation perspectives (especially regarding the American one, see quantitatively informed studies by Blackburn and Lawrence 1995; Finkelstein, Seal, and Schuster 1998; and Schuster and Finkelstein 2008) and from a global perspective (Boyer, Altbach, and Whitelaw 1994; Altbach and Lewis 1996; Forest 2002), numerous studies have been published. In contrast, it is only in the last few years that European comparative academic profession studies have, for the first time, become truly 'data-rich,' following collaborative research efforts in the global 'Changing Academic Profession' (CAP) and the European 'Academic Profession in Europe: Responses to Societal Challenges' (EUROAC) research projects. In the last few years, both projects have given rise to a long list of studies.[1] Both also used the same survey questionnaire, based on the 1991–1993 Carnegie Foundation global survey of the academic profession, which provided a benchmark for comparative studies (Altbach and Lewis 1996: xxii). Consequently, in this book, we follow the 'gold standard' in social sciences (and in higher education studies): The research presented here is based on primary data. In the 2000s, there were at least three global and European (see Altbach 2000; Altbach 2003; Enders 2000; Enders and de Weert 2004) large-scale comparative projects on the changing academic profession and changing academic workplace that were relevant to this book. However, none of the three projects was driven by systematically collected primary quantitative data; therefore, they should be categorized as exploratory studies with some inconsistent or problematic data sources.

Academics' work situations change substantially, and this change is central to the academic profession as a whole, as prior analyses underscore. Enders and de Weert (2009b: 252–253) identified five 'drivers' that were central to changing the nature of the academic profession: the massification of higher education, expansion of research, growing emphasis on the societal relevance of higher education and research, processes of globalization and internationalization, and policies and practices geared toward marketization and managerialism. Similarly, Kogan and Teichler (2007: 10–11) identified three recent trends that were pervasive in higher education: relevance, internationalization, and management. Some other analyses refer specifically to financial constraints, the differentiation of higher education systems, competitive forces, and, moreover, the growing uncertainty of the academic profession: 'We live in times of uncertainty about the future development of higher education and its place in society and it is therefore not surprising to note that the future of the academic profession seems uncertain, too' (Enders and Musselin 2008: 145).

This book discusses a long list of uncertainties related to academic work and life, comparing academics' attitudes, behaviors, and productivity across countries, clusters of academic disciplines, age cohorts, and genders. It is structured around the notion of social stratification in science. It explores various manifestations of stratification in the academic profession across Europe and seeks to understand the extent to which ongoing governance and funding changes are consequential with respect to the work and life of academics.

Several approaches to social stratification in science are used, depending on the context, with research as the core university-sector activity figuring prominently in all of them: The idea of *academic performance stratification* is used in Chapter 1 (discussing research performance differentials across Europe, with specifically defined top research performers contrasted with their lower-performing colleagues); the idea of *academic salary stratification* is used in Chapter 2 (discussing links between income differentials and research performance differentials across Europe, with specifically defined academic top earners contrasted with their lower-earning colleagues); the idea of *academic power stratification* is used in Chapter 3 (analyzing the extent to which European systems are still collegial and the role of academic power distribution across layers of academic positions in European systems); the idea of *international research stratification* is used in Chapter 4 (exploring the links between research productivity differentials and international collaboration differentials, with clearly defined 'internationalists' in research contrasted with 'locals' in research, as well as the role of research internationalization in national award systems and resources distribution in science across Europe); the idea of *academic role stratification* is used in Chapter 5 (exploring intergenerational patterns of academic behaviors, attitudes, and productivity, with 'academics under 40' or 'young academics' contrasted with their older colleagues and with 'academic generations' in academic knowledge production at the forefront); and, finally, the idea of *academic cohort (or age) stratification* is used in Chapter 6 (analyzing changing academic careers with the use of qualitative rather than quantitative material, unique in this book, with a special emphasis on young cohorts of academics seeking stability in academic employment in volatile institutional environments).

The notion of social stratification in science allows for a better understanding of the changing academic profession than a number of competing notions used in the research literature, such as globalization, managerialism, financial austerity, or commodification. This is because the notion of social stratification refers directly to academics and their work and lives. In contrast to the four notions outlined above, our guiding notion in this book is internal rather than external to the academic profession. The issues of persistent inequality in research achievements and in academic knowledge production, the systematic inequality in academic incomes and their (disappearing) link to research productivity, the decreasing role of collegiality in university governance for all, not only the lower layers of academics but, the increasing correlation between internationalization in research and productivity (together with the increasing role of international publications in national reward systems, including access to competitive research funding), and the unexplored role of academic generations—and especially of different types of young academics employed in different countries—go to the very heart of the academic profession. And the above dimensions can be rigorously measured and compared cross-nationally with a unique data set.

Some themes in this book have previously been mentioned in higher education research (in a combination of theoretical and empirical contexts). 'Top research performers,' 'internationalists,' and 'academics under 40' have been studied under different rubrics; however, 'academic top earners' has not been present in the research literature, and none of these prototypical figures in higher education have been studied from a comparative quantitative European perspective using large-scale empirical material. The four faculty categories investigated above, as well as predictors of membership of these categories, have not been studied in cross-national comparative detail thus far. This book links new themes to existing themes and to the extant research literature.

Rare scholarly themes are examined in this book using rare prototypical figures, and our intention is to embed them in a larger scholarly conversation about higher education research (including traditional accounts of the academic profession over the last half century) between the previous generations of scholars. The themes studied indicate new differentiations of the academic profession (with a strong dividing line between the 'haves' and 'have-nots' in terms of publication-derived prestige and research-related resources) along under-researched dimensions from a European cross-national comparative perspective: internationalization in research, academic cohorts, academic incomes, and/or academic teaching/research role orientations. The book's findings have implications for theories of academic productivity, theories of university organization, traditional models of university governance, the economics of science, and policy reform theories.

Higher education research tends to view European academics (and European universities more generally) through the theoretical lenses provided by Anglo–Saxon, predominantly American, ideas about what universities are for and what academics should do; these ideas have been developed over the last half century, including by Logan Wilson, Paul Goodman, John D. Millett, Harold Perkin, Paul Lazarsfeld, Wagner Thielens, Clark Kerr, Martin Trow, Burton R. Clark, and Philip G. Altbach. The type of social imagination and academic imagination applied to universities as institutions and the academic profession as a 'key profession' (Perkin 1969) seems not to have changed much. However, in the meantime, academic realities in Europe have been changing. Consequently, there have been interesting tensions between some traditional ideas in higher education research and some academic realities emerging from the data (as Chapter 2 on high academic incomes indicates).

Transformations of European higher education systems in the last two decades have been substantial and have had a significant impact on the academic profession. The growing complexity of the academic enterprise has led to growing uncertainty about its future. Higher education as a whole has already changed substantially in most European economies, but it is expected to change even more (de Boer et al. 2017; Hüther and Krücken 2018). Perhaps the least susceptible to fundamental changes in the next decade will be the traditional research university, with its taste for research, as it is viewed as crucial for the economic prosperity of regions and nations. All other subsectors of national systems are more susceptible to further changes, heavily affecting the academic profession.

As a recent study of 11 reform processes across Europe emphasizes,

> in higher education, we live in an age of reform. All over Europe, state au-
> thorities frequently adapt their policies and introduce new ones to encour-
> age public higher education institutions to deliver high-quality services in
> an effective and effiocient way. They take forceful initiatives and introduce
> reforms to change the higher education landscape.
>
> (de Boer et al. 2017: 1)

However, governance and funding reforms in Europe have had different tim-
ing, implementation results, and intensities in different systems (Paradeise et al.
2009; Maassen and Olsen 2007), as shown in empirical details through the
governance equalizer model, which captured and graphically presented changes
in governance in England, the Netherlands, Austria, and Germany between
1980 and 2006 (de Boer, Enders, and Schimank 2007) and in the 16 Germany
states in the 2000s (Hüther and Krücken 2018: 119–122). Even though national processes of reform implementation shared rationales and tools—with the
New Public Management (NPM) ideas in the forefront (Musselin and Teixeira
2014; Bleiklie et al. 2017)—reforms remain 'path dependent and most often
incremental' and European higher education systems are reported to 'remain far
from converging toward a unified pattern that would progressively erase borders'
(Paradeise, Reale, and Goastellec 2009: 197, 198). Domestic institutional contexts matter and historical institutions have a 'filtering effect' on international
reform pressures (Dobbins and Knill 2014: 188–189).

Reforms of funding systems were inspired by the NPM doctrine and driven
by the assumption that introducing competition and performance-based funding would increase the performance of systems and institutions; however, every
country uses in practice a combination of different funding options 'having
its own mix, reflecting historical and political developments' (Jongbloed and
Lepori 2015: 443). Funding arrangements are reported to be undergoing 'dramatic changes' (Gläser and Velarde 2018: 1), with the increasing role of project-
based research funding and performance-based funding (Gläser and Laudel
2016). Across Europe, a convergence toward a funding mode is reported:
'about three quarters of the budget is provided by the state as core funds, which
is complemented by third-party funds and student fees' (Jongbloed and Lepori
2015: 449). While the intended scope of governance and funding reforms differs across Europe, as do real effects of implemented reforms, academics are
exposed to permanent reform attempts. The reforms increasingly compel them
to function in the state of permanent adaptation to changing realities (Krücken,
Kosmützky, and Torka 2007). Academics are exposed to both actual reform
implementation and reform debates with their peers and with policymakers,
being reminded by organization studies that reforming universities leads to
further waves of reforms as 'reforms generate reforms' (Brunsson and Olsen
1998: 42–44).

The academic profession has already been fractured into many different academic professions (in the plural), and it is expected to be even more diversified, especially in more vertically stratified systems, with clearly defined top and bottom system layers (see Kwiek 2018a). The increasingly heterogeneous nature of the profession results from

> transformations in employment and working conditions; in their engagement with different activities; in the increased diversification of academic roles; in their different involvement in internationalization processes; and in their participation in decision-making.
>
> (Carvalho 2017: 72–73)

Different directions of academic restructuring in different countries and within particular national systems add to the complexity of the picture, which certainly leads to an overall more stressful working environment. Academics, the core of the academic enterprise, are working in turbulent times. In the last two decades, universities and other higher education institutions, as well as their social and economic environments, have been changing faster than ever before. Today, the academic profession is in the eye of the storm globally, and this book goes beyond change processes in any single European country. It discusses the academic profession and its increasing stratification across Europe, assuming that a theoretically coherent and empirically driven overview of ongoing changes is needed for academics and the general public alike. Examining the national variations of ongoing change through a study of empirical material at the micro level of the individual academic (rather than at institutional or national levels, with their corresponding aggregated data) leads to a better understanding of current realities. Moreover, understanding change is of primal importance to the future shape of the academic profession. Change cannot be effectively opposed nor promoted without such a clear understanding of its drivers and their results.

Not only higher education in Europe (with gross enrollment rates often exceeding 50 percent) but also the academic profession itself are becoming massified, with unclear consequences for individual academics. The end result of this double-massification process is its ever more detailed public scrutiny and ever more sophisticated policy interest. Higher education in general and, by extension, the academic profession are in the public spotlight. Academics are at the core of a multibillion-euro enterprise, but they are also the single most important cost in almost all academic institutions. Therefore, changing realities in which academics function need to be analyzed and understood to enable academics to see more clearly the somehow unexpected context of the large-scale, long-term systemic transformations to which they have been exposed. The general assumption of this book is that the changes directly affecting the life and work of academics will intensify, thereby undermining most principles of traditional academic visions and ideologies or undermining them in most segments of national systems. The drivers of change in higher education across Europe are structurally similar. Before we (the academic profession) decide where we would collectively prefer to be, it would be useful to examine where we are and to see whether and how this goal can be achieved.

Finally, the changes in academic work today are intensive, but, for the first time, they can be assessed in much more detail through large-scale European quantitative research, which adds a refined empirical dimension to the growing research literature on the academic profession. There are ongoing changes in academic work, as well as attempts to measure them and draw valid conclusions from the available empirical material. However, it is also possible that the sheer scale and speed of the changes make it difficult for the community of higher education researchers to interpret them. The inevitable time gaps between data collection and analysis, interpretation, and publication may be more crippling in times of change, as today, than in times of relative stability. It is also possible that we in academic profession studies are actually measuring only the changes of which we are aware; consequently, we may not be measuring the changes of which we are *not* aware and those that are beyond our current analytical frameworks. There may be many reasons why this occurs, the most obvious being the conceptual invisibility of some aspects of change and the resultant lack of proper indicators of change. Consequently, we know much less than we would like to, and we could know, about the changing academic profession in Europe. In academic profession studies, as in any other social research, there are some known knowns and some known unknowns; however, there are also some unknown unknowns of which we are conceptually unaware. This makes social research, including international comparative academic profession studies, extremely exciting and exceedingly rewarding.

Acknowledgements

This book is a product of a journey in my professional life that started in 2009 when Ulrich Teichler of the University of Kassel kindly agreed to Poland's entry to an extant European Science Foundation (ESF) project. For me, it was a highly consequential event in scholarly terms. In the early 2000s, I had been studying the academic profession in two international collaborative research projects coordinated by Philip G. Altbach of Boston College and Jürgen Enders—then of the Center for Higher Education Policy Studies (CHEPS), University of Twente —but there were no follow-up projects. Ulrich Teichler's decision to incorporate me in the ESF project refocused my research interests on international comparative academic profession studies.

I gratefully acknowledge all the friends and colleagues who have made this book possible. First of all, thanks to my colleagues from the EUROAC and CAP projects ('Changing Academic Profession' and 'Academic Profession in Europe: Responses to Societal Challenges') who were responsible for data collection across Europe; without their work, this book would never have been written. My colleagues on the EUROAC national teams included Dominik Antonowicz,

Marie Clarke, Abbey Hyde, Jonathan Drennan, Yurgos Politis, Ester Eva Höhle, Christian Schneijderberg, Nadine Merkator, Gaële Goastellec, Elke Parke, Gülay Ates, Kevin Toffel, Carole Probst, Luminita Moraru, Marko Turk, Bojana Ćulum, Nena Roncević, Jasminka Ledić, Tatiana Fumasoli, Nicolas Pekari, Angelika Brechelmacher, David F. J. Campbell, Timo Aarrevaara, Ian R. Dobson, and Janne Wikström. The EUROAC project was co-funded by the European Science Foundation (ESF) and coordinated by Barbara M. Kehm and Ulrich Teichler.

I gratefully acknowledge all the opportunities to discuss the various chapters of the book as they first versions emerged. Apart from numerous EUROAC seminars across Europe (Kassel, Lausanne, Dublin, Berlin, Vienna, Helsinki, and Poznan), I want to acknowledge the opportunity to prepare (if not always to deliver) keynote speeches and regular conference presentations across Europe and beyond. I am grateful for all the constructive input I received from all of those audiences, both nationally and internationally.

I want to warmly thank my Routledge publishing team, who have been very supportive since this project's inception. My deep gratitude to Jeroen Huisman and Jennifer M. Case, the series editors, who have been waiting for the final manuscript for much longer than originally promised. My special thanks to Helen Perkins, director of SRHE, for her ongoing encouragement and support; and my sincere appreciation to the editors at Routledge, Lucy Stewart and then Sarah Tuckwell, Lisa Font and Natalie Larkin.

I am grateful for all support I have received in the last few years for the Center for Public Policy Studies from all levels of my home university—from rectors and vice-rectors for research, former and current (Bronisław Marciniak, Andrzej Lesicki, Jacek Witkoś, and Ryszard Naskręcki), from former and current deans (Zbigniew Drozdowicz and Jacek Sójka), and from the director of the Institute of Philosophy, Roman Kubicki. Without their unstinting support, writing this book while fulfilling other research commitments would not have been possible.

I want to express my special gratitude to my junior colleagues from the Center for Public Policy Studies: Dr. Wojciec Roszka from the Poznan University of Economics, whose assistance in statistical analysis was absolutely crucial for the success of this research undertaking; Professor Dominik Antonowicz, who was part of the original EUROAC team and conducted 60 semi-structured interviews with Polish academics, as well as participating in all of the EUROAC international seminars; Dr. Krystian Szadkowski, whose day-to-day assistance with ongoing projects was crucial to the completion of this book, and whose Polish transla-tions of several chapters helped me to improve the theoretical frameworks; and the three newcomers to the Center: Professor Emanuel Kulczycki, Dr. Krzysztof Czarnecki, and Jakub Krzeski, who introduced new perspectives from sciento-metrics, welfare state studies, and political philosophy, respectively, to our semi-nars. Finally, I gratefully acknowledge the assistance of Marek Holowiecki in the Center's financial operations and in solving numerous technical problems.

I also wish to acknowledge the academics—more than 17,000 of them— from 11 European countries who gave up time from their own research or with friends and families to complete a dull academic profession questionnaire in the belief that their individual contributions to this research would be meaningful.

Finally, I want to dedicate this book to Natalia and Krystyna—my beloved daughter and wife. I wish Natalia limitless opportunities to develop her talents, to achieve her goals, to live the way she wants. Krystyna and I met 30 years ago, and it was the most important day of my life; living together was never easy, and became even more difficult each time I was finishing a book project. It was no different this time—please accept my apologies for this. Thank you for your unreserved love and powerful support day by day, and year by year![2]

Notes

1 A list of international comparative books includes Locke, Cummings, and Fischer (2011) on governance and management; Teichler and Höhle (2013) on working conditions; Bentley, Coates, Dobson, Goedegebuure, and Meek (2013) on job satisfaction; Kehm and Teichler (2013) on new tasks and new challenges; Teichler, Arimoto, and Cummings (2013) on major findings from the CAP survey; Huang, Finkelstein, and Rostan (2014) on internationalization; Shin et al. (2014b) on teaching and research; Cummings and Teichler (2015) on the relevance of academic work; Galaz-Fontes, Arimoto, Teichler, and Brennan (2016) on biographies and careers; Teichler and Cummings (2015) on recruitment and management; and Fumasoli, Goastellec, and Kehm (2015) on academic work and careers. A list of country-focused books includes Cummings and Finkelstein (2012) on the United States; Arimoto, Cummings, Huang, and Shin (2015) on Japan; and Postiglione and Jung (2017) on Hong Kong. For an overview of papers published in international journals, see Carvalho (2017).

2 The work on this book would not be possible without the support received from the Ministry of Science and Higher Education through its Dialogue grant 0021/ DLG/2016/10 (EXCELLENCE).

Chapter 1

Academic performance stratification

Inequality in the knowledge production

Introduction: built-in undemocracy in individual research performance

In this chapter, we focus on a rare scholarly theme of highly productive academics, statistically confirming their pivotal role in knowledge production across Europe. The upper 10 percent of highly productive academics in 11 European countries studied provides on average about a half of all academic knowledge production as measured by peer-reviewed journal articles and book chapters. In contrast to dominating bibliometric studies of research productivity, we focus not on publication numbers and citation numbers but on academic attitudes, behaviors, and perceptions as predictors of becoming research top performers across European systems. Our chapter provides a (large-scale and cross-country) corroboration of the systematic inequality in knowledge production, for the first time argued for by Alfred Lotka (1926) and Derek J. de Solla Price (1963). We corroborate the deep academic inequality in science and explore in more detail this segment of the academic profession. European highly productive academics—termed research top performers in this chapter—form a highly homogeneous group of academics whose high research performance is driven by structurally similar factors, mostly individual rather than institutional. Highly productive academics are similar from a cross-national perspective and they substantially differ intra-nationally from their lower-performing colleagues.

The academic profession in the countries studied is heavily stratified by academic performance—operationalized in this chapter as research productivity. Academic performance stratification explored in this chapter shows the power of inequality and its roots: the academic community is not 'the company of equals' (Zuckerman 1988: 526). Academic research production—and academic rewards and research resources combined with it—is highly skewed across Europe and its patterns of skewness are surprisingly similar. The stratification by output inevitably leads—in productivity-focused and bibliometrics-obsessed global science—to the stratification by all other types of academic rewards, from citations to honorific awards to individual competitive project funding (none of them analyzed in this book; see Bornmann, Bauer and Schlagberger 2017).

The 'Matthew effect' in science and the traditional cumulative advantage (and cumulative disadvantage) theories developed in sociology of science, from Merton to the Coles, become as relevant today as half a century ago: the distribution of academic rewards is as sharply graded as the distribution of research output.

The growing scholarly interest in research top performers comes from the growing policy interest in research top performance itself. The emphasis on stratification by academic performance leads to the stratification of the academic profession. The inequality in academic knowledge production is more consequential for individual academic careers as it is routinely analyzed with publication and citation data—available at fingertips—to assess academics by hiring committees and research funding panels in national funding agencies. The processes of performance stratification refer directly to academics and indirectly to institutions employing them. Highly graded knowledge production on an individual level is becoming ever more associated with highly graded research funding at the level of departments (or institutions). Across Europe, a small number of scholars produce most of the works and attract huge numbers of citations. Performance determines rewards, and small differences in talent translate into a disproportionate level of success, leading to inequalities in resources, research outcomes, and rewards.

The world of science has always been utterly unequal (Ruiz-Castillo and Costas 2014; Stephan 2012): the intrinsic property of science has been what Derek J. de Solla Price (1963) termed 'essential, built-in undemocracy' (59). Individual performance in science tends not to follow a Gaussian (normal) distribution. Instead, it follows a Paretian (power law) distribution (O'Boyle and Aguinis 2012). Distributions of different social phenomena—such as income, wealth, and prices—show 'strong skewness with long tail on the right, implying inequality' (Abramo, D'Angelo, and Soldantenkova 2017a: 324). Academic knowledge production is not an exception because unproductive scientists work alongside 'top researchers' in academic units, universities, and national systems (Abramo, Cicero, and D'Angelo 2013; Piro, Rørstad, and Aksnes 2016). In more internally competitive and vertically differentiated systems (such as Anglo-Saxon systems), top researchers tend to be concentrated in elite universities, and low performers in less prestigious tiers of the system.

Scientific productivity is skewed, and its skewness has been widely studied in terms of two standard measures of individual performance: publication numbers and citations of publications (Albarrán et al. 2011; Carrasco and Ruiz-Castillo 2014; Ruiz-Castillo and Costas 2014). In a study of 17.2 million authors and 48.2 million publications in Web of Science, Ruiz-Castillo and Costas (2014) show that 5.9 percent of authors accounted for about 35 percent of all publications. The skewness of science implies, as Seglen (1992) showed for the first time, that there will always be authors with huge numbers of publications (attracting huge numbers of citations) accompanied by a number of academics who do not publish and a large fraction of uncited publications. While at the one end of the continnum of research productivity there are research top performers, at the other end there are research non-performers (or simply non-publishers). From among all European countries studied, the highest share of non-performers among full-time academics involved in both teaching and research and employed in the university sector is reported for Poland (as we discuss briefly in a section of Chapter 5).

Scholarly interest in the skewness of science and high individual research performance has been growing exponentially in the last few years. Highly productive academics have been studied mostly intra-nationally and in single fields of knowledge (particularly in economics and psychology). Recent studies on high research performers—based either on publication data or citation data—include research on star scientists (Abramo, D'Angelo, and Caprasecca 2009a; Yair, Gueta, and Davidovitch 2017), star performers (Aguinis and O'Boyle 2014), the most productive scholars, including rising stars and stars overall (Copes, Khey, and Tewksbury 2012), the best versus the rest (O'Boyle and Aguinis 2012), academic stars and productivity stars (Aguinis and O'Boyle 2014), high-performing researchers and superstars (Agrawal, McHale, and Oettl 2017; Serenko et al. 2011).

The growing scholarly interest in research top performers comes also from the increasing emphasis on the role of universities in the global competition between nations and regions and the global competition for talent. Academics are at the center of the global knowledge production and global academic enterprise (Cummings and Finkelstein 2012; Leišyte and Dee 2012; Teichler et al. 2013). Not surprisingly, a question has emerged: 'What makes someone a top researcher?' (Kelchtermans and Veugelers 2013: 273). The objective of this chapter is to study specific characteristics of this unique class of academics: who top performers are, how they work, and what they think about academic work, and to explore the predictors of entering it, from a cross-national comparative perspective. While bibliometric data from international (or national) datasets are perfectly suited for research productivity analyses, they can hardly be used in determining the individual characteristics of top performers, for which large-scale survey data work better.

Top performers are studied here through a bivariate analysis of their working time distribution and their academic role orientation, as well as through a model approach, similarly to 'academic top earners' in Chapter 2 and 'international-ists' in Chapter 4. Odds ratio estimates with logistic regression of being highly productive academics are presented. Consistently across major clusters of academic disciplines, the tiny minority of 10 percent of academics produces about half (53.4 percent of peer-reviewed articles and books chapters) of all European publications (45.6 percent of publications in English and 50.2 percent of internationally co-authored publications). The mean research productivity of top performers across major clusters is on average 8.56 times higher than that of the other academics. Beginning with the remarkable similar productivity distribution patterns across European systems, we pose a general research question: who are these highly productive academics and which institutional and/or individual factors increase the odds of entering this class? Additionally, as high inequality was observed, we were exploring the question whether not only the average research productivity distribution is highly skewed (with a long tail on the right) for all European academics but also for top performers; or, in other words, whether the class of top performers is as internally stratified as that of their lower-performing colleagues.

Highly productive academics as a separate segment of the academic profession are a rare scholarly theme. We consider that because if about one tenth of European academics produce about half of all research output (and 1 in 20 produces about a third), then this distinctive academic population deserves more scholarly attention. Following a handful of previous studies focusing on the theme to varying degrees and with different methodological approaches (Price 1963; Crane 1965; Prpić 1996; Abramo et al. 2009a; Brew and Boud 2009; Postiglione and Jung 2013; and Marquina and Ferreiro 2015), our goal was to explore European research top performers from a cross-national comparative perspective and through large-scale quantitative material. We sought to empirically test the expectations arising out of prior single-nation research.

We explore both the intra-national differences in research productivity between European highly productive academics and the rest of research-involved academics (or 'average' academics, as they are termed in Stephan and Levin 1992: 57–58 and Prpić 1996: 185), as well as cross-national differences and similarities among them. Following prior research on the predictors of research productivity (especially Allison, Long, and Krauze 1982; Allison and Stewart 1974; Wanner, Lewis, and Gregorio 1981; Fox 1983; Stephan and Levin 1992; Ramsden 1994; Teodorescu 2000; Lee and Bozeman 2005; and recently Leišyte and Dee 2012; Shin and Cummings 2010; and Drennan et al. 2013), our guiding questions are as follows. Do research top performers across Europe share the same patterns of working time distribution and the same teaching-research academic role oritentation, both being closely linked to research productivity in the research literature? Are their demographics, patterns of socialization into academia, internationalization and professional collaboration, and overall research engagement similar across Europe? Do they perceive their institutions similarly? In a nutshell, how different are highly productive academics from 'average' academics, how differently do they work and perceive their work, and which factors are positively correlated with high research performance? We use a rather crude measure of survey-derived publication numbers but in this way we are able to seek correlations of high research productivity with various individual- and institutional-level characteristics, unavailable through traditional bibliometric tools.

This chapter is an international comparative study based on extensive quantitative material (using national samples, not merely the material from selected individual institutions or academic fields) rather than the single-nation studies that dominate in the prior non-bibliometric literature on research productivity. While it is very important to measure science through sophisticated bibliometric tools, we argue here that it is still very useful to refer to traditional survey-based individual productivity analyses to explore not only the 'what' of knowledge production but also the 'why' of its production (that is, to explore individual and institutional predictors of high research performance). Through a combination of inferential and logistic regression analyses, we explore highly productive academics as a distinctive (and under-researched) segment of the academic profession. Our research in this chapter contributes to several lines of higher education research: social stratification in science, research productivity, and international comparative academic profession studies, all with a focus on European universities.

Theories of research productivity

Three quotations from the last half century or so show roughly the same phenomenon in science: 'the majority of scientific work is performed by a relatively small number of scientists' (Crane 1965: 714); 'no matter how it is measured, there is enormous inequality in scientists' research productivity' (Allison 1980: 163); and, recently, 'inequality has been, and will always be, an intrinsic feature of science' (Xie 2014: 809). The skewed distribution of scientific output found first by Lotka (1926), and shown by Price (1963), was that about 6 percent of publishing scientists produce half of all papers (Lotka's law, or the inverse square law of productivity, states that the number of scientists producing n papers is $1/n^2$ of those producing one paper; see Kyvik 1989). The relative importance of scientists in the right tail of the output distribution—increasingly termed *stars* in recent bibliometric studies—has endured over time (Agrawal et al. 2017: 1).

The 'superstar effect' refers to markets ('relatively small numbers of people earn enormous amounts of money and dominate the activities in which they engage' Rosen 1981: 845), and the 'Matthew effect' (Cole and Cole 1973; Merton 1968) refers to the science system: a small number of scholars produce most of the works, attract huge numbers of citations, hold prestigious academic positions, and form the disciplines' identity (Cortés, Mora-Valencia, and Perote 2016; Serenko et al. 2011). For Robert K. Merton and Sherwin Rosen, performance determines rewards. In Rosen's 'economics of superstars,' small differences in talent translate into a disproportionate level of success. However, Rosen emphasizes innate talent, and Merton emphasizes external resources (DiPrete and Eirich 2006). Resources and the motivation to publish flow to scientists with high esteem in the scientific community, and that esteem 'flows to those who are highly productive' (Allison and Stewart 1974: 604), as discussed in the Introduction. Cumulative advantage is a general process by which 'small initial differences compound to yield large differences' (Aguinis and O'Boyle 2014: 5). Consequently, Merton's 'Matthew effect' in the system of science inevitably leads to 'haves' and 'have-nots,' or inequalities in resources, research outcomes, and monetary or non-monetary rewards (Xie 2014).

Methods for determining the characteristics of top performers proliferate, and they are studied as individual scientists or scientists embedded in organizational contexts, with reciprocal relationships: how they influence and how they are influenced by their organizations or collaborative networks. The skyline for star scientists (Sidiropoulous et al. 2016) is being sought: stars are those scientists whose performance cannot be surpassed by others with respect to all sciento-metric indexes selected. Apart from stars, the relevant studies focus on the scientific elite or the most highly cited scientists, top researchers (Abramo et al. 2013; Cortés et al. 2016), the academic elite (Yin and Zhi 2016), or prolific professors (Piro et al. 2016). What makes a research star is an all-pervading question in the current productivity-obsessed and number-based academic culture. Star performers ('a few individuals who contribute a disproportionate amount of output') occur in all organizations, including universities. However, a star is a relative position, and identification is possible only by viewing individuals in relation to others' productivity (Aguinis and O'Boyle 2014: 313–315; DiPrete and Eirich 2006: 282).

Research productivity has been an important scholarly topic for a long time (for some original formulations, see Crane 1963; Price 1963; Merton 1968; and Cole and Cole 1973). The literature has identified a number of individual and institutional factors that influence research productivity, including the size of the department, disciplinary norms, reward and prestige systems, and individual-level psychological constructs such as a desire for the intrinsic rewards of puzzle solving (see Leišyte and Dee 2012; Stephan and Levin 1992; Ramsden 1994; and Teodorescu 2000). Faculty orientation toward research is generally believed to predict higher research productivity; as are the time spent on research, being a male academic, faculty collaboration, faculty academic training, years passed since PhD, as well as a cooperative climate and support at the institutional level (Porter and Umbach 2001; Katz and Martin 1997; Smeby and Try 2005; Lee and Bozeman 2005; Fox 2015). The extreme differences in individual research productivity can be explained by a number of theories: we shall focus briefly on the 'sacred spark' theory, the 'cumulative advantage' theory (combined with the 'reinforcement theory'), and 'the utility maximizing theory.'

First, the 'sacred spark' theory presented by Cole and Cole (1973) simply says 'that there are substantial, predetermined differences among scientists in their ability and motivation to do creative scientific research' (Allison and Stewart 1974: 596). Highly productive scholars are 'motivated by an inner drive to do science and by a sheer love of the work' (Cole and Cole 1973: 62). Productive scientists are a strongly motivated group of researchers and they have the stamina, 'or the capacity to work hard and persists in the pursuit of long-range goals' (Fox 1983: 287; Zuckerman 1970: 241). Or, as Paula Stephan and Sharon Levin (1992: 13) argue, 'there is a general consensus that certain people are particularly good at doing science and that some are not just good but superb.'

Second, the 'accumulative advantage' theory developed by Robert K. Merton (1968) holds that productive scientists are likely to be even more productive in the future, while the productivity of those with low performance will be even lower. The accumulative advantage theory is related to the reinforcement theory formulated by the Coles (Cole and Cole 1973: 114), which in its simplest formulation states that 'scientists who are rewarded are productive, and scientists who are not rewarded become less productive.' As Jerry Gaston (1978: 144) points out, reinforcement deals with *why* scientists continue in research activities; and accumulative advantage deals with *how* some scientists are able to obtain resources for research that in turn leads to successful research and publication. Several studies (Allison and Stewart 1974; Allison et al. 1982) support the cumulative advantage hypothesis, without discrediting the sacred spark hypothesis.

Finally, according to the 'utility maximizing theory,' all researchers choose to reduce their research efforts over time because they think other tasks may be more advantageous. As Svein Kyvik (1990: 40) comments, 'eminent researchers may have few incentives to write a new article or book, as that will not really improve the high professional reputation that they already have.' And Stephan and Levin (1992: 35), in discussing age and productivity, argue that 'later in their careers, scientists are less financially motivated to do research. ... with each additional year the rewards for doing research decline.' These three major theories of research productivity are complementary rather than competing: to varying degrees, they are all applicable to the academic profession.

Highly productive academics in the research literature

We distinguish two different approaches in the research literature for exploring individual-level high research productivity. The first approach is to explore it through qualitative material: first, rankings of highly productive academics are created, and then academics in the top ranks are interviewed, with a general research question of 'how can they be so productive?' (Mayrath 2008: 42). Various 'keys to productivity' (Kiewra and Creswell 2000: 155) or 'guidelines for publishing' (Kiewra 1994) are drawn from either targeted academic surveys of productive academics seeking the determinants of high research productivity, or from interviews with 'eminent' or 'prolific' academics, or both. The second approach, in contrast, is to explore high research productivity through quantitative material: surveys of the academic profession in which academic, behavioral and attitudinal data are combined with publication data. In this chapter, we shall use the second, quantitative approach.

The qualitative approach is favored in such soft disciplines as, for instance, educational psychology (Mayrath 2008; Kiewra and Creswell 2000; Patterson-Hazley and Kiewra 2013; Martínez, Floyd, and Erichsen 2011). Carefully collected qualitative material in papers based on 'conversations with highly productive educational psychologists' seeks to answer such questions as 'what factors characterize highly productive educational psychologists?' (Kiewra and Creswell 2000: 136). Qualitative studies based on a varying number of conversations with highly productive academics seek to answer a general question: how do scholars become highly productive? They present a large number of useful tips, and refer to some striking individual examples. However, conversation-based qualitative explorations of highly productive academics, though fascinating, are somehow under-theorized.

Faculty research productivity has been thoroughly explored in the academic literature, mostly in single-nation contexts: especially the United States, the United Kingdom, and Australia (Cole and Cole 1973; Allison and Stewart 1974; Fox 1983; Ramsden 1994), as well as South Korea (Shin and Cummings 2010), but rarely in cross-national contexts (exceptions include Teodorescu 2000; Drennan et al. 2013; and Postiglione and Jung 2013). While most productivity studies did not use national samples and focused on faculty from selected academic fields, especially from the natural sciences, our study uses national samples and refers to all academic fields grouped into five large clusters of disciplines.

International comparative studies in higher education have not generally explored a specific class of highly productive academics; however, they have been mentioned in passing in several single-nation academic profession studies (Crane 1965; Cole and Cole 1973; Allison 1980), but they were not researched in more detail in these studies. Exceptions include a discussion of American 'big producers' in *Little Science, Big Science* by Derek J. de Solla Price (1963), a foundational book for scientometrics; a study of 'star scientists' in the context of gender differences in research productivity in Italy in Abramo et al. 2009a; and studies in the productivity of Croatian 'eminent scientists' in Prpić (1996). Abramo and colleagues (Abramo et al. 2009a: 143) conclude that a star scientist 'is typically a male full professor'; and that, if female, star scientists are primarily concentrated in the lower levels of productivity. They argue that 'to obtain levels of scientific production such as those of a star scientist, the time and energy required for research activities are notably superior to the average, and imply an overwhelming dedication to work' (Abramo et al. 2009a: 154). However, as their work is based on bibliometric data, the authors are unable to go beyond gender, academic rank, institutional type, and academic discipline in their exploration of a 'star scientist profile.' Katarina Prpić (1996) compared the scientific productivity of 'eminent' and 'average' scientists. Her research assumptions were that the patterns of predictors for the publication productivity of eminent scientists would be different from those of 'average' scientists because, in the elite group, 'homogeneity is larger and variability is smaller than in the entire research population' (Prpić 1996: 199).

Recently, Postiglione and Jung (2013) studied 'top tier researchers' in four Asian countries, seeking commonalities shared by them based on the CAP ('Changing Academic Profession') survey. They studied 10 percent of the most and least productive academics through descriptive statistics. They found that highly productive academics emphasize discovery, basic/theoretical research, and social responsibility in science more often than the rest of academics, and spend more time on research than on teaching. They also collaborate more than others, especially in the international domain and perceive their institutions as making decisions about personnel and funding allocation on the basis of performance-based criteria (Postiglione and Jung 2013: 171–177). Also, Marquina and Ferreiro (2015) studied a specifically constructed 'elite group' of academics in six 'emergent' countries, based on the same global academic profession survey. They compared 'elite groups' with the 'rest' of academics: they focused on 'elites' defined as academics with graduate degrees, full-timers, spending more than 10 hours per week on research and preferring research to teaching. Their class of 'elite groups' does not refer directly to research productivity. There are important parallels, though: academics in 'elite groups' are more internationalized in both teaching, research, and publishing; they are overall more satisfied with their work; they spend more time on research and are more research-oriented (Marquina and Ferreiro 2015: 191). Finally, Angela Brew and David Boud (2009: 194), through descriptive analysis, only briefly contrasted 'high research productive' with 'low research productive' academics from six Australian universities, and concluded that high productive academics spend on average about five more hours per week on research and have different priorities—they prioritize research over teaching. The major theories of research productivity as well as studies on highly productive academics, rare as they have been, both provide conceptual underpinning for this chapter.

In this chapter, we explore the personal and institutional characteristics linked to high individual research productivity. This cannot be done through citation analysis: because while the scholarly impact of publications may be more important than sheer publication output, especially for policy purposes, their impact cannot be correlated with individual and institutional predictors of research productivity. While the world of 'measuring science' has moved far beyond self-reported publication data in terms of countries, institutions, research fields (for instance the CWTS Leiden Ranking), and even individual academics, such bibliometric exercises are not able to link research output to individual researchers, academic attitudes, behaviors, and perceptions.

Consequently, our study uses a more traditional research instrument (the large-scale survey). We assume, following Fox (1983: 285), that the principal means of communication in science is the publication process, even though today 'publications' are increasingly linked to their 'where' (in globally ranked academic journals), and their academic 'so what' or scholarly impact (through global impact factors and citation analysis).

The quality–quantity dilemma in academic productivity studies based on survey-derived publication numbers is not easy to solve. This chapter follows the explicit assumption that more productive academics produce more peer-reviewed articles and less productive academics produce fewer peer-reviewed articles—but no link is made here to either the originality of journal articles or their current or future impact in academic disciplines or beyond them, in science or beyond it, in the wider society.

Consequently, from among the four ideal types of academic research production (based on both quantity and quality of published research) suggested by Jonathan R. Cole and Stephen Cole (1973: 91–93) for physicists in their study of social stratification in science—'prolific,' 'perfectionists,' 'mass producers,' and 'silent'—our study tends to focus on the 'prolific' segment in which academics are defined by both the high quantity and high quality of their publications. As Cole and Cole (1973: 111) argued,

> since quality and quantity of research output are fairly highly correlated, the high producers *tend* to publish the more consequential research. ... engaging in a lot of research is in one sense a 'necessary' condition for the production of high-quality work.

Also, Paula E. Stephan and Sharon G. Levin argue (1991: 364) that the prolific scientists they studied have not 'traded quality for quantity by publishing in journals which have lower impact.' Recently, Ulf Sandström and Peter van den Besselaar (2016: 12), using a Swedish dataset of 48,000 researchers and their Web of Science publications, argued that quantity does make a difference because 'the more papers, the more high impact papers,' or to produce high impact papers, 'certain output levels seem to be required.' Finally, as Price (1963: 41) argued along similar lines, 'although there is no guarantee that the small producer is a nonentity and the big producer a distinguished scientist, there is a strong correlation.'

Defining the top perfomers

We explore research productivity defined here, following Daniel Teodorescu (2000: 206), as the 'self-reported number of journal articles and chapters in academic books that the respondent had published in the three years prior to the survey.' A dependent variable studied is being a member of the class of research top performers (as explored through the proxy of the number of peer-reviewed journal articles and book chapters published in the period of 3 years preceding the survey conducted in the 2007–2010 period).

The data used in this book come from the 'European Academic Profession: Responses to Societal Challenges' (EUROAC) project, a sister project to the global 'Changing Academic Profession' (CAP) project (see Carvalho (2017) for a recent overview of the CAP/EUROAC family of studies). The data come from the countries involved in both the CAP and EUROAC projects, with national datasets subsequently cleaned, weighted and merged into a single European dataset.[1] We base our study empirically on the single most important cross-national source of data on academic views, attitudes, perceptions, and behaviors in Europe available today, with all its inherent limitations for comparative research. The quality of the dataset is high (Teichler et al. 2013: 35; Teichler and Höhle 2013: 9) as well as being well-suited for our research purposes. The survey questionnaire was sent out to the CAP countries in 2007 and to the EUROAC countries in most cases in 2010. The total number of returned surveys was 17,211 and included between 1,000 and 1,700 returned surveys from all countries studied, except for Poland where it was higher. Overall, the response rate differed from over 30 percent (in Norway, Italy, and Germany), to 20–30 percent (in the Netherlands, Finland, and Ireland), to about 15 percent in the United Kingdom, 11 percent in Poland, and 10 percent or less in Austria, Switzerland, and Portugal. Overall, both simple random sampling, systematic sampling, and stratified random sampling methods were used, depending on the country (national-level sampling techniques are described for the CAP European countries in RIHE 2008: 89–178, and for the EUROAC countries in Teichler and Höhle 2013: 6–9). However, in most countries, stratified random sampling was used to allow the resulting sample to be distributed in the same way as the population (Hibberts, Burke Johnson, and Hudson 2012: 61–62; Bryman 2012: 192–193). Stratified sampling frames were created and several stratifying criteria were used (for instance, gender and academic position, as in Poland). The stratification of the sample mirrored the population stratification on the stratifying criteria, and mirrored simple random sample in every other way. Random sampling was used to obtain the elements from each stratum.

The relatively low response rate in the United Kingdom, Poland, Austria, Switzerland, and Portugal may have been caused by the increasing number of surveys to which the academic profession is routinely exposed (Mesch 2012). The response rates in these countries have been similar to response rates in several countries studying the academic profession in the last decade: studies in Canada report 17 percent (Jones et al. 2014: 348), in Hong Kong 13 percent (Rostan, Finkelstein, and Huang 2014: 25), in the Republic of Korea 13 percent (Shin et al. 2014: 183), and in Croatia 10 percent (Teichler and Höhle 2013: 8). No groups of academics were systematically excluded from the sampling frame (so 'sampling bias' did not occur: no members of the sampling frame had no or limited chances for inclusion in the sample, Bryman 2012: 187). However, it is not possible to state to what extent the pool of respondents differs from the pool of non-respondents and, consequently, to state whether 'non-response bias' occurs (Stoop 2012: 122). 'Non-response bias' can occur when certain groups of respondents fail to respond or are less likely than others to participate in the survey or answer certain survey questions (Hibberts et al. 2012: 72) or when survey participation is correlated with survey variables (Groves 2006). However, non-response biases are only indirectly related to non-response rates: a key parameter is 'how strongly correlated the survey variable of interest is with response propensity, the likelihood of responding' (Groves 2006: 670). It is conceivable, for instance, that highly productive academics—studied in this chapter—are prone to refuse to participate in the survey because they are very busy; however, they may be inclined to participate in the survey because of a sense of civic (academic) duty, social norms producing a sense of obligation to provide help in the belief that this serves the common (academic) good, combined with a feeling that their answers count (Stoop 2012: 126–128).

In order to explore highly productive academics specifically, we divided the sample of all European academics into two complementary subsamples: academics reporting research involvement and those not reporting this. Then the subsample of research-involved academics was divided into two further subgroups: the first was 'research top performers' (henceforth referred to as 'top performers'), identified

Table 1.1 The distribution of the sample population, by country

	All (Large N)	Full-time employed	Employed in the university sector	Full-time employed in the university sector (N)	Involved in both teaching and research	Full-time employed in the university sector involved in both teaching and research
Austria	1,492	977 65.5%	1,492 100%	977	1,412 94.6%	954 63.9%
Finland	1,374	1,116 81.2%	1,049 76.3%	837	1,193 86.8%	792 57.6%
Germany	1,215	851 70.0%	1,030 84.8%	708	1,098 90.4%	660 54.3%
Ireland	1,126	1,017 90.3%	825 73.3%	742	1,125 99.9%	742 65.9%
Italy	1,711	1,651 96.5%	1,711 100.0%	1,651	1,711 100.0%	1,651 96.5%
Netherlands	1,209	677 56.0%	416 34.4%	298	646 53.4%	266 22.0%
Norway	986	869 88.1%	905 91.8%	809	922 93.5%	766 77.7%
Poland	3,704	3,515 94.9%	1,726 46.6%	1,669	3,659 98.8%	1,643 44.4%
Portugal	1,513	1,236 81.7%	547 36.2%	468	1,174 77.6%	372 24.6%
Switzerland	1,414	827 58.5%	638 45.1%	372	1,245 88.0%	354 25.0%
United Kingdom	1,467	897 61.1%	438 29.9%	356	840 57.3%	266 18.1%
TOTAL	**17,211**	**13,633 79.2%**	**10,777 62.6%**	**8,886 51.6%**	**15,025 87.3%**	**8,466 49.2%**

as academics ranked among the top 10 percent (cut-off points permitting) of academics with the highest research performance in each of the 11 national systems (separately) and in all the five major research field clusters (also separately). The second subgroup was that of the remaining 90 percent of academics involved in research. The distribution of the sample population is shown by country in Table 1.1.

Procedures: the top performers through surveys and its limitations

We use two complementary approaches: statistical inference (independent-samples t-tests for the equality of means and z tests for the equality of fractions performed on the two independent samples applied to almost universal variables in research productivity studies: long research hours and high research role orientation); as well as a multi-dimensional logistic regression model. While most previous studies rely on linear regression models in studying research productivity, this chapter relies on a logistic regression model in seeking country-specific predictors of becoming highly productive. The data relate to the academic behaviors, attitudes, and research productivity of the subpopulation of highly productive academics (the upper 10 percent), contrasted with the subpopulation of the remaining 90 percent of academics; in both cases referring only to those indicating both teaching and research involvement.

To begin with, we shall discuss top performers through a bivariate analysis of the working time distribution and the teaching/research role orientation. Specifically, we shall use statistical inference using t-tests (for the equality of means) and z tests (for the equality of fractions). An independent samples t-test is used when we want to compare the means of two independent populations (research top performers and the rest of academics): by using the sample data we test whether the mean time spent on various categories of academic activity is equal for both populations of academics. The z test for the equality of fractions is used to test the hypothesis that two populations have equal proportions (research role orientation among research top performers and the rest of academics). Although bivariate analyses are limited insofar as they do not control for other important factors that might affect research productivity (Teodorescu 2000: 203), the two selected variables emerge as key in most qualitative and quantitative productivity studies. Therefore, they need separate treatment.

However, a study of multi-dimensional relationships requires a model approach, and therefore odds ratio estimates by logistic regression for belonging to European highly productive academics will be presented, following inferential analyses. Inferential analyses and logistic regression analyses are viewed here as complementary: both approaches are useful for our research purposes.

More specifically, in the section on the working time distribution, an independent two-sample t-test is used. When the variance in the compared populations is equal (Levene's test of homogeneity of variance is used), then Student's t-test is used; otherwise, Welch two sample t-test is used. The test statistic has a t-distribution. Consistent with previous research on the 'working time distribution' in academia (Bentley and Kyvik 2013), we focus here on annualized weekly hours in both teaching periods of the academic year and in non-teaching periods: we assume that 60 percent for the former and 40 percent for the latter time is a good approximation for the vast majority of the European systems studied. Most previous studies of working time patterns are either single-nation or comparative and descriptive (exceptions include Bentley and Kyvik 2013 and Gottlieb and Keith 1997). In the section on teaching/research role orientation, in order to compare fractions, a two-proportion z test is used. The test statistic has a standardized normal distribution. All tests are conducted with a significance level of $\alpha = 0.05$. The details of the multivariate analysis are given in Section 4.2 on logistic regression analysis.

The chapter seeks to contrast research top performers with the rest of academics across 11 European systems, proceeding as follows: first, it identifies top performers by country in the sample; second, it examines their average research productivity (by several proxies) compared with that of the remaining 90 percent of academics, again by country, and third, it examines their share in the total research output—in all three steps, by major clusters of academic disciplines. In these introductory procedures only research productivity data are used. There is a trade off between a disadvantage of using self-reported data (rather than the Scopus or Web of Science data) and publication numbers as the only measure of research performance (rather than a combination of publications, citations, H-index, or other measures used in bibliometrics) in introductory procedures— and an advantage of using individual-level data. Detailed individual-level data can be collected only through a survey instrument. Therefore, in the next set of procedures, behavioral and attitudinal data derived from survey questionnaires can be used as the chapter seeks to compare the working time distribution (with average time investments in teaching, research, service, administration, and other academic duties) and academic role orientation (interests lying primarily in teaching, research or both) of the two classes of academics.

Finally, the chapter seeks to find odds ratio estimates by logistic regression for being in the top 10 percent in research productivity by country, with blocks of different individual and institutional variables. Blocks of individual variables include, for instance, 'socialization to academia' (with such variables as intensive faculty guidance and research projects conducted with faculty), 'internationalization and collaboration' (with such variables as research international in scope or orientation and collaborating domestically), and 'overall research engagement' (with such variables as being a peer reviewer or being an editor of journals/book chapters). The two blocks of institutional variables are 'institutional policies' (for instance, strong performance orientation) and 'institutional support' (availability of research funds and supportive attitude of administration). These variables can be accessed through survey methodology only; the major drawback of this approach being the imprecise nature (compared with detailed bibliometric datasets) of self-reported productivity data.

However, to strengthen the robustness of our productivity analyses, apart from peer-reviewed articles (PRA), three additional measures were used: peer-reviewed article equivalents (PRAE for short), internationally co-authored peer-reviewed article equivalents (IC-PRAE), and English language peer-reviewed article equivalents (ENG-PRAE). Publication counts were converted into article equivalents. The PRAE measure is calculated as the weighted sum of self-reported articles in books or journals (the value of one article equivalent), edited books (the value of two article equivalents), and authored books (the value of five article equivalents) published over the 3-year reference period. The same procedure was used in Røstad and Aksnes 2015: 319; and Bentley 2015: 870; most survey-based studies equate four to six articles to one full monograph. An individually provided share of peer-reviewed publications is applied to each observation (following Bentley 2015). The advantage of using the PRAE measure in this multi-disciplinary study is that it captures publishing through various outlets and does not focus on articles, leaving room for authored books (and edited books), which are still an important outlet in the social sciences and humanities. As Bentley (2015: 870) emphasizes, 'using article equivalents and weighting of books more heavily reflects the relative contribution of the different publication types,' minimizing differences across disciplines.

The internationally co-authored PRAE measure applies the individually provided share of publications co-authored with international colleagues, and the English-language PRAE measure applies the individually provided share of publications published in a foreign language (the language in question in the countries studied is predominantly English). The question about the number of scholarly contributions was thus combined with the question about the percentage of peer-reviewed publications, English-language publications, and internationally co-authored publications. The conversion of publication counts into article equivalents is used in research productivity analyses (especially those focused on productivity correlates) based on survey data in order to make fairer comparisons of productivity across academic fields with dissimilar publication patterns (Kyvik and Aksnes 2015). So the PRAE measure was used to be able to explore more comprehensively cross-disciplinary differences in publication patterns between top performers and the rest of academics, and the IC-PRAE and ENG-PRAE measures were used to explore internationalization patterns in publishing research results between the two groups.

A substantial proportion of publishing in the humanities and social sciences in Europe consists of books and edited books, as opposed to publishing in natural sciences. Article equivalents were used specifically in multi-disciplinary studies involving major clusters of academic disciplines rather than merely science, technology, engineering, and mathematics clusters. (Examples include Ramsden 1994: 213; Gulbrandsen and Smeby 2005: 938; Kyvik and Aksnes 2015: 1441; Teichler et al. 2013: 146–147; Kyvik 1989: 206; Piro et al. 2016: 945; Bentley 2015: 870; and Røstad and Aksnes 2015: 319.) In Poland, the notion of article equivalents has been routinely used in parameterization (a Polish version of a research assessment exercise) and assessments of individual research output for about a decade: currently, a conversion system is used in which most Polish articles as well as all book chapters have a point value of 5 and Polish monographs have a value of 25.

The exact formulation of the productivity question was as follows: 'How many of the following scholarly contributions have you completed in the past *three* years?' (Question D4), with the separate entries for 'scholarly books you authored or co-authored' (D4/1), 'scholarly books you edited or co-edited' (D4/2), 'articles published in an academic book or journal' (D4/3), 'research report/monograph written for a funded project' (D4/4), 'paper presented at a scholarly conference' (D4/5), and 'professional article written for a newspaper or magazine' (D4/6). However, the exact definitions were not provided, assuming their self-explanatory nature. The next question was formulated as follows (D5): 'Which percentage of your publications in the last three years were—peer-reviewed' (D5/6), 'published in a language different from the language of instruction at your current institution' (D5/1), and were 'co-authored with colleagues located in other (foreign) countries' (D5/3)? The questionnaire was explicit about different types of publications and, importantly, European academics are used to routinely counting different publication types for reporting purposes. Survey respondents marked one of a number of nationally determined disciplines. Academics were grouped in five clusters of academic disciplines—that best represent the current structure of the academic professions across Europe (it is difficult to accept the formulation of 'the European academic profession': as Höhle and Teichler (2013: 268) conclude their study on the 'European profession' vs. 'professions in Europe,' 'given the responses to about 50 questions examined in this chapter, we note very few themes which would allow us to talk about a "European" academic profession'). The total number of valid responses was 17,211; however, in this research, academics from 'other disciplines' and those whose work contract did not involve research were excluded. Cases from 'other disciplines' were useless for cross-disciplinary analyses due to their specificity and teaching-only observations were useless for research productivity analyses. Finally, 7,030 observations from five major clusters of academic disciplines (938 top performers and 6,092 lower-performing academics) were used for the analyses.

There are several limitations in this chapter; some of them are more generic and refer to other chapters as well—and others refer to the study of highly productive academics only. First, all the publication data are self-reported and the differences in reporting them can be between nations, academic disciplines, and genders: consequently, to different degrees, respondents 'may present an untrue picture to the researcher, for example answering what they would like a situation to be rather than what the actual situation is' (Cohen, Manion, and Morrison 2011: 404). Although self-reported publication data are not perfect, they do not seem to be subject to any systemic error or systemic bias. Second, due to the anonymization of the collected data, we were unable to study any differences between top performers from institutions of lower academic standing and those from the most prestigious ones. The third limitation comes from a tacit assumption that the major concepts used in the survey instrument in all systems have a somehow similar definition. These terms may have different meanings in the academic perceptions of different countries (for instance, 'teaching' and 'research' may be closely intertwined in such activities as the supervision of doctoral dissertations).

Another limitation is inherent to the structure of the dataset used: in regression analysis, no distinction can be made between single-authored and multiple-authored publications and between national and international publications (except through various proxies like, for instance, 'internationally co-authored publications' or 'publications in English'). Finally, there are two major European systems missing: the French and the Spanish, for which no data in a comparable format were collected.

The top perfomers: a statistical overview

Frequencies of the selected demographic characteristics of the top performers are presented in Table 1.2. About three-quarters are men (73.2 percent), they are predominantly older (seven in ten are at least 40 years old, 69.9 percent), and more than 70 percent (71.1 percent) have at least 10 years of academic experience (calculated as working full-time in the higher education sector beyond teaching and/or working as a research assistant). The mean age of top performers is 47 (standard deviation: 9.96, Figure 1.1). The dominant age groups of top performers differ by academic discipline clusters. On average, the top performers are substantially younger in professions and engineering, and older in the three other clusters (top performers under 40 account for about a quarter of the top

Table 1.2 Sample description: frequencies of selected demographic characteristics, all countries

		Rest (90%)		Top performers (upper 10%)		Total	
		N	%	N	%	N	%
Gender	Male	3,721	61.1	687	73.2	4,408	62.7
	Female	2,371	38.9	251	26.8	2,622	37.3
Age groups	Under 30	702	11.2	51	5.3	753	10.4
	30 to 39	1,982	31.5	240	24.8	2,222	30.6
	40 to 49	1,552	24.6	329	34.0	1,881	25.9
	50 to 59	1,263	20.1	238	24.6	1,502	20.7
	60 and older	798	12.7	109	11.2	906	12.5
Academic experience*	Under 10	2,464	11.7	270	28.9	2,733	39.9
	10 to 19	1,521	25.7	311	33.3	1,832	26.8
	20 to 29	991	16.8	191	20.5	1,183	17.3
	30 to 39	788	13.3	130	14.0	919	13.4
	40 and more	151	2.5	31	3.3	182	2.7
Academic disciplines	Life sciences and medical sciences	2,036	32.3	316	32.7	2,352	32.4
	Physical sciences, mathematics	1,037	16.5	149	15.4	1,186	16.3
	Engineering	716	11.4	107	11.0	822	11.3
	Humanities and social sciences	1,708	27.1	262	27.1	1,971	27.1
	Professions	800	12.7	133	13.8	934	12.9

Note: *Academic experience* means the number of years since one's first full-time job (beyond research and teaching assistant in the higher education/research sector, Question A6).

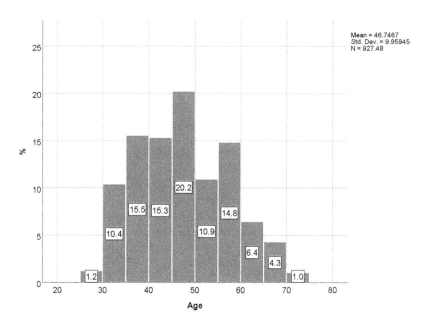

Figure 1.1 Research top performers by age group, all clusters of academic disciplines, and frequency, all countries combined.

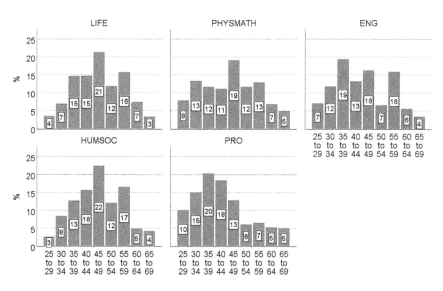

Figure 1.2 Research top performers by age group and cluster of academic disciplines, frequency, all countries combined.

performers in life sciences, physical sciences and mathematics, and humanities and social sciences, compared with 42 percent in professions and one third in engineering; also in professions the share of academics aged 55 and more is the lowest, reaching about one-fifth, see Figure 1.2).

Top performers compared with their lower-performing colleagues share several common features and represent a common professional profile: top performers tend to be male academics with a mean age of about 47, are full professors who collaborate more often nationally and internationally, and publish abroad more often (than the other academics). The top performers' research tends to be international in scope or orientation, they work longer hours and longer research hours, and they are substantially more research-oriented. They focus on basic and theoretical research (somewhat understandably), they sit on national and international committees and boards, and they are peer reviewers and editors of journals or book series more often than their colleagues.

The top perfomers and the national research output

Detailed statistics showing average research productivity through the three article equivalent types (PRAE, IC-PRAE, and ENG-PRAE) by academic disciplines cluster and by group studied (top performers versus the other academics) are shown in Tables 1.3, 1.4, and 1.5.

The mean research productivity in terms of all measures for top performers is, on average, much higher in all clusters of disciplines: about five to ten times higher than for the other academics (see Kwiek 2018b specifically on Poland). Figure 1.3 shows the percentage of the average number of internationally co-authored peer-reviewed articles (IC-PRA) and article equivalents (IC-PRAE) in the average number of peer-reviewed articles (PRA) and article equivalents (PRAE) published in a 3-year reference period for top performers and the rest of academics, by cluster of academic disciplines. For each cluster there are four columns: the first one for the PRA measure, and the remaining three for the PRAE measure. By far the biggest difference in average productivity is in the simplest measure of peer-reviewed articles (PRA), which is reduced substantially if an article equivalent measure is applied (PRAE). Big difference in average productivity is also shown for internationally co-authored publications (IC-PRAE), which shows a powerful role of internationalization in research for productivity: in all clusters, the difference between the four groups of academics is about seven to eight times, and in one (professions) about ten times. Interestingly, top performers produce much more articles and article equivalents, and much more articles and article-equivalents co-authored with international colleagues, but there are significant cross-disciplinary variations rather than intra-disciplinary differences between the two classes of academics (with PHYSMATH and LIFE clusters with a high percentage, and

Table 1.3 Research productivity: peer-reviewed articles (PRA) published in the 3-year reference period, research top performers (10%) vs. the rest (90%). All countries combined

	Rest (90%)						Top performers (upper 10%)					
	Mean PRA	95% confidence interval, lower band	95% confidence interval, upper band	Median	Standard Deviation	N	Mean PRA	95% confidence interval, lower band	95% confidence interval, upper band	Median	Standard Deviation	N
LIFE	3.3	3.1	3.5	2.0	4.1	2,036	22.5	21.2	23.8	20.0	11.9	316
PHYSMATH	3.6	3.3	3.8	2.0	4.0	1,037	21.8	19.6	24.1	20.0	13.8	149
ENGITECH	1.7	1.5	1.9	0.3	2.6	716	17.2	14.4	20.1	13.6	14.7	107
HUMSOC	1.2	1.1	1.3	0.0	1.9	1,708	11.8	10.8	12.9	10.0	8.9	262
PRO	1.2	1.1	1.4	0.0	1.9	800	12.3	11.0	13.6	10.0	7.7	133

Table 1.4 Research productivity: internationally co-authored peer-reviewed articles (IC-PRA) published in the 3-year reference period, research top performers (10%) vs. the rest (90%). All countries combined

	Rest (90%)						Top performers (upper 10%)					
	Mean IC-PRA	95% confidence interval, lower band	95% confidence interval, upper band	Median	Standard Deviation	N	Mean IC-PRA	95% confidence interval, lower band	95% confidence interval, upper band	Median	Standard Deviation	N
LIFE	0.9	0.8	1.0	0.0	2.0	2,036	8.1	7.2	9.0	5.7	8.3	316
PHYSMATH	1.3	1.2	1.5	0.0	2.4	1,037	11.2	9.0	13.4	8.0	13.7	149
ENGITECH	0.3	0.3	0.4	0.0	1.1	716	5.4	4.1	6.7	2.6	6.8	107
HUMSOC	0.2	0.1	0.2	0.0	0.6	1,708	2.5	2.0	3.1	0.4	4.6	262
PRO	0.2	0.1	0.2	0.0	0.6	800	3.3	2.4	4.1	1.3	4.9	133

Table 1.5 Research productivity: English language peer-reviewed articles (ENG-PRA) published in the 3-year reference period, research top performers (10%) vs. the rest (90%). All countries combined (without Ireland and the UK)

	Rest (90%)						Top performers (upper 10%)					
	Mean ENG-PRA	95% confidence interval, lower band	95% confidence interval, upper band	Median	Standard Deviation	N	Mean ENG-PRA	95% confidence interval, lower band	95% confidence interval, upper band	Median	Standard Deviation	N
LIFE	2.8	2.7	3.0	0.8	4.0	1,824	19.9	18.5	21.3	18.0	11.9	283
PHYSMATH	3.4	3.2	3.7	2.0	4.1	946	21.2	18.7	23.7	19.0	14.6	131
ENGITECH	1.3	1.1	1.5	0.0	2.5	649	14.8	12.1	17.4	12.2	13.1	97
HUMSOC	0.5	0.4	0.6	0.0	1.2	1,540	6.8	5.7	7.9	5.0	8.5	235
PRO	0.5	0.4	0.6	0.0	1.2	681	7.1	5.7	8.4	6.0	7.2	113

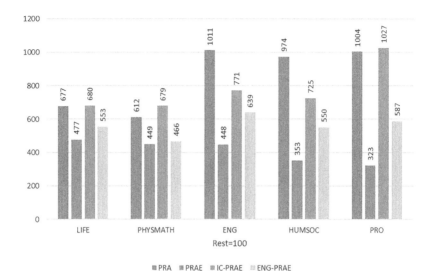

Figure 1.3 Research productivity by cluster of academic disciplines: top performers vs. other academics (productivity of top performers as percentage of productivity of other academics: the Rest = 100%). The
average number of peer-reviewed articles (PRA), peer-reviewed article equivalents (PRAE), internationally co-authored peer-reviewed
article equivalents (IC-PRAE), and English language peer-reviewed
article equivalents (ENG-PRAE) published in a 3-year reference period. For all clusters, the results are statistically significant (in %).
All countries combined.

HUMSOC and PRO clusters with very low percentages, no matter which class
we analyze). The percentage of IC-PRAE in PRAE and of IC-PRA in PRA
is generally similar in all clusters—which may mean that overall structure of
academic production by top performers and by the rest of academics is not
substantially different: the numbers are radically different but the shares are
not (see Figure 1.4, with the highest difference between the two classes for
PRO cluster).

The subsample of academics involved in research from the five major clusters
of academic disciplines was divided into two subgroups: research top performers
(or top performers henceforth), identified as academics ranked among the top
10 percent (cut-off points permitting, from 9.9 percent to 10.5 percent) of academics with the highest research performance in each major cluster of academic
disciplines (separately). The second subgroup was the remaining 90 percent of
academics involved in research. The distribution of the sample population by
cluster and the threshold number of publications (the minimum number of publications to be classified as a top performer) in terms of peer-reviewed articles
(PRA) are presented in Table 1.6. The use of both PRA and PRAE measures
reflects a role played by the two outlets other than articles and book chapters:
books and edited books.

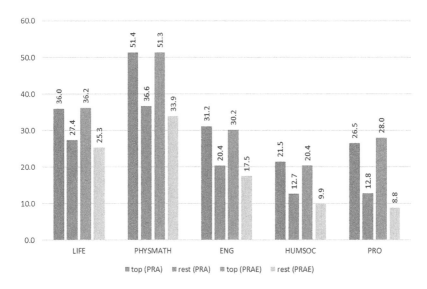

Figure 1.4 Research productivity by cluster of academic disciplines: top performers vs. other academics. The percentage of IC-PRA (and IC-PRAE) in
PRA (and PRAE): the percentage of the average number of internationally co-authored peer-reviewed articles and article equivalents in
the average number of peer-reviewed articles and article equivalents
published in a 3-year reference period. For all clusters, the results are
statistically significant (in %). All countries combined.

Table 1.6 The distribution of the threshold number of publications (the
minimum number to be classified as a top performer) in the sample,
in terms of peer-reviewed articles (PRA), by cluster of academic
discipline and by country

Threshold number of publications (PRA)	AT	FI	DE	IE	IT	NL	NO	PL	PT	CH	UK
LIFE	17	12	15	12	20	20	15	9	12	13.5	11.25
PHYSMATH	12	12	12.6	8	18	17	12	9	6	15	12
ENGITECH	5.6	6	3	11	12	16	5	9	15	8	10
HUMSOC	2	6.5	4.8	12.63	6.3	10	7	8	7	5	8
PRO	2.22	5.94	4.8	10	5	6	6.6	11	7	5.4	6.4

The average research productivity distribution in the case of all academics
for all clusters is highly skewed to the right (Figure 1.5). The figure shows the
percentage of authors on the vertical axis and the number of papers (in brackets)
published on the horizontal axis (see the long tail of productivity on the right
across all clusters; see also a very high percentage of research non-performers
among European academics, all countries combined).

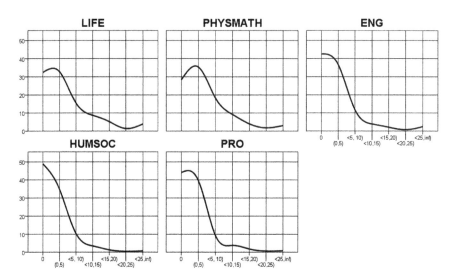

Figure 1.5 All European academics: the distribution of peer-reviewed articles (PRA) published during the 3-year reference period, by cluster of academic disciplines and publication number groups (in percentage). Vertically: percentage of authors, horizontally: number of papers published.

Top performers, as defined in this chapter, provide substance to European research production: without them, it would lose about 40–50 percent of it, depending on the different approaches to defining productivity. The three approaches tested here—the number of articles, peer-reviewed articles, and article equivalents published in the 3-year timeframe studied—lead to slightly different results (see the last three columns in Table 1.7). First, using sheer articles (A), on average, consistently across all European systems studied, slightly less than half (45.9 percent) of all academic research production comes from about 10 percent of the most highly productive academics. In four systems, the share is close to, or exceeds, 50 percent (Austria, Finland, Poland, and Portugal). Second, using peer-reviewed articles (PRA), the share is higher, reaching 53.4 percent, with the share lower than a half for only 3 out of 11 (Italy, Norway, and the UK); and, third, using article equivalents (that is, both peer-reviewed articles, book chapters, books authored and books edited), the share goes down to 37.8 percent, with only Poland reaching a half (50.1 percent). The Polish case is symptomatic for a system in which the traditional role of authored books is very important in moving up the academic ladder (for a doctoral degree, habilitation degree, and the professorship title) and in which edited books are used extensively as a national research communication channel.

This difference is discussed here to show that different approaches to mesasuring productivity lead to different results, both for European academics as a

Table 1.7 Numbers and percentages of journal articles (A), peer-reviewed journal articles (PRA), and peer-reviewed article equivalents (PRAE) produced in the 3-year reference period, by top performers and by the rest of academics, by country (in %)

	Top performers (numbers)			The rest (numbers)			Total (numbers)			Top performers (percentage)		
	Journal articles (A)	Peer-reviewed journal articles (PRA)	Peer-reviewed journal article equivalents (PRAE)	Journal articles (A)	Peer-reviewed journal articles (PRA)	Peer-reviewed journal article equivalents (PRAE)	Journal articles (A)	Peer-reviewed journal articles (PRA)	Peer-reviewed journal article equivalents (PRAE)	Journal articles (A)	Peer-reviewed journal articles (PRA)	Peer-reviewed journal article equivalents (PRAE)
Austria	3,330	2,227	2,833	1,206	545	3,805	4,536	2,772	6,637	73.4	80.3	36.1
Finland	2,445	1,830	1,640	2,435	1,331	2,356	4,880	3,161	3,997	50.1	57.9	37.0
Germany	2,702	1,898	2,013	3,506	1,616	2,528	6,208	3,514	4,542	43.5	54.0	40.1
Ireland	2,419	1,937	1,712	2,684	1,693	2,436	5,103	3,630	4,148	47.4	53.4	40.7
Italy	5,096	4,089	5,281	10,162	5,844	13,630	15,259	9,933	18,911	33.4	41.2	28.0
Netherlands	1,513	1,267	1,190	1,647	1,131	1,348	3,160	2,398	2,538	47.9	52.8	39.7
Norway	1,902	1,577	1,606	2,340	1,751	2,798	4,243	3,329	4,404	44.8	47.4	37.8
Poland	6,767	5,702	3,224	6,831	3,831	3,116	13,599	9,533	6,340	49.8	59.8	50.1
Portugal	1,992	1,686	1,054	1,952	1,234	1,341	3,945	2,920	2,395	50.5	57.7	35.1
Switzerland	2,798	2,160	1,701	3,304	1,864	1,638	6,102	4,024	3,339	45.9	53.7	41.9
UK	1,740	1,471	687	2,475	1,726	872	4,215	3,196	1,559	41.3	46.0	37.9
TOTAL	32,706	25,844	22,943	38,543	22,567	35,867	71,248	48,410	58,809	45.9	53.4	37.8

whole and for academics in individual countries studied. Cross-country differences vary, depending on major communication channels used and the extent to which they are peer-reviewed. For our purposes here, the most useful approach is through peer-reviewed journal articles (PRA).

The top perfomers: a gender distribution

The gender differential in academic productivity rates and the gender stratification in science are highly important issues from the perspectives of public policy (Leathwood and Read 2009; Fitzgerald 2013) and equity, as well as women's status in higher education (Allan 2011). 'No other area in the sociological treatment of scientific careers has received more attention than that of gender. Even in the larger context of stratification research on science, the area of gender has remained the most active' (Hermanowicz 2012: 225).

In this section we explore briefly gender differences in research productivity and, specifically, the gender distribution of research top performers. From a gender perspective, early differences in motivation between male and female academics can have far-reaching consequences for their productivity rates in the future: as Cole and Cole argued (1973: 150–151), even receiving the doctorate may have a qualitatively different meaning for male and female academics. Historically, until a few decades ago, while for male academics, PhD degrees may have been just entry cards to the academic profession, for female academics to have earned the degree was 'in some measure, a triumph.' In some countries, and Poland is the best example, only a minority of women entering the academic profession (as studied through the category of 'new entrants,' or those holding the doctoral degree for no more than 10 years) show a preference for research, compared with the majority of men entering the profession. Polish women academics in the 'new entrants' category show the lowest research interest across all the systems studied. Consistent with the accumulative advantage theory (Allison et al. 1982; Allison and Stewart 1974) and, even more so, consistent with what the Coles referred to as the reinforcement of research activity by the reward system, an early lack of success leads to smaller chances of later scientific success. This is the darker side of the accumulation of rewards in science—it is 'the accumulation of failures—the process of "accumulative disadvantage"' (Cole and Cole 1973: 146; Cole 1979: 78–81). Productivity is heavily influenced by the recognition of early work and, consequently, as the Coles argue: 'if women fail to be as productive in the years immediately following their degree, the social process of accumulative disadvantage may take over and contribute to their falling further behind in the race to produce new scientific discoveries' (Cole and Cole 1973: 151). In other words, as Jonathan R. Cole argued in *Fair Science. Women in the Scientific Community*, the skewed distribution of scientific productivity and of subsequent rewards also results from the process of 'the poor getting poorer':

> the growing inequality between the 'haves' and 'have-nots' of science results in part from a decline in productivity among those scientists who started

their careers as moderately productive researchers, while the elite remain moderately or highly prolific researchers. Potentially, this process can influence the careers of women scientists.

(Cole 1979: 8)

While the 'glass ceiling' for women in science appears to have already been broken (Cummings and Finkelstein 2012: 76 in a US context), globally, academic men have better academic networks and use them more often. Consequently, 'the traditional gender differences in academic work seem to be reproduced through international academic activities' (Vabø et al. 2014: 202). Internationalization in research (for instance, distant conferences, sabbatical leaves abroad, generating international funding with international colleagues)—powered by the opportunities provided by globalization—tends to favor male academics who are less constrained in large-scale international collaboration. As there is a strong correlation between internationalization in research and individual research productivity (see Abramo, D'Angelo, and Solazzi 2011a, 2011b for Italy and Chapter 4), the research productivity of female academics—who are generally more 'internationalized at home' (for instance, in teaching) but less 'internationalized abroad' (for instance, in international collaborative research projects) than male academics—is more affected by the mounting pressures of internationalization than that of male academics. In simple terms, male academics are able to use new internationalization opportunities more effectively.

Not surprisingly, based on the CAP data, Michel Rostan, Flavio A. Ceravolo, and Amy Scott Metcalfe (2014: 130) conclude that

> the prototypical academic figure in international research collaboration is a man, in his mid-50s or younger, working as a professor in a field of the natural sciences at a university in a small, non-Asian and non-English speaking country with a mature economy.

Jisun Jung concluded her study of gender differences in research in China, Australia, the United States, Brazil, and the United Kingdom as follows: 'male academics prefer research, invest much more time in research, have higher publication rates, have diverse funding sources, and are involved in a greater number of international collaborations and academic service activities' (Jung 2015: 176).

The gender gap in research productivity continues and gender differences and inequalities still remain, with 'the permanence of some barriers to women's careers' (Goastellec and Pekari 2013: 76). In general, though, sex differences in productivity are not immune to social change: while women academics used to publish at '50–60 percent' of the male academic rate, now they do so at around '70–80 percent' rate, as Yu Xie and Kimberlee A. Shauman conclude in their *Women in Science. Career Processes and Outcomes* (2003: 182–183) in a US context. The reasons for what Cole and Zuckerman (1984: 218) termed 'the productivity puzzle,' as explored through a systematic multivariate approach, are as follows:

> Women scientists publish fewer papers than men because women are less likely than men to have the personal characteristics, structural positions, and facilitating resources that are conductive to publication. There is very little *direct* effect of sex on research productivity. ... Women and men scientists are located in different academic structures with different access to valuable resources. ... Once sex differences in such positions are taken into account ... net differences between men and women in research productivity are nil or negligible.
>
> (Xie and Shauman 2003: 191–193)

However, as a comparative analysis of micro-level data from nine countries for 1992 and 2007 show, the proportion of women in academia increases and the proportion of full professors who are women also increases (Cummings and Bain 2016: 297). The implications for the scientific productivity of both male and female academics in the Coles' cumulative advantage and reinforcement theories are clear, as Stephan and Levin (1992: 29) emphasize: 'Success breeds success. Consequently, those who enjoy success continue to be productive throughout their lives; those who have less success become discouraged and eventually look to other pursuits for satisfaction.'

The academic career is highly demanding, especially when most young people consider marriage as well as childbirth: 'those who actually decide to build families tend to experience considerable strain, finding they do not have as much time to devote to their work as their colleagues' (Cummings and Finkelstein 2012: 67–68). Gendered patterns of academic work and life can be analyzed both quantitatively (as in our example of male and female top perfomers below) and qualitatively. Qualitative explorations show wider socio-cultural contexts in which statistical findings need to be embedded. A perfect summary of the underlying foundations of the (decreasing but still powerful) academic gender gap as studied through a series of interviews in Anglo-Saxon countries is as follows:

> the academic gender gap has been diminishing for decades, yet it is nonetheless perpetuated by institutional priorities, academic practices, collegial relations, variations in family circumstances, and gendered priorities. Despite major educational, social, and institutional changes, men are still more likely than women to work in departments with a stronger research culture, to receive informal mentoring early in their career, to marry a supportive spouse who takes on most of the household chores, to view themselves as experts, and to receive acknowledgement and recognition for their research and scholarship from editors, publishers, managers, colleagues, and family members.
>
> (Baker 2012: 173)

From a gender perspective applied to our data, the proportion of male academics among research top performers as defined in this chapter is higher than that of female academics but 'productivity concentration indexes' for both genders (linking the percentages of male and female top performers to the percentages of all male and all female academics in national systems) clearly show that the role of highly productive female academics is much higher than traditionally assumed in the literature on gender implications of the social stratification in science.

The mere *share* of women among our top performers as defined in this chapter is not a fair measure. To explore the inequality in academic knowledge production along gender lines, a more sophisticated measuring instrument is needed. Following Abramo et al. (2009a: 143) who focused on 'star scientists' in Italy based on large-scale bibliometric data, we have constructed a similar 'productivity concentration index' for all European countries, for both genders.

The concentration index is a 'measure of association between two variables' based on frequencies data and varying around the neutral value of 1: the percentage of male top performers divided by the percentage of all male academics in a given system, or the share of male academics among top performers divided by the share of male academics among all academics. 'The index of concentration, equaling 1.60, indicates that the relative frequency of this profile among star scientists is over 60% greater than the frequency of the same profile in the entire population' (Abramo et al. 2009a: 143–144). That is, in the case of male academics from the UK (Table 1.8), the productivity concentration index of 1.3 for male academics shows that the relative frequency of male research top performers among all research top performers is 30 percent higher than the frequency of male academics among all academics. Similarly, in the case of female academics from the UK, the productivity concentration index of 0.5 for female academics shows that the relative frequency of female research top performers in all research top performers is 50 percent lower than the share of female academics in all academics.

Universally, across most systems, male productivity concentration indexes are slightly higher than 1 (from 1.1 in Germany, Poland, and Portugal to 1.3 in the UK and Ireland) and female productivity concentration indexes are lower than 1 (from 0.5 in Germany and the UK to 0.9 in Austria, the Netherlands, Poland, and Portugal). In two countries (Austria and the Netherlands), the male productivity concentration index is 1. So, in most countries, male academics are over-represented among top performers, and female academics are under-represented—which is not surprising in the context of the over-representation of male academics in senior ranks for which higher productivity is traditionally reported. In other words, what matters in our analysis is not only the gender distribution of top performers, as shown in the 'frequency' line in Table 1.8 (and the *share* of male top performers, ranging from two-thirds to four-fifths) but also the *relative* presence of male and female academics in the subpopulation of research top performers as measured by a productivity concentration index by genders, as shown in the 'concentration' line in the same table. The concentration

Table 1.8 Gender distribution of top performers by country (numbers and percentages), for all countries. The productivity concentration index is the percentage of male top performers/divided by the percentage of male researchers in a given country; the same applies to female top performers

Items/Countries	AT		FI		DE		IE		IT		NL		NO		PL		PT		CH		UK	
	M	F	M	F	M	F	M	F	M	F	M	F	M	F	M	F	M	F	M	F	M	F
Number	74	31	59	21	74	10	48	22	143	33	35	7	56	14	101	79	24	18	51	11	23	6
Frequency	70.2	29.8	73.2	26.8	88.4	11.6	68.6	32.4	81.4	18.6	83.1	16.9	80.3	19.7	56.1	43.9	58.1	41.9	82.5	17.5	78.7	21.3
Concentration	1.0	0.9	1.2	0.7	1.1	0.5	1.3	0.7	1.2	0.6	1.0	0.9	1.2	0.6	1.1	1.1	1.1	0.9	1.2	0.6	1.3	0.5

of men among top performers is precisely twice that of the concentration of women among top performers in Italy, Norway, Switzerland (1.2 vs. 0.6) and it is slightly lower in Finland, Ireland, and Poland. It is the lowest in Austria and the Netherlands, and the highest in the UK, with a male concentration two and a half times higher.

In the context of the traditional sociology of science and social stratification literature (Wilson 1995; Hagstrom 1965; Merton 1973; Cole and Cole 1973; Zuckerman 1996; Cole 1979), these research results strongly support the argument of the historically growing role of female academics in academic knowledge production: in almost all countries studied, the difference between the *relative* presence of male and female academics in the subpopulation of research top performers is only by a factor of two or less. In the emerging, consistent patterns of inequality in knowledge production, the high role of women academics among highly productive academics is undeniable. The gender productivity gap among research top performers (and the under-representation of female academics in this group) is clearly much lower than expected. However, female academics may find themselves increasingly disadvantaged in the future as a consequence of new public management reforms which are found to have affected them (as the Dutch case shows) more than male academics through a skewed allocation of different academic tasks, with female academics spending more time on teaching and male academics spending more time on research (Leišyte and Hosch-Dayican 2017: 102–103).

There is a long list of caveats in this section, though, leading to reservations of various natures. We will focus on two. First, the research productivity data are self-reported and male academics in some systems may tend to overestimate the number of articles they produce, while female academics may tend to underestimate their number. In other words, different national academic cultures may lead to different levels of overestimation and underestimation of research production contingent on the gender factor. Second, the various systems studied here are differently populated by female academics in general (20–50 percent), and by female academics in the university sector in particular (15–55 percent). Also, there are gender-based choices of research problems, of academic disciplines, and of research styles; including publication patterns, and matters relating to research productivity (Baker 2012). Differences in research styles (for instance, publishing less frequently) between men and women scientists may be linked to the issue of women being 'latecomers to the academic world' (Fisher 2005: 275) and to women frequently embracing a more perfectionist approach to research (Hermanowicz 2012: 229). As Hermanowicz comments on a possible distinctive style adopted by women, 'the perception of a marginal status compels them to adopt extra-high standards of conformity in order to be viewed as legitimate members of the scientific community' (2012: 229)

Not surprisingly, our research shows that female academics already in the top academic ranks are often on average more productive than men in the same ranks, work longer total weekly hours, longer weekly research hours, and are more research-oriented: to reach the highest levels of academic recognition, they had to work in often hostile academic environments (Cole and Cole 1973: 127). Still, as noted above, it would be fundamentally unfair to disregard in our study of highly performing academics the findings from qualitative empirical research on gendered patterns of university-based academic work. There are persistent features of the academic systems studied that are detrimental to gender equality: male and female academics are still unequally distributed in the academic hierarchy and there are gender differences in terms of access to full-time positions in prestigious higher education institutions, access to specific fields, obtaining higher ranks and salaries, or having high publication rates (Goastellec and Pekari 2013: 55). The workload imbalance disadvantaging research in the case of female academics may mean 'stagnation or disruption of an academic career path, especially for women in mid-career levels such as assistant and associate professor, where the criteria for career progression are particularly demanding with respect to research outputs' (Leišyte and Hosch-Dayican 2017: 104). By way of example, this is how the gender gap, including the gender high productivity gap, can be contextualized through qualitative empirical material:

> Men tend to search for full-time positions in high-profile research universities, which provide them with opportunities to carry out funded research, gain scholarly publications, and attain high salaries and esteem from their peers. Conversely, women doctorates express more ambivalence about striving for high-pressure careers and sometimes accept jobs that pay less but are located closer to parents, partners, and friends or that better enable them to manage care work. Because working full-time and being promoted through the ranks require long hours and measurable indicators of research productivity, female PhDs with infants or toddlers may initially accept temporary and part-time positions to help them manage their domestic workload. Others choose employment in teaching universities with less publishing pressure in order to accommodate childrearing without undue stress.
>
> (Baker 2012: 160–161)

Working time distribution and teaching and research role orientation

The first question in this section is whether the working habits of top performers are different from those of the remaining 90 percent of research-involved academics. The second question is whether top performers are more research-oriented (both consistent with the research literature on research productivity, see especially Fox 1992; Bentley and Kyvik 2013; and Shin and Cummings 2010).

We explore here the five dimensions of academic work which were captured by the CAP/EUROAC datasets: teaching, research, service, administration, and 'other' academic activities. The mean for the annualized total working time differential between top performers and the rest of academics is 5.7 hours, ranging from 3.7 hours in Italy to 7.4 hours in Germany and 8.0 hours in Norway. In other words, for example, German top performers, when compared with the rest of (research-involved, as in the whole book) German academics, spend on average an additional 42.6 full working days in academia per year (7.4 hours times 46 working weeks divided by 8 hours per day), and Norwegian top performers spend on average an additional 46 full working days.

We know from previous research productivity studies that longer working hours, and especially research hours, substantially contribute to high productivity: our study shows (with powerful results: p-value <0.001) what exactly 'longer hours' mean for the upper 10 percent of highly productive academics, and shows it from a comparative cross-national perspective. A ticket to enter the class of national top performers differs from country to country, though; and even more so, differs by cluster of academic discipline.

We are interested in the differences in the means of total working hours, and especially the means of research hours, between the two subpopulations in each country and the significance of the results (Table 1.9). Our results are based on two-sided tests assuming equal differences in arithmetic means with a significance level α = 0.05. For each pair with a mean difference significantly different from zero, the symbol of the larger category ('Top' for top performers or 'Rest' for the rest of academics) appears in the column. Tests are adjusted for all pairwise comparisons within a row for each innermost sub-table using the Bonferroni correction. T-tests for the equality of two arithmetic means (Top vs. Rest) were performed for each country for each of the five types of academic activities studied.

As clearly seen in Table 1.9, longer research hours for top performers are statistically significant for a pool of six countries ('Top' symbols in the line of 'research'). But also for a pool of eight countries, longer administration hours for top performers are statistically significant ('Top' symbols in the line of 'administration'). The same applies to service hours (two countries) and hours spent on 'other' academic activities (four countries). Not surprisingly, the same also applies to total working hours in *all* the countries studied. In two countries (Norway and Switzerland), their longer teaching hours are also statistically

Table 1.9 Results of t-tests for the equality of means, top performers (Top) vs. the rest of academics (Rest), all countries. 'How long do you spend on various academic activities?', only full-time academics in universities involved in research (mean per year, 60 percent when classes are in session and 40 percent when classes are not in session)

	AT	FI	DE	IE	IT	NL	NO	PL	PT	CH	UK
Teaching				Rest	Rest		Top	Rest		Top	
Research			Top	Top	Top			Top	Top		Top
Service					Top		Top				
Administration	Top	Top	Top		Top	Top	Top	Top		Top	
Other	Top		Top	Top			Top				
Total	Top	Top	Top	Top	Top	Top	Top	Top	Top	Top	Top

significant. Top performers tend to spend more time on all activities, not only on research. There is a standard working pattern for top performers in most of the countries studied: the time they spend on research is higher. Top performers also spend more time on teaching and on service hours. Specifically, they also spend much more time on administration. 'Science takes time'; and much more scientific production takes much more time. Top performers work (much) longer hours: week by week, month by month, and year by year. Their longer total working time is statistically significant for all countries.

The results of the z test for the equality of fractions performed for all countries (Table 1.10) are based on two-sided tests with a significance level of $\alpha = 0.05$. Tests are adjusted for all pairwise comparisons within a row for each innermost sub-table using the Bonferroni correction.

Z tests for the equality of fractions (Top vs. Rest) were performed for each country for each of the four categories of teaching and research orientation. Correspondingly, as before, for each pair with a fraction difference significantly different from zero, the symbol for the larger category ('Top' for research top performers or 'Rest' for the rest of academics) appears in the column.

As clearly seen in Table 1.10, the research role orientation (answer 3) among top performers is statistically significant in a pool of seven countries ('Top' symbols in the line for 'in both, but leaning toward research,' with no exceptions). Additionally, in a pool of five countries, the strong research role orientation (answer 4) for top performers is also statistically significant, again with no exceptions. The division in role orientation between top performers and the rest of academics is clear (and all differences are statistically

Table 1.10 Results of z tests for the equality of fractions, all countries. Preferences for teaching/research (Question B2: 'Regarding your own preferences, do your interests lie primarily in teaching or in research?'), research top performers (Top) vs. the rest of academics (Rest)

	AT	FI	DE	IE	IT	NL	NO	PL	PT	CH	UK
Primarily in teaching		Rest	Rest	Rest	.a	.a	.a	Rest	Rest		.a
In both, but leaning toward teaching		Rest		Rest	Rest	Rest	Rest	Rest	Rest	Rest	Rest
In both, but leaning toward research		Top	Top	Top		Top		Top	Top	Top	
Primarily in research				Top	Top			Top	Top		Top

Note: .a This category is not used in comparisons because its column proportion is equal to zero or one.

significant): in all the systems studied, top performers are more research-oriented than the rest of academics. Being interested 'primarily in teaching' virtually excludes such European academics from the class of research top performers: their share attains a maximum of 1.1 percent in Ireland. In addition, being interested 'in both, but leaning toward teaching' again almost excludes such European academics from the same class: their share is about 3–8 percent in Finland, Ireland, Italy, the Netherlands, Norway, and the UK, and more in three other countries: Switzerland (10.7 percent), Poland (13.2 percent), and Portugal (21.8 percent). Poland and Portugal are clearly teaching-focused systems, as shown in Chapter 5. Also, the share of top performers whose interests lie 'in both, but leaning toward research' is consistently similar across Europe (about 57–73 percent). Our results show that a research role orientation is a powerful indicator of belonging to the class of the European research elite: as could be expected, being research-oriented is virtually a must for European academics and being teaching-oriented virtually excludes them from this class.

However, the above results about the working time distribution and the teaching/research role orientation among highly productive academics and the rest of academics are not multi-dimensional (the conclusions from the t-test and z test analyses are independent of each other). A study of multi-dimensional relationships requires a model approach with a number of dependent variables, including research hours and research orientation, among several others. Therefore, we present a regression analysis below.

Top performers are examined through a bivariate analysis of the working time distribution and the teaching or research role orientation. Although bivariate analyses are limited as they do not control for other important factors that might affect research productivity (Teodorescu 2000: 203), the two selected variables have emerged as key in numerous productivity studies (Bentley 2015; Bentley and Kyvik 2013; Drennan et al. 2013; Jung 2014; Marquina and Ferreiro 2015; Shin and Cummings 2010). However, a study of multi-dimensional relationships requires a model approach, and, therefore, odds ratio estimates with logistic regression of being a highly productive academic are presented, following inferential analyses.

The class of top performers and how to enter it

In the next step of analysis, we have developed an analytical model to study research productivity based on the research literature, especially quantitative studies of American social scientists by Mary Frank Fox (1992: 295–297), of Australian academics by Paul Ramsden (1994: 211–212), and of academics from ten countries by Daniel Teodorescu (2000: 207). Following Ramsden (1994), we have assumed that 'any sensible explanation of research output must take into account personal (individual) and structural (environmental) factors, and preferably also the interaction between them.' Following the research literature, independent variables are grouped as 'individual' and 'institutional' characteristics in eight clusters (see Table 1.11).

Table 1.11 Faculty research productivity: variables in the model (survey question numbers in parentheses)

Individual variables	Institutional variables
Personal/Demographics	*Institutional policies*
Female (F1)	Strong performance orientation (E4)
Mean age (F2)	Research considered in personnel decisions (E6)
Full-time (A7)	*Institutional support*
Professor (A10)	Availability of research funds (B3)
Socialization	Supportive attitude of administration (E4)
Intensive faculty guidance (A3)	
Research projects with faculty (A3)	
Internationalization and collaboration	
Collaborating internationally (D1)	
Collaborating domestically (D1)	
Publishing in a foreign country (D5)	
Research int'l in scope or orientation (D2)	
Academic behaviors	
Annualized mean research hours (60% in session and 40% not in session) (B1)	
Academic attitudes and role orientation	
Research-oriented (only answer 4) (B2)	
Scholarship is original research (B5)	
Basic/theoretical research (D2)	
Overall research engagement	
National/int'l committees/boards/bodies (A13)	
A peer reviewer (A13)	
Editor of journals/book series (A13)	

There are two questions related to the overall research approach taken. The first question is why estimate a regression model for each of the 11 countries rather than pooling the sample and control for country. The argument for the choice of 10 percent top performers per country (and per major cluster of academic discipline) is that the approach of selecting merely the upper 10 percent of academics, regardless of the country, does not fit the purpose of highlighting cross-national differences among top performers. The factors important in predicting high research productivity in some countries might be irrelevant in other countries. However, we have also developed a single model controlling for country fixed-effects and the two models will be compared briefly in the 'Discussion'

Table 1.12 Odds ratio estimates by logistic regression for being in the top 10 percent in research productivity (by PRA), all countries

	Austria	Finland	Germany	Ireland	Italy	Netherlands	Norway	Poland	Portugal	Switzerland	United Kingdom
Nagelkerke's R²	0.155	0.308	0.210	0.270	0.256	0.207	0.298	0.292	0.672	0.362	0.364
Individual predictors											
Personal/demographics											
Female			0.453*		0.474*						
Age					0.936**						
Full-time			6.203*								
Professor	2.046*		2.98**	5.003***	5.008***		4.242***	2.494**			3.963***
Socialization											
Intensive faculty guidance											
Research projects with faculty					0.457*						
Internationalization and collaboration											
Collaborating internationally		5.371**						1.84**			
Collaborating domestically			2.804**		3.536**		3.979**				
Publishing in a foreign country	4.272*			5.275*			7.434*	2.469***		6.508**	
Research int'l in scope or orient.	2.596**	2.401*							7.538**		
Academic behaviors											
Annualized mean weekly research hours (60% in session, 40% not in session)				1.038**			0.942***	1.028**			1.03*

(Continued)

	Austria	Finland	Germany	Ireland	Italy	Netherlands	Norway	Poland	Portugal	Switzerland	United Kingdom
Academic attitudes and role orientation											
Research-oriented	1.908*										
Scholarship is original research											
Basic/theoretical research											
Overall research engagement											
Nat/int'l committees/boards/bodies	2.416**							2.399***			
A peer reviewer			4.778**	9.65*	2.153*	9.641*		2.726***		26.285**(1)	8.029*
Editor of journals/book series										2.203*	2.707**
Institutional predictors											
Institutional policies											
Strong performance orientation											
Research consid. in HR decisions											
Institutional support											
Availability of research funds										3.497***	
Supportive attitude of admin.											

Note: Results that are not statistically significant are not shown in the Table. '-' – no usable data available (question was not asked); ***p<0.001; **p<0.01; *p<0.05. (1)—These odds ratios need to be treated with caution.

section. The second question is why the regression model is not controlled for academic discipline as a potentially important source of variation: unfortunately, the number of observations per discipline was too small in many cases (often less than 10–15 per cluster of disciplines per country).

In this multivariate analysis, we have dichotomized all category variables through a recoding procedure. We started with 42 personal and institutional characteristics, grouped in eight clusters. We then conducted Pearson Rho's correlation tests to find significantly correlated predictors of the dependent variable. The predictors were entered into a four-stage logistic regression model (as in Cummings and Finkelstein 2012). Multicollinearity was tested using an inverse correlation matrix and no independent variables strongly correlated with others were found. The predictive power of the fourth model (as measured by Nagelkerke's R^2) was the highest for Portugal (0.67), the UK, and Switzerland (both 0.36); for Norway, Ireland, Finland, and Poland, it was in the about 0.27–0.31 range. The predictive power of the models of research productivity estimated by other researchers is not substantially higher (for instance, the average variance demonstrated for 12 European countries studied recently by Drennan et al. (2013: 129) is about 30 percent; and about 30 percent for ten globally studied countries in Teodorescu 2000: 212). In Table 1.12 we present the results of the final, fourth model.

Statistically significant individual and institutional variables

The collection of individual variables emerges as more important than the collection of institutional variables, both in terms of the frequency of occurrence and the size of regression coefficients.

In the first block of individual predictors ('personal/ demographics'), there are four variables: 'female,' 'age,' 'full-time,' and 'professor.' Being a female academic entered the equation in one country only: it is a strong predictor of *not* becoming a top performer in Italy, where the odds ratio value indicates that female academics are about half as likely as male academics to be a top performer. In all other countries, being a male academic is not a predictor of becoming a top performer. While the finding for Italy is consistent with the gender-focused analysis of Italian 'star scientists' in Abramo et al. (2009a), overall, our findings are clearly different from the findings from linear regression analyses in which being a female academic has traditionally been negatively correlated with research productivity.

While in most single-nation and cross-national studies, age is not a statistically significant variable, our model shows that 'age' is a powerful predictor of high research performance in two countries. A one-unit increase (that is, 1 year) in Germany and Italy decreases the odds of becoming a top performer. The two cases demonstrate that the traditional mechanisms of 'accumulative advantage' in academic careers, combined with prior mechanisms of 'reinforcement' in science

(Cole and Cole 1973; Zuckerman 1996; Zuckerman 1988; Allison et al. 1982), do not seem to be at work in all European systems: the traditional long-term accumulation of prestige and resources which comes with age, and which is preceded by prior recognition of academic work, is not so clearly visible in Germany and Italy.

Finally, being a 'professor' (or academic seniority) emerged as the single most important variable in the model, with statistical significance in seven countries. In four of them (Ireland, Italy, Norway, and the UK), being faculty at senior ranks increases the odds of becoming a top performer four to five times, in Germany slightly less than three times, in Poland two and a half times and in Finland twice. This finding confirms the conclusions from previous productivity studies—although certainly academics in European higher education are more likely to be promoted to higher ranks if they are highly productive. Productivity affects being a professor and the relationship may be 'reciprocal' (Teodorescu 2000: 214). Strictly speaking, almost all non-demographic independent variables in our model could also be dependent variables in separate analyses. But as Ramsden (1994: 223) argued, 'identifying correlates of high productivity does not mean that we have identified causal relations.'

In the second block of individual predictors ('socialization': receiving intensive faculty guidance during PhD studies and working with faculty in research projects), to great surprise, especially in the context of the US literature, both variables are either statistically insignificant or, as in Italy, they actually *decrease* the odds of becoming top performers (inconsistent with findings in Horta and Santos 2016 who focused on the impact of publishing during doctoral studies on future productivity). Unfortunately, the following could not be tested: a long line of research in which current affiliation matters (through contacts or halo effects), whether graduates of major universities are more likely to be highly productive than graduates of minor universities, and whether the next generation's most productive scientists come from a highly selected group of previous top scientists (Crane 1965). A common explanation for the two systems could be that in 'academic oligarchy' types of systems, doctoral students receive faculty guidance more by working for senior faculty, possibly as a cheap academic labor force, rather than independently working with them. According to the 'reinforcement' theory (Zuckerman 1996; Fox 1983), later productivity is substantially influenced by the early recognition of research work, so young academics receiving intensive faculty guidance in specific Polish and Italian systems may have lower odds of becoming top performers later in their careers due to not pursuing their independent research strongly enough early in their careers.

The third block of individual predictors ('internationalization and collaboration') emerges as the single most important grouping in predicting high research productivity: each of the four variables at least doubles the odds of becoming a top performer. The four variables are as follows: 'collaborating internationally,' 'collaborating domestically,' 'publishing in a foreign country,' and 'research international in scope or orientation.' These variables enter the equation in all countries except one (the Netherlands).

Domestic collaboration influences high research productivity in four countries (Germany, Italy, Norway, and the UK). 'Publishing in a foreign country' emerged as a powerful predictor in five smaller or peripheral higher education systems: Austria, Ireland, Poland, Switzerland, and Norway, as with small academic markets it makes it more necessary for prolific academics to publish internationally. Also, 'research international in scope or orientation' increases the odds in three countries. In the block of 'academic behaviors,' contrary to previous research conclusions from linear regression models (most recently in Cummings and Finkelstein 2012: 58; Shin and Cummings 2010: 590; and Drennan et al. 2013: 127), annualized mean weekly research hours emerged as determinative predictors only in three countries (Ireland, Poland, and the UK): a unit increase of 1 hour (in annualized research hours per week) increases the odds of being a top performer by a 2.8–3.8 percent on average (*ceteris paribus*). In other words, in these three countries, an increase of 10 annualized research hours per week leads to an increase in the odds by between a quarter and one-third. In Norway, surprisingly, annualized mean weekly research hours emerged as predictors decreasing the odds. In all the other countries, a high research time investment is not a determinative predictor of becoming a top performer.

Again, in the block of 'academic attitudes and role orientation,' contrary to the findings from previous linear regression models, research orientation emerged as a powerful predictor of research productivity in only one country, with $Exp(B) = 1.91$ for Austria. In all other countries, it was not a determinative predictor. Also, the view of scholarship as 'original research' and the emphasis on 'basic/theoretical research' do not emerge as correlated with high research productivity in any country.

Surprisingly, while in descriptive statistics (as in Postiglione and Jung 2013) and in inferential analyses based on t-tests for the equality of means and z tests for the equality of fractions presented above, both long research hours (academic behaviors) and high research orientation (academic attitudes) emerge as important characteristics of top performers, following the almost universal findings in the research productivity literature, here, a multi-dimensional model approach supports these findings in selected countries only. Finally, and understandably in the context of previous literature, being a peer reviewer (in the block of 'overall research engagement') emerges as a powerful predictor of becoming a top performer: it increases the odds in six countries—five times in Finland, eight times in the UK, and nine times in the Netherlands and Ireland. It may effectively mean at least two things: first, it pays off to be a reviewer; and, second, reviewers are the right persons in the right place in the current science systems.

The importance of variables differs from country to country, but the overall determinative power of individual-level predictors (blocks 1 through 6) is much stronger than those of institutional-level predictors (blocks 7 and 8), consistent with previous research on productivity (Ramsden 1994: 220; Shin and Cummings 2010: 588; Teodorescu 2000: 212; and Cummings and Finkelstein 2012: 59). As Drennan et al. (2013: 128) concluded in their recent study, 'institutional factors were found to have very little impact on research productivity.' This finding is also consistent with the conclusion about the American professoriate that 'intrinsic motivations' rather than 'institutional incentive structures' (Finkelstein 1984: 97–98, Teodorescu 2000: 217) stimulate research productivity. In general, the institutional-level predictors are statistically significant in only one case in one country (Switzerland). Surprisingly in the context of previous research (Wanner et al. 1981; Fox 1983), two institutional predictors are not statistically significant in any of the countries studied: 'availability of research funds' and 'supportive attitude of administration' (except for Switzerland in the case of research funding). This might mean that, generally, neither institutional policies nor institutional support substantially matter in becoming a top performer.

Interestingly, while the conclusions from linear regression models indicate that institutional-level predictors of research productivity are weak, in our logistic regression model the conclusions indicate that they are actually statistically insignificant. In particular, research funds and academic climate (good academic-administration relationships) do not enter the equations in any country in the model. Also, the strong performance orientation of institutions is statistically insignificant in all countries except Switzerland. Institutional variables are more applicable to public policy than individual variables because they may be amenable to change—to learn more about the optimal conditions for highly productive academics, 'management patterns can be changed more easily than individual interests and attitudes' (Ramsden 1994: 224).

Discussion

We have used two complementary approaches to explore the unique class of European research top performers: statistical inference and a multi-dimensional logistic regression model. The findings from statistical inference show two clear cross-national patterns applicable to top performers: longer working hours (in most working time categories) and higher research orientation. In only three countries do the rest of academics actually spend more time than top performers on any of the studied activities: this is teaching in Ireland, Italy, and Poland. The results from these three countries provide strong support for a thesis about an antagonistic or competitive relationship between teaching and research (as argued by Fox (1992) who discussed 'mutuality' and 'competition' between teaching and research), at statistically significant levels: while highly productive academics in these countries spend more time on research, the rest of academics spend more time on teaching. In these countries, as Fox (1992: 303) argued, teaching and research 'are at some odds with each other.' Top performers work (much) longer total hours every week, all year round. Their longer total working time is statistically significant for all countries. From a statistical inference approach, top performers are also more research-oriented than the rest of academics. The most salient difference between the two sub-populations can be seen in three structurally similar systems having a similar teaching/research time distribution: in Ireland, Portugal, and Poland only about half of the 'rest' of academics are research-oriented. They are nominally involved in research but they are not research-oriented in their self-declared role preferences. In general, the distribution of research role orientation is almost universal across all the countries studied. Consequently, highly productive academics are almost universally more intra-nationally different from 'average' academics, and almost universally more similar to top performers in other countries.

Our study draws attention to the fact that there are important differences in those conclusions from linear regression models detailed in previous studies, both single-nation and cross-national, and the conclusions derived via a multiple regression model from predictors of belonging to a distinctive group of the European research elite as defined in this chapter. The internationalization of research, national and international research collaboration, international publishing, academic seniority, as well as high levels of overall research engagement emerge as powerful correlates of high research productivity. Also, in both cases, the overall determinative power of individual-level predictors is stronger than that of institutional-level predictors (as in Ramsden 1994: 223; Shin and Cummings 2010: 586; and Cummings and Finkelstein 2012: 58).

While in t-test and z test analyses, both research hours and research orientation strongly characterize top performers, a multi-dimensional model approach through regression analysis, surprisingly, supports these findings in selected countries only. From among individual variables, both age and academic seniority (being a professor) are important predictors of high research productivity. However, surprisingly, neither annualized research hours, nor research orientation (traditionally, the two most important predictors of research productivity) emerged as powerful predictors of high research productivity in more than three and two countries, respectively. This is perhaps the most perplexing result of our research: while in inferential analyses, these are critical variables in all the systems studied, in multi-dimensional analyses, their role is considerably smaller than expected. The specific case of working time distribution and research role orientation clearly shows that a combination of several approaches is more fruitful than a reliance on any of them separately.

There is also an interesting tension between the conclusions drawn from 11 multiple regression models and the single model controlling for country fixed-effects. The difference is in focus: highly productive academics being explored as nested in the context of national systems or explored independent of the context. While in the first model, in the block of personal/demographic variables, both age and gender entered the equation in two countries; in the single model for European academics being female was statistically insignificant but mean age was also significant, decreasing the odds of becoming a top performer (Exp(B) = 0.984). While in the first model working full-time was statistically significant only in one country (Germany), in the single model being employed full-time is statistically insignificant; also, while in the first model being a professor (or academic seniority) increases the odds in most countries from two to five times, in the single model it increases the odds by 140 percent. The two socialization variables were not significant in either of the models (except for Italy in the former). The internationalization and collaboration variables increase the odds by between 180–380 percent (depending on the country) in the first model, and by a mere 30–50 percent in the second model. In both models, research being international 'in scope or orientation' increases the odds. Also in both models, higher mean weekly research hours increase the odds (Exp(B) = 1.038–1.030 and Exp(B) = 1.012, respectively). However, self-declared research role orientation in the first model is statistically significant in only one country, and in the second, single model, it is statistically significant, increasing the odds by 26 percent. Also, the research engagement variables increase the odds in the first model by 65–240 percent and in the single model by a mere 55–100 percent. As for institutional-level variables, in the first model they are statistically significant in only two countries and in the single model they are statistically insignificant. In the single model, with Poland as a reference category, being a German, Norwegian, or Austrian academic increases the odds by 115–865 percent. Nagelkerke's R^2 is 0.204.

The differences in conclusions from our two different logistic regression models (with top performers differently defined; in Europe as a whole or separately in European systems) are smaller than expected: in the context of previous single-nation studies, the insignificance of gender in the single model comes as a surprise. The emergence of academic seniority as a predictor of high research productivity in the single model is consistent with previous studies; the statistical significance of the research role orientation in only one country in the first model (and its significance in the single model) come as a surprise. This may imply that there is a growing tension between self-declared research role orientation and research productivity in Europe. While European academics increasingly view themselves as research-oriented, research orientation emerges as a much less statistically significant predictor of becoming a top performer than expected from previous research. In contrast, research time investments emerge as significant predictors in both the first model (in three countries) and in the single model.

The overall relative insignificance of institutional predictors in the first model and its small significance (Exp(B) = 1.267) in the second model in the case of highly productive academics may provide further support for the 'sacred spark' theory of productivity (Cole and Cole 1973): regardless of administrative and financial institutional settings, some faculty—and they may be our 'research top performers'—will always show greater inner drive toward research than others. Also, Peter James Bentley and Svein Kyvik, in their global study of 13 countries, found more support for this theory than for the competing 'utility maximization theory' (Stephan and Levin 1992). As the Coles (1973: 71) argued, 'to be successful, a scientist must have the self-discipline to work long hours and to work productively. Such self-discipline and motivation probably explains at least as much variance in scientific success as native ability.' Top performers as defined in this chapter seem to fit this description perfectly. The 'accumulative advantage' theory (combined with 'reinforcement theory') found only partial support in the study: age is not a significant predictor in most systems studied, and academic seniority (or professorships), although a significant predictor in most systems, is reciprocally linked to productivity.

Concluding reflections

In this chapter we have followed several research paths. First, we have focused on the rare scholarly theme of highly productive academics. Their role in knowledge production across all 11 European systems studied is pivotal: without these 10 percent of academics, national academic outputs would be halved. Second, we have presented an international comparative study based on solid quantitative material rather than the single-nation studies that dominate previous research. Third, in contrast to bibliometric studies of research productivity, we focused on academic attitudes, behaviors, and perceptions as the predictors of becoming research top performers. Our study provides a large-scale and cross-national corroboration of the systematic inequality in knowledge production, suggested for the first time by Alfred Lotka (1926) and Derek de Solla Price (1963). What we may term the '10/50 rule' holds strongly across Europe (with the upper 10 percent of academics producing 50 percent of all peer-reviewed publications).

European highly productive academics are a highly homogeneous group of academics whose high research performance is driven by structurally similar factors which cannot be easily replicated through policy measures. The variables increasing the odds of entering this class are individual rather than institutional. From whichever institutional and national contexts they come, they work according to similar working patterns and they share similar academic attitudes. Highly productive academics, as they emerge from this study, are similar from a European cross-national perspective and they substantially differ intra nationally from their lower-performing colleagues. They are a universal academic species and they share roughly the same burden of academic production across Europe.

Our study draws attention to the fact that there are important differences in those conclusions from linear regression models with the correlates of research productivity detailed in previous studies and the conclusions from a multiple regression model with predictors of belonging to the European research elite. Our study shows the gender of academics as a very weak predictor, their age as a powerful predictor, and academic seniority and internationalization as the most important predictors. Contrary to most previous findings based on linear regression models, both annualized mean weekly research hours and research role orientation only emerged as powerful predictors of becoming a research top performer in several countries. In line with most previous research, though, institutional-level predictors emerged as statistically insignificant.

The study also shows a considerable tension between the conclusions from inferential results and logistic regression results. Surprisingly, while in inferential analyses both long research hours and high research orientation emerge as critical characteristics of top performers, a multi-dimensional model approach supports these findings in selected countries only. While in inferential analyses, these are crucial variables in all the systems studied, in multi-dimensional analyses, their role is small. We conclude, therefore, that a combination of several approaches provides a better empirical insight into the European research elite. It is hard to entirely disregard the finding that being research-oriented is virtually a must to enter to the class of research top performers in Europe and being teaching-oriented virtually excludes European academics from this class. This finding has strong policy implications, especially for hiring new academic staff.

Therefore, based on the combination of inferential and multiple regression findings, European research top performers emerge in this study as much more cosmopolitan (the power of internationalization in research), much more hard-working (the power of long overall working hours and long research hours), and much more research-oriented (the power of a single academic focus) than the rest of European academics, despite differentiated national contexts.

The European academic knowledge production hinges on European top performers. Kyvik (1989: 209) came to similar conclusions about the skewness of Norwegian productivity (the most prolific 20 percent of the faculty produced 50 percent of the total research output) and Abramo et al. (2009a: 143) presented similar findings about Italian productivity patterns (12 percent of authors accounted for 35 percent of the total research output, averaged among the disciplinary areas).

This research shows that consistently across major clusters of academic disciplines, top performers produce about half (53.4 percent) of all European peer-reviewed publications (as well as 45.6 percent of publications in English and 50.2 percent of internationally co-authored publications). Their mean research productivity across major clusters is much higher (on average, 8.56 times) than that of the other academics. Strong cross-disciplinary differences are observed, however.

Interestingly, the average research productivity distribution is highly skewed (with a long tail on the right) not only for all European academics in the sample, which could have been expected, but also for its segment of top performers. The upper 10 percent of academics is as internally stratified as the lower-performing 90 percent, with a very small number of very high publishers: the right tail of the productivity distribution tends to behave exactly as the entire productivity distribution. This result is consistent with recent findings by Yair et al. (2017: 5) who showed in a sample of Israel Prize laureates that the tail of excellence may behave as the entire productivity distribution. In a similar vein, Abramo, D'Angelo, and Soldatenkova (2017a: 334) found the same pattern in the Italian national research system: 'research productivity distribution for all fields is highly skewed to the right, both at overall level and within the upper tail.' This is also the case across Europe.

The most instructive example comes from life sciences (with 2,352 cases and the highest number of statistically significant differences between the two subpopulations among several academic activities studied). The top performers in life sciences, on average, seem to follow all traditional accounts of productive academics in the sociology of science. On average, they work many more hours per week and, specifically, they have the traditional working time distribution attributed to high publishers (Fox 1983; Hagstrom 1974) according to which research-time allocations compete directly with teaching-time allocations (Fox 1992; Kyvik 1990; Ramsden 1994), or the only relevant difference is in general between research time and non-research time (Stephan 2012). Their average weekly teaching time is much shorter, and their research time is much longer; in addition, they spend more hours on administration (presumably more research involves more research grants, which require more administrative work; alternatively, these academics are more often heads of research groups or medium-level administrators, such as directors and deans).

However, limitations of the dataset used mean that three streams of research studied in literature could not be followed in this chapter. First, it was not possible to study differences between top performers from institutions of lower academic standing and those from the most prestigious institutions, knowing that minor and major universities (as in Agrawal et al. 2017; and Crane 1965) may provide more and less favorable academic settings and attract more and less talented students and academics, respectively. Location and affiliation may matter not only for recognition but also for high research productivity, which could not be verified with the dataset used. It could not be studied whether top performers gravitate toward institutions and departments in which research is a priority. Neither within-department (and institution) nor between-department (or institution) variability could be studied, as in Perianes-Rodriguez and Ruiz-Castillo (2015) and in Becker and Toutkoushian (2003).

Second, top performers could not be linked to individual institutions. For this reason, a study of the impact of highly productive academics on the general productivity of their academic units—or of the asymmetry of knowledge production between the within-unit top performers and the within-unit other academics across different institutions—could not be performed (following Piro et al. 2016 who studied Norwegian universities, with the conclusion that their overall productivity impact on units is modest). Top performers may increase the productivity of those present in the organization, and they may also increase the productivity of newly hired members due to their reputation (Agrawal et al. 2017). However, with the instrument used, this could not be explored. And, third, only a cross-sectional study could be performed; thus, no changes over time could be analyzed (for instance, the identification of the persistence of top performance over time as in Kelchtermans and Veugelers (2013), or the length of periods of the stardom of stars as in Abramo et al. (2017b) could not be explored).

Based on the Carnegie dataset of the academic profession, Philip G. Altbach and Lionel S. Lewis (1996: 24) argued, without much further detail, that 'actual productivity is in fact limited to a minority of the profession.' Paul Ramsden's (1994: 223) conclusions in his study of research productivity based on surveys of

890 academics from 18 Australian institutions were similar: 'most publications are produced by a small proportion of the total number of staff.' Also, Mary Frank Fox (1992: 296), based on surveys of 3,968 American social science academics, argued that 'few people produce many articles and many publish few or none.' Therefore our guiding research puzzle was as follows: is this the case across European systems too? Our findings consistently show that such productivity distribution patterns strongly hold for almost all European higher education systems and for all five major clusters of academic disciplines.

Consequently, our empirical findings show that there are different 'academic professions' in European universities, with a small share of highly productive researchers and a large share of relatively middle to low productive academics. Cross-national similarities among highly productive academics are as strong as the intra-national differences between them and the remaining research-involved academics in their national systems.

The distribution of academic knowledge production in Europe is highly skewed toward highly productive academics. The policy implications for this historically consistent pattern of research productivity are more important in systems in which research funding is increasingly based on individual research grants (such as Poland following the 2008–2012 wave of reforms) than in systems with primarily institutionally based research funding (such as Italy, Abramo et al. 2011a), and are different for competitive and non-competitive systems in Europe (or with strong 'up or out' vs. 'once in—forever in' employment policies). A major emergent policy dilemma is whether to support more high-performing academics (wherever they are located) or highly ranked institutions, with the option of concentrating high-performing academics in highly ranked institutions, leading to a growing national research concentration in selected institutions only. Additionally, the tension between teaching and research is likely to increase in systems in which more competitive research funding systems are introduced.

Policy conclusions regarding knowledge production as viewed through the proxy of publishing articles and book chapters are perplexing: if European systems dismissed its top performers (the upper 10 percent of their research-active academics), they would lose on average about half of their national academic production. And if European systems dismissed the bottom half of their research-active academics in terms of research productivity, they would lose less than 6 percent of their national knowledge production (in the case of research-active academics employed full-time in the university sector, the loss would be 8.5 percent).

Consequently, a new typology of the academic profession across Europe emerges, based on the measurable contribution to knowledge production: in the research-active segment of the academic profession, there are research top performers, research middle performers (high-middle and low-middle), and research non-performers, or no-publishers. (These are the Coles' 'silent scientists,' whose share among full-time academics employed in the university sector ranges from less than 10 percent in Ireland, Italy, the UK, and the Netherlands to more than 40 percent in Poland.)

On top of that, both higher education institutions in general and universities in particular are populated by non research-active faculty, an additional segment of research non-performers. The academic behaviors and academic attitudes of research top performers are worlds apart from those of both middle performers and non-performers. And in terms of research productivity, there is no single 'academic profession' (as has always been the case in the last half a century), only 'professions' in the plural. 'Academic professions' in the plural appear in a similar vein in Enders and Musselin (2008: 127) when they refer to the growing internal differentiation of the academic profession; in Marginson (2009: 110) when he summarizes the impact of globalization on the stratification 'between those with global freedoms and those bound to the soil within nations or localities'; and in Teichler (2014b: 84) when he explores the validity of the traditional Humboldtian teaching-research nexus in Germany and restricts it solely to a group of German 'university professors.' The growing stratification of academics across Europe is the name of the game in town, and the persistent inequality in academic knowledge production is one of its major dimensions.

We have explored in this chapter a distinctive subgroup of highly productive academics from a cross-European comparative perspective to show the complexities inherent in the 'academic profession' concept. The disaggregated picture of faculty research performance in Europe highlights a powerful divide between research top performers and the rest of academics, which does not seem to have been studied so far from a European comparative perspective.

Note

1 We worked on the final data set dated June 17, 2011 created by René Kooij and Florian Löwenstein from the International Centre of Higher Education and Research—INCHER-Kassel.

Chapter 2

Academic salary stratification

Productivity and income

Introduction

This chapter examines highly paid academics—or academic top earners—employed across universities in ten European countries. It argues that while, in the Anglo-Saxon countries, the university research mission typically pays off at an individual level, in Continental Europe, it pays off only in combination with administrative and related duties. Seeking future financial rewards through research does not seem to be a viable strategy in Europe, but seeking satisfaction in research through solving research puzzles is also becoming difficult, with the growing emphasis on the relevance and applicability of research. Thus, both the traditional investment motivation and consumption motivation to perform research (Levin and Stephan 1991) decrease, creating policy implications.

This research differs from existing salary studies in its focus, sample, and method. It goes beyond previous work that has studied academic salaries either in single institutions (Katz 1973; Ferber 1974; Fox 1985), multiple institutions (Hamermesh, Johnson, and Weisbrod 1982; Konrad and Pfeffer 1990; Ward 2001), or national systems (mostly the United States, as in McLaughlin, Montgomery, and Mahan 1979; Gomez-Mejia and Balkin 1992; Bellas 1993; Fairweather 1993; Barbezat and Hughes 2005; Fairweather 2005; Melguizo and Strober 2007). It goes beyond a more traditional approach, which examines the relationships between academic salary and its correlates through only bivariate correlational analyses, by using both logistic regression analyses and bivariate correlational analyses. This research examines the relationships between academic salaries and academic behaviors and productivity in a single institutional type, the European university, exploring one sub-category of academics: academics employed full-time and involved in both teaching and research. Finally, this chapter explores predictors of becoming an academic top earner from a comparative cross-national European perspective.

The massification of the academic profession

The massification of higher education inevitably leads to the massification of the academic profession, with dramatic consequences—especially outside of

Europe—in terms of its social and financial standing (with 'desacralization' of the profession going on, its borders becoming blurred, Yudkevich 2016: 2). As a global collection of 28 country studies emphasized, 'without significant salaries and appropriate contracts and conditions of service, the profession cannot thrive—and indeed cannot perform quite well. Without conditions that permit a secure career, competitive with alternatives in the labor market, the entire academic enterprise will falter' (Altbach et al. 2012: 3). Even though salaries are only a single element in a larger picture of the academic research environment, it is a highly important element and a major component of institutional budgets. For a long time, academic salaries have been under-valued as a research topic and, consequently, largely under-researched in higher education studies. However, in the last two decades, academic salary studies have been booming, with more than a hundred publications. The financial instability of the academic profession across developed countries, with powerful national variations, has helped to drive this research. However, there are only a few cross-national comparative salary studies focusing on more than two countries (Shen and Xiong 2015), in addition to two collections of national case studies (Rumbley, Pacheco, and Altbach 2008; Altbach et al. 2012).

The expansion of the university system in Europe began in the 1960s, together with the expansion of the academic profession. While the early decades of the expansion of the academic profession in Europe were the 'Golden age' of the welfare state, what followed was 'permanent austerity' (Nixon 2017). The ability to generate revenues for ever increasing public spending across Western Europe has been declining for four decades now and there has been a growing competition among various public services for public funding. All major European systems have been spending more on higher education and academic research in the 2005–2015 period (OECD 2016) but there may be limits to average academic salary growth due to sheer numbers of academics. Not only are there ever more academics, there are also ever greater numbers of full professors who are at the top of pay scales. As academic work is highly labor-intensive, in all systems and all (non-profit) universities, academic (and other) salaries are the biggest cost category. Cost containment meant in the last few year, inter-alia, growing shares and numbers of part-time and project-based academics (the Netherlands, Austria), freezing promotions to higher ranks (Ireland), and reducing salary levels (Romania and Bulgaria).

As in every other sector of economy, the number of highly paid positions in higher education is limited, despite the expansion of the systems. Most academics globally cannot live a middle-class lifestyle with their academic salary alone (Altbach 2015: 7). Academic salaries are clearly context-sensitive and the frame of reference in the last half a century has been the category of professionals. A traditional view is that academics tend to trade-off 'pecuniary' and 'non-pecuniary' elements of their work (or tend to assess 'non-pecuniary advantages' of academic work higher than its 'pecuniary disadvantages,' Ward and Sloane 2000). Self-selection into academic jobs by individuals 'who place a relatively high ranking on non-pecuniary aspects of work' has often been reported (Ward and Sloane 2000: 297). As Armey (1983: 37–38) points out, 'faculty members often trade income for freedom' because 'monetary compensation is not all, not even the most important.' As the Coles (1973: 45) stress in their study of the social stratification in science, 'in science, unlike society at large, location in the stratification system is not determined by the amount of money earned. … In science money does not have important symbolic value.' A recognition for outstanding research—rather than money earned and property owned—is

> the pillar which supports the entire scientific society. Without just rewards for research well done, science would probably deteriorate. Furthermore, unless there is recognition of excellence, the bases for assigning individuals to different positions in the system will seem totally arbitrary.
>
> (Cole and Cole 1973: 75–76)

The reward system operates in such a way as to encourage the creative scientists to be productive.

The ongoing stratification of the academic profession in terms of academic salaries is increasingly related to the teaching/research role orientation and ever more competitive funding made available to European academics in national and international quasi-markets of competitive research funding. Consequently, the teaching-orientation, so far especially correlated with gender (women academics traditionally being more teaching-focused and spending more time on teaching and less time on research compared with male academics) seems to reinforce the gender salary gap.

There are growing cross-disciplinary disparities in academic salaries in largely 'unstructured' systems exemplified by the US system; those disparities across European 'structured' systems seem to be more restrained (Stephan 2012). The major issue for European universities is the lure of corporate and industry work in some areas, and its lack in other areas, leading to cross-disciplinary tensions over salary levels. The academe-industry gap refers in different degrees to different areas and there is a tension between more curiosity-driven research in lower-paid academia and more applied research in higher-paid industry. Currently, freedom to pursue one's own research project 'compensates for much lower monetary rewards in academe. Urging scientists to focus on more applied research projects might cause selection of academics into industry,' as implications of the Careers of Doctorate Holders project show (Balsmeier and Pellens 2016: 25).

Institutions with more open salary systems, notably in the United States, are more able to attract top-quality researchers from institutions with less open salary systems, notably those in Continental Europe. Academics across large parts of Continental Europe are still typically civil servants paid largely based on a single well-defined fixed-salary system (Altbach et al. 2012). Consequently, 'universities in the US have greater leeway than those in most other places to reward performance and to pay high salaries to attract star researchers' (Stephan 2012: 1).

However, in the last two decades, most European systems have tended to introduce various forms of merit pay, moving very slowly away from fixed-salary systems (Enders and de Weert 2004: 18–19; and national case studies in Altbach et al. 2012). And opening possibilities for stronger academic pay stratification.

Traditionally, the full-time professoriate could expect a salary 'putting its members in the middle or upper-middle class of society' (Altbach 2003: 16). The attractiveness of academia as a career is affected by 'the general standing of the profession, and the overall levels of pay that it attracts' (Marginson 1991: 42). There is the 'declining desirability of the faculty position' in Europe (Huisman, de Weert, and Bartelse 2002: 158):

> poor academic pay is undoubtedly a factor behind the drain of young brains to the private sector. There is increasing awareness, however, that the problem cannot be fixed simply by creating more positions and increasing salaries. The fundamental problem in Europe is the loss of appeal of the faculty job.

As Goastellec et al. (2013: 105) summarize recent literature on the professoriate, the overall impression is 'one of crisis, decline and a loss of prestige and status ... there is a sense of good-bye, a literature of regret.'

These are recurrent themes; however, they are not our focus. Our focus is not the—adequate or inadequate, and ever more often inadequate than adequate— level of academic salaries across Europe and the future of the academic profession but their patterns and intra-national and cross-national differentiations, and predictors of belonging to the class of highly paid academics. Our focus in this sense are 'internal' aspects of university salaries (or salary scales *within* the profession) rather than their 'external' aspects (or their development in relation to other sectors of society, following Finkenstaedt's distinction (2011: 184). From a larger perspective, research on academic salaries has important policy implications because faculty salaries are usually the largest single item in academic budgets.

The reward structure in science and differences in salary regimes

Academics have always been heavily stratified, as have been academic institutions, the consequence being dispersion in university salaries. Its reason is that 'individuals and universities are not homogeneous. Individuals receive differentials which compensate them for ability and motivation, length of training and past job experience' (Williams, Blackstone, and Metcalf 1974: 277). Differentials are both prestige-related and salary-related.

The reward structure in science consists of two components (Stephan 2010). First, science is governed by the priority system, a reward system that encourages the production and sharing of knowledge. Scientists are motivated to perform research 'by a desire to establish priority of discovery' (Stephan 2010: 2) because recognition in science depends on 'being first' (Stephan 1996: 1202); consequently, 'there are no awards for being second or third' (Stephan 1996: 1202), following Hagstrom who back in the 1960s argued that 'scientists prize the recognition that comes from being the first to present a discovery, and they compete strenuously to obtain it' (1965: 99). Also, second, the reward structure in science consists of remuneration. As Stephan argues along the lines of the economics of science, 'compensation in science is generally composed of two parts: one portion is paid regardless of the individual's success in races, the other is priority-based and reflects the value of the winner's contribution to science' (Stephan 1996: 1202).

This is the role of publication numbers and their quality, and citations in raises and promotions in universities. In testing the high research productivity-high prestige-high salary link, we go beyond the traditional account in which scientists are rewarded for their research performance 'by the community of scientists engaged in research on similar topics' (Gaston 1978: 2) and see whether high research performance, apart from the traditional academic recognition (as discussed in Introduction), is complemented by higher salaries.

Academic positions, like other jobs, provide both extrinsic rewards (salaries and other material benefits) and intrinsic rewards (derived from academic work) (Blau 1994: 80). Poor salaries are a major impediment to effective faculty recruitment; however, 'job choices of academics are less responsive to salary differences than those of persons in the same specialties in other employment' (Blau 1994: 81). There is a number of interrelated critical issues: 'levels of compensation, perceived trends in compensation, compensation relative to competing labor market sectors, and perceptions of equitable treatment all serve to influence choices to enter (or exit) faculty employment' (Schuster 1992: 1542). The national 'academic market place' (Caplow and McGee 1958), 'academic labor markets' (Williams et al. 1974; Schuster 1992; Fairweather 1995) or 'markets for academics' (Musselin 2010)—combined with emergent 'global labor markets' for scientists (Marginson 2009)—determine who academics are today and who they will be in the future. They produce (or fail to produce) the requisite talent in academe. The international academic labor market, like the academic profession itself, is highly stratified, with language as a key element. And the national dimension weighs heavily in academic labor markets because of what Christine Musselin termed the 'university configurations' particular to each country (2004: 112–116).

A typology of salary systems is useful to see the difference between the United States and Europe, and changes over time. While the United States represents a combination of 'unstructured' and 'structured' salary systems, the nine European countries studied in this chapter represent 'structured' salary systems (noted in Hansen's entry on 'Salaries and Salary Determination' in Clark and Neave's *Encyclopedia*, Hansen 1992: 1478–1479): academics across Continental Europe are most often civil servants and paid accordingly. While unstructured, merit-based systems attempt to reward performance, in structured systems academics are paid largely based on a single, well-defined fixed-salary schedule.

There are inevitable implications for academic work in European-type structured systems: indifference to differences in performance from the perspective of salaries: 'Faculty members of considerable merit are underrewarded while other less meritorious faculty members may be overrewarded relative not only to what they produce each year but also to their cumulative performance record' (Hansen 1992: 1478).

Institutions with unstructured salary systems, notably in the United States, are more able to attract top quality researchers from institutions with structured salary systems, notably from Europe. As Stephan points out,

> unequal pay among researchers contributes significantly to a nation's success in attracting the best and the brightest. Universities in the US have greater leeway than those in most other places to reward performance and to pay high salaries to attract star researchers. Pay inequality is not the norm abroad.
>
> (Stephan 2012: 1)

Between two ideal type systems there is a continuum that blends elements of both. In the last two decades, most European systems tend to introduce various forms of merit pay, moving slowly away from the extreme of a pure structured salary system (Marginson 2009: 106; Enders and de Weert 2004: 18–19; selected European country chapters in Enders and de Weert 2004 and in Altbach et al. 2012). However, the challenge in trying to reward individual merit hinges on the definition of merit (Hansen 1992: 1481): 'internally determined merit' (assessment of contribution to one's own institution) is in sharp contrast to 'externally determined merit' (assessment by other institutions or based on publication record). In increasingly stratified European systems, 'externally determined merit' based on research achievements tend to matter more in upper echelons of institutions, and 'internally determined merit' tends to matter more in lower echelons of institutions, more focused on teaching and service missions.

Models of academic salaries: human capital and prestige generation

Existing theories of faculty pay can be categorized into market models and institutional models, which view academic pay as a function of either market competition or institutional forces, respectively (Fairweather 2005: 403). Two market models attribute changes in faculty salaries, at least in part, to changes in supply and demand: one school emphasizes the homogeneity of national academic markets based on research and prestige (research output is highly valued in research-oriented institutions, and highly productive academics are paid more), and the other school emphasizes the segmented character of national academic markets (teaching-oriented institutions value teaching over research, and top teachers are paid more). The institutional theories of faculty pay emphasize that pay is an expression of institutional norms and values, regardless of institutional missions, and that institutional forces can dictate salary levels: 'institutions that actually value teaching will pay their productive teachers the most, whereas institutions valuing research will pay their productive researchers the most' (Fairweather 2005: 403).

In a standard human capital model (as used by Hamermesh et al. 1982), academic earnings are a function of research productivity (on the demand side), as well as any factors that affect the equilibrium supply of labor. Faculty salary is also viewed as indirectly related to productivity because more productive academics are likely to be promoted faster and promotions mean higher financial rewards.

Scientists' engagement in research can be either investment-motivated (seeking future financial rewards), consumption-motivated (seeking research puzzles), or both (Thursby, Thursby, and Gupta-Mukherjee 2007). While the investment motive implies a decline in research productivity over one's career, the consumption motive does not imply such a decline (Levin and Stephan 1991). A 'taste for science' (Roach and Sauermann 2010)—that is, for nonpecuniary returns—causes scientists to choose academia over industry. Academics with different abilities and tastes in terms of nonpecuniary returns choose different careers: basic or applied research in academia or industry (Agarwal and Ohyama 2013). Time spent on research reduces current earnings but increases future earnings, as in investment models of human capital. On average, scientists become less productive as they age (Levin and Stephan 1991; Stephan and Levin 1992; Kyvik 1990), with changing research productivity over the lifecycle and productivity in systems with aging academic cohorts being important research focuses.

From the perspective of the economics of higher education, specifically the concepts of labor economics, academic compensation is influenced by a number of factors related to the demand for higher education services and the supply of qualified individuals for faculty positions (Toutkoushian and Paulsen 2016: 324). From this perspective, academics have acquired human capital (skills and talents that an individual can obtain through education, training, and experience in the labor market) and endowed human capital (natural ability and talent) (Toutkoushian and Paulsen 2016: 351). In academic labor markets, academics can have large variations in their levels of both types of human capital. The connection between human capital and academic salaries follows from the effects of human capital on productivity, which in turn influences pay (Toutkoushian and Paulsen 2016: 353). As Toutkoushian and Paulsen (2016: 353) point out,

> if faculty compensation is determined in part by an individual's productivity in teaching, research, and public service, then salaries should be correlated with productivity. Human capital theory would thus predict that faculty with more acquired and endowed human capital would, on average, have higher salaries than other faculty.

Economic models of academic salary determination have been predominantly based on the human capital theory (embedded in analyses of for-profit firms and treating higher education institutions accordingly); in the prestige model of salary determination, universities behave as both firms and non-profit institutions, or 'hybrids' (Melguizo and Strober 2007: 634). In the prestige model, academic salaries are viewed as returns on the generation of prestige (for the individual academic, as well as the institution). Non-profit higher education institutions act largely as 'prestige maximizers,' just like for-profit companies act as 'profit maximizers':

> Not only are institutions seeking to maximize prestige, so are departments and faculty members. Institutions seek to increase their prestige vis-à-vis other institutions; departments seek to increase their prestige vis-à-vis other departments in the same field at other institutions (and also, for purposes of resource allocation vis-à-vis departments in their own institution); and faculty members seek to increase their own reputation among colleagues, within their own institution, but most especially nationally and internationally among their academic peers.
>
> (Melguizo and Strober 2007: 635)

While human capital salary models focus on individuals' research, teaching, and public service productivity, a potential alternative model focuses on individuals' prestige generation, mostly through publications, research grants, patents, and awards, that is, productivity. Both the human capital model and the prestige model state that higher productivity (defined for different areas, with publications being at the forefront) should lead to higher academic incomes.

Institutions will spend the money on valued activities—rather than show them as 'profit,' as shown in *In Pursuit of Prestige* (Brewer, Gates, and Goldman 2002: 20). Prestige is largely a rival good, based on relative, rather than absolute, measurement, and accumulating prestige is a zero-sum game (Brewer et al. 2002: 30). Academia is becoming ever more competitive, and competitiveness is encouraged by deliberate government policies: 'at the centre of all this is prestige, at all levels from the national system to the individual' (Blackmore 2016: 1). Universities—as well as academics—compete in prestige markets. In particular, there is a strong link between individual and institutional prestige:

> In maximizing their individual prestige, faculty members simultaneously maximize the prestige of their departments and institutions. Faculty members increase their own prestige by publishing articles and books, obtaining research grants and patents, being elected to various national academies, and garnering prestigious and well-publicized prizes. And when the renown and influence of their faculty members grow by these means, the prestige of the departments and institutions that employ these faculty grows commensurately.
>
> (Melguizo and Strober 2007: 635)

The maximization of prestige, in this theoretical framework, is strongly correlated with faculty salaries. Academics who help their institution to become prestigious are rewarded by the institution with higher salaries: more articles and books published in prestigious outlets, more prestigious research grants, more patents, etc. lead to higher institutional prestige, which consequently, albeit not directly, leads to higher individual salaries. That is, 'the currency in which institutions are paid for faculty research is prestige. As a result, institutions provide financial rewards to scholarly output,' with faculty salaries being viewed as returns on the generation of prestige (Melguizo and Strober 2007: 639).

Following the logic of this salary model, in the context of our research, highly productive academics should be disproportionately over-represented among highly paid academics. Because more time spent on teaching means less time spent on research and vice versa, or there being only 'research' and 'non-research' time investments (Levin and Stephan 1991: 115), academics spending, on average, more time on research should be receiving higher average salaries. Spending more time on teaching, in turn, should have a negative or, at best, neutral effect on one's salary (Katz 1973; Dillon and Marsh 1981; Konrad and Pfeffer 1990; Fairweather 1993).

However, there is a difference between spending time on research, being research-focused, and being highly productive as compared with one's peers: highly productive academics can also have more formal responsibilities as leaders, deans, heads of departments, etc. and still have co-authored publications with their post-docs or other early-stage researchers. The chance to have longer lists of co-authored publications may increase for selected academics with more institutional power, and institutional power increases with age and seniority (Stephan and Levin 1992). Finally, the willingness of academic institutions to adjust financial rewards to productivity—possible in different European systems to different degrees—creates institutional challenges and tensions among academics (Teixeira 2017: 43). So far, academic performance stratification discussed in Chapter 1 seems to be operating parallel to, and independently from, academic salary stratification studied in this chapter. An examination of possible over-representation of academic top earners among highly productive academics will show the extent to which the former stratification type overlaps with the latter.

Defining academic top earners

Income data used in this chapter were available for the following ten countries: Austria, Finland, Germany, Italy, the Netherlands, Norway, Poland, Portugal, Switzerland, and the United Kingdom. Academic incomes have not been explored in detail so far (except for Shen and Xiong 2015, a study mostly descriptive, and Nanbu and Amano 2015, a single-nation study on Japan).

In technical terms, we divided the sample of all academics who reported their incomes in the ten above-mentioned countries into academic 'top earners' and 'the rest.' As elsewhere in this book, our focus was on a subsample by downsizing all national samples to full-time academics in the university sector and excluding all part-timers and all academics employed in polytechnics and 'other academic institutions.' On the one hand, a better cross-national data comparability was achieved; on the other, the subsamples represented national higher education realities to varying degrees only.

Top earners are defined as those in the 80th percentile of gross academic income—the upper 20 percent of academics in each of the five major clusters of academic disciplines (separately), in each country (separately), cut-off points permitting. We did not want to combine all full-time academics from the university sector into a single subset, because the vast majority of top earners would then come from Switzerland and none would come from Poland or Portugal (based on the nominal values of their salaries). We also wanted to explore all the systems and examine national-level top earners cross-nationally. By looking at the intra-national patterns, we avoided the issue of changing conversion rates over time (in the case of the four non-eurozone European countries: Norway, Poland, Switzerland, and the UK) and the issue of different levels of national affluence, highly determining the *levels* of national academic salaries (but presumably not salary *patterns*).

Additionally, we restricted our subsample of top earners and the rest: we have explored only academics who are at least 40 years old and have at least 10 years of academic experience. This was done to avoid comparing academics across radically different age cohorts with different seniority levels and, especially, different job characteristics. Analyzing top earners and the rest of academics across all age cohorts and all career stages and seniority levels would significantly increase the number of observations but would also lead to potentially erroneous results with regard to the time spent on research. Analyzing only older academics with longer academic experience (longer time passed since first full-time employment) leads to more robust results. However, this is the second-best approach, the best approach being a study of smaller age cohorts and seniority and career-stage cohorts separately, which is not possible due to the radically decreased numbers of observations by country and academic discipline cluster in such a case. In a lifecycle view, faculty devote more time to research early in their careers and less time to research later on (see, e.g., Thursby et al. 2007; Levin and Stephan 1991). In the US context, achieving tenure is a critical point, as is a Habilitation degree (a postdoctoral degree that exists in various versions) in a number of European systems, including the majority in our sample: Germany, Poland, Finland, Switzerland, Austria, Portugal, and Italy. Consequently, in Europe, academics aged 40 and over are already a relatively homogeneous cohort. 'The rest' of academics is defined here as the remaining 80 percent of academics who are at least 40 years old and have at least 10 years of academic experience.

The number of valid cases with income and disciplinary data in the selected cohort is 3,586, including both top earners (N(TE) = 649, or 18.1 percent) and the rest of academics (N(R) = 2,937, or 81.9 percent) (see Table A.1 in the Statistical Appendices). About two-thirds of academics in the sample are male,

Table 2.1 Sample description: frequencies of selected demographic characteristics, all countries combined

		Employed full-time in the university sector, involved in both teaching and research (all responses)		Employed full-time in the university sector, involved in both teaching and research (responses with valid income data)	
		N	%	N	%
Gender	Male	3,174	65.9	2,488	66.9
	Female	1,639	34.1	1,230	33.1
Age	40–44	1,035	21.4	796	21.3
	45–49	1,098	22.7	789	21.2
	50–54	754	15.6	599	16.1
	55–59	938	19.4	723	19.4
	60 and more	1,011	20.9	825	22.1
Academic experience*	10–19	1,527	41.3	1,188	39.6
	20–29	1,176	31.8	958	32.0
	30 and more	992	26.8	852	28.4
Clusters of academic disciplines**	Hard sciences	2,558	55.5	2,031	56.6
	Soft sciences	2,051	44.5	1,554	43.4

Note: *'Academic experience' means the number of years since one's first full-time employment ('beyond research and teaching assistant in higher education/research sector,' Question A6). **The 'hard sciences' cluster includes 'physical sciences and mathematics,' 'life sciences and medical sciences,' and 'engineering,' while the 'soft sciences' cluster includes 'humanities and social sciences' and 'professions' (Question A2).

Table 2.2 Sample description: frequencies of selected demographic characteristics, all ten countries combined, academic top earners only

		N	%
Gender	Male	489	82.8
	Female	102	17.2
Age	40–44	44	7.4
	45–49	87	14.7
	50–54	88	14.8
	55–59	146	24.5
	60 and more	230	38.6
Academic experience*	10–19	127	23.2
	20–29	179	32.7
	30 and more	241	44.1
Clusters of academic disciplines**	Hard sciences	346	58.1
	Soft sciences	249	41.9

Note: The *'academic experience' and **the 'hard sciences' cluster are defined as in Table 2.1 above.

with the age cohorts for academics aged at least 40 and academic experience cohorts being relatively evenly distributed. The distribution of the sample population by country and the frequencies of selected demographic characteristics are shown in Table 2.1 (all academics) and Table 2.2 (top earners only) below. The non-response rate pertaining to the gross annual salary question ranged from as low as 0.6 percent in the UK and 1.1 percent in Poland to as high as 31.2 percent in Switzerland and 47.4 percent in Austria. Not all respondents provided all the relevant data: for instance, not all academics employed full-time in the university sector provided data on their income (see column with 'responses with valid income data'), and not all top earners provided full data on gender, age, academic experience, and/or cluster of academic discipline. We excluded all academics who indicated 'no answer' (missing data), '0' salary, as well as excessively high and excessively low amounts earned.

Specific and generic limitations

The results of research in this chapter should be interpreted in light of several limitations, specifically those related to the sample, methods, procedures, and dataset. First, while this research goes beyond the limitation of being a single-institution study, as is the case with the majority of papers on academic incomes published in the last four decades, and thus it is not a case study, the national-level sampling techniques differed across the ten countries studied (see Teichler and Höhle 2013: 6–9; and RIHE 2008: 89–178), as did the ways in which the survey questionnaire was distributed (paper, on-line, or combined), the response rates, the distribution of academics across various institutional types and various forms of employment, etc. These could have influenced the final results. Second, the analyses are based on self-declared data that were provided by academics voluntarily, with some items potentially being viewed as more sensitive in some countries than in others (important in this chapter: income and research productivity). Specifically, the analyses are based on self-reported annual gross income, and there are substantial differences between taxation systems across Europe, with the same gross income leading to vastly different net incomes.

Third, we use a rather crude measure of research productivity, which is defined as the number of peer-reviewed articles published in a 3-year reference period. The survey does not allow an examination of journal quality (and especially does not allow to a distinction between top-tier journals and others) or the examination of citation counts. However, to strengthen the robustness of our productivity analyses, as in Chapter 1 and Chapter 5, we have used three fractionalized versions of the dependent variable: peer-reviewed article equivalents (also capturing authored and edited books), internationally co-authored article equivalents, and foreign language (here, English) article equivalents. We were unable to examine individual academics' research outputs and link them to institutional tiers based on national prestige ladders in the ten countries, rather than merely to linking them to institutional types (such as 'universities' in our case, as opposed to 'polytechnics' and 'other higher education institutions'). We were also unable to define the selectivity of the employing institution (and of the PhD graduation institution) or its wealth, size, or current national or international ranking. Finally, with the dataset in question, we were also unable to study how patterns of academic salaries change over time intra-nationally and cross-nationally.

On top of these specific limitations, more generic limitations linked to cross-country comparisons in higher education in general, given the differences in academic traditions across national systems, must be mentioned. Comparative higher education has its potentials, as well as its limits (Teichler 1996; Altbach et al. 2012), and moving from single-nation studies to cross-national studies, which involves the emergence of international datasets, the institutionalization of cross-national research, and the emergence of large international research teams, introduces new tensions, sometimes leading to 'dynamic relationship between planning, design, execution, challenges and opportunities' (Hoffman and Horta 2016: 41). International research collaboration in comparative research is a 'two-sided medal': the social diversity of research team members can 'positively influence as well as hinder the comparative research process' (Kosmützky 2018: 11–12; see also Kosmützky 2015).

Analytical frameworks in higher education research have mostly been produced for national, rather than cross-national, interpretive purposes. The knowledge base for cross-national studies increases (and the CAP/EUROAC dataset used here provides a new type of comparative data: primary, disaggregated, and self-produced by researchers, rather than the secondary, national-level, aggregated data commonly collected by the state), but international comparative research in higher education is seldom grounded in ideal research designs with clearly defined hypotheses. Datasets such as ours are clearly produced in heterogeneous national higher education settings: national academic traditions lead to strong differences in national career opportunities, research funding availability, dominant missions in various institutional types, dominant academic activities in various system subsectors, preferred academic role orientations, favored publication outlets, etc. The meanings of such basic terms as, e.g., 'professor,' 'young academic,' 'competitive research funding,' and 'academic duties' differ from country to country and must still be translated into a common set of concepts to organize data analysis. Consequently, the best approach is to use a semi-structured research design that reflects the wealth of options in higher education (with enough room for the application of internationally incompatible variables; in the EUROAC project, 480 in-depth semi-structured interviews were conducted across seven European countries, but the qualitative material is not used in this chapter). All in all, however, despite inherent limitations, cross-national studies of the academic profession create new insights with interesting institutional policy and national policy implications.

Academic income and working time distribution

In this section and the next one, we explore differences in working time distribution and productivity differentials between academic top earners and the rest of academics, specifically among older (aged 40 and more) and more academically experienced (10 or more years since the first employment) cohorts to avoid the exploration of groups of academics with significantly different job profiles.

Here, we explore five dimensions of academic work that were captured by the dataset: teaching, research, service, administration, and 'other' academic activities. We focus on average weekly hours in the teaching periods of the academic year, as well as in its non-teaching periods. We annualize these hours, assuming that 60 percent for the former period and 40 percent for the latter period represents a good approximation for the majority of the ten European systems studied (regarding the average length of the teaching and non-teaching periods during an academic year across Europe, see Bentley and Kyvik 2013, who use a similar 66.6/33.3 ratio in a global study of 13 countries). We explore the differences in the means of various categories of working hours (by academic activity) between the two subpopulations in each country (see Table 2.3). As in Chapter 1, our results are based on two-sided tests assuming equal differences in arithmetic means with a significance level of $\alpha = 0.05$. For each pair with a mean difference significantly different from zero, the symbol of the larger category ('Top' for top earners and 'Rest' for the rest of academics) appears in the column. T-tests for the equality of two arithmetic means ('Top' vs. 'Rest') were performed for each country for each of the five types of academic activities studied, as well as for total working hours.

Previous studies on academic salaries have strongly suggested that longer research hours contribute strongly to higher salaries (e.g., Katz 1973; Hamermesh et al. 1982; Fairweather 2005): our study shows that while top earners in three European countries indeed work statistically significantly longer 'total hours,'

Table 2.3 Working hours differentials. Results of t-tests for the equality of means for top earners (top) vs. the rest of academics (rest) in ten countries. Question B1: 'Considering all your professional work, how many hours do you spend in a typical week on each of the following activities? (when "classes are in session" and when "classes are not in session").' Only academics who were employed full-time in universities and involved in both teaching and research were considered (annualized mean weekly hours)

	PL	DE	AT	FI	IT	NL	NO	PT	CH	UK
Teaching hours										Rest
Research hours										Top
Service hours	Top					Top	Top		Top	
Administration hours	Top	Top		Top			Top			
Other hours		Top					Top			
Total hours		Top		Top					Top	

most importantly, in seven countries, they work longer 'service' (four countries) and/or 'administration' hours (four countries; see either 'Rest' or 'Top' symbols for each country).

Interestingly, statistically significant working time differentials between top earners and the rest of academics do not exist for teaching and research time investments, except in the UK, where there is clearly a different pattern: top earners, on average, spend 6.35 hours more per week on research, and the rest of academics spend, on average, more than 5 hours more on teaching. Previous research findings generally showed a strong positive correlation between research hours and salary levels and also a negative or no correlation between teaching hours and salary levels (Katz 1973; Dillon and Marsh 1981; Melguizo and Strober 2007; Hamermesh et al. 1982; Konrad and Pfeffer 1990; Fairweather 2005). Our research on the European sample does not confirm these findings. The traditional link between higher time investments in research and higher incomes—consistently demonstrated (mostly for Anglo-Saxon countries, especially the United States) in the last half a century—does not currently seem to hold across Continental Europe. Interestingly, from the perspective of future academic careers, top earners tend to spend more time (than the rest of academics) on all academic activities *except* for teaching and research, and they especially spend more time on administration and service. There is one qualification, however: the time measured is the current time, not the time spent a decade earlier, which may have led to their current positions.

We are unable, unfortunately, to explore further the details of 'service,' 'administration,' and 'other academic duties' time investments (although we have good indications from our accompanying qualitative material based on 480 interviews with academics conducted across seven countries: higher incomes seem to be increasingly linked to academic posts of directors and deans held by academics; however, our subsample does not include non-academics or administrators who do no research: top earners as defined here are all involved in research). The (annualized) total weekly working time differential between top earners and the rest of academics—in the three countries in which it is statistically significant—ranges from 5.5 hours in Finland to 7.5 hours in Germany and to 8.25 hours in Switzerland. In other words, for example, German top earners in the university sector, when compared with the rest of (full-time employed) German academics, spend on average an additional 43.1 full working days in academia per year (7.5 hours times 46 weeks divided by 8 hours per day).

Academic income and research productivity

The analysis of individual research productivity involves three measures: 'peer-reviewed article equivalents' (PRAE), 'internationally co-authored peer-reviewed article equivalents' (IC-PRAE), and 'English language peer-reviewed article equivalents' (ENG-PRAE). The PRAE measure—as in Chapter 1—is calculated (following Bentley 2015) as the weighted sum of self-reported articles in books or journals (1 point), edited books (2 points), and authored books (5 points) published over the period of 3 years prior to the survey execution. An individually provided share of peer-reviewed publications is applied to each observation. The PRAE measure captures publishing through various outlets and does not focus only on articles, leaving room for authored books and edited books, which are still a major outlet in the social sciences and humanities in some European systems. The IC-PRAE measure applies the individually provided share of publications co-authored with international colleagues, and the ENG-PRAE measure applies the individually provided share of publications published in a foreign language (assuming that the language in question in all countries, except for the UK, is predominantly English, as descriptive statistics shows). In the majority of the countries studied (for Austria, the Netherlands, and Switzerland, there are no statistically significant results), top earners are, on average, much more academically productive in the 3-year reference period (see 'Top' in all lines in Table 2.4).

The productivity differential between top earners and the rest of academics, as defined in this chapter, is high and statistically significant, mostly at a high level (p-value <0.001), especially in the case of peer-reviewed article equivalents. In

Table 2.4 Research productivity and high academic income, summary. Results of t-tests for the equality of means for top earners (Top) vs. the rest of academics (Rest) in ten countries. Group with a significantly larger mean (Top or Rest) shown by country. Question D4/3, 'How many of the following scholarly contributions have you completed in the past *three* years?', was combined with Question D5, 'Which percentage of your publications in the last three years were peer-reviewed (PRAE), were published in a language different from the language of instruction at your current institution (ENG-PRAE), or were co-authored with colleagues located in other (foreign) countries (IC-PRAE)?' The results presented in the chart below represent 'articles published in an academic book or journal,' 'scholarly books you authored or co-authored,' and 'scholarly books you edited or co-edited.' Only full-time academics employed in universities and involved in both teaching and research were included.

	PL	DE	AT	FI	IT	NL	NO	PT	CH	UK
Peer-reviewed article equivalent (PRAE)	Top	Top		Top	Top		Top	Top		Top
Internationally co-authored article equivalent (IC-PRAE)	Top	Top		Top			Top			Top
Foreign language article equivalent (ENG-PRAE)	Top	Top		Top	Top		Top	Top		

seven countries—Poland, Germany, Finland, Italy, Norway, Portugal, and the United Kingdom—it is, on average, in the 80–140 percent range. Only on Italy is the differential lower, at 43 percent (the reason could be that Italian academics show the highest average individual productivity among the European countries studied (see Kwiek 2015c). For instance, in the UK, the average number of peer-reviewed article equivalents published in the 3-year reference period by the rest of academics is 4.63, while the equivalent number for top earners is 11.3, or 144.06 percent more. In the case of internationally co-authored article equivalents, the difference is even higher: 180.49 percent for Poland, 178.05 percent for the UK, 145.56 percent for Germany, and 100 percent for Finland (the 95 percent confidence interval for the difference of means and other statistical details are provided in Table A.2 in the Statistical Appendices).

Our analysis shows (see graphically Figures 2.1 and 2.2) that the upper 20 percent of academics in terms of incomes (or our 'top earners') in the majority of countries studied are substantially more productive and produce much more internationally co-authored publications than the rest of academics (from the same older age cohort). While they work on average longer 'administrative' and 'service' hours (rather than research hours), they are much more academically productive.

Is higher academic income positively correlated with better research performance, even though it does not seem to be positively correlated with research time investments? Are top earners disproportionately represented among highly

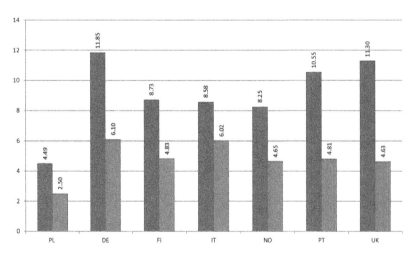

Figure 2.1 Academic productivity and high academic income: top earners vs. the rest of academics (from the same older cohort). The average number of 'peer-reviewed article equivalents' published in a 3-year reference period (top earners in black, the rest of academics in gray). Only full-time academics employed in universities and involved in both teaching and research are included. Only countries with statistically significant results are included.

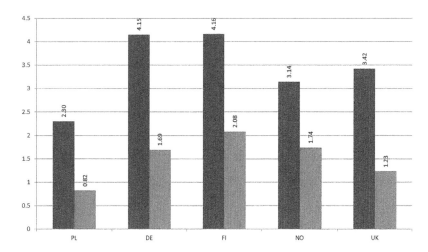

Figure 2.2 Academic productivity and high academic income: top earners vs. the rest of academics (from the same older cohort). The average number of 'internationally co-authored article equivalents' published in a 3-year reference period (top earners in black, the rest of academics in gray). Only full-time academics employed in universities and involved in both teaching and research are included. Only countries with statistically significant results are included.

productive academics (defined here in a similar manner as top earners—and differently from top performers in Chapter 1 due to the number of observations with salary data needed—as academics located in the upper 20 percent of research productivity, a pool created separately for major academic disciplines and for each country and then merged)? Yes, they definitely are. For instance, in Germany, on average, 43.1 percent of highly productive academics are highly paid academics (top earners) and, on average, 73.3 percent of the rest of academics are not top earners (see Table 2.5). Our analysis shows that, on average, 31.8 percent of national highly productive academics are among national top earners—from almost 80 percent in the United Kingdom to about 40 percent in Finland, Germany, and Portugal and 30 percent in Norway. The only exception is Poland, where highly productive academics are not overrepresented among top earners, constituting merely 22.9 percent of top earners. Poland has a strict national-level fixed salary scheme. A chi-square test of independence was conducted: there is significant interdependence between the two variables in the six above-mentioned countries. The significance level for all the countries is 0.10 (Table 2.6).

However, the above results are not multi-dimensional (the conclusions from the t-test analyses are independent of one another), and, as such, can be misleading (for instance, the relationship between salary and publication numbers may be influenced by seniority). A study of multi-dimensional relationships requires the model approach presented below.

Table 2.5 The share of top earners among highly productive academics. Only countries with statistically significant results are included

		Rest (non-top earners)	Top earners
Finland	Rest (non-highly-productive academics)	74.5	25.5
	Highly productive academics	59.5	40.5
Germany	Rest (non-highly-productive academics)	73.3	26.7
	Highly productive academics	56.9	43.1
Norway	Rest (non-highly-productive academics)	82.7	17.3
	Highly productive academics	66.5	33.5
Poland	Rest (non-highly-productive academics)	85.3	14.7
	Highly productive academics	77.1	22.9
Portugal	Rest (non-highly-productive academics)	79.9	20.1
	Highly productive academics	57.3	42.7
United Kingdom	Rest (non-highly-productive academics)	69.4	30.6
	Highly productive academics	22.0	78.0
TOTAL	Rest (non-highly-productive academics)	77.5	22.5
	Highly productive academics	68.2	31.8

Table 2.6 Chi-square independence test statistics

Statistics	AT	FI	DE	IT	NL	NO	PL	PT	CH	UK
Chi-square	0.455	3.637	3.493	1.364	0.229	7.636	7.666	3.41	0.54	10.698
df	1	1	1	1	1	1	1	1	1	1
p-value	0.5	0.057	0.062	0.243	0.633	0.006	0.006	0.065	0.462	0.001

The class of academic top earners and how to enter it

Like all regression analyses, logistic regression is a form of predictive analysis. It is used to explain the relationship between one dependent binary variable and one or more independent variable(s). Logistic regression assumes that the dependent variable is a stochastic event and proceeds in terms of likelihoods. The log odds of an event are estimated. The question in this section is how does the probability of being in the upper 20 percent of academic incomes change with changes in various independent variables?

Studies on academic salaries focus on various aspects of academic work: publications and teaching/research abilities (Katz 1973), male and female salaries vis-à-vis research performance (Ferber 1974), the role of citations (Hamermesh et al. 1982), institutional emphasis on research (Konrad and Pfeffer 1990), publications in top-tier journals (Gomez-Mejia and Balkin 1992), the maximization of prestige (Melguizo and Strober 2007), academic ranks and strategies to succeed financially (McLaughlin et al. 1979), teaching vs. research (Fairweather 2005), and others.

One persistent dimension of earnings inequality is gender. The gender salary gap has drawn research attention (initially in Anglo-Saxon countries) since the early 1970s (as summarized in Bellas 1993; Fox 1985; Barbezat and Hughes 2005). While it is uncertain whether gender differences 'reflect differences in human capital or productivity between individuals, discrimination by universities or supply decisions by workers,' a common thread that runs through the literature is the 'evidence of the existence of gender differences in salary' (Ward 2001). 'Sex stratification' is reported within the academic profession, and the 'cost of being female' in science is being explored (Bellas 1993: 62). The picture of the United States in the 1980s, as reported by Fox (1985), was as follows: academic tasks (teaching and research) were divided by sex, workplaces were segregated by sex (institutions, fields, and areas) and activities were stratified by sex. Men occupied more superordinate academic ranks and positions, and women occupied more subordinate ranks and positions. There are also growing cross-disciplinary disparities in academic salaries in more open salary systems (as exemplified by the US system). The disparities across generally less open systems, such as European systems, seem to be more restrained (Stephan 2012).

Research consistently shows scholarly productivity as the strongest correlate of faculty pay; teaching has been typically shown to be unrelated to, or to be a negative factor in faculty compensation (see Katz 1973; McLaughlin et al. 1979; Dillon and Marsh 1981; Hamermesh et al. 1982; Konrad and Pfeffer 1990; Fairweather 1993; Gomez-Mejia and Balkin 1992; Fairweather 2005; Melguizo and Strober 2007). The quality of research (as measured by citations, a proxy for the extent of a scholar's influence on the work of other researchers) is rewarded by the academic market:

> an additional reference adds more to salary than does the publication of an additional book or article. This interpretation of the reward structure in economics will, we hope, not be entirely lost on younger academics choosing how to allocate their time.
>
> (Hamermesh et al. 1982: 481)

Unfortunately, citation studies cannot be undertaken based on the dataset we use. As Fairweather (2005: 401) summarizes his several studies, 'faculty who taught less and published more received the highest average salaries regardless of type of 4-year institution or academic discipline.' The regression results show that spending more hours in the classroom continues to be related to a lower basic salary for faculty members at all types of institutions studied, and publishing productivity continues as a significant positive factor in pay at all types of institutions (Fairweather 2005: 416–417). Teaching remains a negative factor in pay.

Finally, also 'reputational capital' (Moore, Newman, and Turnbull 2001) and 'reputation' are related to academic pay. Moore and colleagues (2001), in their study on academic economists, provide empirical arguments that academic pay is strongly correlated with what they term 'reputational capital,' which goes beyond the quantity of publications and includes both their quality (for instance, first-tier and second-tier publications only) and citations. They conclude that 'there are significant monetary returns to high-quality research in the economics profession' (Moore et al. 2001: 668): 'individuals who publish a smaller number of frequently cited papers add more to their reputational capital than individuals who publish a greater number of less frequently cited papers' (Moore et al. 2001: 670). The 'quality' of one's scholarly research, measured by the frequency of the references to that work, has a major impact on academic salaries, as Hamermesh et al. (1982: 481) showed for the first time (for academic economists): 'an additional reference adds more to salary than does the publication of an additional book or article.'

Based on the research literature and given the limitations of the dataset at our disposal, specifically the lack of a link between individual observations and bibliometric data, we developed an analytical model to study academic salaries. Specifically, we employed selected variables found in McLaughlin et al. (1979), Gomez-Mejia and Balkin (1992), Fairweather (1993), Melguizo and Strober (2007), and Shen and Xiong (2015). In this multivariate analysis, we dichotomized all category variables through a recoding procedure. We started with 42 personal and institutional characteristics, which were grouped into eight clusters: personal/demographics, socialization, internationalization, academic behaviors, academic attitudes and role orientation, overall research engagement, institutional policies, and institutional support. We then conducted Pearson Rho's correlation tests to find significantly correlated predictors of the dependent variable. High intercollerations among the predictors (multicollinearity) were tested using an inverse correlation matrix because a correlation matrix refers only to pairwise correlations of independent variables. On the main diagonal of an inverse correlation matrix, there are values without unequivocal interpretation; however, they show how strongly a given variable is correlated with all other variables. The interpretation is performed in such a way that all variables with diagonal values higher than 4 are removed from analysis. In our case, there was only one such value ('peer-reviewed article equivalent,' diagonal value: 4.222); however, because it did not significantly exceed the conventional boundary value of 4, it was left in the model. Also, principal component analysis (PCA) was performed to determine whether any variables, due to their high level of correlation, could be grouped into homogeneous groups. No significant interdependence between any of the variables was found.

We also used two robustness checks. The first was an examination of pairwise correlations, particularly between the status of professors, age, and the

Table 2.7 Odds ratio estimates, obtained via logistic regression, of being in the top 20 percent in terms of total gross academic income for all nine countries

	AT	CH	DE	FI	IT	NO	PL	NL
Nagelkerke's R^2	0.302	0.608	0.61	0.822	0.449	0.298	0.286	0.598
Personal/demographics								
Age			1.124**	1.287*	1.174***		1.043*	1.201*
Female							0.379**	
Professor	12.419***a	15.171**a	77.322***a	2588.019***a	8.334***	3.267**	3.219**	78.745**a
Cluster of hard sciences			5.14*	44.523**a			0.43**	
Years since first full-time appointment				0.814*		1.045*		
Academic behaviors								
Annualized (proxy: 60 percent in session, 40 percent not in session) mean weekly teaching hours			0.925*			0.953*		
Annualized mean weekly research hours								
Annualized mean weekly service hours		1.17**					1.104***	
Annualized mean weekly administrative hours				1.466**		1.061*	1.07*	
Annualized mean weekly other hours		1.241*						
Academic attitudes and role orientation								
Research-oriented ('Primarily in research')				68.817**a	2.573*			
Teaching-oriented ('Primarily in teaching')			34.68*a					
Basic/theoretical research		7.39*						
Applied/practically oriented								
Commercially oriented/intended for technology transfer				0.004**a	2.312*	5.656**		

(*Continued*)

	AT	CH	DE	FI	IT	NO	PL	NL
Internationalization and collaboration								
Collaborating internationally in research								
Research international in scope or orientation				33.982*a				
Overall research engagement								
A peer reviewer				7.447*				
Editor of journals/book series								
National/international committees, boards, and bodies								
Being a highly productive academic (the upper 20 percent)						2.521*	3.559**	
Scholarly books authored or co-authored	0.598*			3.071*				
Peer-reviewed article equivalents published			0.94*					
Internationally co-authored article equivalents published			1.187*	0.611**				
Foreign language article equivalents published				1.358**	1.034*			
Papers presented at a scholarly conference				0.885**				
Patents or inventions	2.283*			9.99*				
Constant	0.199***	0.005***	0***	0**	0***	0.038***	0.015**	0**

Note

Results that are not statistically significant are not shown in the Table. * p<0.05, ** p<0.01, *** p<0.001; a—these odds ratios must be treated with caution.

productivity measures. It may be that most of the effect of research productivity is captured by the professor variable. The status of professors was moderately and positively correlated with age (r = 0.33), which is understandable. We used five productivity measures: scholarly books authored or co-authored, peer-reviewed article equivalents, internationally co-authored article equivalents, foreign language article equivalents and papers presented at scholarly conference. The correlation between the status of professor with our productivity measures was indeed positive but weak (in the r = 0.11–0.18 range). The second robustness check was to run the model without the professor variable and see how the results changed. We ran a pooled model across all countries with the professor variable and without it. In both models, all productivity-related variables were statistically insignificant. However, in the former model, the professor variable somehow inherently included several variables traditionally associated with being a professor (such as being a peer reviewer, being an editor of journals or book series or belonging to national or international committees, boards and bodies, which were all statistically insignificant). When the professor variable was removed from the model, all these variables emerged as significant. Surprisingly, there was a difference between productivity-related variables (which were insignificant) and prestige-related variables (which were significant only in the model without the professor variable).

The model was estimated using a stepwise backward elimination based on the Wald criteria, so only significant variables were included in the models for each country. We estimated a regression model for eight of the ten countries to highlight cross-national differences among top earners (for Portugal and the UK, the character of data did not allow the use of the maximum likelihood estimator). The models were fitted correctly: neither over-fitting nor under-fitting occurred. Only meaningful variables were included, and all meaningful variables were included. Each observation was independent. The predictive power of the fourth model, as measured by Nagelkerke's R^2, was generally high, and it was the highest for Finland (0.82), followed by Switzerland, Germany, and the Netherlands (in the 0.60–061 range); it was 0.45 for Italy and in the range of 0.29–0.30 for Austria, Norway, and Poland. The total average variance demonstrated for the eight countries was 49.66 percent. In Table 2.7, we present the results of the fourth model, which is the final model.

Statistically significant variables

Institutional variables did not enter into the equation in any of the countries studied. The importance of individual-level variables differs from country to country. In the first block of individual predictors ('personal/ demographics'), age entered into the equation in the majority of countries. Age is a strong predictor of being an academic top earner in Germany, Finland, Italy, Poland, and the Netherlands: on average, a one-unit increase (i.e., 1 year) increases the odds of being a top earner by as much as 29 percent in Finland and 20 percent in the

Netherlands, as well as by 17 percent in Italy, 12 percent in Germany, and 4 percent in Poland (*ceteris paribus*) for the specific older academic cohort explored here. This finding is consistent with the conclusions of Melguizo and Strober (2007) and McLaughlin et al. (1979), who emphasized positive correlations between age and salaries. In Norway, where age did not enter into the equation, the predictor 'years since first full-time employment' (or academic age) did: on average, a 1-year increase in academic age increased the odds of becoming a top earner by 5 percent and, unexpectedly, decreased the odds of becoming a top earner by 18 percent in Finland. The only exceptions in our pool of countries were Austria and Switzerland, where neither age nor academic age was statistically significant.

Interestingly, being a female academic entered into the equation only in Poland. It is a very strong predictor of *not* being a top earner there. In Poland, the odds ratio value indicates that female academics are, on average, highly unlikely (about one-third as likely as male academics) to be top earners (Exp(B) = 0.379). It is important to remember that the cohort studied is aged 40 and more and has a minimum of 10 years of academic experience. In all other countries, being a female academic is not a statistically significant variable. This finding does not confirm the conclusions of earlier academic salary studies (Fox 1985; Bellas 1993; Ward 2001; and Balkin and Gomez-Mejia 2002), specifically the research findings of a long list of Anglo-Saxon pay equity studies focused on gender salary gaps (Barbezat and Hughes 2005). However, it is consistent with more recent studies (e.g., Melguizo and Strober 2007), which show limited correlation between gender and earnings and the potential impact of institutional and/or national policy corrective actions. This research explores highly paid European academics, rather than all academics, and the odds of entering this peculiar group. Being a professor (or academic seniority) emerged as an important variable in the model, with statistical significance in all countries; however, the odds ratios for five of these countries should be treated with caution. In the other countries, being of a senior rank increases the odds of being a top earner by about eight-fold in Italy and about three-fold in Norway and Poland. Again, consistent with previous studies, European academics are certainly more likely to be promoted to higher ranks if and when they are older (Barbezat and Donihue 1998) as their publication lists become longer, which is consistent with human capital (Becker and Toutkoushian 2003; Toutkoushian and Paulsen 2016) and prestige models of academic salaries (Melguizo and Strober 2007). Professorship and academic seniority certainly affect academic income levels, as we would expect from human capital theory, and the relationship is reciprocal (Fairweather 2005; Katz 1973): correlates of high incomes do not necessarily indicate causal relationships. The cluster of hard sciences entered into the equation in two countries, with ambiguous results. The decrease in the odds of becoming a top earner in this cluster in Poland (Exp(B) = 0.43) is consistent with recent analyses of the Polish academic profession in which university salaries in the natural sciences and life sciences are lower than the institutional average (Kwiek 2015c).

In the block of 'academic behaviors,' annualized mean research hours per week did not emerge as a determinative predictor of becoming a top earner in any country. In a similar vein, only in Poland and Germany did annualized mean weekly teaching hours emerge as a determinative predictor: on average, a unit increase of 1 hour decreased the odds of becoming a top earner by about 5 percent in the former and 7 percent in the latter (*ceteris paribus*), which is consistent with the vast teaching/research trade-off literature. This is perhaps the most perplexing finding of this research project: contrary to most of the extant literature (specifically Katz 1973; Dillon and Marsh 1981; Hamermesh et al. 1982; Fairweather 1993) in the majority of the European countries studied, neither teaching nor research hours are statistically significant predictors of higher academic incomes.

In the case of teaching/research time investments, the results of the bivariate analysis and regression analysis point in the same direction. Traditionally, long research hours were reported to be strongly correlated with higher academic incomes, and long teaching hours were reported to be correlated with lower academic incomes. Our research does not support these claims in the specific case of European academics. However, previous research was predominantly focused on Anglo-Saxon academics and on all incomes rather than higher incomes. There is an important qualification: the measure used refers to the current time only; past time investments in research cannot be grasped with the instrument used. Annualized mean weekly service hours, in turn, entered into the equation in two countries (Switzerland, where a unit-increase of 1 hour per week increases the odds of becoming a top earner by about 17 percent on average, and Poland, where such an increase in mean weekly service hours increased the odds of becoming a top earner by about 10 percent on average). Annualized mean weekly administrative hours entered the equation in three countries (increasing the odds by about 47 percent in Finland, 6 percent in Norway, and 7 percent in Poland on average and *ceteris paribus*). Finally, 'other' hours emerged as a strong predictor in Switzerland (increasing the odds of becoming a top earner by about 24 percent on average). However, 'total working hours' did not enter into the equation in any of the countries studied, which may indicate the importance of a specific working time distribution rather than long working hours (in contrast to the case of European research top performers analyzed in Chapter 1 for whom all types of hours, except for teaching hours, were longer). In the case of teaching/research time investments—as well as administration and service time investments—the results of the bivariate analysis and the regression analysis again point in the same direction, consistent with McLaughlin et al. (1979: 32), who link individual strategies to succeed financially with academic rank ladders and suggest avoiding too much teaching in the early stages of one's career and focusing on administration in the later stages of one's academic career: 'an administrative assignment for an established professor will increase the likelihood for salary increases.'

In the 'academic attitudes and role orientation' block, being interested 'primarily in research' emerged as a strong predictor in only one country, Italy (increasing the odds of becoming a top earner by more than two-and-a-half-fold on average). This was surprising in the context of the existing literature, in which the research role orientation matters considerably in terms of higher salaries (e.g., Stephan 1996; Konrad and Pfeffer 1990). Characterizing one's primary research as 'commercially oriented or intended for technology transfer' substantially increases the odds of becoming a top earner in two countries: by almost two-and-a-half-fold in Italy and by about 5.7-fold in Norway. An interest in 'basic/theoretical research' increases the odds of becoming a top earner by 7.4-fold in Switzerland. Overall, different academic attitudes and role orientations (especially a preference for teaching or research) did not emerge as statistically important (the same results were achieved in the bivariate correlational analysis, which is not reported here due to space limits). In the 'internationalization and collaboration' block, no predictors entered the equation.

Finally, inconsistent with the conclusions from most of the literature referred to in Section 2 (especially Gomez-Mejia and Balkin 1992; Fairweather 1993; and McLaughlin et al. 1979), in the 'overall research engagement' block, selected academic research-related and prestige-related activities, as well as high research productivity, did not emerge as highly determinative. High individual academic productivity—being a highly productive academic, defined as being in the upper 20 percent of the productivity scale and measured separately for major clusters of academic disciplines—entered into the equation in only two countries, increasing the odds in Poland (more than three-and-a-half-fold on average) and in Norway (more than two-and-a-half-fold on average, in both cases *ceteris paribus*). In other countries, high academic productivity did not have a statistically significant effect on becoming a top earner. Being a peer reviewer emerged as a significant variable in the model in only one country, Finland (with Exp(B) = 7.447). Sitting on national and international committees, boards and bodies did not emerge as significant in any of the countries. The same was true for being an editor of a journal (or a book series). Having a patent or invention within the reference period of three years emerged as significant in two countries (Austria, Exp(B) = 2.283 and Finland, Exp(B) = 9.99).

Also, the variables related to publications (such as scholarly books authored or co-authored, peer-reviewed article equivalents published, internationally co-authored article equivalents published, and foreign language article equivalents published) did not emerge as unambiguous determinative variables in most of the countries studied. For instance, books published increased the odds of becoming a top earner substantially (three-fold) in Finland, but decreased them in Austria. Also, peer-reviewed article equivalents published entered into the equation in only one country: they actually decreased the odds of becoming a top earner by 6 percent in Germany. Finally, another dimension of research activities—the number of papers presented at a scholarly conference—actually decreased the odds of being a top earner in Finland (by 11 percent) and was statistically insignificant in all other countries.

Finally, a third robustness check was performed by running the model with a higher cut-off point. We examined the upper 15 percent (instead of the upper

20 percent), as contrasted with the rest of academics, and compared the differences. The predictive power of the fourth model, as measured by Nagelkerke's R^2, was roughly the same, being slightly higher for five countries (Austria, Switzerland, Italy, Norway, and Poland) and slightly lower for the remaining three (Germany, Finland, and the Netherlands). The total average variance demonstrated for the eight countries was similar (50.11 percent). As in the first model, being a female academic emerged as a statistically significant variable (in Italy, Norway, and Poland), and the odds ratio values indicate that female academics are, on average, highly unlikely (about one-third to one-fourth as likely as male academics) to become top earners (Exp(B) = 0.274–0.379). The hard sciences cluster emerged as statistically significant, substantially decreasing the odds of being among the top earners in four countries (Austria, Italy, Norway and Poland, with Exp(B) = 0.248–0.360). Annualized mean weekly research hours were shown to decrease the odds of becoming a top earner in Austria, Italy and Poland (with Exp(B) = 0.926–0.969). Annualized mean weekly service hours, in turn, increased the odds of becoming a top earner in all countries, except Austria and Finland (with Exp(B) = 1.066–1.201), as did annualized mean weekly 'other' hours in Germany and Italy (with Exp(B) = 1.057 and Exp(B) = 1.090, respectively). Also, similar to the first model, a research orientation increases the odds of becoming a top earner (in Austria and Italy), papers presented at scholarly conferences decrease these odds (in Austria and Finland) and having a patent or invention increases these odds (in Austria and Finland).

Thus, overall research engagement—as studied through many variables in the model—proves to be largely statistically insignificant as a predictor of belonging to the class highly paid academics. Relatively weak correlations between various research-related activities (such as being a highly productive academic or the number of peer-reviewed article equivalents, conference papers, etc.), various prestige-related academic activities (such as being a journal editor or sitting on national and international scientific committees) and academic incomes are largely inconsistent with earlier studies of the academic profession. These results do not confirm the results of the bivariate analysis and indicate that the use of parallel methods is more useful than a focus on single methods. The split revealed in this research may be related both to the more general ideas organizing research-based academic careers and academic salaries and, more practically, to greater leeway due to the better funding of American universities from which samples had been drawn. There is also an important distinction to be made between the determinants of academic incomes in general and the predictors of high academic incomes studied in this chapter.

Discussion and concluding reflections

This chapter is an empirically based comparative study of highly paid academics in Europe. We have examined ten European systems, and our focus was restricted to full-time academics involved in both teaching and research who were employed in a specific institutional type: the university. A class of academic 'top earners' (from the age cohort of 40 years old and more having a minimum of 10 years of academic experience) was examined to explore various aspects of their working time distribution and research productivity. Finally, the predictors of becoming an academic top earner were examined from a cross-national European perspective.

To a large extent, the findings obtained via a multi-dimensional model approach support the findings of inferential statistics: interestingly, in the context of previous (mostly) single-nation studies, research time for the academic cohort studied is not positively correlated with high incomes, teaching time is not negatively correlated with high incomes, and there is almost no correlation between the research role orientation or gender and high incomes. Interestingly, the strong correlations between high productivity and high incomes seen in the bivariate analysis are not confirmed in the regression analysis. The research focus of this chapter was on high incomes in an older cohort of academics and the odds of receiving them, rather than—as in traditional academic salary studies— all academics and all academic incomes in general. Consequently, this research explores cross-national academic salaries via new questions (top earners, as contrasted with the rest of academics, and the predictors of being a top earner) applied to new (that is, older) academic cohorts in new (that is, European) national settings.

This research has two types of implications: implications for current theoretical models and assumptions in salary studies, as well as policy implications for institutions and national systems. Starting with the former, our findings tend to suggest that the traditionally explored link between higher time investments in research and higher academic incomes—consistently demonstrated for Anglo-Saxon countries over the last four decades (as in Katz 1973; Konrad and Pfeffer 1990; Fairweather 1993; Gomez-Mejia and Balkin 1992; Fairweather 2005; Melguizo and Strober 2007)—may not hold across Europe today as strongly as in Anglo-Saxon systems. As Fairweather (1993: 629) expressed, the traditional view is that 'faculty who spend more time on research and who publish the most are paid more than their teaching-oriented colleagues,' and the American academe is moving toward 'a single faculty reward structure, one dependent on publishing, spending time on research, and minimizing involvement in instruction.' National academic labor markets in Europe, as is clear from this research, are homogeneous and research-based, rather than segmented (Fairweather 2005): teaching-oriented institutions do not seem to be paying their top teachers more, while all institutions tend to pay their highly productive academics more. For European universities, academic pay does not seem to be influenced—as in labor economics (Toutkoushian and Paulsen 2016)—by the demand for higher education services or the supply of qualified individuals. According to our results, highly productive academics are disproportionately over-represented among highly paid academics across Europe: on average, 31.8 percent of top national highly productive academics are among national top earners, with this percentage ranging from almost 80 percent in the United

Kingdom to about 40 percent in Finland, Germany, and Portugal. The correlations between high incomes and high performance are strong. The academic performance stratification tends to overlap with the academic salary stratification.

Given that European higher education research stands in the shadow of its American counterpart, especially in terms of its basic theoretical frameworks, this chapter suggests a more sustained focus on cross-national differences in higher education and on the role of various national traditions in the academic enterprise in the future. We suggest rethinking the potential over-reliance on American research findings in discussing academic salaries in non-American contexts. While North America has traditionally been viewed as able to provide the most extensive and relevant research, higher education research infrastructures in other world regions have been developing over the last two decades, with thousands of academics active in the field in Europe, Latin America, Australia, and Asia (Jung et al. 2018; Carvalho 2017).

The results of our analysis are not consistent with traditional academic salary research, which tends to emphasize strong positive correlations between salaries and long research hours, combined with a strong research focus; however, our results are consistent with those of traditional research in terms of showing correlations between high salaries and high productivity. The interesting point is that individual productivity also includes co-authored productivity. Therefore, high productivity must not necessarily be correlated with longer research hours. One indication that the high earners in our sample may be involved in the extensive supervision of collective research grants and/or leading research groups, heading departments or faculties, etc. is the finding that they tend to spend more time on administration, service, and other academic duties. For instance, top earners in Germany and Switzerland work, on average, 8 more hours per week than the rest of academics in the same older cohorts. This indicates, on average, 5 more administrative hours in Germany and 10 more service hours in Switzerland, with no statistically significant difference in traditionally explored teaching and research hours.

Thus, the US salary system (with highly differentiated salary levels across institutions) and European salary systems (with low national pay differentials) certainly have one point in common: the higher average research productivity of highly paid academics. However, while in the United States, longer research hours, a stronger research focus, and higher research productivity seem to pay off directly, in Europe, only higher research productivity seems to matter directly in determining individual salary levels. On top of that, high productivity determines high salaries only in combination with more time being spent on non-research academic activities outside the traditional teaching and research dyad.

At a policy level, a more direct research–income link in the United States as compared to European countries might result in the stronger siphoning of research-focused academics with higher 'tastes for science' (Roach and Sauermann 2010) (those who want to have better salaries and do not want to be involved in university administrative duties) from European to American universities. Academic salaries and the distribution of research/non-research time are at the core of the traditional university enterprise. The questions of what to do (proportions of teaching, research and administration time, and whether to conduct basic or applied research) and where to be (at which institution, in academia or industry, and possibly in which national system) are looming not only for individual academics but also at the institutional and national levels, guiding institutional (Pinheiro, Benneworth, and Jones 2012) and national (Musselin and Teixeira 2014; Enders, Boer, and Westerheijden 2011) higher education reform agendas. Our research strongly supports findings about the 'asymmetric international mobility' of talented scientists between Europe and the United States, as recently studied by Janger and Nowotny (2016). While top researchers certainly attract other top researchers and the attractiveness of an academic job increases with its salary, job choice is 'not driven by the remuneration package alone' (Janger and Nowotny 2016: 1679). There seems to be a '"global" view on which [academic] jobs are attractive, explaining the international mobility of scientists towards countries where jobs with these characteristics are more common' (Janger and Nowotny 2016: 1681). As is well-known from studies of academic careers, 'the ability of an occupation to attract high-level recruits depends to a great extent on the prestige of the occupation, working conditions, and perceived opportunities in the occupation' (Cole and Cole 1973: 234).

This research shows that while in Anglo-Saxon countries, the university research mission traditionally pays off at an individual level, in Europe, it pays off in combination with administrative and related duties. Seeking future financial rewards through research in Europe seems difficult, except for highly productive academics, but seeking satisfaction through solving research puzzles is also becoming more difficult than ever before because of the growing emphasis on the relevance and applicability of fundable research (Teichler et al. 2013). Thus, because both the traditional 'investment motivation' and the 'consumption motivation' for research (Levin and Stephan 1991) are scarce in European academia today, national-level and institutional-level policies may need to be rethought so that the best and brightest will still seek and maintain academic employment in European higher education in the context of an 'exodus of European researchers' (Docquier and Rapoport 2012: 715). Certainly, the conditions of the academic profession vary from country to country across the continent, with Switzerland being the most attractive and Poland being the least attractive (in the sample studied) when viewed through the proxies of average academic job satisfaction, average salary level, and willingness to leave the academic profession. There are many employment options to choose from today, and studies of the academic profession show an ever-shorter list of 'non-pecuniary advantages' and an ever-longer list of 'pecuniary disadvantages' (Ward and Sloane 2000) for academic positions in European universities. The intersection of high research performance and high academic salaries is one of the most consequential testing grounds for the attractiveness of the academic profession in the future.

Chapter 3

Academic power stratification

Collegiality and university governance

Introduction

This chapter examines the applicability of selected theoretical models of university governance to the 11 analyzed higher education systems. In particular, we test the applicability of a collegial model—believed to be in decline or co-existing with more managerial models that appear in different guises in most parts of Europe (Marini and Reale 2016). The aim was to assess the extent to which European universities in selected systems operate according to the traditional collegial model of the 'community of scholars,' and to explore cross-national differences. A detailed study of selected variables and specifically constructed indexes reveals cross-national differences in the power of academic collegial bodies as perceived by European academics, as measured by the influence of those bodies on academic decision-making and the power of the government and external stakeholders. The major theoretical concepts are drawn from studies of university governance by Olsen (2007), McNay (1995), and Birnbaum (1988).

As a point of departure, we consider that the following observation may no longer hold true for European higher education systems: 'Unfortunately, there is little research on the extent to which *models* of governance represent the *beliefs and behaviors* of people in the higher education governance structure' (Rhoades 1992: 1377, my emphasis). In fact, these 'models' and the 'beliefs and behaviors' of European academics can already be systematically comparatively studied by reference to rigorous primary quantitative data. The core of the proposed approach is to juxtapose extant theoretical models of university governance and comparative data on the beliefs and behaviors of the academic profession in 11 European systems. National data on views, attitudes, and behaviors facilitate a cross-national comparative analysis of changing governance models and dynamics of belief and behavior. In other words, traditional university governance models serving as Max Weber's ideal types can be measured against large-scale comparative data.

University governance: broader and narrower perspectives

In higher education research, university governance is viewed from both broader (e.g., Huisman, Maassen, and Neave 2001; Neave and van Vught 1994) and narrower perspectives (e.g., Shattock 2006; Tight 2012). From a broader perspective, governance refers to the changing relationship between the university and the state—that is, to a new 'social contract' (Maassen and Olsen 2007), especially as globalization and Europeanization challenge and reshape the role of nation states and welfare states (Carvalho and Santiago 2015), the role of public and private sectors in the provision of social services (Kwiek 2013a and 2018c), and the growth of markets/quasi-markets in higher education.

In these broad contexts, concepts such as the rise of the 'evaluative state' and 'steering at a distance' have emerged in higher education research (Neave and van Vught 1991). In continental Europe's 'triangle of coordination' between higher education institutions and academics, the state, and the market, policy changes 'were mostly formulated as a recalibration of the powers of governments versus the higher education institutions. Only in the 1990s ... the concept of market mechanisms became more dominant in the policy and steering debates' (Huisman 2009: 3). As argued by Magalhães and Amaral (2009: 187), the changing relationship between states and higher education systems means that 'states have started to promote an apparent deregulation—by inducing institutions to go to the market, to self-regulation and to competition between themselves—as a more efficient form of regulation.' Consequently, from a broader perspective, there is an ongoing 'search for a new pact' between universities and society (Maassen and Olsen 2007: 181).

In contrast, from a narrow perspective, 'university governance is defined as the constitutional forms and processes through which universities govern their affairs. ... [G]overnance extend[s] right through senates and academic boards to faculty boards and departmental meetings,' and governance is considered to be effective when 'these levels of governance work together productively' (Shattock 2006: 1). This perspective is shared by the 'how to' literature on managing academic institutions and by those leadership studies that focus on senior management roles (Tight 2012: 132–135); we refer to both of these approaches in various parts of our analysis. In exploring collegiality, we have adopted a narrow view of governance, focusing on micro- and meso-level academic phenomena. To operationalize Olsen's visions of the university, on the other hand, we take a broad approach to governance that looks beyond the micro level of individual academics and the meso level of institutions to the macro level of state-university relationships.

In taking a broad approach, we were especially interested in the 'less state, more market' simplification of New Public Management ideas in relation to universities across Europe. The so-called 'governance analytical perspective' provides a 'general analytical framework for studying all kinds of coordination problems among actors' (de Boer et al. 2007: 138). Following the analysis of university governance in England, the Netherlands, Austria, and Germany as proposed by de Boer, Enders, and Schimank, we took a bird's eye view of European universities using their five dimensions: 'state regulation' (top-down authority); 'stakeholder guidance' (intermediary bodies as goal-setters and advisers); 'academic self-governance' (as institutionalized in collegial decision-making at universities); 'managerial self-governance' (university leaders as internal goal-setters, regulators and decision-makers); and 'competition for scarce resources' (mostly in 'quasi-markets'). De Boer et al. argued that 'a configuration of governance is made up of a specific mixture of the five dimensions at a particular point of time' (2007: 139).

Looking at the last decade of changes in European universities, it seems that state regulation in most systems is high and on the rise, but managerial self-governance, external guidance, and competition are low in most cases, though also on the rise. Academic self-governance remains mostly high and is only beginning to decline (at different rates in different systems). In contrast, the picture in Poland is only beginning to resemble the situation in Western Europe in terms of direction of change. At present, the major difference is Poland's exceptionally high level of academic self-governance.

This chapter takes the cross-national comparative analysis to a different level, 'stepping down even further to the micro-level of the day-to-day work of individual academics and research groups' (de Boer et al. 2007: 150). In assessing the various European forms of university governance, we refer to both narrow approaches (as in Birnbaum and McNay's focus on intra-institutional academic phenomena) and broad approaches (as in Olsen's focus on both the intra-institutional meso level and the macro level of state-university relationships), which are seen here as complementary.

Models of university governance

In organization theory, university governance has been understood in terms of different 'cognitive frames' (Birnbaum 1988: 84), 'images' and 'metaphors' (Morgan 1986), and 'models' (Clark 1983). Following Birnbaum, we understand a model as

> an abstraction of reality that, if it is good enough, allows us to understand (and sometimes to predict) some of the dynamics of the system that it represents. Models are seldom right or wrong; they are just more or less useful for examining different aspects of organizational functioning.
>
> (Birnbaum 1988: 83)

Additionally, following Lave and March's *Introduction to Models in the Social Sciences*, we can view a model as 'a simplified picture of a part of the real world. It has some of the characteristics of the real world, but not all of them. It is a set of interrelated guesses about the world' (Lave and March 1993: 3).

In mapping the contours of institutional and systemic changes, it is useful to work with typologies. The empirical data make it possible to position European systems in relation to each other and to assess higher education systems against existing models of university organization and governance. Among the countries studied, Poland is exceptional in that the political and scientific isolation of the Communist period meant that its universities were not included in the Western European and American models of university governance then being developed.

For present purposes, we identified three useful typologies of university governance by Robert Birnbaum, Ian McNay, and Johan P. Olsen. Birnbaum distinguished between four major models of academic organization: 'collegial,' 'bureaucratic,' 'political,' and 'anarchical' (1988: 83–174). McNay proposed four models of university organization co-existing in time in different mixes: 'collegium,' 'bureaucracy,' 'corporation,' and 'enterprise' (1995: 105–112). Finally, Olsen argued for four 'stylized visions' of the university: 'a rule-governed community of scholars,' 'an instrument for shifting national political agendas,' 'a representative democracy,' and 'a service enterprise embedded in competitive markets' (2007: 30).

Using complex new international empirical data, we analyzed organizational patterns in European higher education systems. Rather than constructing a new typology, we assessed the applicability of the selected existing typologies to real patterns of functioning. As the analyzed typologies and models refer to universities, our empirical data referred only to universities (as elsewhere in the book) rather than to whole higher education systems. In particular, we investigated the extent to which the reality of these European systems aligns with the academic collegial models of Olsen, Birnbaum, and McNay. Olsen's *institutional* model of the university as a 'community of scholars' (in principle, paralleling Birnbaum's and McNay's 'collegium' models) is empirically tested below. It is also briefly empirically contrasted with Olsen's *instrumental* models—in particular, the model of the university as an 'instrument for shifting political agendas,' which has become increasingly important across Europe.

We had to choose between two approaches: to examine in very general terms the extent to which traditional university governance typologies and models are applicable in European universities (focusing on Olsen, Birnbaum, and McNay), or to focus on the governance model common to all three typologies (the collegial model), testing the assumption that this model would be a good fit for the Polish case but less so for other European cases. Following an initial assessment based on a review of the research literature, we pursued the second approach, 'testing' for the 'community of scholars' collegial model that Poland seemed likely to manifest much more strongly than most other European systems (including Portugal and Italy, defined as 'professorially coordinated systems' by Teichler et al. 2013: 191).

A review of the literature on university governance in Poland, viewed as a special case for historical reasons, clearly indicates coordination by senior academics and their collegial bodies as the prevailing form among Clark's three patterns of coordination (by senior academics, by the state, or by the market). As an expression of deep aversion to state and external intervention following the collapse of Communism, the Humboldt-oriented model offered the academic community what Dobbins and Knill described as 'the best of both worlds,' in which 'the state continued to finance higher education in full but remained nearly powerless with regard to teaching, research, administration, and procedural matters' (2009: 424).

In Polish universities, linking to the collegial model of university governance in the three typologies, autonomy is construed as 'delegating all authority to collegial bodies,' given the threat that 'locating too much authority in the collegial bodies (the senates and the faculty boards) could restrict the autonomy of the institution as a whole' (Białecki and Dąbrowa-Szefler 2009: 197). They further observe that the version of autonomy professed by the Polish academic community 'is often construed as independence from the expectations and aspirations of the professional communities corresponding to the academic disciplines' (2009: 197). In similar vein, Dobbins stressed that Poland maintains 'most features typical of academic self-rule' and is 'relatively insulated from socio-economic stakeholders' (2015: 24, 25). Following the collapse of Communism in 1989, universities became fully autonomous, and decision-making power was returned to 'high-ranking academics who governed by means of academic senates' (Dobbins 2015: 24; Antonowicz 2016).

Here, however, we focus on cross-national differences across Europe and a possible clustering of countries based on perceptions of academic collegiality.

Academic collegiality defined

Following Birnbaum (1988), and adapting his four major models of university organization (collegial, bureaucratic, political, and anarchical), Kathleen Manning's *Organizational Theory in Higher Education* defines the collegial model of university organization by reference to such features as circular communication and consensus decision-making, leadership as first among equals, socialization of new faculty members, academic freedom, tenure, and self-governance as a system of shared governance for making collective institutional decisions (Manning 2013: 40–48; Aarrevaara 2010). Collegiality centers on 'conferring, collaborating, and gaining consensus,' where the underlying assumption is that conflict can be eliminated through consensus-based discussion (Austin and Jones 2016: 125). Most of these features can be studied by reference to variables within the dataset used here.

Birnbaum defines a 'collegial system' in terms of the following characteristics:

> An emphasis on consensus, shared power, common commitments and aspirations, and leadership that emphasizes consultation and collective responsibilities are clearly important factors. ... It is a community in which status differences are deemphasized and people interact as equals, making it possible to consider the college as a community of colleagues—in other words, as a collegium.
>
> (Birnbaum 1988: 86–97)

However, as Birnbaum defines it, a 'collegium' comprises senior, tenured academics but does not include the non-tenured class of assistants, as our empirical findings will show. Much of their interaction is informal; the institution
is egalitarian and democratic, and members of the administration and faculty
'consider each other as equals.' There is an emphasis on 'thoroughness and
deliberation,' and decisions are made by consensus. The administration is understood to be 'subordinated to the collegium and carries out the collegium's
will.' Administrators tend to be 'amateurs' rather than professionals; the leader
is elected rather than appointed, and he or she is not seen by faculty as a 'boss'
but rather as 'first among equals.' There is 'general agreement on the expected
and accepted relationships' between administrators and faculty; informal norms
control academic behavior more powerfully than written rules and regulations,
and leaders are selected by their colleagues because they are seen to exemplify
their institutions' norms (Birnbaum 1988: 87–101).

Similarly, McNay links his model of 'collegium' to one of Clark's 'basic values'
of 'liberty' or 'freedom' in higher education (1983: 247–249). In this model, the
role of central authorities is 'permissive' and its management style is 'consensual.'
The role of the administration is to be the servant of the academic community,
and the timeframe in organizational thinking is 'long' (McNay 1995: 109). In
similar vein, Clark notes that collegiality is

> the form of authority about which the profession expresses the greatest
> pride. It has democratic, anti-bureaucratic overtones, as decisions are to be
> made not by a boss but by a group of peers; equality is operationalized in a
> one-person one-vote procedure.
>
> (1987b: 384)

As summarized by Gary Rhoades, the 'collegial model' of academic governance

> emphasizes nonhierarchical, cooperative decision making and the significance
> of faculty self-determination. Various campus constituencies are knit together
> by common interests and by a sense of academic community that legitimizes
> the concerns of these parties. Members of that community participate colle-
> gially in administering the affairs of the organization. The concerns of the
> faculty are particularly influential in the process of academic self-governance.
>
> (1992: 1377)

Finally, Olsen's four models or 'stylized visions' of university organization and
governance (Olsen 2007: 28–33) generally coexist in time as 'enduring aspects
of university organization and governance. The mix of visions varies over time
and across political and cultural systems.' As he further notes,

> if support is conditional and a question of degree and the four visions are
> both competing and supplementing each other, there will in some periods

and contexts be a balance among the different visions. In other periods and contexts one vision may generate reform efforts, while others constrain what are legitimate and viable solutions.

(2007: 36–37)

Olsen's theoretical views find support in the results of recent quantitative studies of the survival of collegiality in managerially led European universities—that is, the cultures of collegialism and of managerialism can coexist without necessarily trading off one another (Marini and Reale 2016: 13). In the following sections, we assess the applicability of Olsen's first model to the empirical data from the 11 selected European systems. We then present an 'Index of Government Influence' and an 'Index of Academic Entrepreneurialism' as alternative operationalizations of Olsen's second model. Finally, we discuss collegiality by operationalizing Birnbaum's and McNay's models of 'collegium.' Specifically, we construct an 'Index of Collegiality' to assess European systems, showing the relative power of collegial bodies among other academic actors involved in decision-making.

The analytical power of the three indexes lies in their *relativity*, as the relative positioning of European higher education systems is more important than absolute values on these indexes. The indexes for specific countries are aggregated, averaged, and produced according to the percentages of academics who agree or strongly agree with selected statements (sometimes in reverse scale order). In other words, the indexes are derived directly from primary data reflecting the views of the academic profession in particular systems. For instance, some European systems can be characterized as more 'collegial' or more 'entrepreneurial,' based on perceptions that are internal to academic institutions rather than according to external national or institutional statistics.

An *internal* perspective of this kind reveals issues that are often hidden behind data aggregated at the level of the higher education sector or its institutions or at state level. The micro-level perspective of individual faculty members is useful for all higher education stakeholders, either in terms of self-knowledge or in understanding how institutions are affected by long-term reform pressures.

In general, we explore the extent to which *theoretical* models of university governance fit the *reality* of European systems—that is, the extent to which these models fit the empirical data on the 'beliefs and behaviors' of academic professions in Europe mentioned at the beginning of this chapter. The answers can only be contextual and relative; pragmatically, we position these European universities in relation to those in other European countries in order to assess the models' applicability in various systems.

The data referred to here are confined to the subsample of academics employed full-time in the university sector (as defined by the 11 national teams) and involved in both teaching and research. Consequently, as in several other chapters, the total number of observations is 8,466. In principle, the applicability of theoretical models of university governance to the reality of European universities might be assessed by any of three research designs on a continuum of quantitative, mixed, and qualitative methods (Creswell and Plano Clark 2011). While our approach is more quantitative, the qualitative material collected in five countries (Finland, Germany, Ireland, Poland, and Switzerland) is also useful. Although we decided not to refer directly to the qualitative material, the present account is indirectly underpinned by about 480 reports based on semi-structured, in-depth interviews with academics based on a common protocol. This decision was informed by methodological assumptions—in particular, a more quantitative approach best addressed our research questions, especially as the qualitative material, is available for only 5 of the 11 countries studied.

Apart from the more generic limitations discussed in Chapter 1, some specific limitations apply here. The first of these is the inability to compare academic perceptions across academic generations, as cohort effects in academic perceptions of university governance and academic collegiality cannot easily be studied using cross-sectional datasets. Cohort effects refer to intergenerational comparison at a given moment in time of academics employed under different conditions and at different times; in this regard, it is difficult to disentangle age effects from cohort effects. While we can analyze various academics' perceptions by age (under 40, in their 40s, 50s, and 60s), they still belong to different academic generations. We could not, for instance, ask the same generation of academics the same question at a different point in time. The second limitation is the inability to compare academic perceptions of university governance and academic collegiality across individual institutions. Instead, we could compare only large clusters (e.g., *universities* versus *other higher education institutions*). Nor did our dataset enable us to investigate on a per-institution basis what is often referred to as 'colleague climate'—encouragement of research as reflected in institutional prestige and linked to notions of collegiality (Blau 1994: 238; Finkelstein 1984: 97; Fox 2015). As anonymization of the collected data precluded any links between individual academics and specific institutions, we were unable to explore how perceptions might differ between academics from more and less prestigious institutions. In this regard, there were two extremes; while Austria and Italy have only 'universities,' seven types of institution can be distinguished in Poland.

A third limitation relates to cross-national analyses of higher education systems. While higher education research has relied heavily in recent years on cross-national studies (as well as single-nation studies), potential caveats may be more relevant for Poland than for any of the other selected European countries. The results presented in other chapters indicate that Poland may differ more from the cluster of ten Western European countries than any two countries differ within the cluster. For example, it is very difficult to classify Poland within existing and emergent typologies in terms of dominant academic role orientation (teaching/research). In a book based on CAP data, Shin et al. (2014b) elaborated a typology of 'research focused systems' (all continental European systems), 'teaching focused systems' (Mexico, Brazil, Argentina, Malaysia, and South Africa), and 'teaching and research balanced systems' (USA, Canada, UK, and Australia). In a parallel formulation, a distinction has been drawn between 'emergent' and 'mature' higher education systems, in which all 'emergent' systems are 'teaching focused systems' (Locke et al. 2011).

The question, then, is where Poland should be located in the above typologies in this solely cross-European study. Does Poland differ so much in its teaching and research behaviors and attitudes that it should be lumped together with non-European ('teaching focused' and 'emergent') systems, despite clearly belonging historically to the European (previously Humboldtian or Napoleonic) family of university systems? Based on data collected in a comparable format, is Poland distinct enough to be excluded from the continental European family of 'research focused systems'? The provisional answer is that Polish higher education is moving rapidly toward a highly stratified system, in which a small number of research-intensive universities attract the bulk of available research funding, leaving the vast majority of increasingly teaching-focused institutions with limited access to funding in an ever more competitive setting (Kwiek 2018d). From a global perspective, however, Poland is much more 'research focused' than 'teaching focused,' although certainly lower in research intensity (funding), research interest (academic role orientation), and research involvement (time), along with Ireland and Portugal (for more detail, see Chapter 5).

The uncertainties about where Poland belongs (and does not belong) in recent international typologies link to uncertainties about how best to answer our question about the applicability of the selected governance models to the European data. Like most concepts in higher education research, these were formulated in the United States over the last half century. Our analysis is rooted in a tacit assumption that the principal concepts used in the survey instrument have a somewhat similar meaning across all 11 systems. Clearly, however, these terms may be used in different ways, not only across countries but in Poland as compared to the other ten countries. This limitation is highlighted by Daniel Teodorescu in his cross-national study of research productivity, where he refers to the risk associated with 'applying the findings of Western literature on publication productivity to other national contexts' (Teodorescu 2000: 219)

We can only assume that 30 years after the collapse of Communism, these concepts are more similar than before in Poland and the ten other European countries.

The institutional vision of the university: a 'rule-governed community of scholars'

We begin by analyzing the applicability of Olsen's first model—the university as 'a rule-governed community of scholars'—to the realities of European universities. This model is related to Birnbaum's 'collegial' model, Baldridge's 'university collegium,' and McNay's 'collegium.' In this model, which we link below to selected variables from our European dataset, the university is understood as an institution with the following characteristics. 1) It has its own constitutive and normative and organizational principles. 2) It exhibits a shared commitment to scholarship and learning, basic research and the search for the truth, irrespective of immediate utility and applicability, political convenience or economic benefit. 3) It is expected to benefit society as a whole rather than specific 'stakeholders' or those who are able to pay. 4) Neutral competence is the only source of legitimate authority. 5) It exhibits collegial organization, has elected leaders, and is organized by academic discipline. 6) Its activities and results are assessed by the internal norm of scholarship (peer review), where truth is an end in itself, and the system evolves through internal, organic processes rather than by external design (Olsen 2007: 30–31).

Our research question asked to what extent European universities in different systems exhibit the characteristics specified in Olsen's model. To that end, we linked Olsen's ideas to selected variables to see whether different European systems could be positioned in relation to each other. Based on the university governance literature, the initial hypothesis was that, with its unique historical trajectory as the only post-Communist system in the sample, Poland would be more representative of a 'community of scholars' system than most of the other European systems here.

We analyzed five statements from the dataset that best fit Olsen's first model with regard to the following issues: scholarship and research, the character of primary research undertaken, and research funding. While not all parameters of the model were reflected in the dataset, at least five statements linked directly to Olsen's ideas. Using a five-point Likert scale (see Table 3.1), the five statements analyzed here were as follows:

- 'Scholarship includes the application of academic knowledge in real-life settings' (B5/2). The Netherlands, followed by Poland, ranked *lowest* (39.0 percent agreeing).
- 'Faculty in my discipline have a professional obligation to apply their knowledge to problems in society' (B5/8). Poland, followed by the Netherlands and Switzerland, ranked *lowest* (38.1 percent agreeing).
- 'Emphasis of your primary research: applied/practically oriented' (D2/2). Poland, followed by the Netherlands and Switzerland, ranked *lowest* (45.5 percent answering *very much*).
- 'Emphasis of your primary research: commercially oriented/intended for technology transfer' (D2/3). Poland, followed by Switzerland and Norway, ranked *lowest* (9.8 percent answering *very much*).
- 'External sponsors or clients have no influence over my research activities' (D6/3). Norway, followed by Austria and Switzerland, ranked highest (64.8 percent agreeing).

There is a clear cross-disciplinary pattern here, in that the Polish, Swiss, Norwegian, and Dutch systems differ substantially from the other European systems on most of the items related to Olsen's 'community of scholars' model. Poland ranks lowest in three of the four categories in which a lower rank means that

Table 3.1 Aspects of the 'community of scholars' ideal, percent agreeing (by country; full-time faculty employed in the university sector involved in both teaching and research; answers 1 and 2 combined on a five-point Likert scale (1-*strongly agree* to 5-*strongly disagree* and 1-*very much* to 5-*not at all*)

	PL	DE	AT	FI	IE	IT	NL	NO	PT	CH	UK
Application in real-life settings	55.9	65.4	61.4	81.1	77.0	59.0	39.0	60.9	75.0	*	56.8
Professional obligation to address problems of society	38.1	47.3	57.1	58.2	63.1	61.8	44.3	50.3	70.5	46.0	56.7
Emphasis on practically oriented research	45.5	67.4	61.4	62.7	61.4	60.6	55.8	58.3	69.6	57.9	69.5
Emphasis on commercially oriented research	9.8	19.0	14.2	19.6	14.0	15.3	15.9	13.8	20.1	12.4	15.6
No influence of external sponsors	59.6	51.2	63.8	47.7	45.7	52.7	55.3	64.8	48.1	61.3	38.3

Note: * the question not asked in Switzerland.

the system is closer to the model: professional obligation to apply knowledge to societal problems (the other two lowest-ranking systems were the Netherlands and Switzerland); practical orientation in research (the other two lowest-ranking systems were again the Netherlands and Switzerland); and commercial orientation in research (the other two lowest-ranking systems were Switzerland and Norway). The Netherlands and Poland also ranked lowest in application of scholarship in real-life settings. Finally, Norway ranked highest in lack of external sponsor influence on research (a higher rank means the system is closer to the model studied); the two other highest-ranking systems were Austria and Switzerland. The systems that least fit the 'community of scholars' pattern were Portugal, Finland, and the United Kingdom. Although only through a limited number of parameters could be shown (because of the limited number of relevant dataset variables) Polish, Dutch, Swiss, and Norwegian universities emerge as closest to the Olsen model.

Most significantly, Polish universities proved to be most isolated from the needs of society and from the economy's needs and were closer to the idea of the Ivory Tower than any other European system studied here. This reflects academics' beliefs, which are crucial to academic performance. (Poland has been criticized in this regard in recent international reports published by the World Bank, OECD, and the European Commission.) This disappointing picture is confirmed by institutional, national higher education, and research and development statistics (based on parameters such as total income from industry or share of total income from industry, in terms of both national and institutional budgets). The same picture is confirmed by our analysis of the views and beliefs of Polish academics as compared with those in the other ten systems.

There is no obvious or necessary link between academic collegiality (either in the sense of universities as 'communities of scholars' or, as we show later, in terms of the power of elected academic bodies) and limited links to the external social and economic world. Wherever you are in Europe, collegiality does not imply the separation of universities from the outside world, especially with regard to the economy. The Polish case seems to reveal an uncommonly high level of interiorization of traditional academic norms by the academic profession. These are historically associated with the ideal of the Ivory Tower and go hand in hand with an exceptionally low level of readiness to connect professionally with the outside world.

The instrumental vision of the university: an 'instrument for shifting political agendas'

In Olsen's second model of the university—the university as an 'instrument for shifting national political agendas' (one of his three instrumental models)—the university is viewed as

> a rational tool for implementing the purposes and policies of democratically elected leaders. It is an instrument for achieving national priorities, as defined by the government of the day. The University cannot base its activity on a long-term pact based on constitutive academic values and principles and a commitment to a vision of civilized society and cultural development. Instead research and education is a factor of production and a source of wealth or welfare. The University's purposes and direction of growth depend on shifting political priorities and funds more than on scholarly dynamics. A key issue is applicability and utility of research for practical problem-solving, such as defense, industrial-technological competition, health and education. ... Change in the University is closely linked to political decisions and change.
>
> (Olsen 2007: 31)

For present purposes, we translated the model into variables found in our dataset. While those variables cannot capture all aspects of the model as described, at least two aspects can be analyzed in more detail: government influence on academic decisions and academic entrepreneurialism. We then assessed the applicability of Olsen's second model to the European case by means of two composite indexes: the 'Index of Government Influence' and the 'Index of Academic Entrepreneurialism.'

In both cases, a high ranking would indicate a good fit between the model and the current reality as described by academics in a given country.

On the 'Index of Government Influence,' Poland ranks by far the lowest in Europe (Table 3.2). The index represents the aggregated and averaged value of responses to Question E1; 'At your institution, which actor has the primary influence on each of the following decisions?' On this index, the response of interest was *Government or external stakeholders*. Other response options included *institutional managers, academic unit managers, faculty committees/boards, individual faculty*, and *students*. What matters here is not the absolute index values for particular countries but the relative ranking of these systems. Poland is by far the lowest ranking country on the composite index, suggesting that the influence of government (and 'external stakeholders') on the 11 aspects selected for cross-national analysis is very limited, and certainly the lowest in Europe. On this index, the only significant difference is between Germany (highest rank) and all other countries, and between Poland (lowest rank) and all other countries. Poland is slightly above the European average in only two academic contexts: faculty promotions and determining budget priorities. On all other counts, it is either lowest or one of the lowest.[1]

On the second composite index linked to Olsen's model of university organization—the 'Index of Academic Entrepreneurialism', shown in Table 3.3—Poland and Italy rank lowest in Europe. This index comprises five items that are usually linked with academic entrepreneurialism in the research literature. Germany ranks highest on this index, followed by a cluster of three countries: Finland, the Netherlands, and the United Kingdom. The results for Germany are consistent with Teichler's conclusion that the Humboldtian legacy 'is not that of an "ivory tower". Rather, university professors in Germany underscore practice-oriented approaches in research' (2014b: 85). In contrast, the Humboldtian legacy in Poland accounts for the relative isolation of university-based research from social and economic needs.

Based on our brief analysis of the two composite indexes related to Olsen's second model of the university as an 'instrument for shifting national political agendas,' we can conclude that this model does not seem to fit the reality of the Polish higher education system (as perceived by Polish academics) and only partly fits the reality of the Italian higher education system. As compared with other European systems, this model is least applicable to the Polish system as perceived by Polish academics. The emergent conflict between the vision of the university shared by the Polish academic community (the value-based, autonomy-driven 'community of scholars' model) and the policy-making community's vision (instrumental, externally driven) centers on what Bowen and Schuster term 'basic values' (1986: 53), which are 'derived from long academic tradition and tend to be conveyed from one generation to the next.' While this conflict between Olsen's institutional and instrumental visions has a history of several decades in the other Western European systems analyzed here, this is not the case in Poland, where this value-driven conflict is only beginning to emerge. However,

Table 3.2 Index of Government Influence (Question E1): At your institution, which actor has the primary influence on each of the following decisions? (full-time faculty only, universities only; answer: Government or external stakeholders (percent))

	Austria	Finland	Germany	Ireland	Italy	Netherlands	Norway	Poland	Portugal	Switzerland	UK	Mean
Selecting key administrators	23.1	2.4	8.7	2.2	6.0	24.5	1.1	0.6	2.2	11.1	0.9	6.0
Choosing new faculty	4.3	0.3	4.5	0.7	2.9	0.0	1.6	0.0	0.0	11.6	0.3	2.0
Making faculty promotion and tenure decisions	0.8	0.2	2.2	0.7	4.2	0.0	2.5	1.7	0.7	1.5	0.0	1.9
Determining budget priorities	8.4	4.1	5.3	3.8	1.8	0.7	1.9	5.2	8.1	10.5	3.9	4.5
Determining the overall teaching load of faculty	0.9	3.6	100.0	0.2	2.3	0.0	3.8	0.1	0.8	5.3	0.5	11.2
Setting admission standards for undergraduate students	15.8	9.7	10.7	16.6	6.4	5.7	12.8	0.7	12.0	13.4	2.7	8.3
Approving new academic programs	6.5	14.8	8.7	0.9	2.2	5.0	0.0	2.1	6.4	6.7	2.1	4.8
Evaluating teaching	0.7	5.1	2.1	1.1	0.9	4.0	1.9	0.5	3.5	3.0	5.6	1.8
Setting internal research priorities	2.1	0.5	2.6	1.8	3.1	0.3	1.3	0.4	1.1	0.1	0.6	1.5
Evaluating research	5.8	13.8	7.6	9.9	15.0	16.3	19.3	2.6	30.8	3.9	19.6	11.0
Establishing international linkages	0.7	0.0	0.2	0.4	0.9	1.4	0.2	0.9	1.1	1.8	0.0	0.7
TOTAL (Index)	69.2	54.5	152.7	38.3	45.9	57.9	46.5	14.8	66.6	69.0	36.2	53.7

Table 3.3 Index of Academic Entrepreneurialism (Question E1): To what extent does your institution emphasize the following practices? (full-time faculty only, universities only; from 1-very much to 5-not at all; combined responses 1 and 2, very much and a lot) (percent))

	Austria	Finland	Germany	Ireland	Italy	Netherlands	Norway	Poland	Portugal	UK	Mean
Performance based allocation of resources to academic units	43.9	61.3	55.3	28.0	29.4	63.9	54.1	36.6	18.6	39.6	**41.0**
Considering the practical relevance/applicability of the work of colleagues when making personnel decisions	21.6	27.1	20.7	13.9	10.1	19.4	18.1	14.4	9.2	25.9	**16.6**
Recruiting faculty who have work experience outside of academia	19.5	15.4	29.1	13.5	7.0	17.7	12.7	9.8	25.7	14.2	**13.9**
Encouraging academics to adopt service activities/entrepreneurial activities outside the institution	9.0	7.1	53.2	25.6	14.6	17.3	14.0	9.4	29.0	29.2	**18.3**
Encouraging individuals, businesses, foundations etc. to contribute more to higher education	34.7	21.8	49.7	45.7	22.3	23.7	20.4	19.5	34.6	34.2	**27.6**
TOTAL (Index)	**128.7**	**142.7**	**208.0**	**126.7**	**83.4**	**142.0**	**119.3**	**89.7**	**117.0**	**143.1**	**117.4**

this most collegial (and 'professorially coordinated') system seems likely to be brought into line with other European systems following structural reforms to be introduced in 2018, which were previously attempted in 2009–2012.

Based on a preliminary data analysis along the lines described above (using the same subsample of university academics but with different variables), we conclude that Olsen's other instrumental models of the university (as 'service enterprise embedded in competitive markets' and as 'representative democracy') do not fit the majority of European countries studied here.[2]

To sum up, we argue that Olsen's first (institutional and collegial) model best fits the realities of the Polish higher education system as perceived by the country's academic community. In addition, the model better fits the perceived realities in the Netherlands, Norway, and Switzerland than in the other countries studied. However, the second (instrumental) model was found to be least influential in Poland as compared with all other countries, where there is very little government influence and much more academic entrepreneurialism. Although currently perceived as irrelevant by Poland's academic community, these characteristics are massively promoted in the new wave of Polish reforms and may gain ground in coming years with state-supported changes in funding and governance mechanisms. At present, the two models seem incompatible in Poland, and the logic of current Polish reforms dooms both to ongoing conflict, grounded in the incommensurability of the academic profession's traditional academic values and norms and the alternative values and norms promoted by higher education policymakers and reformers. The experiences of other European systems and the political economy of reforms suggest that, in the years ahead, academic values and norms may gravitate gradually toward the instrumental model. In this way, Polish higher education may become less isolated from 'external' social and economic issues as organizational and funding mechanisms are fundamentally transformed.

Perceived influences on university decision-making

In exploring the perceived influence of various actors on university decision-making (as discussed above in relation to the index of government influence), we are especially interested in the influence of traditional collegial bodies on academic decisions. Following Birnbaum (1988) and McNay (1995), academic collegiality is understood here as the power of academic collegial bodies at faculty and departmental levels. As McNay argues in his 'collegium' model,

> If the main tasks of the university are teaching and research, most developments will spring from these two activities and decisions will be based within the structures where they are organized—mainly discipline-based departments—within a frame of reference set by peer scholars in the international community.

(1995: 106)

In the survey instrument, the power of academic collegial bodies is contrasted on the one hand with the power of governments, external stakeholders, and institutional managers, and of academic unit managers and individual faculty members on the other. The response options concerning influential actors in academic decision-making included *government or external stakeholders, institutional managers, academic unit managers, faculty committees/boards, individual faculty*, and *students*. (For present purposes, we omitted the category of students.) The following academic decision contexts were considered most essential at the stage of survey instrument design and were therefore explored in detail:

- Selecting key administrators.
- Choosing new faculty.
- Making faculty promotion and tenure decisions.
- Determining budget priorities.
- Determining the overall teaching load of faculty.
- Setting admission standards for undergraduate students.
- Approving new academic programs.
- Evaluating teaching.
- Setting internal research priorities.
- Evaluating research.
- Establishing international linkages.

To examine the role of faculty committees/boards in decision-making, we constructed the composite 'Index of Collegiality' by aggregating and averaging answers indicating that these were primary influencers. Across Europe, collegial academic bodies were found to be most influential in Switzerland and Poland (Table 3.4). The Index of Collegiality is by far the highest for these two countries, clearly supporting the finding in the section on the institutional vision of the university above (based on a different set of variables) that Swiss and Polish universities follow the 'community of scholars' model. Swiss academic bodies are most influential in Europe in all but two of the 11 issues. (Ireland and Italy rank highest in approving new faculty programs, and the Netherlands and Poland rank highest in establishing international linkages.) Polish academic bodies are ranked second most influential in choosing new faculty, promotion, and tenure, teaching loads and evaluation, and establishing international linkages. In all areas, Swiss academic bodies are more influential than the European average. Polish bodies are most influential only in determining teaching load, approving new academic programs, and evaluating teaching. As measured by this index, collegiality as the relative power of collegial bodies is very high in Switzerland and Poland and high in the United Kingdom, Portugal, Italy, Ireland, and the Netherlands as compared with the other countries. The Swiss and Polish systems are perceived by academics as highly collegial, in the sense that academic collegial bodies are seen to play an exceptionally powerful role in academic decision-making.

Table 3.4 Index of Collegiality (Question E1): At your institution, which actor has the primary influence on each of the following decisions? (full-time faculty only, universities only; answer: 'Faculty committees/boards' (percent))

	Austria	Finland	Germany	Ireland	Italy	Netherlands	Norway	Poland	Portugal	Switzerland	UK	Mean
Selecting key administrators	8.9	22.0	20.3	18.5	7.4	1.5	15.5	8.5	18.1	41.5	28.7	13.5
Choosing new faculty	32.0	32.7	38.5	44.8	34.9	55.2	32.9	47.2	55.6	59.8	41.9	40.2
Making faculty promotion and tenure decisions	4.3	47.0	12.9	58.0	33.6	37.0	32.5	60.4	50.1	73.7	52.2	40.3
Determining budget priorities	2.6	23.7	11.2	19.5	20.7	15.2	20.4	22.5	8.5	44.4	27.1	18.9
Determining the overall teaching load of faculty	9.6	24.2	0.0	14.0	45.1	41.1	21.4	68.5	52.3	67.4	29.2	35.8
Setting admission standards for undergraduate students	18.0	42.5	27.1	38.7	53.9	38.6	41.2	33.8	41.2	58.1	44.0	39.3
Approving new academic programs	21.0	41.3	25.0	68.2	68.9	28.4	0.0	73.7	54.3	60.4	57.0	55.7
Evaluating teaching	11.1	22.4	25.2	23.0	34.7	31.5	20.1	44.0	23.6	36.0	32.3	29.6
Setting internal research priorities	2.7	14.9	12.7	22.1	12.2	29.7	15.2	15.2	32.2	36.9	15.2	15.3
Evaluating research	11.7	18.7	20.7	26.9	32.4	31.0	18.1	27.3	27.9	37.5	22.3	24.8
Establishing international linkages	1.5	7.3	5.9	10.2	5.9	20.8	4.5	16.7	15.3	11.6	9.3	9.2
TOTAL (Index)	123.3	296.6	199.6	344.1	349.7	329.9	221.7	417.7	379.2	527.1	359.3	322.6

Table 3.5 Views on institution management and governance, full-time faculty only, universities only (Questions E4 and E5) on a five-point Likert scale (from 1—strongly agree to 5—strongly disagree; responses 1 and 2 combined, percent agreeing or agreeing strongly)

	Austria	Finland	Germany	Ireland	Italy	Netherlands	Norway	Poland	Portugal	Switzerland	UK	Mean
Strong emphasis on the institution's mission	37.9	55.4	37.7	52.3	19.8	52.2	41.3	19.6	46.4	45.5	56.5	**35.5**
Good communication between management and academics	18.8	32.0	19.0	18.9	26.0	26.4	34.6	21.7	28.9	35.4	20.6	**25.0**
Top-down management style	62.9	52.5	44.9	75.9	52.0	53.1	29.6	51.4	45.4	42.4	59.2	**51.7**
Collegiality in decision-making processes	22.4	26.2	27.8	17.3	15.8	32.6	24.5	26.9	36.3	43.9	19.7	**24.2**
Strong performance orientation	49.9	59.3	0.0	54.3	21.7	71.2	51.8	57.7	37.8	45.3	71.9	**47.7**
Cumbersome admin. process	75.3	57.3	71.0	80.1	53.2	53.8	55.6	70.0	55.3	52.4	70.7	**63.6**
Supportive attitude of administrative staff toward teaching activities	26.1	25.7	27.6	29.9	18.9	48.4	43.6	29.8	31.5	41.4	39.7	**29.2**
Supportive attitude of admin. staff toward research activities	33.7	25.1	24.7	51.0	17.1	35.8	36.0	24.1	15.7	50.3	38.6	**28.4**
Professional development for administrative/management duties for individual faculty	39.1	24.8	20.5	46.2	4.6	26.0	10.2	16.3	9.6	45.6	35.4	**20.6**
Top-level administrators providing competent leadership	39.1	40.9	34.0	27.4	32.2	41.8	37.8	24.8	42.5	39.3	22.0	**33.2**
I am kept informed about what is going on at this institution	56.9	44.4	50.9	33.7	41.3	44.0	38.0	34.8	35.6	40.7	32.0	**41.4**
Lack of faculty involvement is a real problem	63.3	28.7	44.3	59.6	39.2	28.2	34.8	18.4	55.1	32.6	38.4	**38.0**
Students should have a stronger voice in determining policy that affects them	42.6	28.4	40.	33.8	30.9	13.9	27.7	29.6	26.6	23.8	28.8	**31.3**
The administration supports academic freedom	41.5	23.7	38.5	38.7	47.2	49.6	30.8	17.9	40.8	50.6	46.9	**35.3**

Returning to the theoretical model, the major features of McNay's 'collegium' model are very strongly reflected in the perceptions of Swiss and Polish academics. Here, *freedom* is a stronger value than *equity, loyalty*, or *competence* (Clark 1983). *Collegiality* is more important than the other three models (*bureaucracy, corporation*, and *enterprise*), and the role of the government is *permissive* rather than *regulatory, directive*, or *supportive* (as in the other three models). Management style is *consensual* rather than *formal/rational, political/tactical*, or *developed leadership* (as in the other three models). Finally, the administration serves the *academic community* rather than the *committee, chief executive*, or external or internal *clients* (as in the other three models). From another perspective, Western European reports characterize the Polish higher education system as too 'democratic' in the sense that academic collegial bodies are responsible for too many aspects of university functioning.

When asked directly about *top-down management style* and *collegiality in decision-making processes* in their institutions (Table 3.5), European academics responded as follows. Top-down management style is most often reported by academics in Ireland, followed by Austria and the United Kingdom. Collegiality is ranked highest in Switzerland, followed by Portugal and the Netherlands. Interestingly, while Polish academics perceive academic collegial bodies as very powerful, responses agreeing or strongly agreeing with the other two issues above is almost exactly the average for the 11 countries (51.4 percent for top-down management and 26.9 percent for collegiality).

Surprisingly, the perception of academic collegial bodies as highly influential does not correspond to more general perceptions of their influence, as seen in the responses concerning top-down management style and collegiality. This may indicate that different levels of collegiality are considered natural in different national systems—for example, as opposed to Switzerland, the strong influence of faculty committees/boards in Poland is *not* viewed as a generally high level of academic collegiality or as a generally low level of top-down management. In light of the findings concerning the most influential actors in management and decision-making, the fact that relatively few academics agree that their institutions are collegial indicates the pivotal role of academic collegial bodies.

The junior–senior split in the academic profession

Finally, we explore the distribution of influence and authority across academic career stages as an aspect of university governance. Here, the research question is whether European collegiality is actually a 'collegiality of seniors' as the research literature strongly suggests.

The junior–senior dimension is much discussed in higher education research (e.g., Finkelstein et al. 1998; Enders 2000); for example, Neave and Rhoades analyzed the 'deep rift' between the full professoriate and the 'assistant class' in European academia (1987: 211–212). One of the strongest dividing lines in European higher education systems is between seniors and juniors as different academic ranks. In some of these countries, the postdoctoral or habilitation degree plays a fundamental role as the entry ticket to the lower class of senior academics (as against the higher class of full professorship). Across European countries, juniors are not equal partners, and their voice in university matters is heard only when their research role is stronger, which comes with age. In short, institutional authority has always related to authority within the discipline of science. In countries where institutional promotion is based strictly on assessment of research achievements, those with higher research prestige are always more influential than juniors, whose research prestige is necessarily lower. In most of the European countries included here, juniors experience what Teichler (2014b: 65) termed 'a long period of high selectivity and dependence,' during which they are 'expected to survive a long period of dependence and social uncertainty—mostly more than 10 years—before becoming independent and socially secure scholars.' Here, we focus on this dependence.

Academic position and power stratification in European systems is most fully expressed by the differing academic influence of 'professors' (as nationally defined) and 'new entrants' to the academic profession (defined for present purposes as those awarded PhD degrees in the ten years preceding the survey). Based on an extensive review of the literature on stratification of the academic profession and of science (Cole and Cole 1973; Zuckerman 1979; Finkelstein et al. 1998; Schuster and Finkelstein 2006; Enders 2000; Enders and de Weert 2009a), our initial hypothesis was that professors would be much more appreciative than new entrants of how universities are currently organized in their own countries. This hypothesis proved false for all of the countries studied.

Surprisingly, the pervasive lack of perceived *personal* influence among new entrants (as compared with professors) on academic policy making was not associated with negative perceptions of current university organization in any of these countries. Indeed, young academics across Europe seem substantially more appreciative of the status quo. This is significant for the political economy of reforms, which assumes that reforms should defer to those internal stakeholders who stand to benefit most and are therefore likely to strongly support reform (and the reformers). Across all the European systems analyzed here, the professorial class is more critical of the organizational status quo.

Restricting our analysis for a moment to Poland, Polish new entrants exhibit much lower personal influence in quantitative terms than full professors at department, faculty, and institutional levels. Their responses to the question 'How influential are *you*, personally, in helping to shape key academic policies?' show that one fifth believe they are 'not at all influential' at department level, rising to more than half at faculty level and four-fifths at institutional level (see Figure 3.1). This effect is much less pronounced among full professors; less than 5 percent, rising to about 10 percent at faculty level and about 40 percent at institutional level.

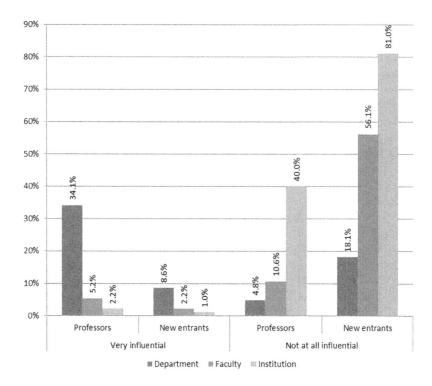

Figure 3.1 Responses to Question E1: How influential are you, personally, in helping to shape key academic policies? (by career stage and age group, Polish academics (percent)).

The two contrasted career stages (and, in the Polish case, age groups) also differ substantially in their views on management and administration. In general, new entrants are much more appreciative of how their institutions are currently managed, and they seem much more satisfied with the institutional status quo. Surprisingly, substantially more of them agree (and strongly agree) that there is good communication between management and academics in their institutions, as well as collegiality in decision-making processes. A much smaller proportion of new entrants report a top-down management style while more believe that top-level administrators provide competent leadership, and that they are kept informed about what is going on. The distribution of views across career stages and age groups is shown in Table 3.6.

The substantial generational differences in academic satisfaction can be explored through several proxies. In the survey, academics were asked to respond to such statements as *This is a poor time for any young person to begin an academic career in my field*; *If I had my time again, I would not become an academic*; and *My job is a source of considerable personal strain*. More than four in ten (43.0

Table 3.6 Views on institution management and administration; Polish
academics by career stage and age group (full professors and new
entrants only), full-time academics (universities only) on a five-
point Likert scale (from 1—*strongly agree* to 5—*strongly disagree*;
responses 1 and 2, 4 and 5 combined) (percent)

		Career stage		Age group			
		New entrants	Full professors	Under 40	40s	50s	60s and above
Good communication between management and academics	Agree	56.8	36.4	55.2	52.7	42.7	33.7
	Neither agree nor disagree	26.2	32.6	28.6	28.9	32.4	32.0
	Disagree	17.0	30.9	16.1	18.4	24.9	34.3
Top-down management style	Agree	21.5	34.1	19.1	21.3	30.7	29.6
	Neither agree nor disagree	22.2	28.0	23.3	22.8	23.5	31.7
	Disagree	56.4	37.9	57.7	56.0	45.8	38.7
Collegiality in decision-making processes	Agree	50.1	27.7	50.0	41.0	34.6	21.3
	Neither agree nor disagree	29.9	31.8	27.9	38.5	32.8	38.9
	Disagree	20.0	40.5	22.1	20.4	32.7	39.8
Top-level administrators providing competent leadership	Agree	48.9	39.8	52.5	44.4	42.2	28.1
	Neither agree nor disagree	31.4	31.7	29.8	31.7	34.5	30.7
	Disagree	19.7	28.5	17.7	23.9	23.3	41.2
I am kept informed about what is going on at this institution	Agree	43.1	25.4	42.2	38.0	27.5	25.2
	Neither agree nor disagree	28.7	26.9	25.1	28.1	31.0	24.0
	Disagree	28.2	47.7	32.7	33.8	41.6	50.8

percent) of new entrants to Polish universities agree with the first statement,
and almost as many (40.3 percent) are stressed by their job. A smaller propor-
tion (16.1 percent) would not now choose to become academics. As shown in
Table 3.7, professors across Europe agreed less often with all three statements.
The most pessimistic academics (both new entrants and professors) are found in
Austria, Italy, and the United Kingdom. Professors (but not new entrants) from
Germany are most stressed by their work, followed by both professors and new
entrants in the Netherlands and the United Kingdom.

These findings were confirmed in the interviews. For instance, young Polish
academics often reported feeling more stressed, overworked, and frustrated than
their older colleagues. They also reported feeling increasingly that they were on

Table 3.7 Perceptions of academic faculty: academic satisfaction (proxies) by academic stage (professors (P) vs. new entrants (NE)), full-time academics (universities only) by country

	AT		FI		DE		IE		IT		NL		NO		PL		PT		CH		UK		Total	
	P	NE	P	NE	P	NE	P	NE	P	NE	P	NE	P	NE	P	NE	P	NE	P	NE	P	NE	P	NE
This is a bad time for any young person to begin an academic career in my field.	71.0	73.4	47.6	45.6	34.4	40.4	41.3	50.5	72.7	73.8	30.7	33.0	26.3	18.5	35.2	43.0	34.8	35.5	31.9	34.6	43.5	56.6	51.0	49.0
If I had my time again, I would not become an academic.	9.2	16.4	8.0	17.4	11.0	18.9	8.0	13.5	11.6	8.0	13.7	12.2	16.3	15.4	13.6	16.1	15.0	16.0	12.6	15.9	21.2	32.8	10.9	16.3
My job is a source of considerable personal strain.	34.5	45.6	48.4	46.5	51.4	37.0	37.8	45.6	26.7	33.9	61.4	57.3	35.0	34.4	24.5	40.3	39.2	46.6	35.3	39.8	54.7	54.8	35.1	41.5

their own, with ever more competition between individuals and institutions and increasing professional uncertainty and financial instability. They share these uncertainties and instabilities with their colleagues in Europe (Teichler and Höhle 2013) and internationally (Yudkevich, Altbach, and Rumbley 2015).

Beyond the widely discussed differences related to gender, institutional type, institutional rank, and academic field (studies of differentiation offering explanations as opposed to studies of diversity; see Huisman 1998), investigation of the academic profession by academic generation as elaborated here and in Chapter 5 reveals a further line of differentiation. Intra-national differences between generations are often greater than cross-national differences between those generations, and, in this respect, the Polish data differ little from the other countries here. Across all European systems, recent performance-oriented changes in rules governing promotions and distribution of research funds are driven by structurally similar factors that may account for the academic profession's lack of cross-generational homogeneity. In Poland, a generational gap overlaps a rank gap, while in other countries it is not the case.

Across all these countries, there is a clear pattern of influence and authority. In all countries (see the 'very influential' column in Table 3.8), professors are much more influential than new entrants at all three levels (department, faculty, and institution). However, in three countries (Germany, Austria, and

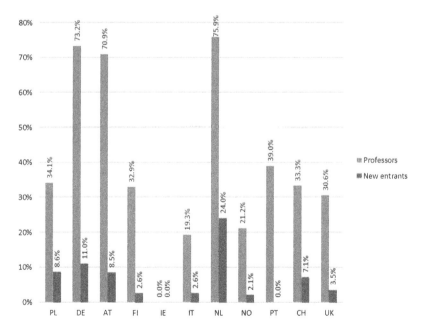

Figure 3.2 Responses to Question E1: *How influential are you, personally, in helping to shape key academic policies?* ('very influential', 'department' level, professors vs. new entrants by country (percent)).

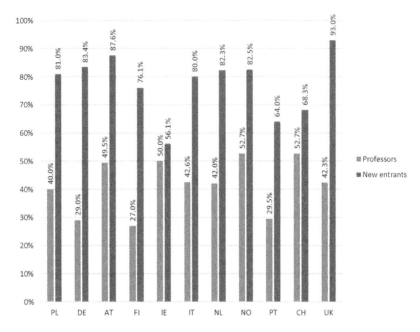

Figure 3.3 Responses to Question E1: *How influential are you, personally, in helping to shape key academic policies?* (not at all influential, 'institution' level, professors vs. new entrants by country (percent)).

the Netherlands), 70–75 percent of professors are very influential at the lowest (departmental) level, as compared with only 20–40 percent in all the other countries. New entrants report being very influential more often than average only in the Netherlands (24.0 percent); about 7–10 percent of new entrants report being very influential in Germany and Austria from the first cluster, followed by Poland and Switzerland, where there is a high level of collegiality (i.e., power of collegial bodies). In all the other countries, the share is 2–4 percent. However, the very high influence of professors at department level does not translate into very high influence at faculty or institution levels. As might be expected, professors are less likely than new entrants to report having no influence at the institutional level. In a majority of countries, the proportion of new entrants who feel powerless at this level reaches 80 percent, as compared with 40–50 percent among professors (mean for professors: 37.7 percent; mean for new entrants: 77.5 percent). The smallest share of least influential professors is in Germany, Finland, and Portugal while the United Kingdom, Austria, and Germany report the largest share of least influential new entrants.

In general, the European academy exhibits a strong generational divide. Across all systems, the split between professoriate and new entrants is very clear. From the generational perspective adopted here, collegiality can be viewed as a 'collegiality of seniors,' to which juniors have only limited access.

Table 3.8 Responses to Question E1: How influential are you, personally, in helping to shape key academic policies? (European academics by career stage and by country (percent))

		Very influential		Somewhat influential		A little influential		Not at all influential	
		Professors	New entrants	Professors	New entrants	Professors	New entrants	Professors	New entrants
PL	Department	34.1	8.6	44.0	27.6	17.1	45.6	4.8	18.1
	Faculty	5.2	2.2	37.7	6.6	46.6	35.0	10.6	56.1
	Institution	2.2	1.0	6.8	1.3	51.0	16.8	40.0	81.0
DE	Department	73.2	11.0	19.7	44.1	3.6	28.2	3.5	16.6
	Faculty	22.7	0.8	54.2	8.6	17.1	29.6	6.1	61.1
	Institution	10.9	0.7	22.8	4.9	37.3	11.1	29.0	83.4
AT	Department	70.9	8.5	23.0	21.6	0.0	33.0	6.1	36.8
	Faculty	17.9	1.0	44.2	4.9	27.9	19.0	9.9	75.2
	Institution	7.2	0.5	8.0	1.6	35.3	10.3	49.5	87.6
FI	Department	32.9	2.6	51.5	25.8	10.0	57.3	5.5	14.4
	Faculty	8.7	0.4	43.5	6.7	35.4	34.6	12.5	58.3
	Institution	4.0	0.5	22.9	2.4	46.0	21.0	27.0	76.1
IE	Department	0.0	0.0	59.7	25.9	27.4	43.5	12.9	30.5
	Faculty	0.0	0.0	23.2	11.9	53.6	30.8	23.2	57.2
	Institution	0.0	0.0	17.5	9.1	32.5	34.8	50.0	56.1
IT	Department	19.3	2.6	52.1	26.8	22.5	39.6	6.1	31.1
	Faculty	7.8	0.7	38.2	9.0	42.9	36.0	11.0	54.3
	Institution	2.8	1.0	11.6	3.1	43.0	16.0	42.6	80.0
NL	Department	75.9	24.0	20.1	45.8	4.0	22.2	0.0	8.1
	Faculty	8.7	1.4	63.6	21.9	21.1	37.7	6.7	39.0
	Institution	1.3	0.7	13.7	1.7	43.0	15.3	42.0	82.3
NO	Department	21.2	2.1	36.4	20.6	27.8	39.1	14.6	38.2
	Faculty	5.9	0.2	19.8	2.6	31.5	18.7	42.7	78.5
	Institution	5.5	0.6	13.4	5.5	28.5	11.3	52.7	82.5
PT	Department	39.0	2.3	41.9	30.3	17.6	45.7	1.5	21.7
	Faculty	19.7	3.6	30.6	10.5	38.5	36.8	11.2	49.1
	Institution	7.6	3.3	33.6	2.5	29.3	30.1	29.5	64.0
CH	Department	33.3	7.1	40.5	17.9	19.1	44.5	7.1	30.5
	Faculty	6.5	1.6	22.8	4.9	55.9	25.3	14.9	68.2
	Institution	3.0	1.9	16.4	5.0	27.9	24.9	52.7	68.3
UK	Department	30.6	3.5	52.6	17.3	15.5	38.7	1.3	40.5
	Faculty	5.3	0.2	48.2	4.7	26.2	19.6	20.3	75.5
	Institution	5.6	0.0	15.3	2.4	36.7	4.6	42.3	93.0

Concluding reflections

This chapter explored the extent to which two selected university governance models are applicable to European systems, testing the applicability of the collegial model of the university (Olsen's 'rule-governed community of scholars') as compared with the managerial model (Olsen's 'instrument for shifting political agendas'). Analysis of the academic attitudes and beliefs linked to these two models of university organization enabled us to define the relative positioning of European higher education systems.

The results of our research can be summarized as follows. With reference to Olsen's theoretical models of university organization and Birnbaum's and McNay's notions of academic collegiality, Polish and Swiss universities can be said to embody the traditional collegial model of the university as a 'community of scholars' to an extent unparalleled in other European countries. In line with the management and governance literature, this study confirms that the defining feature of Swiss and Polish universities is their powerful collegiality. The influence of collegial bodies on academic decision-making is highest in these two countries. In contrast, the influence of government and external stakeholders is lowest in Poland (but high in Switzerland). In Polish universities, the level of academic entrepreneurialism, which is usually linked to managerial rather than collegial management styles, is the lowest in Europe. It follows that the Polish and Swiss higher education systems are the most collegially coordinated 'republics of scholars' in Europe, although in Poland there are ever-increasing national and international pressures for reform.

In the case of Poland, pressures for reform have created a conflict between the institutional vision of the university shared by the academic community (a value-based 'community of scholars') and the instrumental vision shared by the policy-making community (an externally driven national, goal-oriented 'organization'). As a conflict between 'fundamental values' (Bowen and Schuster 1986: 53) that cannot be easily reconciled, this is crucial at the level of policy. While the conflict between the Olsenian institutional vision and the vision of the university as an instrument of national political agendas has been a feature for several decades now of the other Western European systems studied here, that conflict is only now emerging in Poland.

As the most collegial ('professorially coordinated'/'republic of scholars') system in Europe, Poland is still awaiting implementation of reforms that will bring it closer to other European systems that are already governed by instrumental logic and large-scale government-led reforms. However, one lesson to be learned from those Western European reforms is that they tend to lead unavoidably to 'further reforms,' as policymakers in recent decades have tended to view universities as 'incomplete' organizations (Brunsson 2009). As organizations that remain 'incomplete,' Polish universities are likely to be seen as 'work in progress' in the coming years to a much greater extent than the academic profession wishes or imagines, leading to a further wave of value-driven conflicts.

Notes

1 The highest rank for Germany results from the impact of a single variable: 'determining the overall teaching load of faculty'; which disappears if this variable is disregarded due to the specificity of the German system. Similarly, 0 percent for the variable 'choosing new faculty' (in the Netherlands, Poland, and Portugal) requires an explanation: governments and external stakeholders in these countries do not have any influence on employment policy at the lowest, institutional level; additionally, in the Netherlands and in the UK (more precisely in England) they do not have any influence on making faculty promotions; and in Norway, they have no influence on approving new study programs, as confirmed in the literature.

2 In the third model, the university is 'an economic enterprise or a service station operating in regional or global markets. ... The University is governed and changed by its sovereign customers. Research and higher education are commodities, bundles of goods to be sold in a free market. Competition and achieving profit and other individual gains are key processes' (Olsen 2007: 33). And in the fourth model, the university is an interest group democracy, with high participation of students and unions of employees (Olsen 2007: 32).

Chapter 4

International research stratification

International collaboration and productivity

Introduction

In this chapter, first, international research collaboration (IRC) and international research orientation (IRO) are studied at the micro-level of individual academics from the university sector. Both are studied cross-nationally, cross-disciplinarily, and cross-generationally. This chapter differs from most existing internationalization literature in its sample (Europe) and focus (patterns of internationalization in research), using more standard methods (a multivariate model approach). In the context of changing incentive and reward systems in European academic science, which are becoming more output-oriented, as discussed in Chapter 1 on research top performers and Chapter 2 on academic top earners, it may be ever more important for individual academics to cooperate internationally in research. International research collaboration tends to be correlated with higher research productivity; and it may be ever more important to co-publish internationally, as international multi-authored publications tend to exhibit higher citation rates. The major issue is that 'internationalists' increasingly compete with 'locals' (defined as academics collaborating and not collaborating internationally) in university hierarchies of prestige and for access to project-based research funding across Europe. Evidence is presented here that co-authoring publications internationally is still a rare form of research internationalization in Europe (50.8 percent of academics co-author publications internationally). However, as compared with other world regions, the percentage of European academics collaborating internationally in research (63.8 percent) is very high.

Second, in this chapter the correlation between international research collaboration and individual research productivity is examined. Research productivity and international publication co-authorship of 'internationalists' and 'locals' are systematically compared. In all countries and all clusters of academic disciplines studied, international collaboration in research is strongly correlated with substantially higher research productivity. Internationalization in research increasingly plays a stratifying role, though: more international collaboration tends to mean higher publishing rates and those who do not collaborate internationally may be losing more than ever before in terms of resources and prestige in the process of 'accumulative disadvantage,' which means that more productive academics receive ever more resources and prestige, and those less productive are rewarded marginally or not rewarded at all. This is more acute in systems in which project-based funding is more important than core funding for research. The competition is becoming a pervading feature of European research landscape and local prestige combined with local publications may no longer suffice in the apparently never-ending race for resources and academic recognition. Huge cross-disciplinary and cross-national differences apply but, in general terms, this chapter shows a powerful role of internationalization of research for both individual research productivity and the competitiveness, in terms of both volume and quality, of national research outputs. Cross-disciplinary and cross-country differences are explored.

International research collaboration (IRC) has captivated the imagination of the academic profession and organized the research policy steps taken by governments worldwide. Policy-makers and funding agencies have encouraged IRC in the expectation that it will produce higher impact rates in science and technology, foster publications, and improve the quality of training (Jeong, Choi, and Kim 2014; Landry and Amara 1998). European Union research funding programs and academic mobility programs enhancing IRC at a regional level have been present for two decades now. While the world seems to collaborate in research mostly on a nation-by-nation basis, Europe is exceptional in terms of its long-term, large-scale regional research collaborations (Hoekman, Frenken, and Tijssen, 2010; Georghiou 1998). Consequently, European academics should not only be highly involved in IRC but also exhibit high international research orientation.

Academic work can be viewed through academic attitudes (how academics perceive their work), through academic behaviors (how they actually work), or both, as elsewhere in this book. Our dataset enables us to refer to both attitudinal characteristics and actual behaviors from an international comparative perspective. Consequently, here, IRC is viewed as a specific academic behavior, and international research orientation (IRO) is viewed as a specific academic attitude (Cummings and Finkelstein 2012). This chapter addresses four specific research questions: a behavioral question about the patterns of European academics' IRC; an attitudinal question about the patterns of IRO (both of these questions are considered cross-nationally and cross-disciplinarily, and the latter is considered cross-generationally); a behavioral question about the patterns of international publishing, including international publication co-authorship (cross-nationally and cross-generationally); and, finally, a mixed attitudinal-behavioral question regarding the predictors of IRC, or what makes some academics more prone to collaborating with international colleagues in research than others, across Europe. This chapter follows the other chapters in its focus: it explores a single institutional type, the European university, across 11 European countries and one sub-category of academics, academics employed full-time in the university sector and involved in both teaching and research.

Internationalists and locals in academic research production

Academic disciplines on the one hand, and academic institutions on the other, affect the patterns of academic attitudes and behaviors at an individual level (Clark 1983), in this case the patterns of IRO and IRC. Both IRO and IRC are highly discipline-sensitive. Previous research suggests that the 'collaborative imperative' dominates in academic science, especially in hard disciplines, though it is less prevalent in soft ones (Lewis 2013; Kyvik and Larsen 1997). In some disciplines, such as the humanities, the 'lonely scholar' model still dominates, while in others, only IRC, especially internationally co-authored publications, leads to academic recognition (Lewis, Ross, and Holden 2012) and, increasingly, access to national and international competitive research funding (Jeong et al. 2014; Melin 2000). 'Internationalists' or 'cosmopolitans' (academics involved in IRC and/or publishing internationally) increasingly compete with 'locals' (academics not involved in IRC and/or not publishing internationally) in university hierarchies of prestige across Europe (Wagner and Leydesdorff 2005). Internationalists/cosmopolitans and locals are also competing for access to funding from national research funding agencies, especially in the hard sciences (Smeby and Gornitzka 2008). Consequently, following the Matthew effect in patterns of international connectivity, a 'small attractive elite' might be dominating international research collaboration, especially in its voluntary, informal mode. In traditional accounts of social stratification in science (Merton 1973; Cole and Cole 1973; Zuckerman 1970), internationalists tend to compete for international recognition—and locals tend to do research and publish for national research markets.

With one reservation, though: when examining the inclusion or exclusion in the international academic community, different types of approaches to internationalization need to born in mind: Enders (2006: 16–17) makes a useful distinction between 'would-be internationalization,' with partners not always considered on equal terms (represented in our sample by Poland), 'must-be internationalization,' with international cooperation considered indispensible (Switzerland, Norway, Finland, or the Netherlands), 'two-arena' countries (Germany), with powerful national-langauge publication markets, and 'armchair internationalization' (the United Kingdom), with internationalization by importing. In different countries, national academic cultures promote or hinder internationalization in research to different degrees and for different reasons.

Academics are central to the success of internationalization in research: they can be more or less (or not at all) internationally minded in their research. The imperative to internationalize is reported to be stronger in smaller and more peripheral countries:

> For systems on the periphery, the imperative to internationalize is strong and unambiguous. … For core systems and those closer to the core, especially

large systems, the motives are weaker and more ambiguous. There is simply less at stake. ... In all cases, the decision to 'engage' internationally comes down to the decision of individual academic staff and their institutions.

(Finkelstein and Sethi 2014: 237–238)

In theoretical approaches to IRO, the traditional 'cosmopolitan/local' distinction has often been used. In Robert K. Merton's sociology of science (Merton 1973: 374), outstanding scientists tend to be 'cosmopolitans,' oriented to the wider 'national and trans-national environments,' and 'locals' tend to be oriented 'primarily to their immediate band of associates.' Alvin Gouldner in his 'cosmopolitan-local' ideal types has contrasted academics who are more loyal to their employing organization and less research-oriented (that is, locals) with academics who are less loyal to their organization and more research-oriented (that is, cosmopolitans). Gouldner's data-based pure types of organizational loyalty and professional commitment have been reformulated in both organizational studies and higher education research (Glaser 1963; Abrahamson 1965; Rhoades et al. 2008; Smeby and Gornitzka 2008). However, the distinction did not refer originally to internationalization in research (focusing on organizational roles and professional identities); the distinction connected to norms about professionals, including academics, with the concept of 'mobility' in its center. Immobile, parochial, and institution-oriented academics (loyal to inside reference groups) were contrasted with mobile, cosmopolitan, career-oriented academics (loyal to outside reference groups)—in an American context of the mid-century rise of science and federal research funding (Abrahamson 1965). Gouldner defined reference groups as those groups with which individuals identify and to whom they refer in making judgments about their own performance: cosmopolitans and locals differ sharply in their identification. Their frame of reference in conducting research and publishing research results is fundamentally different, leading them to seek different sources of recognition and to have different trajectories of academic careers (Wagner and Leydesdorff 2005).

The level of IRO differs across academic disciplines, soft sciences being in general more local, and hard sciences being more global or internationalized: reward systems operate differently not only across countries but also across disciplines. In short, seeking international recognition within discipline-sensitive national reward systems in science may be more (or less) 'necessary' (Kyvik and Larsen 1997: 260). The level of IRO depends also on what Richard Whitley (2000: 220) termed 'the structure of reputational audiences,' different for different disciplines: reputation comes from different audiences, lay groups, or groups of colleagues, national or international. Locals produce knowledge for local research markets and audiences; internationalists produce it for international markets and audiences, or both local and international ones (Kyvik and Larsen 1997). IRO is a function of individual propensity combined with disciplines, institutions, and national reward structures within science: finally, at an individual level, IRO leads to a personal decision to internationalize more (or less) in research. The level of international orientation depends on the researchers themselves (Wagner and Leydesdorff 2005). Faculty internationalization is reported to be disproportionately shaped by deeply ingrained individual values and predilections rather than institutions and academic disciplines (Finkelstein, Walker, and Chen 2013). Institutional-level pressures to internationalize—from a policy perspective—may not work.

The internationalists–locals distinction in research orientation has been analyzed under different rubrics, including the peripatetic–indigenous dichotomy (Welch 1997) and the internationalists–insulars opposition (Cummings and Finkelstein 2012). However, the classical two-dimensional model of high commitment to research and high professional commitment (cosmopolitans) contrasted with high commitment to institution and high organizational loyalty (locals) leads also to different conceptualizations of IRO: apart from pure cosmopolitans and pure locals in research, there can also be 'mixed types' and 'neither types' of academics: those combining international and local research orientation, and those generally uninterested in research (Grimes 1980). There emerge two more classes: 'local-cosmopolitan' scientists on the one hand, with dual orientation (Glaser 1963), and 'drones' or systematic non-producers, with limited contribution to the overall academic enterprise (Harman 1989), on the other. In an American context, the contrasted types of 'local cosmopolitans' and 'cosmopolitan locals' (Rhoades et al. 2008) in research offer alternative models of a professional, beyond the dichotomy of either strong international research orientation, or strong local research orientation.

International research collaboration

IRC is strongly correlated with IRO. Impediments to IRC are reported to be related to macro-level factors (geopolitics, history, language, cultural traditions, country size, country wealth, and geographical distance), institutional-level factors (reputation and resources), and individual-level factors (Georghiou 1998; Luukkonen, Persson, and Sivertsen 1992). IRC patterns have been shown both in single-nation research and in global research (Wagner and Leydesdorff 2005). IRC has its benefits and its costs (Katz and Martin 1997). Specifically, transaction costs (Georghiou 1998) and coordination costs (Cummings and Kiesler 2007) are higher in international than in national research collaboration. In collaborative research, national or international, there is a trade-off between an increase in additional publications and research funds and the minimization of transaction costs (Landry and Amara 1998). Having multiple universities involved in research collaboration complicates coordination and worsens the outcomes of projects (Cummings and Kiesler 2007). Research collaboration with highly productive scientists generally increases individual productivity, while collaboration with low-productivity scientists is reported to decrease it (Lee and Bozeman 2005).

In the context of changing incentive and reward systems in European science, which are becoming more output-oriented (Kyvik and Aksnes 2015), it is ever more important for individual academics to cooperate and, specifically, to cooperate internationally (as well as to co-publish internationally). Multiple-institution papers are more highly cited than single-institution papers, and papers with international co-authors are more highly cited than papers with domestic co-authors (Narin and Whitlow 1990). Performance-based funding modes are increasingly used across Europe, and the broad awareness of international research-based university rankings makes scholarly publishing more than an individual matter and links them closely to institutional and/or departmental funding and prestige. However, in highly competitive science systems, IRC may be primarily motivated by reward structures. As Wagner and Leydesdorff (2005: 1616) argue, 'highly visible and productive researchers, able to choose, work with those who are more likely to enhance their productivity and credibility.'

IRC is the most demanding type of contact between researchers: 'it presupposes attractiveness, international visibility, and often involves significant commitment by the researcher' (Smeby and Gornitzka 2008: 48). It also involves the entire research process (Smeby and Trondal 2005). Research collaboration at an individual level, both national and international, is reported to be ruled by researchers' 'pragmatism' ('when there is something to gain, then a particular collaboration will occur; otherwise, it will not') and by their 'self-organization' (individual rather than institutional determination of 'with whom to cooperate and under which forms') (Melin 2000: 39). IRC can be viewed as an emergent, self-organizing, and networked system. The selection of partners in IRC and locations for research is most often based on choices made by the researchers themselves. What matters in more spontaneous or bottom-up collaborations is 'the individual interests of researchers seeking resources and reputation' (Wagner and Leydesdorff 2005: 1616). However, the role of the state through funding and higher education internationalizatiojn initiatives is critical (Horta 2009a).

According to resource allocation theory, the resources that academics and their teams can invest in research, in terms of their commitment and time, are always limited. Consequently, the decision to engage in research teamwork, including international research teamwork, 'is ultimately a resource allocation decision by which members must decide how to best allocate their limited resources' (Porter, Itir Gogus, and Yu 2010: 41), with time often being a more valuable research resource than funding (Katz and Martin 1997). The consumption of time due to various additional requirements can reduce the time and energy available for actual research activities (Jeong et al. 2014).

Research collaboration can be studied both between and within the individual, group, department, institution, sector, and national levels. In this research, following Katz and Martin (1997), IRC, at an individual level, means collaboration between academics located in different countries (and not between academics with different nationalities located in the same country or in the same institution), while intra-national collaboration means collaboration within a single country. However, international collaboration rests upon a much larger base of domestic activities (Georghiou 1998; Wagner 2006).

IRC can be either formal or informal (within or outside formal agreements and externally funded projects), and international publication co-authorship always requires a published product as an outcome of the cooperative efforts (Georghiou, 1998; Melin and Persson 1996). Not every IRC leads to internationally co-authored publications. There are many cases of collaborations that are not 'consummated' in a co-authored paper (Katz and Martin 1997). The writing of co-authored papers does not necessarily imply a close relationship between the authors (Luukkonen et al. 1992). Traditionally, IRC has been dominated by informal collaboration, which does not require international scientific agreements (Georghiou 1998). Scientists often 'self-select fellow collaborators ... simply because the collaborator offers new ideas or complementary capabilities' (Wagner 2006: 3).

This chapter is focused on international research collaboration and assumes the researcher-based view rather than the research-based view (Jeong, Choi, and Kim 2011). Thus, the unit of analysis is the individual academic, as elsewhere in the book. Apart from the 'solo research' mode in science, internal collaboration (within the same organization), domestic collaboration (within the same country), and international collaboration (between countries) must be clearly differentiated (Jeong et al. 2011: 969). Collaboration is largely a matter of social convention among scientists and therefore difficult to define; what constitutes a collaboration varies across organizational levels and changes over time (Katz and Martin 1997). Research collaboration can be defined as a 'system of research activities by several actors related in a functional way and coordinated to attain a research goal corresponding with these actors' research goals or interests' (Laudel 2002: 5). Thus, collaboration presupposes that a shared research goal is defined by activities rather than by the actors involved, and the term is reserved for research that includes personal interactions. Given this definition, collaboration need not be focused on publishing articles. Collaborations may have no publication objectives at any point. Broader notions of collaboration are not easy to measure, and, therefore, many studies of research collaboration 'begin and end with [a] co-authored publication' (Bozeman and Boardman 2014: 2–3).

For IRC to emerge, two preconditions must be met: motivation on the part of the researcher and his or her attractiveness as a researcher to international colleagues (Kyvik and Larsen 1994; Wagner 2006). The ability of any actor to join international research networks depends on his or her attractiveness as a partner (Wagner and Leydesdorff 2005). 'Visibility is a basic condition for being potentially interesting to other scientists, but one also has to be attractive in order to be actively sought out by others' (Kyvik and Larsen 1994: 163).

Overall, the international dimension in *research* has been under-studied ('less discussed and more assumed as a natural and implicit element,' de Wit 2002: 96) in the international higher education stream of literature (see Deardorff et al. 2012). Although internationalization-related shifts in 'research' come under the pillar of 'internationalization at home' (Knight 2012), the theme is largely undiscussed. The present chapter, through the concepts of IRO and IRC, intends to highlight this somehow neglected area, using theoretical insights from academic profession studies, sociology of science, and scientometrics.

Measuring internationalization of research

There are two approaches to 'measure' the internationalization of research in a national higher education system. One approach is *external* to the system and relies on such secondary data as, for instance, the national statistics on input and output in academic research. In particular, the aggregated national academic research production can be compared internationally, either through the international publication reports or through the international citation reports. The other approach is *internal* to a national higher education system and relies on academic behavioral and attitudinal data, voluntarily provided by the academic faculty in a consistent, internationally comparable format. The former approach relies on the aggregate macro-level national data, the latter on the disaggregate micro-level (that of individual academics) data. Both approaches are highly complementary. Until recently, due to the scarcity of the reliable international data, only the former approach was used in Europe for international comparative quantitative purposes. Now, with new datasets, the latter approach is becoming highly useful for both research and public policy objectives.

As in most chapters in this book, a subsample of European academics from 11 countries who were employed full-time in the university sector and involved in both teaching and research (49.1 percent, or 8,466 observations) is used. About 60 percent of academics in the sample are male, and about 40 percent are female. About 60 percent come from hard academic fields, and about 40 percent come from soft academic fields. The age cohorts and academic experience cohorts are relatively evenly distributed. A sample description in terms of selected demographic characteristics is presented in Table 4.1.

As elsewhere in the book, six major clusters of academic disciplines were studied: life sciences and medical sciences, physical sciences and mathematics, engineering, humanities and social sciences, professions (which included teacher training and education science; business and administration, economics; and law in the questionnaire), and other fields. Both inferential statistics and a multivariate model approach were used.

The exact questions regarding IRC and IRO in the survey were formulated as follows: 'How would you characterize your research efforts undertaken during this (or the previous) academic year?—Do you collaborate with international colleagues?' (Yes/No; question D1/4); 'How would you characterize the emphasis of your primary research this (or the previous) academic year?—international in scope or orientation' (on a five-point Likert scale between 1, indicating 'very much,' and 5, indicating 'not at all,' with answers 1 and 2 combined, question D2/5; other options included 'basic/theoretical,' 'applied/practically oriented,' 'commercially oriented,' 'based in one discipline,' and 'multi-/interdisciplinary').

Table 4.1 Sample description: frequencies of selected
demographic characteristics, only academics
employed in the university sector and involved
in both teaching and research, all 11 European
countries combined

		N	%
Gender	Male	5,102	62.1
	Female	3,113	37.9
Age	Under 35	1,699	20.8
	35–44	2,532	31.0
	45–59	2,876	35.4
	60 and more	1,041	12.8
Academic experience*	Under 7	2,431	29.2
	7–15	2,422	29.1
	16 and more	3,476	41.7
Academic fields	Soft	3,455	42.9
	Hard	4,590	57.1

Note: *'Academic experience' means the number of years since one's
first full-time employment ('beyond research and teaching assistant
in higher education/research sector').

Importantly, no explanation or guidance was given in any of the 11 countries
regarding the terms 'international,' 'research' (and its variants), 'research international in scope or orientation,' or 'international collaboration in research.' We
did not want to complicate the academic profession survey with 400 variables.

Therefore one limitation of this approach in this chapter is the survey instrument's inability to distinguish between IRC based on nationality (for instance,
Polish and German academics working together at a Polish or German university) or location (for instance, two German or two Polish academics working in
different countries) or between different modes and intensities of IRC (from
exchanging e-mails with international colleagues to attending international conferences and writing joint international project proposals). Consequently, the behavioral concept of international collaboration in research was measured crudely
(a simple 'Yes' or 'No' answer), and different individual perceptions of internationalization were lumped together and averaged. International co-authorship
and international publishing were also crudely measured (through self-declared
percentages of peer-reviewed internationally co-authored journal articles and
book chapters, regardless of publication numbers, so that the publishing patterns lump high research performers together with low research performers).
However, the chapter leads to several important cross-national conclusions.

There are several other limitations relevant specifically for this chapter. The
first is our inability to compare academics across individual institutions: we can
only draw comparisons between large clusters of them. We are therefore unable to study differences in the internationalization of research and in research

productivity between academics from institutions of lower academic standing and those from most prestigious ones (all we could do was to distinguish between a broad cluster of 'universities' and a broad cluster of 'other higher education institutions' in each system studied). The next limitation is our inability to compare the internationalization of research and research productivity across academic generations: cohort aspects cannot be easily studied through cross-sectional datasets. Cohort effects mean that academics employed under different conditions and in different times are being intergenerationally compared at a given moment in time, and it is difficult to disentangle age effects from cohort effects. We can analyze academics by age brackets (e.g., academics under 40, in their 40s, 50s, and 60s), but they still belong to different academic generations as they were employed under different conditions. Even more so, the employment conditions—such as, for instance, high or low competition for academic jobs—generally differed between countries and, to an extent, between academic fields. The two academic disciplines with changing employment conditions, access to research funding, and access to academic jobs over time are the humanities and particle physics (Cole and Cole 1973; Ziman 1994).

International research collaboration and international research orientation

IRC differs substantially from IRO: the former represents academic behaviors (studied together with international publishing patterns in this chapter), and the latter represents academic attitudes. However, it is useful to study their patterns concurrently. In terms of IRO, on average, about two-thirds of European academics characterize their primary research as 'international' (mean: 63.1 percent), with about three-quarters of academics in Ireland, Italy, and the Netherlands and less than one-half in Poland reporting this (Figure 4.1). In terms of IRC, on average, two-thirds of academics collaborate internationally (mean 63.8 percent), with this number ranging from about one-half in Poland, Germany, and Portugal to about three-quarters in the Netherlands, Austria, Ireland, Switzerland, and Finland.

Two cases are interesting from a cross-national perspective. First, in Austria, Finland, and Switzerland, the percentage of internationally collaborating academics is considerably higher than the percentage of academics who view their research as international in scope or orientation, while in Italy, exceptionally in Europe, it is the other way around—the percentage of internationally collaborating academics is considerably lower than the percentage of academics who view their research as international in scope or orientation (by 15 percentage points). In most countries, the percentages of the attitudinal and the behavioral dimensions of internationalization are roughly similar. These two cases suggest that attitudes toward research internationalization can substantially differ from actual internationalization behaviors. The attitudinal concept of 'international research' can have national variations in meaning, apart from cross-disciplinary

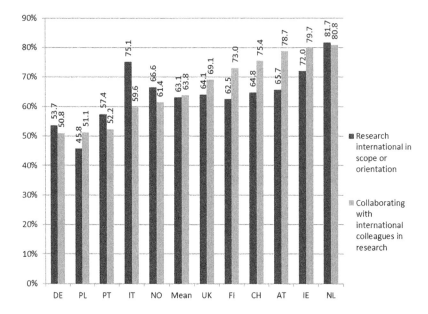

Figure 4.1 Internationalization in research: average percentage of academics whose research is international in scope or orientation and who collaborate in research with international colleagues, only academics employed in the university sector and involved in both teaching and research, by country.

differences (Kyvik and Larsen 1997). In most countries, internationalization attitudes match internationalization behaviors. In some countries, however, average real international collaboration is more common than average declared internationalization attitudes, and in Italy real collaboration is substantially less common than declared internationalization attitudes. The case of the Italian research internationalization has been discussed (Abramo et al. 2011a; Rostan et al. 2014), and our research confirms the previous findings, according to which the internationalization attitude/behavior discrepancy in Italy is high.

From a cross-disciplinary perspective, consistent with previous studies (Hoekman et al. 2010; Rostan and Ceravolo 2015; Lewis 2013), in terms of IRC, academics in the cluster of physical sciences and mathematics are by far the most internationalized in research (with about three-fourths being 'internationalists'), and academics in the cluster of professions are the least internationalized (with only about half of them being 'internationalists,' see Figure 4.2). Surprisingly, in light of previous studies, the level of research internationalization, as viewed through the proxy of international collaboration in research, is similar for the cluster of humanities and social sciences on the one hand and the clusters of engineering, life sciences, and medical sciences on the other hand (with about 60–65 percent of researchers in both categories being 'internationalists').

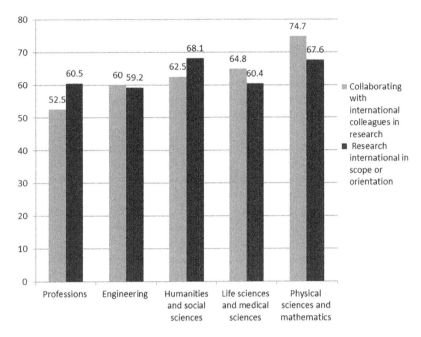

Figure 4.2 Internationalization in research: percentage of academics whose research is international in scope or orientation and who collaborate in research with international colleagues, only academics employed in the university sector and involved in both teaching and research, by major clusters of academic disciplines.

However, in terms of IRO, interestingly, academics in the humanities and social sciences are, on average, slightly more internationalized than academics in the physical sciences and mathematics and substantially more internationalized than academics in the life sciences and medical sciences.

The disciplinary patterns of IRC and IRO are similar to the country patterns. In some disciplines, such as in the physical sciences and mathematics, a higher share of academics actually collaborate internationally than characterize their research as international. In others, notably in the humanities, social sciences, and professions, it is the other way around, leading to substantial cross-disciplinary differences in the understanding of what 'international research' is. (The relationship between an international scope or orientation in research and major clusters of academic disciplines is statistically significant, with Chi-sq = 49.4, sig<0.001, as is the relationship between international collaboration in research and major clusters of academic disciplines, with Chi-sq = 122.4, sig<0.001).

Viewed through a double lens of IRC and IRO, European academics can be classified into four distinctive groups. Two of them—traditionally studied in research literature as 'internationalists' or 'cosmopolitans' or 'globals'—and 'locals' (Merton 1973; Abrahamson 1965; Kyvik and Larsen 1997; Finkelstein et al.

2013)—are those who collaborate internationally and view their research as international in scope or orientation (answers Yes and Yes, about half of all academics, 49.4 percent, see columns 'Table percent' in Table 4.2) and those who do not collaborate internationally and do not see their research as international in scope or orientation (answers No and No, about one-fifth of all academics, or 19.9 percent). Our findings do not confirm Smeby and Gornitzka's (2008: 37) claim about Norwegian academics that given the overall rise in IRC, the distinction between locals and cosmopolitans is no longer valid and we are 'all cosmopolitans.'

However, there are also two other groups, jointly comprising about 30 percent of European academics, which seem to complicate the otherwise simple (and dichotomous) picture of research internationalization: those who collaborate internationally but do not view their research as international (answers Yes and No, 16.7 percent of academics) and those who do not collaborate internationally but characterize their research as international (answers No and Yes, 14 percent of academics). The relation between an international scope or orientation in research and international collaboration is statistically significant, with Chi-sq = 778.12, sig<0.001. Interesting tensions between internationalization in research in behavioral terms (collaboration that is actually undertaken) and in attitudinal terms (a characterization of the emphasis in research, regardless of the various research efforts undertaken) emerge. The tensions have been examined globally by Rostan et al. (2014: 122), who concluded that

> there are countries where academics' attitude toward research and their actual research behavior match almost perfectly, either signaling a high degree of internationalization of research as in the United Kingdom or a low degree of internationalzliation as in Brazil. In others, attitudes and behaviors sharply diverge, such as in China and Japan.

Table 4.2 International research collaboration by international research orientation, percent by column, only academics employed in the university sector and involved in both teaching and research, all countries combined

		Research international in scope or orientation			
		No		*Yes*	
		%	*Table %*	%	*Table %*
Collaboration in research with international colleagues	No	54.3	19.9	22.1	14.0
	Yes	45.7	16.7	77.9	49.4

Note: Column percent (1 and 3 separately) add to 100. Table percent (2 and 4 together) add to 100. Chi-sq = 778.12, sig<0.001.

Certainly, cross-disciplinary differences emerge. In some disciplines, research can be not international in content but can still require international collaboration (for instance, in STEM fields). In others, research can be international in content and can be conducted as solo research, with no international collaboration (for instance, in language studies or anthropology). IRC has always been most conveniently measured by international co-authorships, though there has been some criticism of equating the two (Katz and Martin 1997; Lee and Bozeman 2005).

While, in very general terms, the traditional notion of 'internationalists'/'- cosmopolitans' and 'locals' seems to capture the differences in various aspects of internationalization in research very well, when applied to a micro-level of individual academics and their self-declared academic attitudes and academic behaviors, these terms seem to miss almost one-third of European academics. Consequently, a traditional dichotomous typology does not serve the academic professions in Europe well. Apart from internationalists and locals, there are also academics who are involved in international collaboration (behaviors) but do not characterize their research as international (attitudes), as well as academics who are not involved in international collaboration but do characterize their research as international. Internationalists and locals represent pure types of academics in the sense that their academic attitudes roughly match their academic behaviors, and the latter two types represent mixed types in the sense that these two factors do not match.

Our research findings will be more robust when cross-national patterns of internationalization are studied through academic behaviors—that is, IRC (and international publishing)—rather than IRO, or academic attitudes. This approach is adopted below.

International publishing: cross-national patterns

Apart from a straightforward approach to IRC ('Do you collaborate with international colleagues?'), its three proxies are considered in this section: self-declared percentages of internationally co-authored publications, percentages of publications in international journals, and percentages of publications in English. Three thresholds were used: 'at least 1 percent' (very low intensity), 'at least 25 percent' (medium intensity), and 'at least 50 percent' (high intensity) of one's academic works. The 1 percent threshold allows us to determine the share of academics who are effectively *not* involved in international publishing. The other two thresholds allow us to see the intensity of international publishing from cross-national (and cross-generational in the next section) perspectives.

At the medium level of intensity, on average, about three-quarters of European academics report publishing in a foreign language (74.1 percent), about two-thirds (63.9 percent) report publishing in international journals, and about one-third (28.9 percent) report publishing in co-authorship with international colleagues (Table 4.3). Huge cross-national differentiation applies, with the Netherlands

Table 4.3 International publishing: mean percent of academics who recently co-authored publications with colleagues from other countries, who published in foreign journals, and who published in a foreign language (only academics employed in the university sector and involved in both teaching and research), by level of intensity and country

Academics who have recently...	co-authored publications with international colleagues (by intensity thresholds)			published in international journals (by intensity thresholds)			published in a foreign language (by intensity thresholds)		
	>1%	>25%	>50%	>1%	>25%	>50%	>1%	>25%	>50%
Austria	62.1	35.6	16.4	85.5	71.7	59.9	86.4	72.7	61.1
Finland	46.9	26.3	12.4	76.7	64.9	53.8	79.8	69.9	59.3
Germany	44.6	24.0	9.1	71.6	57.2	42.1	86.8	75.3	59.9
Ireland	58.0	28.8	12.4	83.6	66.6	53.2	.	.	.
Italy	43.5	21.3	9.9	66.8	55.4	46.3	79.2	67.3	58.4
Netherlands	70.0	41.7	21.2	–	–	–	96.6	90.2	82.5
Norway	47.0	29.6	13.0	–	–	–	93.1	85.3	74.5
Poland	25.4	24.1	12.3	77.3	67.6	57.6	74.0	71.8	50.7
Portugal	47.7	25.7	8.8	60.4	58.7	38.9	75.7	65.9	48.1
Switzerland	65.4	38.6	19.4	78.7	68.3	51.9	79.7	68.6	57.1
UK	48.5	22.3	7.7	77.5	64.4	55.2	.	.	.
TOTAL (weighted mean)	50.8	28.9	13.0	75.3	63.9	51.0	83.5	74.1	61.3

Note: In the Netherlands and Norway, the question about publishing in international journals was not asked. In Ireland and the UK, the foreign language question was excluded from the analysis. The questions were as follows: 'Which percentage of your publications in the last three years were co-authored with colleagues located in other (foreign) countries' (D5/3), 'published in a foreign country' (D5/4), and 'published in a language different from the language of instruction at your current institution?' (D5/1).

and Switzerland showing the highest shares of internationally co-authored publications at both the medium- and the high-intensity levels (about 40 percent and 20 percent), far above the European averages. Not surprisingly, given the low public and private funding for research and high teaching loads, the country with the highest share of academics not co-authoring publications with international colleagues is Poland (about three-quarters, with the European average being about 50 percent).

This research shows a striking difference between the three modes of international publishing: publishing in a foreign language and in a foreign country on the one hand and co-authoring publications with international colleagues on the other. The latter type of publishing, consistent with the prior literature (Melin and Persson 1996; Smeby and Gornitzka 2008), is a much rarer form of research internationalization in Europe. About one-half of academics (49.2 percent) did

not co-author any publications internationally within the 3-year reference period, and, on average, about one in four of them (28.9 percent) co-authored their
publications internationally with a medium level of intensity, and about one in
eight (13 percent) co-authored their publications with a high level of intensity.
Compared with other world regions, the percentage of academics collaborating
internationally in research (63.8 percent), as well as publishing internationally
and co-authoring publications internationally, is very high (Finkelstein et al. 2013
on the United States; Rostan et al. 2014 on mature and emerging countries).

Collaboration and publication co-authorship: cross-generational patterns

IRC varies not only by country and discipline but also by academic generation. Academics enter universities in different eras and thus encounter different career opportunities and academic norms. A general change in the norms
of appropriate academic behavior in which international collaboration figures
prominently would contribute to explaining changes in productivity and collaboration patterns across all academic generations (Kyvik and Aksnes 2015).
A cross-generational perspective complements traditional perspectives—cross-
national, cross-institutional, and cross-disciplinary. A cohort approach to the
academic profession has had limited use thus far (see Marquina and Jones
2015; Shin, Arimoto, Cummings, and Teichler 2014; and Jung, Kooij, and
Teichler 2014).

From a cross-generational comparative perspective, in most of the countries
studied, the highest share of academics collaborating with international partners
in research is among older and oldest generations (see Table 4.4). Not surprisingly, in the context of existing single-nation literatures (Smeby and Gornitzka
2008; Kyvik and Larsen 1997), IRC needs time to grow and certainly needs
access to funding, which increases with age (Jeong et al. 2014).

In none of the countries studied was the share of internationally collaborating
academics the highest for the youngest academic cohort, those who had entered
the profession since 2001 (consistent with Jung et al.'s (2014) global conclusion that senior academics' careers appear to be more international than those
of junior academics). Substantial cross-country differences apply, however. By
far, the least internationalized oldest generation of the academic profession in
Europe exists in the UK and Italy, with slightly more than half of academics collaborating internationally, and the least internationalized youngest generation
of the academic profession in Europe exists in Germany, Poland, and Portugal
(Table 4.4). There is an interesting difference between these three countries and
the Netherlands, Ireland, and the UK, where the share of internationalists among
the youngest generation reaches 80 percent, as compared with 40–45 percent
for the former. Country size explains the Dutch case (small systems tend to
cooperate internationally more frequently than larger ones, Smeby and Trondal
2005; Kyvik and Larsen 1997), but this does not explain the Portuguese case,

Table 4.4 International research collaboration: percent of academics collaborating internationally in research (only academics employed in the university sector and involved in both teaching and research), by country and academic cohort (the year range of the first academic job)

	2001– 2010 %	1991– 2000 %	1981– 1990 %	Before 1981 %
Austria	70.4	80.9	86.7	85.9
Finland	64.4	77.1	87.0	87.5
Germany	39.0	56.2	72.2	63.9
Ireland	80.4	76.6	81.2	77.4
Italy	61.3	65.6	60.3	52.5
Netherlands	80.7	82.4	81.3	76.8
Norway	53.5	60.5	67.7	75.8
Poland	45.4	47.3	57.9	55.3
Portugal	43.8	54.6	60.5	72.7
Switzerland	69.1	93.2	90.7	82.6
UK	77.6	60.5	84.2	55.1
TOTAL (weighted mean)	62.3	68.6	75.4	71.4

Table 4.5 International publication co-authorship: percent of academics who have recently co-authored publications with colleagues in other countries, only academics employed in the university sector and involved in both teaching and research, by country and academic cohort (the year range of first academic job)

	Academic generation 2001–2010 (by intensity threshold)		Academic generation 1991–2000 (by intensity threshold)		Academic generation 1981–1990 (by intensity threshold)		Academic generation before 1981 (by intensity threshold)	
	>25%	>50%	>25%	>50%	>25%	>50%	>25%	>50%
Austria	35.5	16.7	39.3	20.1	35.9	14.5	25.8	10.7
Finland	21.4	11.2	27.7	13.9	32.5	14.1	25.5	9.8
Germany	23.2	9.9	27.6	9.7	18.0	6.0	24.3	7.4
Ireland	31.4	13.6	26.8	12.4	19.4	9.0	28.6	10.2
Italy	21.2	11.4	27.1	11.3	22.7	10.6	14.0	6.8
Netherlands	51.0	27.9	44.6	24.1	33.1	13.3	31.0	13.1
Norway	31.5	13.4	27.9	14.0	29.6	12.2	30.8	10.7
Poland	20.1	8.9	20.0	12.3	24.7	12.2	30.6	16.0
Portugal	29.0	9.3	25.5	9.8	21.6	5.7	31.6	9.0
Switzerland	40.2	22.1	38.5	17.9	51.7	19.0	33.5	23.1
UK	18.0	8.7	23.8	7.3	34.3	13.1	11.8	0.0
TOTAL (weighted mean)	27.4	13.0	28.5	13.3	27.4	11.7	23.6	10.4

which is an equally small system (as opposed to the Polish and German cases, which represent relatively large higher education systems and internal research and publication markets).

Applying a generational approach to international co-authorship leads to the following results (Table 4.5): there are clearly three European countries in which the youngest academic generations (those entering university employment from 2001 to 2010), at both the medium and high publication intensity levels, have the highest share of internationally co-authored publications. The leaders in this regard are the Netherlands and Switzerland, followed by Austria. In terms of international co-authorship, the least internationalized systems among the youngest academic generation are Germany, Poland, Italy, Finland, and the UK.

Collaboration and research productivity

The relationships between international cooperation and research productivity have been widely discussed in research literature, with a general assumption that collaborative activities in research, including international collaborative activities, tend to increase research productivity (Teodorescu 2000; Godin and Gingras 2000; Lee and Bozeman 2005; Shin and Cummings 2010; Abramo et al. 2011a). International research collaboration is most often found to be a critical factor in predicting high research productivity while domestic collaboration is most often found not to be significant. But as Sooho Lee and Barry Bozeman (2005: 673) pointed out, 'despite the ubiquitous nature of collaboration in science, the benefits of collaboration are more often assumed than investigated. ... Do those who collaborate more tend to have more publications?' Yes indeed, they tend to, and very much so, as we shall clearly show below in the case of international collaboration. The rule does not seem to work in the case of domestic collaboration.

We shall analyze two specific aspects of internationalization in research: first, the correlation between international academic cooperation in research and academic productivity (following Daniel Teodorescu's (2000: 206) definition of research productivity as a 'self-reported number of journal articles and chapters in academic books that the respondent had published in the three years prior to the survey') and, second, the correlation between international academic cooperation in research and the co-authorship of publications with international colleagues (at the aggregated European level, across five major clusters of academic disciplines; globally, see Rostan et al. 2014).

As already noted, academic disciplines (together with academic institutions) determine both the patterns of academic attitudes and the patterns of academic behaviors: in our case, international orientation in research as an attitude and international publishing patterns as a behavior. The notions of Burton R. Clark's 'small worlds, different worlds' and Tony Becher and Paul R. Trowler's 'academic tribes and territories' are as important to cross-disciplinary patterns of international cooperation as Karin Knorr Cetina's 'epistemic cultures' and Mary

Henkel's 'academic identities.' These studies show, through different concepts and based on different empirical material, that cooperation patterns (and international cooperation patterns) are discipline-sensitive. The national and international collaboration intensity is not uniform across different academic fields (Abramo et al. 2009a). As Jenny M. Lewis (2013: 103) showed on a sample of academics interviewed in Australia, New Zealand, and the UK, research in 2008 in these countries was done 'alone' by about two-thirds of academics in the humanities and only by one in fourteen academics in science (65.6 percent vs. 7.4 percent); it was done 'with others' by only one in seven in the humanities and by three-quarters in sciences (13.5 percent vs. 75.3 percent; for the rest of academics, the option was 'mixed'). We shall study here the cross-disciplinary differences in detail.

The first question in this section is how strongly international collaboration in research is correlated with higher than average research productivity and whether the relationships found hold across all academic disciplines. Responses to the question 'How many of the following scholarly contributions have you completed in the past three years?' with the number of peer-reviewed 'articles published in an academic book or journal' were analyzed. The analysis was conducted with reference to the two separate classes of 'internationalists' and 'locals.' We define 'internationalists' in this section as academics indicating their involvement in international research collaboration and 'locals' as academics indicating their lack of involvement in it. The independent samples t-test was used: it is a parametric statistical test used for testing a null hypothesis of equality of the means in two independent subpopulations.

Across all clusters of academic disciplines, the difference in productivity rates between 'internationalists' and 'locals' is statistically significant at a high level (p-value< 0.001, see Table 4.7). Those academics who were collaborating with international colleagues in research had published on average substantially more peer-reviewed articles in academic books or journals than their colleagues in the same cluster of academic disciplines who were recently *not* collaborating internationally.

As shown in Table 4.6, the percentage of academics collaborating internationally in research across Europe is high and it is the activity reported on average by two-thirds of academics. There are huge cross-disciplinary and cross-national differences, though. The share of 'internationalists' varies significantly across major clusters of academic disciplines. Consistently with previous studies, academics in the cluster of physical sciences and mathematics are by far the most internationalized in research (three-quarters of them are collaborating internationally) and academics in the cluster of professions are the least internationalized (only about half of them are collaborating internationally). Surprisingly in the light of previous studies, the level of internationalization as viewed through the proxy of international collaboration in research is similar for the humanities and social sciences on the one hand, and engineering on the other hand (about 63–65 percent of academics are collaborating internationally). The 'European

Table 4.6 Percentage of academics collaborating internationally in research, by cluster of academic disciplines and country, only academics full-time employed in the university sector and involved in both teaching and research (in percent)

Cluster of academic disciplines	European field mean*	DE	AT	FI	IE	IT	NL	NO	PT	CH	UK	PL	Discipline cluster mean
Life sciences and medical sciences	64.8	58.7	84.4	77.4	80.7	58.6	79.3	66.7	55.6	71.7	83.3	54.8	70.1
Physical sciences, mathematics	74.7	72.0	88.3	84.7	80.0	71.4	91.7	68.5	54.2	83.3	71.4	72.4	76.2
Engineering	60.0	26.9	76.1	75.0	74.0	58.2	86.4	66.1	68.3	75.4	61.6	26.8	63.2
Humanities and social sciences	62.5	51.8	82.2	73.4	83.6	56.9	80.4	59.3	64.9	-	61.0	47.5	66.1
Professions	52.6	34.6	56.1	63.6	84.6	42.0	67.5	42.7	54.6	77.8	25.0	38.3	53.3
Country mean	63.0	48.8	77.4	74.8	80.6	57.4	81.1	60.7	59.6	77.1	60.5	48.0	66.0

Note: '-'—missing data. *'European field mean' shows the average percentage for all academics combined; 'field mean' averages means from all countries.

Table 4.7 Peer-reviewed articles published by European academics in an academic book or journal by international collaboration in research ('internationals'—Yes, and 'locals'—No) and cluster of academic disciplines. Only academics full-time employed in the university sector and involved in both teaching and research (in percent)

Cluster of academic disciplines	International collaboration	N	%	Mean no. of peer-reviewed articles (3 years)	SE	95% confidence interval for mean		T-test for equality of means	df	p-value
						LB	UB			
Life sciences and medical sciences	Yes	1,542	64.8	7.48	0.26	6.97	7.98	10,927	2285	<0.001
	No	837	35.2	3.34	0.18	2.98	3.71			
Physical sciences, mathematics	Yes	887	74.7	6.92	0.32	6.28	7.55	6,654	1159	<0.001
	No	301	25.3	3.06	0.25	2.56	3.55			
Engineering	Yes	502	60.0	5.19	0.43	4.35	6.03	6,391	799	<0.001
	No	335	40.0	1.61	0.20	1.23	2.00			
Humanities and social sciences	Yes	1,249	62.5	3.34	0.17	2.99	3.68	6,983	1905	<0.001
	No	749	37.5	1.62	0.12	1.39	1.85			
Professions	Yes	503	52.5	3.81	0.27	3.28	4.33	6,367	901	<0.001
	No	455	47.5	1.67	0.18	1.31	2.03			

field mean' column in Table 4.6 shows the mean percentage for all European academics studied in a given cluster of academic disciplines (regardless of the country), while the 'Discipline cluster mean' column shows the mean of the countries' means (that is, takes into account differences in national populations per cluster of disciplines).

Huge cross-national differences apply, as seen in Table 4.6; there are clearly four categories of countries in our sample: international research 'leaders,' 'followers,' 'moderates,' and 'laggards.' The most highly internationalized systems in research in Europe, or research internationalization leaders, are the relatively small systems of Ireland and the Netherlands (on average more than four in every five Irish and Dutch academics are collaborating internationally), followed by Austria, Switzerland, and Finland, internationalization followers (about three-quarters of academics). The two least internationalized systems, or internationalization laggards, are relatively big systems of Poland and Germany, with slightly less than half (about 48 percent) of all academics collaborating internationally. The remaining countries are internationalization moderates. Surprisingly, the patterns of internationalization of Polish and German systems are almost identical in all five clusters of academic disciplines: the highest for physical sciences and mathematics (over 70 percent) and life sciences and medical sciences (in the 50–60 percent range), the lowest for professions (in the 30–40 percent range), and for engineering (slightly below 30 percent). Both systems are among the biggest in Europe, with powerful hierarchical differences and strictly defined career ladders, and are rooted in Humboldtian, nation-oriented ideals of the university (see Kwiek 2016).

'Internationalists' (lines 'Yes' in Table 4.7) across all clusters of academic disciplines had published on average at least twice as many peer-reviewed articles as 'locals' (lines 'No' in Table 4.7), with a large differentiation between clusters. (Similarly, the 'volume' of international collaboration, which we are unable to measure here based on the survey instrument used, is reported on the basis of a bibliometric analysis to be 'positively correlated to productivity,' Abramo et al. 2011a: 642). In some clusters of academic disciplines, 'internationalists' produced on average more than 200 percent (222.35 percent in engineering) and about 120–130 percent (in life sciences and medical sciences, physical sciences, mathematics, and professions) more articles in the reference period. In humanities and social sciences, they produced about 100 percent (106.17 percent) more articles. 'Internationalists' in life sciences and medical sciences, the cluster academic disciplines with the highest productivity rate, produced on average 7.48 articles (and it was 123.95 percent more than 'locals' who produced on average 3.34 articles). The 95 percent confidence interval for mean (e.g., 6.97 articles as a lower bound and 7.98 articles as an upper bound in the case of life sciences and medical sciences) indicates that the 6.97–7.98 interval covers the number of articles with 95 percent of certainty; similarly 'internationalists' in the humanities and social sciences, the cluster of academic disciplines with the lowest productivity rate, produced on average 3.34 articles and 'locals' produced on average 1.62 articles. The cluster of academic disciplines with the highest productivity rate differential between 'internationalists' and 'locals' in Europe is clearly engineering: with the average productivity rates of 5.19 articles for the former group and 1.61 articles for the latter group. It is useful to remember at this point that the measure used here is 'peer-reviewed articles,' which in all clusters of academic disciplines severely reduces the number of articles compared with a sheer measure of 'articles' (for instance, in humanities and social sciences, the measure of 'peer review' reduces the number of articles by half).

As Table 4.8 clearly demonstrates, in all countries and in all clusters of academic disciplines studied, international collaboration in research is correlated with a substantially higher number of publications. Only for the Netherlands, the most highly internationalized system in Europe, the results are not statistically significant. If we assume that the mean number of publication of locals is 100 percent, then the discipline mean for internationals varies from about 200 for the cluster of humanities and social sciences to more than 320 for the cluster of engineering, and the country mean for internationals varies from about 190 in Poland and the United Kingdom to almost 450 in Austria (based on two clusters only). The average of country means is 241. International collaboration pays off most in terms of knowledge production in the cluster of engineering (on average, academics collaborating internationally produce more than three times more publications), and the least for the cluster of humanities and social sciences

Table 4.8 Percentage of peer-reviewed articles published by academics collaborating internationally in research in an academic book or journal (no international collaboration in research = 100 percent), by cluster of academic disciplines (in percent); Only academics full-time employed in the university sector and involved in both teaching and research (in percent)

	European cluster mean*	DE	AT	FI	IE	IT	NL	NO	PT	CH	UK	PL
Life sciences and medical sciences	224		324	292	282	276	208	400	268	135	244	117	204
Physical sciences, mathematics	226		645	589	313	190	181	98	333	362	998	266	293
Engineering	322		513	1147	282	226	223	233	528	300		274	538
Humanities and social sciences	206		122	187	309	347	291	134	219	786	248	190	164
Professions	228		227	1559	212	309	352	257	301	125	51	86	151
Country mean	241		371	447	299	270	237	206	287	206	207	194	187

Note: * 'European cluster mean' shows the average percentage for all academics from a given cluster of disciplines combined.

(about twice more). Results were statistically significant for seven countries in the cluster of life sciences, six countries in the cluster of physical sciences and mathematics, five countries in the cluster of engineering, and four in the cluster of professions.

Collaboration and publication co-authorship

We will draw an important distinction here to view internationalization in research from one more angle. There seems to be a fundamental difference between internationalization as research *collaboration* and internationalization as *international co-authorship* of research publications. The former is more informal, the latter is more formal (Rostan et al. 2014: 136). Presumably, only a fraction of international collaboration activities lead to internationally co-authored publications. Academics can collaborate internationally and still be *not* involved in cross-border knowledge transfer, that is, joint academic publishing. International publication co-authorship occurs at a more individual level than international collaboration, and at the individual level, some preconditions have been identified in research literature. As Jens-Christian Smeby and Ase Gornitzka (2008: 43) argue in their study of the changing internationalization of Norwegian academics across two decades, the integration of researchers into transnational academic communities is dependent on two separate factors: a motivation on the part of the researcher and his/her attractiveness as a researcher to international colleagues. Another relevant factor is the availability of resources (Smeby and Gornitzka 2008: 38).

Thus the second aspect of internationalization in research studied in this section is the difference in the *proportion* of internationally co-authored publications between the subsample of 'internationalists' and the subsample of 'locals' in Europe. In our analysis, the difference is statistically significant at a high level (p-value< 0.001) across all clusters of academic disciplines. While research productivity was analyzed above in correlation with international collaboration across different clusters of academic disciplines, now the intensity of international publication co-authorship is analyzed in correlation with international collaboration across clusters of academic disciplines.

At an aggregated European level, the differences between 'internationalists' and 'locals' are consistent across all clusters of academic disciplines. And they can be summed up in a single statement: 'no international collaboration, no international co-authorship.' The average proportion of internationally co-authored publications for 'internationalists' differs across clusters of academic disciplines (see Table 4.9): consistently with previous research results which link international research collaboration with higher research productivity across disciplines (for instance, Shin and Cummings 2010), it is the highest for physical sciences and mathematics (34.67 percent) and the lowest for humanities and social sciences (only 14.20 percent) and professions (19.14 percent). There is a powerful relationship between being involved in international cooperation in research and

Table 4.9 Percentage of articles by European academics published in an academic book or journal coauthored with colleagues located in other (foreign) countries, by international collaboration in research and cluster of academic disciplines (in percent). Only academics full-time employed in the university sector and involved in both teaching and research (in percent)

Cluster of academic disciplines	International collaboration	N	%	Mean percentage of peer-reviewed articles	SE	95% confidence interval for mean		T-test for equality of means	df	p-value
						LB	UB			
Life sciences and medical sciences	Yes	1,542	64.8	34.67	0.89	32.92	36.42	20.662	2070	<0.001
	No	837	35.2	6.69	0.73	5.25	8.13			
Physical sciences, mathematics	Yes	887	74.7	41.00	1.23	38.60	43.41	15.450	1081	<0.001
	No	301	25.3	6.16	1.18	3.84	8.48			
Engineering	Yes	502	60.0	25.02	1.34	22.39	27.65	9.373	760	<0.001
	No	335	40.0	6.57	1.19	4.22	8.92			
Humanities and social sciences	Yes	1,249	62.5	14.20	0.70	12.83	15.57	11.602	1701	<0.001
	No	749	37.5	2.39	0.49	1.43	3.35			
Professions	Yes	503	52.5	19.14	1.25	16.69	21.59	11.173	832	<0.001
	No	455	47.5	2.54	0.60	1.36	3.71			

international co-authorship of articles in books and journals. The difference in the share of the latter type of publications between 'internationalists' and 'locals' is huge: the average rate of international co-authorship for 'internationalists' is between four to five times higher in such clusters of academic fields as engineering, life sciences, and medical sciences).

Academics *not* collaborating internationally report no more than merely 7 percent of their publications being internationally co-authored in the three 'hard' fields and no more than merely 3 percent in the two 'soft' fields only. The highest difference in the share between academics collaborating and not collaborating internationally is in professions and the lowest difference is in engineering. In the most internationalized cluster of academic disciplines (physical sciences and mathematics), the share of internationally co-authored publications for 'internationalists' is 35.67 percent while the share for 'locals' is only 6.69 percent.

The pattern is consistent for both academics collaborating internationally and those not collaborating internationally across all clusters of academic disciplines studied. Those not collaborating internationally produce only a marginal percentage of their publications as co-authored with colleagues from other countries. Their share in the academic profession in Europe is substantial, though: about four out of ten academics in professions and engineering, about three out of ten in humanities and social sciences, and life sciences and medical sciences, and about a quarter of all academics in physical sciences and mathematics do not collaborate internationally. If internationally co-authored publications count for national systems, then the only way to have more of them is through increased international research collaboration. There are strong patterns across Europe linking collaboration and international co-publishing, with some variations, though (as can be seen from the detailed national data in Table A.3 in the Satistical Appendix): for instance, Switzerland exhibits the smallest difference between internationalists and locals in terms of the share of internationally co-authored publications (in all clusters of disciplines for which Swiss data were available).

Finally, two reservations need to be made about this section. The first reservation is about the direction of causality in the research productivity–international cooperation relation and the existence of a number of indirect factors enhancing international cooperation. The identification of high research productivity correlates (e.g., international collaboration) does not mean the identification of causal relations (Ramsden 1994: 223). International cooperation in research may be generally undertaken by more productive academics as such academics are sought by most productive academics across all systems (Smeby and Try 2005). Also more productive academics tend to have better access to funding for international cooperation (Lee and Bozeman 2005: 677; Smeby and Trondal 2005: 463; Geuna 1998). The cooperation with productive academics generally increases individual research productivity but the cooperation with non-productive academics generally decreases it, as already mentioned (Katz and

Martin 1997: 5; Lee and Bozeman 2005: 676). In some cases, the costs of international cooperation (travel, subsistence, the time spent on project preparation, administration and reporting) may exceed individual and/or institutional benefits (Katz and Martin 1997: 16). International cooperation involves numerous individual and institutional 'transaction costs' (Abramo et al. 2011a). On top of that, individual benefits my be incommensurable with institutional costs.

The second reservation is about an important difference between publication numbers and their scientific significance. Numbers do not determine scientific value but it is often assumed in the studies on the social stratification in science that a higher number of publications may lead to more significant research than a lower number of them:

> since quality and quantity of research output are fairly highly correlated, the high producers *tend* to publish the more consequential research. The gist of the matter is that engaging in a lot of research is in one sense a 'necessary' condition for the production of high-quality work
> (Cole and Cole 1973: 111; see Abramo et al. 2011b: 630; Rostan et al. 2014: 141)

A high level of output might be a condition for high-quality papers. In a similar vein, Derek J. de Solla Price, one of the founding fathers of bibliometrics, had already argued in the 1960s in his study on *Little Science, Big Science* that there is 'a significant correlation between qualitative solidness and quantitative solidness' (Price 1963: 77). In this sense, we explore research productivity through a rather crude measure of peer-reviewed publication numbers (rather than through a journal impact factor and citation analysis) but in this way we are able to seek correlations with international research collaboration, and, especially, to show how *not* collaborating internationally impedes individual research productivity and, at the level of national higher education systems, total national academic output.

Predictors of international research collaboration

Finally, in an attempt to explain IRC, a multivariate model approach is adopted in this section. The predictors of IRC are explored. The research literature on IRC based on the core CAP/EUROAC dataset is scarce, and its geographical focus is global or single-nation (Rostan and Ceravolo 2015; Rostan, Ceravolo, and Metcalfe 2014; Finkelstein and Sethi 2014; Finkelstein et al. 2013; Jung et al. 2014). The choice of independent variables in this section was guided by conceptual frameworks that had already been applied to the core dataset, along with some modifications. The modifications included the use of independent variables that were relevant in the European context, as well as a focus on a subset of institutions (universities only), a subset of academics (employed full-time and involved in both teaching and research activities), and international collaboration as a straightforward dichotomous dependent variable.

The decision to collaborate internationally in research is always made by an individual academic working in an academic institution in a national setting. In general, following Blackburn and Lawrence's (1995) work on academic activities, the individual and contextual factors involved in the shaping of international activities of European academics were combined in the model. Clark's matrix (1983: 28) shows academic work to be embedded in institutional types and academic disciplines. However, in this model, only a single institutional type, the European university, was explored. Six clusters of academic disciplines were used. The relevant factors included individual biographical features, organizational and professional features, and structural/contextual (country-related) features characterizing the wider context within which international research activities are performed (see a global analysis in Rostan and Ceravolo 2015).

The intensity of IRC tends to differ by the type of research conducted. The survey instrument used allowed us to characterize one's primary research emphasis as either basic/theoretical or applied/practically oriented, with intensity being measured on a five-point Likert scale from 'very much' to 'not at all.' At the level of individual variables, gender; age, through the proxy of academic cohorts (Jung et al. 2014); and father's tertiary education, as a proxy of the social and cultural capital provided by academics' families, were used. Also, a single predictor related to socialization within academia (earning a doctoral degree abroad) and a single predictor related to the academic profession (the academic rank of the professor) were used. Finally, three independent variables related to national contexts were used: the countries studied were classified as English-speaking or non-English-speaking; as small, medium, or large in terms of population size (Kyvik and Larsen 1997); and as lower, middle, or high in terms of their economic status or wealth (Luukkonen et al. 1992), as summarized in Table 4.10.

The logistic regression results for the dependent variable 'collaborates with international colleagues in research' (yes–no dichotomy) are presented below. The independent variables were dichotomized through a recoding procedure; some variables were inherently dichotomous (male/female: Yes or No; PhD achieved

Table 4.10 National contextual variables: Population and wealth

	Population (2017)		GDP per capita (2016)
Small	< 15 million: AT, FI, IE, NO	Lower	< 20,000 USD: PL
Medium	15–40 million: PL, NL	Middle	20,000–50,000 USD: AT, DE, FI, IT, NL, UK
Large	> 40 million: DE, IT, UK	High	> 50,000 USD: IE, NO

abroad: Yes or No etc.). Pearson Rho's correlation tests were used to find significantly correlated predictors of the dependent variable. Large intercollerations among the predictors (multicollinearity) were tested using an inverse correlation matrix because a correlation matrix refers only to pairwise correlations of independent variables. Also, principal component analysis (PCA) was performed to determine whether any variables, due to their high levels of correlation, could be grouped into homogeneous groups. No significant interdependence between any of the variables were found. The relevant reference categories selected in the model were as follows: belonging to 'other' academic disciplines, an emphasis on 'applied' research, being a female academic, belonging to the oldest academic cohort (entering the academic profession before 1981), one's father's education being 'non-tertiary', not earning a PhD abroad, not being a professor, working in a large country, and working in a country with a high level of economic status.

Table 4.11 shows the logistic regression results for the dependent variable, controlling for the above independent variables. In the block of variables representing clusters of academic disciplines, academics working in the cluster of physical sciences and mathematics are more likely to collaborate with international colleagues in their research (consistent with Rostan et al.'s findings 2014 and Cummings and Finkelstein's findings 2012), and those working in the professions cluster are less likely to collaborate as compared with 'other disciplines' (here and in each case below, *ceteris paribus*). For the other clusters, the results are statistically insignificant. In the block of variables representing research emphasis, only the combined (both basic and applied) variable is statistically significant, and engaging in combined research significantly increases the odds of IRC as compared with an emphasis on applied research only. Gender emerges as highly correlated with IRC (consistent with Rostan et al. 2014; and inconsistent with Cummings and Finkelstein's US case, 2014). Being male significantly ($Exp(B) = 1.69$) increases the odds of IRC as compared with being female, as does having entered the academic profession between 1981 and 1990, increasing the odds by about 40 percent as compared with the oldest academic generation. As an individual variable, one's father's education emerged as a statistically insignificant predictor. Surprisingly, the only academic socialization variable used in the model, defined as earning a PhD abroad—decreases the odds of IRC (consistent with Kyvik and Larsen's findings 1997), as does the academic profession variable of rank, with being a full professor decreasing the odds of IRC. Results from a multivariate model approach are consistent with results from a cross-generational section, assuming that professors belong mostly to the oldest generation in most European systems.

Finally, the three contextual (country-related) variables entered the equation. Consistent with previous literature, being an academic in an English-speaking country (Ireland and the United Kingdom in the sample) decreases

Table 4.11 Predictors of international research collaboration, only academics employed in the university sector and involved in both teaching and research

	B	S.E.	Sig.	Exp(B)
Cluster of academic discipline				
Life sciences and medical sciences				
Physical sciences and mathematics	0.489**	0.148	0.001	1.63**
Engineering				
Humanities and social sciences				
Professions	−0.589***	0.145	0.000	0.555***
Other—reference category				
Research emphasis				
Basic				
Combined	0.392***	0.085	0.000	1.48***
Applied—reference category				
Gender				
Male	0.525***	0.067	0.000	1.69***
Female—reference category				
Academic cohort				
2001–2010				
1991–2000				
1981–1990	0.395**	0.115	0.001	1.484**
Before 1981–reference category				
Father's education				
Tertiary				
Non-tertiary—reference category				
PhD achieved abroad				
Yes	−0.381***	0.073	0.000	0.683***
No—reference category				
Professor				
Yes	−0.866***	0.112	0.000	0.421***
No—reference category				
English-speaking country				
Yes	−0.768***	0.118	0.000	0.464***
No—reference category				
Country size				
Small	0.815***	0.097	0.000	2.259***
Medium				
Large—reference category				
Country's economy status				
Lower				
Middle	0.478***	0.105	0.000	1.613***
High—reference category				
Constant	1.006***	0.222	0.000	2.736***

the likelihood of IRC. Being an academic in a small country (with a small higher education system) radically increases the odds of IRC (the small countries in the sample being Austria, Finland, Ireland, and Norway). Finally, working in a country located in the middle of the wealth scale (as measured by GDP per capita) also increases the odds of IRC as compared with working in a high-income country.

In the next step of analysis, the contextual variables of language, country size, and country wealth were removed from the model, and nine countries were added, with the UK acting as a reference country (globally, the same procedure was applied in Rostan et al. 2014). The logistic regression results from this model do not differ substantially from the results of the first model. What did prove useful, however, was further exploring the block of country variables. The net effect of the country of current employment on the odds of collaborating with international colleagues in research is presented in Figure 4.3 in the form of B coefficients of logistic regression for each country (the yellow squares are the B coefficients). The major finding is a clear contrast between Finland and Poland, even though both countries are located on the global 'scientific periphery' (Kyvik and Larsen 1997) due to their languages and their small 'national scientific size' (Luukkonen et al. 1992). Academics working in Finland

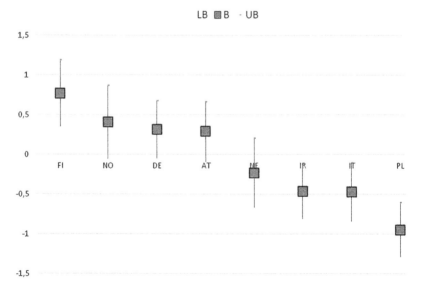

Figure 4.3 Net effect of the country of current employment on the odds of collaborating with international colleagues in research. B coefficients for countries with 95 percent confidence intervals. Only academics employed in the university sector and involved in both teaching and research.

are more than twice $(\text{Exp}(B) = 2.158)$ as likely to collaborate with international colleagues in research as compared with their colleagues from the UK, and academics working in Poland are less than half as likely to do so as compared with those in the UK $(\text{Exp}(B) = 0.389)$. Poland and Finland are at two visible extremes in Figure 4.3. This difference may be linked to divergent research policies over the last two decades, with a focus on internationalization in research in Finland and the long-term 'deinstitutionalization' of the research mission (Kwiek 2012) in Polish universities and their persistent underfunding regarding research. Also, working in Ireland or Italy decreases the odds of collaborating internationally. For all other countries, the model does not yield statistically significant estimates (see the 95 percent confidence interval for the mean: lower and upper bound crossing the zero line for Norway, Germany, Austria, and the Netherlands).

Discussion and concluding reflections

In this chapter, international research collaboration (IRC) and international research orientation (IRO) have been studied at the micro-level of individual academics from the university sector ($N = 8{,}466$, 11 European systems). Both were studied cross-nationally, cross-disciplinarily, and cross-generationally, or by country, cluster of academic disciplines, and academic generation. This chapter differs from most existing internationalization-related literature in that it is focused on the internationalization of academic research, rather than the internationalization of higher education from a cross-country comparative perspective (de Wit 2002) or international higher education (Deardorff et al. 2012). It differs from most existing literature in its sample (Europe) and focus (the individual academic as a unit of analysis and patterns of internationalization in research, respectively), using more standard methods (a multivariate model approach).

The factors influencing internationalization are becoming increasingly complex and competitive, the research-based competition for major world rankings being a prime example. The traditional international cooperation and exchange is becoming overshadowed by 'competition for status, bright students, talented faculty, research grants, and memberships in networks' (Knight 2010: 211). And status and recognition are granted to academics and academic institutions primarily through research outcomes—prestigious publications and grants alike, especially international. Assuming that internationalization-related shifts in 'research' come under the pillar of 'internationalization at home' (Knight 2012), the concepts of IRO and IRC were discussed, using theoretical insights from international academic profession studies, sociology of science, and scientometrics.

Evidence was presented that co-authoring publications internationally is a rare form of research internationalization in Europe as compared with publishing in a foreign language or in a foreign country. About half of European academics (49.2 percent) do not co-author publications internationally, and, on average, about one in four (28.9 percent) do so with a medium level of intensity, and only about one in eight (13.0 percent) do so with a high level of intensity or internationally co-author at least one-quarter and one-half of their work, respectively. As compared with other world regions, the percentage of European academics collaborating internationally in research (63.8 percent), as well as publishing in international journals, publishing in a foreign language, and co-authoring publications internationally at the medium and high intensity levels, is very high (Huang, Finkelstein, and Rostan, 2014; Rostan and Ceravolo 2015).

From a cross-generational perspective, rarely used in comparative IRC studies (Jung et al. 2014), in none of the 11 countries studied was the share of internationally collaborating academics the highest for the youngest cohort. At the same time, a striking cross-national differential within the youngest European generation of academics was found, with the share of internationally collaborating academics ranging from 80 percent (in the Netherlands, Ireland, and the UK) to 40 percent (in Germany, Poland, and Portugal). This cross-national differential among new entrants into the academic profession may be a strong barrier to intra-European research collaboration in the future.

The predictors of IRC have been explored using a multivariate model approach. Cross-disciplinary variations in IRC emerged as substantial, with academics in the physical sciences and mathematics cluster and academics combining basic and applied research being more likely to collaborate internationally. Gender emerged as highly correlated with IRC. Being male significantly increased the odds of IRC (by 69 percent) as compared with being female, which has heavy institutional policy implications for academic careers. Being an academic in an English-speaking country decreases the likelihood of IRC, and being an academic in a small country radically increases the likelihood of IRC. Also, working in less affluent European countries increases the odds of IRC as compared with working in high income countries. The findings regarding the negative impact of having an international doctoral degree and being a full professor, although somewhat counter-intuitive in both US and global contexts, can be explained by some degree of discrepancy between one's current academic location and the location where one's socialization to academia occurred and by generally older age of professors (and the entire graying academic profession) in Europe as compared with the global average.

This chapter also shows that research productivity of European academics is strongly correlated with international research collaboration: the average research productivity rate of European academics involved in international collaboration (whom we term 'internationalists') is consistently higher than the rate of

European academics *not* involved in international collaboration (whom we term 'locals') in all clusters of academic disciplines and in all countries studied.

The international publication co-authorship is also powerfully correlated with international research collaboration: the average rate of international co-authorship for 'internationalists' is much higher than this rate for 'locals.' Academics *not* collaborating internationally report no more than merely 7 percent of their publications being internationally co-authored in the 'hard' fields and no more than merely 3 percent in the 'soft' fields studied. Thus in a specific case of publishing in co-authorship with international colleagues, the policy lesson is simple: 'no international collaboration, no international co-authorship.'

These results lead to strong policy implications: large-scale international publication co-authorships are on average only possible if produced by 'internationalists' on the basis of their international collaboration. Only a negligible fraction of publications from nationally isolated science (produced by 'locals') can be internationally co-authored, and internationally co-authored publications are strictly related to collaborative activities with international colleagues. And if cross-border activities are to involve more than 'a small attractive elite' (Smeby and Gornitzka 2008: 39), incentives combined with resources are a necessary precondition. Consequently, what Sooho Lee and Barry Bozeman (2005: 693) termed 'the collaboration-as-synergy assumption' held by policy-makers (strongly believing that scientific collaboration has positive effects on research productivity) affects not only 'particular research awards' but also 'entire programs of research policy'. Consequently, any national system focused on increasing the international visibility of its knowledge production needs to install the internationalization of research in the center of its national research policy (Norway being a prime example, see Gornitzka and Langfeldt 2008).

The distinction between 'internationalists' and 'locals' seems to permeate European research. Some systems, institutions, and academics are consistently more internationalized in research than others. For 'internationalists' the international academic community is a reference group, while 'locals' publish predominantly for the national academic community. Internationalization increasingly plays a stratifying role, though: more international collaboration tends to mean higher publishing rates (combined with higher citation rates) and those who do not collaborate internationally may be losing more than ever before in terms of resources and prestige in the process of 'accumulative disadvantage' (Cole and Cole 1973: 146). The competition is becoming a permanent feature of European research landscape, and local prestige combined with local publications may no longer suffice in the race for resources and academic recognition.

Huge cross-disciplinary and cross-national differences apply but, in general terms, this chapter shows a powerful role of internationalization of research for both individual research productivity and the competitiveness of national research outputs.

International research collaboration and international research orientation are critically important in European academia given newly emergent university hierarchies of prestige, academic incentive and reward systems, and gradually redefined access to competitive research funding. Enhanced IRC, especially that leading to international publishing in top-tier journals, contributes to the emergence of new stratification in the academic professions in Europe along the divide between internationalists and locals. From a global perspective, Europe is a highly interesting case because the IRC across the continent is not only programmatic in major European Union (EU) and national-level research policy documents but also massively funded from national and EU sources.

Chapter 5

Academic role stratification

Patterns in teaching, research, and productivity across academic generations

Introduction

Despite the increasing role of 'third mission' activities in European universities (Pinheiro et al. 2012), teaching and research are still the two fundamental dimensions of the academic enterprise. However, there have been relatively few quantitative comparative studies of teaching and research in the academic profession from a European perspective (as opposed to American and global studies). Most European studies of this kind have focused either on a very small cluster of countries or are based on qualitative material in combination with publicly available aggregated statistical data. This chapter departs from this trend by focusing on quantitative differences in distribution of teaching and research time and teaching and research role orientation across academic generations—specifically, by comparing young academics (i.e., those under 40) with their older colleagues across six European higher education systems.

Before the massification and diversification of higher education, research was the core academic duty in all modern universities. In the social stratification of science, research results were a determining factor across all types of academic system, including 'the institute university' in Germany, the 'collegiate university' in Great Britain, the 'academy university' in France, the 'graduate department university' in the United States, the 'applied university' in Japan, and the 'communist university' across Central and Eastern Europe (see Clark 1995). According to Clark, universities were 'places of inquiry' with national variations, especially in the golden age of postwar expansion (see Introduction). However, in the last few decades, the universal generic forces that Clark described as 'research drift' and 'teaching drift' have tended to 'dissolve the research-teaching-study nexus. They pull research away from the settings of advanced teaching and learning and, in turn, shift teaching and study away from the locales characterized as places of inquiry' (Clark 1995: 209). As a consequence of this tendency, there emerged academics who are more 'teachers' and academics who are more 'researchers,' and the traditional Humboldtian idea of the modern university applies now only to selected parts of higher education systems:

> In modern systems of higher education, it is increasingly clear, not all academic staff will be or should be researchers. It is also everywhere the case

that full-time research becomes a career in its own right. As a result, 'teachers' and 'researchers' in some considerable part become two groups separated by task and location.

(Clark 1995: 209)

In the postwar period, as noted above, only research achievements determined academic prestige, which was the core of the academic enterprise; reputation was 'the main currency for the academic' (Becher and Kogan 1980: 103), and this derived from research (Clark 1983; Clark 1987a; Altbach 2012). Individual research output was the criterion of performance in science, leading to the uneven distribution of academic awards and career opportunities discussed in Chapters 1 and 2. As John Ziman noted, 'scientific ability is very unevenly distributed' and 'research is not an egalitarian profession. It is a rigorous pursuit, where incompetent performance, as signaled by persistently low achievement, eventually clogs up the system' (1994: 259). Yet although the massified university is characterized by 'low achievement' in research, there is no clogging up of the university system, as the analysis of research non-performers in the next section clearly shows.

Higher education in Continental Europe has traditionally been distinguished by its ability to combine the two core university missions of teaching and research. In this respect, the Humboldtian tradition has remained surprisingly strong across Europe but generally not in other world regions. This is especially true in developing countries where higher education systems have expanded rapidly in recent decades (Forest 2002; Shin 2014; Shin et al. 2014). In the postwar period, the role of research in academia was clearly defined:

it is research, as a task and as a basis for status, that makes the difference. ... The minority of academics who are actively engaged in research lead the profession in all important respects. Their work mystifies the profession, generates its modern myths, and throws up its heroes.

(Clark 1987a: 102)

Academic prestige and institutional promotions still relate almost exclusively to research achievements, and the increasing competition for external research funding globally is based largely on individual research output. As discussed in Chapter 6, academics must meet certain expectations in terms of research achievement at different stages of their academic career in order to attract research funding. Not surprisingly, today, as half a century ago, 'in the culture of the university, it seems, academic distinction and publications go together' (Ramsden 1994: 207).

This chapter explores intergenerational and cross-national patterns in the teaching/research divide in European systems, using large-scale comparative data on research and teaching time allocation (academic behaviors), teaching or research role orientation (academic attitudes), and intergenerational patterns in research productivity across academic age cohorts. To begin, academics routinely involved in publishing their research results ('publishers') will be contrasted with 'non-publishers' or 'non-performers' (see Chapter 1)—that is, academics employed full-time in the university sector who are involved in both teaching and research but have no peer-reviewed publications.

Non-publishers in academia

According to traditional accounts of the scientific community, full-time academics employed in European universities who do *not* conduct research should not be regarded as scientists. For example, in one of the earliest comprehensive analyses of American universities (*The Scientific Community*), Hagstrom (1965: 43) claimed that published articles and books, as well as papers read at society meetings, are 'the most important channel of communication from the standpoint of the larger community. Those who do not contribute at all through this channel cannot be considered scientists.' In a similar vein, Wilson (1995) argued that

> intellectual inquiry, unlike the growing of mushrooms, is not carried on in hidden recesses away from the public gaze. There is the necessity for bringing results to light in the form of publication, for in the academic scheme of things results unpublished are little better than those never achieved.
>
> (197)

Others have also insisted that non-publishers do not belong to the larger academic community, including Lazarsfeld and Thielens (1958) and Caplow and McGee (1958), Millett (1962), and Goodman (1962). Millett noted that scholars are permanently subject to the critical scrutiny of their peers:

> each published article, each book review, each research project recorded, each participation in professional discussion, each book—all are carefully observed and remembered. No faculty member can escape the judgment of his colleagues or university and in the scholarly world at large.
>
> (Millett 1962: 82)

Analyzing the 'publish or perish' issue, a recurrent theme in the last half century, Caplow and McGee argued that members of the academic profession must be both teachers and researchers who are 'in essence, paid to do one job, whereas the worth of their services is evaluated on the basis of how well they do another' (1958: 82).

No publications implies no research, which does not fit the traditional profile of the European university. Nevertheless, our survey results show that there are thousands of non-publishers across European universities (and not just in 'other higher education institutions') who are nominally involved in both teaching and research. Is non-publishing increasingly compatible, then, with academic work in massified universities? Differences in institutional and national academic cultures may explain differing levels of individual research productivity—including none at all—at least in some periods. (As our study covered a 3-year reference period, those academics who reported zero peer-reviewed publications within that period were classified as non-publishers.)

While institutions of lower academic standing may minimize the significance of academic research, those of higher academic standing may exert normative pressure on faculty members to become more intensely involved in research (Blau 1994: 24). However, even in academic cultures favorable to research activities, outcomes are uncertain and uneven; according to the so-called Ortega hypothesis, 'experimental science has progressed thanks in great part to the work of men astoundingly mediocre, and even less than mediocre' (Cole and Cole 1973: 216). In the same context, Blau made the following observations.

> Much emphasis on research will induce some faculty members, though not all, to become involved in research; only a portion of those engaged in research will succeed in obtaining results worth reporting; and not all of these will actually write a paper or a book. The process goes on beyond this point: some of the reports written will never be published, and a mere fraction of the published papers will later be found to have made original contribution to knowledge. Yet it takes large numbers of scientists and scholars who are engaged in research for a minute fraction of them significantly to advance scientific progress and human understanding.
>
> (1994: 241)

Similarly, the normative pressures to conduct and publish research may be much lower in some countries than in others (see Kwiek 2012 on the 'deinstitutionalization' of the research mission at Polish universities, followed by its 'reinstitutionalization' in the last wave of reforms; and Wolszczak-Derlacz and Parteka 2010 on institutional productivity). In an age of massified universities, perhaps the scale of research non-performance should not be surprising. Nevertheless, the fact that the share of non-publishers exceeds 40 percent in a country like Poland (across all academic clusters and age groups in the university subsector) indicates a drift away from the traditional Humboldtian role of combined teaching and research (that is, publishing) in European universities.

Among self-reported research-involved faculty employed full-time in the European university sector (as distinct from those who are not involved in research and those working part-time or in the non-university sector), consistent non-publishers are consistent research non-performers. Their massive number should be surprising from the traditional perspective that prevailed before the emergence of the massified university. Now, perhaps, the scale of the phenomenon is unsurprising, and in some systems non-publishing is tolerated despite corrective measures such as research assessment exercises at departmental, institutional, and national levels. In these countries, the 'occupational culture' does not seem to exert what Wilson (1995: 196–197) described as 'definite pressures to overcome individual inertias and deflections,' and his 'publish or perish' credo does not seem to apply. While Poland is a prime example, the share of non-publishers exceeded 15 percent in five of the 11 countries studied, indicating a similar (if less dramatic) drift to teaching across Europe. Other related patterns are more generally evident; for example, the share of research non-performers in non-university sectors is higher than in the university sector, and the share of research non-performers among part-time academics is higher than among those employed full-time, for all countries studied and regardless of size of non-university sectors and share of part-time employment (which differs significantly across Europe).

The share of research non-performers by country varies widely, from more than 40 percent of Polish academics and 15–20 percent of Finnish, Portuguese, Norwegian, and Germans to less than 10 percent of Irish, Italian, Dutch, and British academics (full-time employed, teaching- and research-involved, university sector only, Table 5.1). In all countries other than Poland and Germany, there is also a gender difference in research non-performers among full-time university faculty (Table 5.2). In most countries, the share of female research non-performers is at least 50 percent higher—notably in Switzerland, where 23.5 percent of female academics are research non-performers as opposed to a mere 7.8 percent of males. In several countries, the gender split of non-performers is closer: a very high 42–44 percent for both genders in Poland, 20–21 percent in Finland, and a very low 5–7 percent for both genders in Italy and the UK. In relation to the age of non-publishing academics, perhaps surprisingly, the highest percentage is under 40 in most cases. The exceptions are Poland, Italy, and the UK, where most non-publishers are aged 60 or over. Across disciplines, the engineering cluster has the highest average percentage of non-publishers in most of the countries surveyed (Table 5.3), with almost 40 percent in Finland and almost 35 percent in Germany—two countries with very high patenting rates.

Perhaps early in their careers, non-performers may realize that they are unable to compete with their peers in terms of major research achievements and publication, and they may voluntarily choose other channels. In this context, Cole and Cole hypothesized that

Table 5.1 Percentage of non-publishers (A—'articles and book chapters,' question not asked in Poland; PRA—'peer-reviewed articles and book chapters') by country among full-time academics involved in both teaching and research (universities only)

	FI	DE	IE	IT	NL	NO	PL	PT	CH	UK	Mean
Non-performers (A)	20.2	15.4	9.1	5.4	2.7	15.9	-	18.3	12.4	5.7	24.7
Non-performers (PRA)	38.0	33.0	16.0	31.4	10.3	23.5	43.2	27.2	21.8	8.9	38.7

Table 5.2 Percentage of non-publishers (no A - 'articles and book chapters' published in a 3-year reference period) by gender, age, and country among full-time academics involved in both teaching and research (universities only)

	Male	Female	Total	Under 40	40s	50s	60 and above
Finland	19.5	20.9	20.2	26.8	15.1	14.1	14.2
Germany	17.2	9.3	15.4	24.4	7.6	6.4	10.7
Ireland	7.0	10.6	9.1	9.2	7.0	12.2	8.8
Italy	4.9	6.5	5.4	4.3	5.4	3.9	7.1
Netherlands	1.3	7.7	2.7	2.9	2.1	2.7	3.0
Norway	13.8	18.6	15.9	19.8	12.9	15.9	11.3
Poland*	44.2	42.2	43.2	44.9	40.2	38.0	51.3
Portugal	15.4	21.1	18.3	22.8	16.1	15.7	11.7
Switzerland	7.8	23.5	12.4	18.3	2.6	2.5	14.2
United Kingdom	4.8	5.6	5.1	2.0	8.1	9.8	10.5

Note: * PRA measure (peer-reviewed articles and book chapters) applied to Poland.

Table 5.3 Percentage of non-publishers (no A - 'articles and book chapters' published in a 3-year reference period) by academic cluster and country (full-time academics, universities only)

	Life sciences, med. sciences	Physical sciences, mathematics	Engineering	Humanities and social sciences	Professions	Total
Finland	9.6	14.7	39.0	9.9	21.0	20.2
Germany	13.4	16.2	34.7	3.7	7.1	15.4
Ireland	9.9	11.8	4.0	10.0	10.2	9.1
Italy	5.4	4.5	8.4	4.9	4.8	5.4
Netherlands	6.5	2.3	3.9	0.8	1.6	2.7
Norway	10.9	12.6	31.7	10.5	28.3	15.9
Poland*	43.5	52.8	55.3	42.7	35.5	43.2
Portugal	14.2	11.4	20.3	16.6	29.1	18.3
Switzerland	8.8	4.0	0.0	13.8	23.8	12.4
UK	2.4	0.0	21.6	6.0	13.5	5.7

Note: * PRA measure (peer-reviewed articles and book chapters) applied to Poland.

physicists who are not successful in achieving national recognition are likely to adopt local people as reference groups and drop the national scientific elite as a meaningful reference group. Physicists in the 'minor leagues' will spend their time teaching, doing administrative work, and even doing a small amount of research for the fun of it. Many of these physicists probably achieve a satisfying degree of satisfaction in their local environments. Local prestige probably goes a long way to make up for failure to achieve national recognition.

(Cole and Cole 1973: 260–261)

The reference to 'minor leagues' applies in particular to those involved in 'minor universities' (Crane 1965). Certainly, in an age of massification, it is not realistic to expect that every European academic will publish, but one might still expect *university* academics to publish. In Europe, universities' prestige rests almost entirely on research and publications as measured nationally and internationally. Given the increasing role of competitive research funding in most European systems, it may be difficult to accommodate unproductive scholars in the university sector, leading to further academic role stratification. In the era of the massified university, it seems likely that more research will increasingly be conducted in fewer institutions by fewer academics.

The generational divide: the academic profession as academic cohorts

Adopting a generational approach to the academic professions in Europe, the present chapter centers on patterns of academic work, academic attitudes, and research productivity among academics under 40 as compared with those in older age brackets. As academics under 40 have usually held their PhD degree for no more than a decade or so, they are still in their 'formative years' (Teichler 2006). For present purposes, we assumed that comparing academic cohorts or generations by age and by academic rank ('professor' and 'new entrant') might prove more revealing than either a general bipartite junior-senior split (as in Teichler and Höhle 2013) or a tripartite split such as junior/middle rank/professor (Enders and Teichler 1997), early-career/mid-career/late-career (Shin et al. 2014), or novel/intermediate/consolidated (Marquina et al. 2015).

In every country, the academic profession comprises not only academics from various fields and institutional types and males and females of different ranks (all in changing percentages over time) but also different academic generations (Finkelstein et al. 1998). At different times, different proportions of young and older academics are employed, and those in the most prestigious positions (chairs, full professorships etc.) usually serve as role models and mentors for new entrants (Hagstrom 1965; Brechelmacher et al. 2015). In Europe's graying systems, the proportion of older academics is on the rise, creating various intraprofessional tensions.

As has been argued throughout this book, the academic profession varies widely across Europe; in his study, Jürgen Enders put it this way: 'faculty are the heart and soul of higher education and research. But they are not one heart and one soul' (Enders 2006: 9). Instead, increasingly stratified and differentiated 'academic professions' (Enders and Musselin 2008; Teichler 2014b) are emerging, and Enders (2006: 9) suggested four 'axes of differentiation': 'the discipline or academic specialty, the sectoral or institutional dividing line, the internal ranking system, and national differences—all of which may affect structures, practices and cultures in academe.' This chapter explores another important line of differentiation—between academic cohorts or generations—across six countries that best illustrate the contrast. From the sample of 11 countries for which data are available, two clusters were selected for in-depth analysis. The differences were most vivid in Finland, Switzerland, and the United Kingdom on the one hand and in Ireland, Poland, and Portugal on the other. With regard to teaching and research, the cross-generational contrast between these clusters is surprisingly stark in terms of how academics under 40 work and think about their work.

The time allocated to teaching and research is linked to both individual and institutional factors. For academics, 'time-economy' matters (Gottlieb and Keith 1997: 416), and research time competes directly with teaching time (as well as with time spent on administration and service), creating academic role conflicts (Marsh and Hattie 2002: 611). The amount of time available is always limited; our dataset shows that only a small minority of academics (mostly full professors in selected clusters of disciplines) work longer than 55 hours per week on average. The scarcity of time reflects both the nature of the contemporary academic profession and the scarcity of public resources; across the globe, research time is considered a luxury in many areas of higher education. As Clark asserted,

> for professors concerned about saving hours for research, time spent teaching is time diverted. It may be mandated, but it steals time away from something more basic and is seen as more of a burden; more time for research is not.
>
> (1987a: 72–73)

In an American context too, Mary Frank Fox reported that academics who publish frequently

> are not strongly investing in *both* research and teaching. Rather, they appear to trade off one set of investments against another ... research and teaching activities do not represent aspects of a single dimension of interests, commitments, and orientations, but are different dimensions that are at odds with each other. With respect to publication productivity, the sets of teaching and research variables are competitive, not complementary.
>
> (1992: 301)

The permanent competition between teaching and research time investments is a core theme in higher education studies because it is closely linked to academic prestige and allocation of awards, as we show in the Introduction. As discussed in Chapter 2, highly productive academics—that is, top research performers—are overrepresented among highly paid or top earning academics. Basic patterns of academic time distribution at individual level are at the center of debate about the future attractiveness of the academic profession. Heavy teaching loads (in Central and East European countries such as Russia, Ukraine, and Romania, as well as Poland in our sample) make research involvement and high achievement more difficult and less probable.

In this chapter, we examine the teaching/research competition hypothesis closely across academic generations. Demand overload and increasing external pressures on time in ever more competitive working environments are widely reported across all of the 11 European countries studied. Many previous empirical studies have shown that, as Hattie and Marsh (1996: 529) noted in their scarcity model account, 'the common belief that research and teaching are inextricably entwined is an enduring myth. At best, research and teaching are very loosely coupled.' Indeed, the 'teaching-research relation is close to zero' (Marsh and Hattie 2002: 628) and 'either non-existent or, where it appears, too modest to conclude that one necessarily enhances the other' (Centra 1983: 388; see also Fox 1992). For institutions, too, different time allocation patterns matter, and faculty's time is increasingly measured, reported, and accounted for. Following Bentley and Kyvik (2013: 330), we assume that 'faculty time is a core and valuable institutional resource. In research universities ... research time is scarce and must be carefully managed.' Time economy differs across generations of academics, and we explore differences in time investment in quantitative terms.

According to Ryder's classical account,

> a cohort may be defined as the aggregate of individuals (within some population definition) who experienced the same event within the same time interval .... The cohort record is not merely a summation of a set of individual histories. Each cohort has a distinctive composition and character reflecting the circumstances of its unique origination and history.
>
> (1965: 845)

The idea of a research design based on academic cohorts or generations was informed by Stephan and Levin's influential study *Striking the Mother Lode in Science. The Importance of Age, Place, and Time* (1992). They argued that 'many conditions that lead to RPRT [the right place at the right time] are not specific to the individual but, rather, specific to a generation. This means that success in science depends, in part, on things outside the control of the individual scientist' (1992: 4). Two decades later, Stephan returned to the idea of 'cohort effects';

> A distinguishing characteristic of the market for scientists and engineers is the presence of cohort effects. Careers of scientists and engineers are affected by events occurring at the time their cohort graduates. ... Some scientists graduate when jobs are plentiful; they have a choice among jobs and have little difficulty obtaining funding for their research. Their careers flourish. ... Others graduate when jobs are considerably less plentiful.
>
> (2012: 174–175)

As in the European context (although this is never mentioned), 'the 60-year-old is not only 25 years older than the 35-year-old but was also born in a different era when values and opportunities may have been significantly different' (Stephan and Levin 1992: 58). The present study is based on cross-sectional data; it would always be preferable to use longitudinal data, but, as this was not possible, we are examining only a snapshot of cross-generational differences at a point in time. The survey will be repeated in 2018, capturing another point in time, at least for Poland.

Academic generations appear infrequently in academic profession studies, probably because of the limited available data. Marquina and Jones recently suggested (2015: 1349) that different generations of academics may 'experience and understand academic work in quite different ways.' Our research seeks to explore those differences on the basis of a more general observation that cohorts are individuals who come of age at approximately the same time and who

> share similar experiences or receive similar exposure to the unique events that characterize their lives. These common experiences may mark each one for life, and as a result, members of different cohorts may exhibit differences in behavior, values, and intellectual abilities.
>
> (Stephan and Levin 1992: 115)

Among previous studies of the academic profession focusing on academic generations, cohorts, and career stages, Finkelstein et al. (1998: 103) looked at two distinct academic generations in American higher education: 'new entrants' (those in the first seven years of their academic careers) and 'seniors.' They concluded that the two cohorts differed less in what they did than in terms of who they were. In their recent study of 'academic boomers,' 'sandwich generation,' and 'new generation' academics in Korean higher education (hired during different periods since 1981), Shin et al. (2015: 1407) suggested that personal and institutional characteristics only partly explain differences between academics, who 'share similar perceptions and experiences even though they are in different age groups or academic ranks, if they have experienced a similar socio-economic environment.' In an earlier study, Shin et al. (2014) analyzed Korean academics' teaching and research activities, role preferences, and time budget at three career stages (under 40, 41–55, and 56 and more). Their findings indicated an increasing research orientation among the younger generation, with negative policy implications. In a study of Norwegian academics, Kyvik and Aksnes (2015: 1451) explained the increase in publication productivity over a 30-year period in generational terms and identified four key factors: younger generations' better qualifications, their increased research collaboration, improved research conditions, and the introduction of incentive and reward systems.

In her study of research productivity by career stage among Korean academics, Jung (2014: 87–88) categorized academics as 'fledglings,' 'maturing academics,' 'established academics,' and 'patriarchs,' arguing that 'academics tend to experience changes in terms of their interests, values, or performance according to their career stage.' Finally, Santiago, Carvalho, and Cardoso (2015) studied perceptions of governance and management in Portuguese higher education among 'younger,' 'middle,' and 'older' academic generations; they found no differences between these groups in terms of their preferred management model. Primary cross-national data on 'generational change and academic work' (Marquina and Jones 2015) have been analyzed only recently, following extensive research within the CAP and EUROAC projects.

Points of departure

Issues of data collection and analysis have already been discussed (notably in Chapter 1). Here again, we focus on academics involved in both teaching and research and employed full-time in the university sector. Selected demographic characteristics of academics from the six selected countries are summarized in Table 5.4. We have classified academics across those six countries into four age cohorts: under 40 ('young academics'), 40–49, 50–59, and 60 or over. We explore five items here: total weekly self-reported work hours, total weekly self-reported teaching hours, total weekly self-reported research hours, self-reported orientation to teaching versus research, and number of peer-reviewed articles and book chapters published in the previous three years. The major independent variable was age. The six selected countries (Finland, Switzerland, the United Kingdom, Ireland, Poland, and Portugal) represent all the major European models of higher education (Humboldtian, Napoleonic, Anglo-Saxon, and a post-communist hybrid model).

Based on the extensive literature review, our initial hypotheses were as follows. First, in all types of European higher education system—pre-Humboldtian (Ireland), Humboldtian (Germany and Italy), and post-Humboldtian (the United Kingdom, Norway, and the Netherlands) (Schimank and Winnes 2000) as represented in our dataset, any major differences in research orientation are likely to arise between academic disciplines because, inter alia, different academic 'territories' or disciplinary groupings (hard pure, soft pure, hard applied, and soft applied) are linked to different academic 'tribes' or cultures (Becher and Trowler 2001).

Second, for some disciplines, especially those grouped together here under the heading 'life sciences and medical sciences,' research orientation is likely to be higher than average across all systems and age groups. For other disciplines, especially those grouped under the heading 'humanities and social sciences,' research orientation is likely to be lower than average.

Third, female academics are likely to be more teaching-oriented than male academics across all academic disciplines, in all countries, and across all age groups (Gottlieb and Keith 1997), to the extent that 'although the women, like the men, would prefer to be teaching less, if both genders were to get their wishes, the women would still be teaching considerably more than their male counterparts,' as has been shown in America (Finkelstein 1984: 198; Finkelstein et al. 1998: 69) and in global contexts (Forest 2002: 65). As Brew and Boud pointed out, 'a consistent finding is that women publish less than men. This has considerable political and ethical implications' (2009: 192).

Fourth, new male entrants are likely to be more research-oriented than new female entrants (Finkelstein et al. 1998: 77) across all academic disciplines (Schuster and Finkelstein 2006: 90–91), and their publication productivity is likely to be higher (Zuckerman 1991: 43; Cole and Zuckerman 1991: 170; Kyvik and Olsen 2008: 449).

Among other initial hypotheses, older academics (and especially mid-career academics in their 40s and 50s) across all systems are likely to work longer hours than both their younger and older colleagues; both are likely to work longer hours on both teaching and research, as well as on administrative issues. Part of their research time is likely to be stolen by 'service, administration, and other academic duties,' but overall research orientation is likely to decline steadily with age, regardless of discipline (Stephan and Levin 1992: 25–74). New entrants in 'soft' disciplines are likely to be less research-oriented than full professors, and new entrants in 'hard' disciplines are likely to be more research-oriented than full professors. While research hours are likely to decrease with age, total working hours are likely to increase with age and with career stage. Full professors are likely to exhibit the strongest research orientation and to work the longest hours across all systems and academic clusters, and female full professors are likely to work longer hours more frequently than male full professors.

Finally, we also hypothesized that there would be major intra-national differentials in research and teaching behaviors and attitudes in European universities between academic cohorts and between clusters of academic disciplines; and between academics in more research-intensive systems with high levels of public academic research funding and academics in more teaching-intensive systems with limited public academic research funding. We further hypothesized that a country's academic-research funding profile would be reflected in academics' teaching and research attitudes and behaviors, and especially in average weekly hours spent on research. Although these initial hypotheses proved useful in analyzing the dataset, the above assumptions differed in most instances from the realities exposed by our quantitative analysis.

Teaching time and research time investments across academic generations

Having already explored the full dataset of 11 systems to identify clusters of similar systems, this chapter examines the differences between two clusters: research-focused Type 1 systems (represented here by Finland, Switzerland, and the United Kingdom) and teaching-focused Type 2 systems (represented here by Ireland, Poland, and Portugal).

The stark difference between the clusters in terms of time invested in teaching and in research is clearly seen in Figures 5.1 and 5.2. In Finland, Switzerland, and the United Kingdom (Type 1), young academics spend much less time on teaching and much more time on research than their young colleagues in Ireland, Poland, and Portugal (Type 2). In Type 2 systems, teaching remains at the same high level for all academic cohorts while remaining low for Type 1 academics under 40 and increasing for older cohorts. Conversely, research is low and relatively stable for all generations in Type 2 systems but is very high for young academics in Type 1 systems, decreasing with each generation. Taking teaching and research as the two core academic activities, Figure 5.3 shows the distribution of teaching,

Table 5.4 Sample description: selected demographic characteristics by country, academics involved in both teaching and research and employed full-time in the university sector

		Finland		Switzerland		United Kingdom		Ireland		Poland		Portugal	
		N	%	N	%	N	%	N	%	N	%	N	%
Gender	Male	403	61.1	248	69.5	207	62.1	274	53.4	778	49.5	141	53.7
	Female	256	38.9	109	30.5	126	37.9	239	46.6	794	50.5	121	46.3
	Under 40	354	52.8	213	59.0	214	61.3	324	50.0	555	34.9	255	64.5
	40–49	149	22.3	73	20.1	66	18.8	182	28.1	418	26.3	81	20.5
	50–59	130	19.3	53	14.8	53	15.1	111	17.1	352	22.1	54	13.6
	60 and older	37	5.6	22	6.1	17	4.8	31	4.8	267	16.8	5	1.4
Academic experience*	Under 10	307	52.1	160	56.8	211	63.2	247	41.9	438	27.7	180	48.2
	10–19	152	25.8	68	24.2	78	23.2	209	35.5	397	25.1	106	28.4
	20–29	93	15.7	37	13.1	28	8.5	75	12.7	321	20.2	63	16.7
	30–39	38	6.4	17	5.9	14	4.2	46	7.8	336	21.2	25	6.7
	40 or more	0	0.0	0	0.0	3	0.9	12	2.0	92	5.8	0	0.0
Academic disciplines	Life sciences and medical sciences	146	21.9	195	54.1	153	43.9	178	27.5	579	36.4	85	21.6
	Physical sciences, mathematics	97	14.5	34	9.3	58	16.6	82	12.7	186	11.7	38	9.6
	Engineering	156	23.2	3	0.7	35	10.1	56	8.6	48	3.0	97	24.7
	Humanities and social sciences	166	24.8	71	19.7	75	21.6	173	26.7	616	38.7	84	21.4
	Professions	105	15.6	58	16.2	28	7.9	159	24.5	163	10.2	90	22.7

Note: * Academic experience means number of years since first full-time job beyond research and teaching assistant in higher education/research sector (Question A6).

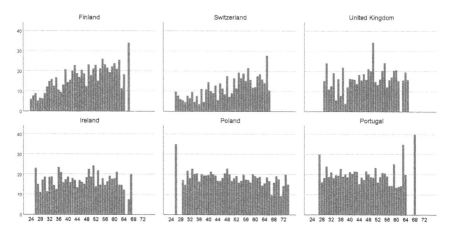

Figure 5.1 Time spent (hours per week) by faculty on teaching-related activities (when classes are in session), by age and country among academics involved in both teaching and research and employed full-time in the university sector.

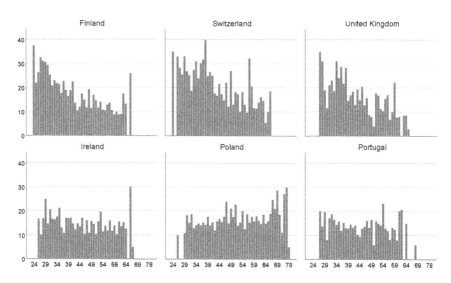

Figure 5.2 Time spent (hours per week) by faculty on research-related activities (when classes are in session), by age and country among academics involved in both teaching and research and employed full-time in the university sector.

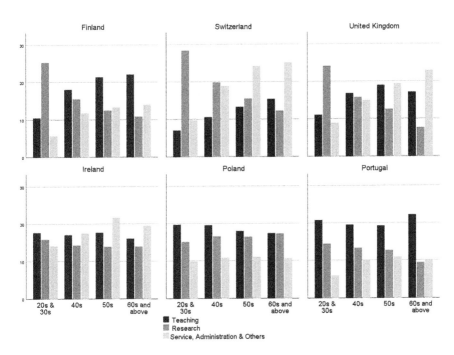

Figure 5.3 Average time spent (hours per week) on various academic activities (when classes are in session): teaching, research, and all other activities combined (service, administration etc.) by age group and country among academics involved in both teaching and research and employed full-time in the university sector.

research, and all other activities combined by age group for both Type 1 and Type 2 systems. Time spent on all other academic activities combined (see 'Service, administration and others') generally increases with age, but in Type 1 systems, especially in Switzerland and the United Kingdom, the level is surprisingly high for older cohorts (at 20–25 hours per week).

In both types of system, the difference in average time allocation between teaching and research (when classes are in session) across different age groups is striking; for instance, while 'young academics' in Switzerland spend an average 28.5 hours per week on research activities, those in Finland average 26 hours, those in Poland and Portugal spend about half that time on research (15.1 and 14.1 hours, respectively).[1] Conversely, while young Swiss academics spend an average 7.1 hours per week on teaching-related activities and their Finnish counterparts average 9.9 hours, their Polish and Portuguese colleagues spend an average of about 20 hours on such activities—week by week, month by month, and year by year. It is important to note that those described here as 'academics under 40' are not doctoral students or postdoctoral researchers but full-time staff members with teaching and research duties.

In Switzerland and Finland, research time decreases sharply among older age groups while teaching time increases sharply with age. In contrast, there is a relatively stable distribution of teaching and research time across all age groups in Poland and Portugal. There are marginal differences in teaching and research time allocation across young, mid-career, and older academics in these countries, with the most stable system of time distribution across academic generations in Poland, where time allocation seems frozen across all age groups.

In terms of average time investment, then, academics under 40 in research-focused Type 1 systems are very high research performers and very low teaching performers while older academics are high teaching performers and low research performers. (We will explore intergenerational differences in teaching or research role orientation and the issue of actual research productivity across generations in later sections.) In research-focused Type 1 systems, then, there seems to be a powerful intergenerational division of labor. In Switzerland and Finland, weekly research time drops dramatically from about 26–28 hours per week (about 25 hours in the UK) for academics under 40 to about 12 hours (8 hours in the UK) for academics in their 50s and 60s. In contrast, both young and older academics in teaching-focused Type 2 systems are consistently high teaching performers and stable medium (or low) research performers. The pattern of time allocation in teaching-focused Type 2 systems is relatively constant across all age groups, with very high (by comparison) average weekly teaching time and low to very low (by comparison) average research time throughout an academic career as shown in Figures 5.1, 5.2, and 5.3.

The pattern of average time allocation is highly gender-sensitive; in both research-focused Type 1 and teaching-focused Type 2 systems, female academics (all age groups combined) spend more time on teaching activities (other than in Switzerland, where the difference is marginal). The starkest gender differential is in the United Kingdom, where female academics spend on average 6.4 (58 percent) more weekly hours on teaching and almost 9 hours less (60 percent) on research; both differences are statistically significant (Table 5.5). In Ireland and Poland, too, the differences in teaching-research time distribution by gender are statistically significant.

Importantly, the gender differential cannot be exclusively linked to historical differences in employment patterns or job profiles (Table 5.6). In all six countries, female academics under 40 spend more time on teaching (other than in Switzerland, where the difference is negligible), and less time on research. Again, the United Kingdom provides the most striking example: young female academics spend an average 8.1 (92 percent) more hours on teaching-related activities each week, and 9.2 less hours (a mere 52 percent) on research-related activities; again, both differences are statistically significant.

In the United Kingdom, the intra-national gender differential in teaching-research time distribution is higher than the cross-national differential between the United Kingdom and teaching-focused Type 2 systems (Ireland, Poland,

and Portugal). The gender differential does not generally apply to Type 2 systems; in Ireland, Poland, and Portugal, the only statistically significant differential relates to research time, averaging up to 4.7 hours in Ireland and 4.4 hours in Poland (Table 5.5). As predicted by cumulative advantage theory (Allison et al. 1982; Allison and Stewart 1974) and reinforcement of research activity by the reward system, an early lack of success reduces the likelihood of later scientific success, which is clearly linked to research time investment. As productivity is heavily influenced by recognition of early work, 'if women fail to be as productive in the years immediately following their degree, the social process of accumulative disadvantage may take over and contribute to their falling further behind in the race to produce new scientific discoveries' (Cole and Cole 1973: 151).

With regard to 'the disciplinary shaping of the profession' (Becher 1987), we explored whether the research-focused Type 1 and teaching-focused Type 2 intergenerational teaching-research behavioral patterns were consistent across clusters of academic disciplines.[2] Average hours spent on teaching and research were disaggregated into hours for different academic clusters, and then into hours for different age groups. In the former, generational-blind analysis of 'all academics' revealed substantial diversity in academic behaviors within national systems. Additionally, intra-national disciplinary differences between 'hard' fields and 'soft' fields in research-focused Type 1 systems were *higher* than cross-national differences between Type 1 and Type 2 systems in 'soft' areas. For instance, Swiss and Finnish academics spend much more time on research in 'hard' fields and the same amount of time in 'soft' areas when compared with Polish and Portuguese academics.

Further disaggregation into academic clusters and age groups yields a still more complex picture. For young academics only, the differences between research-focused Type 1 and teaching-focused Type 2 systems are much more pronounced. In Switzerland and Finland, young academics in life sciences and medical sciences and in physical sciences and mathematics spend on research on average about 30 hours a week as compared with Poland at 17–18 hours and Portugal at 12–14 hours. What is especially surprising is that while the time spent on research for *all* academics in two soft areas (humanities and social sciences and professions) is similar for both types of system, there is a fundamental difference between the two systems for *young* academics.

Figure 5.4 presents the average weekly teaching and research time allocation of academics under 40 by country and academic cluster. While young academics in teaching-focused Type 2 countries (Ireland, Poland, and Portugal) spend on average 16–24 hours a week on teaching-related activities in all clusters, life sciences and medical sciences academics in Finland spend twice as many hours on teaching-related activities as those in Switzerland. Interestingly, academics in the 'soft' clusters of humanities and social science in five of the six countries (other than Switzerland) spend almost the same long hours teaching. While

Table 5.5 Academics of all age groups combined: Time spent (hours per week) by faculty on various academic activities (when classes are in session) by gender and country among academics involved in both teaching and research and employed full-time in the university sector

		M	F	t	df	p-value	Group with significantly larger mean
Finland	Teaching	13.6	17.6	-3.545	601	<0.001	F
	Research	19.6	19.4	0.191	601	0.849	—
	Service	2.5	1.5	2.432	601	0.015	M
	Administration	5.1	3.6	2.960	601	0.003	M
	Other academic activities	2.8	1.8	3.307	601	0.001	M
	TOTAL hours	**43.6**	**44.0**	**-0.408**	**601**	**0.683**	**—**
Switzerland	Teaching	9.5	8.8	0.648	331	0.517	—
	Research	23.0	25.0	-1.086	331	0.278	—
	Service	5.5	4.2	1.094	331	0.275	—
	Administration	6.4	5.2	1.540	331	0.125	—
	Other academic activities	3.7	3.3	0.591	331	0.555	—
	TOTAL hours	**48.2**	**46.4**	**1.114**	**331**	**0.266**	**—**
United Kingdom	Teaching	11.9	18.3	-3.859	217	<0.001	F
	Research	22.4	13.6	4.745	217	<0.001	M
	Service	1.2	1.3	-0.170	217	0.865	—
	Administration	7.1	10.6	-2.887	217	0.004	F
	Other academic activities	2.5	4.4	-2.811	217	0.005	F
	TOTAL hours	**45.1**	**48.1**	**-1.965**	**217**	**0.051**	**—**
Ireland	Teaching	16.4	18.6	-2.590	489	0.010	F
	Research	16.3	13.0	3.570	489	<0.001	M
	Service	2.4	2.1	0.686	489	0.493	—
	Administration	10.8	10.6	0.349	489	0.728	—
	Other academic activities	4.1	4.2	-0.202	489	0.840	—
	TOTAL hours	**50.1**	**48.5**	**1.423**	**489**	**0.155**	**—**
Poland	Teaching	17.7	20.3	-5.113	1506	<0.001	F
	Research	16.8	15.5	2.211	1506	0.027	M
	Service	3.3	2.8	1.927	1506	0.054	—
	Administration	4.5	4.2	1.184	1506	0.237	—
	Other academic activities	3.1	3.1	-0.182	1506	0.855	—
	TOTAL hours	**45.3**	**45.9**	**-0.617**	**1506**	**0.537**	**—**
Portugal	Teaching	18.6	21.4	-2.522	237	0.012	F
	Research	13.9	14.1	-0.188	237	0.851	—
	Service	1.7	0.8	2.625	237	0.009	M
	Administration	5.1	3.5	2.278	237	0.024	M
	Other academic activities	2.6	1.8	1.801	237	0.073	—
	TOTAL hours	**41.9**	**41.6**	**0.207**	**237**	**0.836**	**—**

Table 5.6 Academics under 40 only: Time spent (hours per week) by faculty on various academic activities (when classes are in session) by gender and country among academics involved in both teaching and research and employed full-time in the university sector

		M	F	t	df	p-value	Group with signif. larger mean
Finland	Teaching	9.0	13.0	−2.624	305	0.009	M
	Research	25.6	24.4	0.702	305	0.483	—
	Service	1.7	0.9	1.446	305	0.149	—
	Administration	2.7	2.0	1.563	305	0.119	—
	Other acad. activities	2.1	1.4	2.174	305	0.030	F
	TOTAL hours	**41.1**	**41.7**	**−0.597**	**305**	**0.551**	**—**
Switzerland	Teaching	7.2	6.9	0.224	190	0.823	—
	Research	29.2	27.2	0.842	190	0.401	—
	Service	2.1	4.1	−1.810	190	0.072	—
	Administration	3.2	4.2	−1.749	190	0.082	—
	Other acad. activities	3.4	2.6	0.942	190	0.347	—
	TOTAL hours	**45.1**	**45.0**	**0.033**	**190**	**0.974**	**—**
United Kingdom	Teaching	8.8	16.9	−3.431	122	0.001	M
	Research	26.8	17.6	3.473	122	0.001	F
	Service	0.8	1.2	−0.842	122	0.401	—
	Administration	4.5	8.3	−2.795	122	0.006	M
	Other acad. activities	1.8	3.4	−2.620	122	0.010	M
	TOTAL hours	**42.7**	**47.4**	**−2.712**	**122**	**0.008**	**M**
Ireland	Teaching	16.9	18.4	−0.940	178	0.349	—
	Research	18.5	13.8	2.693	178	0.008	F
	Service	1.8	1.0	1.986	178	0.049	F
	Administration	8.6	8.8	−0.151	178	0.880	—
	Other acad. activities	3.3	4.1	−1.048	178	0.296	—
	TOTAL Hours	**49.1**	**46.0**	**1.682**	**178**	**0.094**	**—**
Poland	Teaching	19.3	20.3	−1.040	509	0.299	—
	Research	17.6	13.2	4.555	509	0.000	F
	Service	3.0	2.6	0.896	509	0.371	—
	Administration	4.2	4.2	−0.050	509	0.960	—
	Other acad. activities	2.8	2.8	0.055	509	0.956	—
	TOTAL hours	**46.9**	**43.1**	**2.633**	**509**	**0.009**	**F**
Portugal	Teaching	18.4	21.5	−1.920	111	0.057	—
	Research	15.3	15.2	0.07	111	0.944	—
	Service	1.3	0.4	2.263	111	0.026	F
	Administration	2.7	2.6	0.135	111	0.893	—
	Other acad. activities	1.5	1.8	−0.521	111	0.603	—
	TOTAL hours	**39.2**	**41.5**	**−0.994**	**111**	**0.323**	**—**

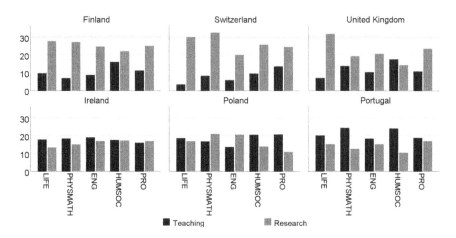

Figure 5.4 Academics under 40 only: Average time spent (hours per week) by faculty on teaching and research (when classes are in session) by academic discipline cluster and country among academics involved in both teaching and research and employed full-time in the university sector.

research-focused Type 1 academics in 'hard' clusters spend much longer hours on research than on teaching, this difference is much smaller in engineering.

In research-focused Type 1 systems, then, academics under 40 across all clusters of disciplines consistently invest more time in research than both their colleagues in teaching-focused Type 2 systems and their older colleagues and are consistently relieved from teaching across all hard disciplines. In contrast, young academics across all disciplines in teaching-focused Type 2 systems consistently invest more time in teaching and (comparatively) less time in research.

Teaching and research role orientation across academic generations

A further question is whether patterns of time investment overlap with patterns of academic role orientation. Our research shows that European systems studied through academic attitudes can be grouped into exactly the same research-focused Type 1 and teaching-focused Type 2 systems studied through academic behaviors. In the survey, academics were asked the following question about role orientation: 'Regarding your own preferences, do your interests lie primarily in teaching or in research?' There were four possible answers: 'primarily in teaching,' 'both, but leaning toward teaching,' 'both, but leaning toward research,' and 'primarily in research.' For the purposes of this chapter, we are especially interested in the distribution of academics whose orientation is 'primarily in research' (characterized here as 'hardcore research-oriented faculty') across systems, age groups, and academic clusters. Table 5.7 shows the distribution of teaching/ research role orientation for academics from all age groups across the two system types. In research-focused Type 1 systems (Finland, Switzerland, and the United Kingdom), the share of hardcore research-oriented academics ranges between 30 and 40 percent; in teaching-focused Type 2 systems (Ireland, Poland, and Portugal), it is in the 7 to 12 percent range. These high and low hardcore research orientation figures seem to mirror high and low research time investment in the two systems.

As in the previous section, we are specifically interested here in academics under 40. In the six selected countries, research orientation decreases with age— highest for the youngest cohort and lowest for the oldest (Table 5.8). In both system types, high or low research time investment among young academics is accompanied, respectively, by high or low research orientation. While hardcore research-oriented faculty comprises 35–50 percent of young academics in Type 1 systems, it remains in the 7–18 percent range in Type 2 systems. Interestingly, while the figure for Ireland and Portugal is roughly the same as for all age groups combined, the share increases by half (from 12.2 to 18.1 percent) among Polish academics. Presumably, the greater intra-national cross-generational differences in Poland relate to the new performance-based funding for research, which was first discussed at the time of survey execution. Figure 5.5 highlights the stark differences between Type 1 and Type 2 systems for academics of all age groups combined (left bar) and for young academics (right bar).

From a cross-disciplinary perspective, there are substantial cross-national and intra-national differences in hardcore research orientation. More detailed intra-generational analyses of academic clusters revealed huge differences in Europe behind the aggregate pictures. There is a contrast between the attitudes of young and old generations of scholars working in research-oriented disciplines and those working in humanities and social sciences. Additionally, there are intergenerational gender differences in research orientation across academic

Table 5.7 Academics of all age groups combined: preferences for teaching/ research (Question B2: *Regarding your own preferences, do your interests lie primarily in teaching or in research?*) by country (percent) among academics involved in both teaching and research and employed full-time in the university sector

Orientation	Finland	Switzerland	United Kingdom	Ireland	Poland	Portugal
Primarily teaching	7.4	2.6	4.6	3.8	7.9	6.3
Both (but leaning toward teaching)	15.4	20.3	10.9	26.9	29.6	39.0
Both (but leaning toward research)	44.0	49.3	44.0	59.1	50.3	47.6
Primarily research	33.2	27.7	40.5	10.2	12.2	7.1

Table 5.8 Hardcore research-oriented faculty (all countries) by age group
(Question B2; answer 4 only: *Primarily research*) (percent) among
academics involved in both teaching and research and employed
full-time in the university sector

Age group	Finland	Switzerland	United Kingdom	Ireland	Poland	Portugal
Under 40	46.2	33.8	52.7	11.6	18.1	7.3
40–49	31.5	25.9	40.5	10.4	12.9	5.6
50–59	16.8	16.8	23.5	7.1	6.3	11.3
60 and above	14.4	0	3.3	8.1	6.5	1.4

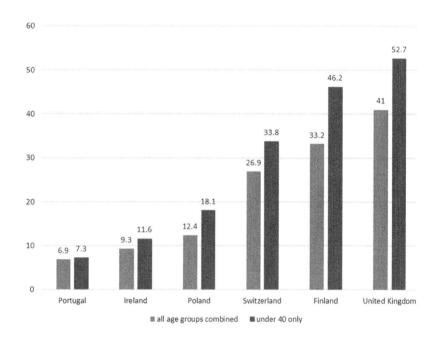

Figure 5.5 Hardcore research-oriented faculty, all countries and all age groups
combined plus academics under 40 only by country (Question B2;
answer 4 only: *Primarily research*) (percent) among academics involved in both teaching and research and employed full-time in the
university sector.

clusters within particular countries, with powerful implications for recruitment
and employment policies.

In all research-focused Type 1 systems, the share of young academics who are
heavily involved in research (i.e., interested 'primarily in research' and referred to
here as 'hardcore research-oriented faculty') is systematically two to three times
higher than in teaching-focused Type 2 systems (and the figure falls to less than
10 percent among Swiss and British academics in their 60s). This slide in research

orientation with age is greatest in the United Kingdom (by about 50 percentage points). (As the next section shows, this declining research orientation for the oldest age group is reflected in research productivity.) In contrast, the slide in research orientation is much smaller in teaching-focused Type 2 systems.

The crucial issue for future generational shifts in the European academy is that the overall national research orientation in research-focused Type 1 systems may be still growing as young academics gradually become mid-career academics. In contrast, in teaching-focused Type 2 systems, succeeding generations do not seem able to change the low overall research preference. As research orientation is stable across all age groups in Poland, Portugal, and Ireland, no fundamental or sizeable generational shift can be expected toward research orientation. To increase research orientation in these systems, natural generational succession will not suffice; instead, there is a need for targeted policy measures to address the selection, retention, and promotion of academics.

Research productivity in STEM disciplines across academic generations

Finally, we analyzed cross-generational patterns of research productivity. Research-dominated time distribution and role orientation are the two major predictors of research productivity (see Fox 1992; Cole and Cole 1973; Ramsden 1994). In this section, we explore generational differences in research productivity, focusing on peer-reviewed journal articles and book chapters and excluding the other productivity measures used in Chapter 1. The single measure of 'peer-reviewed articles published in an academic book or journal' (PRA) was applied to academics across all four major cohorts (Tables 5.9 and 5.10) and to the two contrasted academic cohorts (academics under 40 and academics in their 50s) (see Tables 5.11 and 5.12). To enhance comparability of results, the three STEM (science, technology, engineering and mathematics) academic clusters were selected for further analysis, including 'life sciences and medical sciences,' 'physical sciences, mathematics,' and 'engineering,' as well as a single 'STEM combined' cluster comprising the three clusters. In contrast to Chapter 1, the measure of 'peer-reviewed article equivalents' (PRAE) was not used, as books and edited books are used as publication channels in the STEM cluster much less often than in the humanities and social sciences.

We have explored both cross-national and intra-national differences in research productivity by age and academic cluster in the two types of higher education system. It is most interesting that, at the aggregated level of national systems, there are no discernible patterns in research productivity that would differentiate research-focused Type 1 and teaching-focused Type 2 systems.

Tables 5.11 and 5.12 show percentage difference and difference in article numbers between two academic cohorts (academics under 40 and those in their 50s) across the three STEM clusters and in the combined STEM cluster. In two clusters and in the combined cluster, the difference is much higher for

Table 5.9 Average research productivity by age group (peer-reviewed articles published in an academic book or journal (PRA)) by academic cluster and country among academics involved in research and employed full-time in the university sector

	Life sciences and medical sciences				Physical sciences, mathematics			
	Academics under 40	Academics in their 40s	Academics in their 50s	Academics in their 60s and older	Academics under 40	Academics in their 40s	Academics in their 50s	Academics in their 60s and older
Finland	2.5	7.5	11.8	12.9	4.3	6.5	6.7	4.4
Switzerland	3.8	13.7	10.0	9.2	4.0	13.4	21.3	10.8
United Kingdom	2.4	11.5	7.9	6.0	5.5	10.5	34.0	12.0
Ireland	4.1	5.2	8.6	2.7	3.3	3.0	5.1	3.4
Poland	2.4	3.1	3.3	3.2	4.1	2.9	2.0	1.9
Portugal	7.3	11.3	4.6	13.6	3.1	9.9	3.0	3.1

Table 5.10 Average research productivity by age group (peer-reviewed articles published in an academic book or journal (PRA)) by academic cluster and country among academics involved in research and employed full-time in the university sector

	Engineering				STEM combined			
	Academics under 40	Academics in their 40s	Academics in their 50s	Academics in their 60s and older	Academics under 40	Academics in their 40s	Academics in their 50s	Academics in their 60s and older
Finland	2.0	3.8	2.1	10.7	2.7	6.0	7.5	11.0
Switzerland	15.0			5.0	4.0	13.6	11.2	9.0
United Kingdom	2.9	6.2	2.8	1.0	3.5	11.0	7.0	6.5
Ireland	5.9	5.2	9.8	3.8	4.3	4.6	8.2	3.1
Poland	5.9	3.2	3.7	0.5	2.7	3.1	2.9	2.6
Portugal	2.4	4.8	8.4	0.0	4.3	8.3	7.2	4.5

Table 5.11 Average academic productivity (peer-reviewed articles published in an academic book or journal (PRA)) (under 40 vs. 50s only) by academic cluster and country among academics involved in both teaching and research and employed full-time in the university sector

	Life sciences and medical sciences				Physical sciences, mathematics			
	Academics under 40	Academics in their 50s	% difference	Difference in article numbers	Academics under 40	Academics in their 50s	% difference	Difference in article numbers
Finland	2.5	11.8	475.5	9.4	4.3	6.7	155.0	2.4
Switzerland	3.8	10.0	266.5	6.3	4.0	21.3	529.1	17.3
United Kingdom	2.4	7.9	322.3	5.4	5.5	34.0	614.4	28.5
Ireland	4.1	8.6	207.5	4.4	3.3	5.1	153.7	1.8
Poland	2.4	3.3	137.0	0.9	4.1	2.0	47.9	-2.1
Portugal	7.3	4.6	62.9	-2.7	3.1	3.0	94.3	-0.2

Table 5.12 Average academic productivity (peer-reviewed articles published in an academic book or journal (PRA)) (under 40 vs. 50s only) by academic cluster and country among academics involved in both teaching and research and employed full-time in the university sector

	Engineering				STEM combined			
	Academics under 40	Academics in their 50s	% difference	Difference in article numbers	Academics under 40	Academics in their 50s	% difference	Difference in article numbers
Finland	2.0	2.1	105.7	0.1	2.7	7.5	274.2	4.8
Switzerland	15.0				4.0	11.2	282.8	7.2
United Kingdom	2.9	2.8	98.3	-0.1	3.5	7.0	202.9	3.6
Ireland	5.9	9.8	167.7	4.0	4.3	8.2	192.7	3.9
Poland	5.9	3.7	62.4	-2.2	2.7	2.9	105.3	0.1
Portugal	2.4	8.4	351.6	6.0	4.3	7.2	166.9	2.9

research-focused Type 1 systems than for teaching-focused Type 2. For instance, for LIFE, the difference is in the 266.5–475.5 percentage range for Type 1 and in the 137.0–207.5 percentage range for Type 2. The only exception is Portugal at 62.9 percent, representing a decrease in average productivity. In the combined STEM cluster, the increase in average productivity across the two academic cohorts is in the 202.9–274.2 percentage range for Type 1 systems, and in the 105.3–192.7 percentage range for Type 2.

Importantly, the radical system differences in average working time distribution and academic role orientation discussed in the two previous sections *do not* translate into any discernible difference in research productivity patterns across generations, as older generations consistently publish more than younger generations across all STEM clusters of academic disciplines across Europe. However, as Tables 5.9 and 5.10 show, average productivity declines for the oldest generation of academics across all clusters.

Based on existing evidence of the decline of productivity with age in the United States (Stephan and Levin 1992: 156), Italy (Bonaccorsi and Daraio 2003: 75), and Norway (Kyvik and Olsen 2008: 455), we assumed that from an intra-national perspective, academics under 40 in research-focused Type 1 systems would exhibit higher research productivity than their older colleagues. The argument would be that young academics spend substantially more time on research activities and exhibit much higher research orientation. Although not yet well established in academic and professional networks and 'cumulative advantage' is only just beginning to help them to access resources (Merton 1973; Stephan and Levin 1992), they nevertheless have a unique opportunity (by comparison with older age groups) to combine their high research orientation with more available research time. In contrast, we assumed that young academics in teaching-focused Type 2 systems who are as heavily involved in teaching as their older colleagues would exhibit lower research productivity than those older colleagues.

Our general hypothesis was that average research productivity in both research-focused Type 1 and teaching-focused Type 2 systems disaggregated by age group would align closely with changes in research orientation and involvement by age group. In Type 1 systems, then, average productivity should be higher among young academics and lower among older academics. In contrast, average productivity should be steadily increasing across all age groups in Type 2 systems.

Surprisingly (but consistent with sociological theories of cumulative advantage and reinforcement) (Merton 1973; Cole and Cole 1973), research productivity patterns proved similar in both research-focused Type 1 and teaching-focused Type 2 systems, and no clear inter-systemic differences were observed. In both systems, research productivity increases consistently with age, and research productivity is highest by far among academics in their 50s. However, one significant difference is that academics in their 50s in Type 1 systems are substantially more productive (numerically and by a very high percentage) than their colleagues under 40; in Type 2 systems, they are only marginally more productive. For the combined STEM cluster in Type 1 systems (Finland, Switzerland, and United Kingdom) they are two to three times more productive, and for Type 2 systems (Ireland, Poland, and Portugal), they exhibit average research productivity that is the same (Poland), slightly higher (Portugal), or twice as high (Ireland) (Tables 5.11 and 5.12).

The goal of this chapter was to rigorously examine whether, at the empirical micro-level of the individual, 'interests, time commitments, and orientation to teaching ... are associated with depressed publication productivity. The parallel research and non-teaching related professional investments are associated with enhanced publication productivity' (Fox 1992: 297–298). As our data show, this is less clear at the aggregated level of national systems. Unexpectedly (in light of previous studies of research productivity), strongly *decreasing* research-related time investments by academic cohort in all research-focused Type 1 systems leads to strongly *increasing* research productivity by academic cohort. Academics under 40 were no more productive than those in their 50s in any cluster of disciplines in any of the selected countries.

However, the increase in research productivity for academics in their 50s as compared with those under 40 differs consistently between research-focused Type 1 and teaching-focused Type 2 systems. In Type 1 systems, these differences are huge; in Type 1 systems overall, research productivity increases steadily with age and is highest among academics in their 50s, declining among those in their 60s. In contrast, the differences in research productivity across age groups are much smaller in Type 2 countries. Cumulative advantage and reinforcement theories, internationalization, professionalization, and networking effects do not seem to operate in teaching-focused Type 2 systems to the same extent as in research-focused Type 1 systems.

Aside from powerful cross-national differences, there is evidence of powerful intergenerational and interdisciplinary differences in research productivity by academic cluster. Different countries excel in research productivity in different academic disciplines for academics under 40 and those in their 50s. The dynamics of intergenerational difference are strongly differentiated by academic cluster—for instance, Finland exhibits the highest percentage *increase* in research productivity for the 'under 40' to 50s age groups in the cluster of life sciences and medical sciences (475.5 percent), and in the cluster of physical sciences and mathematics in the United Kingdom (614.4 percent).

Discussion and concluding reflections

This chapter does not engage directly with the long-standing controversy about 'mutuality' (or 'complementarity') versus 'competition' between teaching and research activities (Gottlieb and Keith 1997; Ramsden and Moses 1992); nor does it contrast theories of integrated academic roles with theories of segmentation and conflict (Fox 1992). Rather, the focus here is on patterns of academic

194 Academic role stratification

behavior (teaching and research time allocation), academic attitudes (teaching or research role orientation), and research productivity from cross-national and intergenerational perspectives.

To identify intra-national and cross-national differences, young academics (under 40) were systematically compared with older generations of academics. The point of departure was that there is no longer a single academic profession. Instead, there are increasingly stratified and differentiated 'academic professions,' both nationally and cross-nationally (Enders and Musselin 2008). In science, increasing age stratification increases differences between academic cohorts or generations and is closely interrelated with academic role stratification.

From a cross-national perspective, this chapter confirms that in research-focused Type 1 European systems (represented here by Finland, Switzerland, and the United Kingdom), young academics exhibit fundamentally different academic behaviors and academic attitudes than their older colleagues. They work differently, and they think differently about their work, especially in relation to research. In contrast, academics of all generations in teaching-focused Type 2 systems (represented here by Ireland, Poland, and Portugal) work and think in largely similar ways. These differences between the two types of higher education system are clear-cut. Our analysis shows that the stratification of academic role (teaching/research) permeates not just national systems but (even more so) academic cohorts or generations within and across these systems. Intra-national differentiation between cohorts of academics is starker than cross-national differentiation.

Cross-sectional data were analyzed to expose patterns and to cluster European countries accordingly. These patterns (and Type 1 and Type 2 clustering of other systems) should be further tested in other parts of the world and in the various subsectors of national higher education systems.

Research-focused Type 1 and teaching-focused Type 2 higher education systems can be viewed as Weberian ideal types, or as two 'models' of higher education in the sense proposed by Lave and March:

> A model is a simplified picture of a part of the real world. It has some of the characteristics of the real world, but not all of them. It is a set of interrelated guesses about the world. Like all pictures, a model is simpler than the phenomenon it is supposed to represent or explain. ... We construct models in order to explain and appreciate the world. Sometimes we call our simplifications theories, paradigms, hypotheses, or simply ideas.
>
> (1993: 3)

In these terms, Type 1 and Type 2 systems would be 'simply ideas,' or 'interrelated guesses' about empirically observed differences. Research-focused Type 1 systems are characterized by 'strong young research performers' and teaching-focused Type 2 systems by 'strong young teaching performers,' referring to what academics under 40 predominantly do and how they tend to view their teaching/research role orientation (as compared with academics in all older age groups). Type 1 systems may also be described as intergenerational 'research to teaching' systems, and Type 2 as intergenerational 'teaching to teaching' systems. What matters is that the two types are strikingly different, and the national systems in each cluster are strikingly similar.

In fact, European academics under 40 emerge from this research not only as located in different countries but as belonging to two different species in terms of academic role stratification. The disaggregated individual micro-level teaching/research divide proved to be stronger than expected. With the aggregated statistical data from bibliometrics, it would be impossible to use sophisticated tools measuring working time distribution and academic role orientation (using age cohorts as units of analysis would be possible at best, if bibliometric datasets were combined with academic faculty registers).

In research-focused Type 1 systems (Switzerland, Finland, and the United Kingdom), young academics exhibited a strong research orientation and invested three to four times more time in research. In older age groups, decreasing research commitment was accompanied by a substantial decline in time spent on research. In contrast, time allocation and academic role orientation in the teaching-focused Type 2 systems (Ireland, Poland, and Portugal) were stable across academic age groups. Across age groups, there were no obvious or major tensions between academics' self-declared role orientation and actual average teaching and research hours. Academics seemed to be doing what they prefer to be doing (unless what they are doing actually influences their preferences as a means of avoiding permanent discomfort at work). Low research orientation among young academics in teaching-focused Type 2 systems was associated with medium to low research hours. As average research hours were low or medium but stable across all age groups, there was no evidence of intergenerational conflicts caused by sharply declining research interests and research hours with age.

Interestingly, in both Type 1 and Type 2 systems, there was no observed correlation between the distribution of research time and orientation across age groups and research productivity across age groups. In other words, academics under 40 in Type 1 systems who invest much longer hours in research and have a much higher research orientation than their older colleagues did not exhibit higher average research productivity. The analysis provides powerful support for the argument that average productivity increases with age (though not beyond the age of 60) only by virtue of cumulative advantage and increased internationalization, professionalization, and networking levels that accrue over time. The findings indicate that research time and orientation may matter less for research productivity than age, as shown by average productivity of academics under 40 as compared with academics aged 60 or more.

On this evidence, the academic profession is hugely stratified in terms of both age and academic role, especially in Type 1 systems. Age stratification is closely related to academic role stratification, which means that there are huge intergenerational differences between young and older academics in Type 1 systems.

In Switzerland, Finland, and the United Kingdom, the academic universes of young and older academics seem fundamentally different, with a powerful intergenerational clash between highly research-involved academics under 40 and the low research orientation and heavy teaching loads of academics in their 50s. However, this intergenerational clash is concealed by the intergenerational distribution of research productivity, which rises consistently with age in all clusters of disciplines.

The following question therefore emerges: as a young generation of academics gradually replaces older generations in research-focused Type 1 systems, will there be a sharp increase in research orientation? Additionally, as there is no conspicuous intergenerational divide in time investment and research orientation in teaching-focused Type 2 systems, will Type 1 contrast even more starkly with Type 2, where no such generational replacement is conceivable?

National academic recruitment and promotion policies seem increasingly important in national systems that are less research-oriented. These teaching-focused Type 2 systems (here, Ireland, Poland, and Portugal) aspire to catch up in terms of individual research productivity and total national research output with more research-oriented systems. In these circumstances, who is recruited and who is retained (and, in particular what research attitudes and behaviors they exhibit) may define the future of the teaching/research divide in Europe. In the long run, competition between systems that encourage research-oriented attitudes and research-focused academic behaviors and those with low research orientation and teaching-focused academic behaviors seems fundamentally difficult. The trans-European gap in academic knowledge production may be growing ever wider, and the present analysis suggests that academic performance stratification at country level as well as among individual academics may yet become much starker.

For young academics in teaching-focused Type 2 systems (represented here by Ireland, Poland, and Portugal), very high teaching hours and very low research orientation may in the future effectively prevent them from matching the research achievements of young academics in major research-focused Type 1 European systems (represented here by Finland, Switzerland, and the United Kingdom). High levels of teaching involvement effectively reduce the number of hours for research, and low research orientation does not create the intraprofessional tensions necessary for the promotion of national-level changes. The absence of obvious intergenerational conflicts regarding role orientation in these countries comes at the cost of relatively low research performance, both among young academics and nationally. The Type 1-Type 2 stratification of 'young research performers' competing with 'young teaching performers' at the individual micro-level is undoubtedly a global phenomenon (see Shin et al. 2014). This clearly reinforces the global vertical or hierarchical stratification of higher education (Marginson 2016c) at both system and institutional levels, which is beyond the scope of this book.

Notes

1 In the survey instrument used, 'research' is taken to mean 'reading literature, writing, conducting experiments, fieldwork' and 'teaching' is taken to mean 'preparation of instructional materials and lesson plans, classroom instruction, advising students, reading and evaluating student work.' While the two terms are used in this uncomplicated fashion, they may be closely intertwined for some academics. The 'overlapping nature' of academic duties is clearly a methodological problem (Bentley and Kyvik 2012: 533–534) that cannot be easily resolved unless the survey instrument employs more specific categories.

2 As elsewhere in the book, we studied five major clusters of academic disciplines: 'life sciences and medical sciences' (referred to in the survey questionnaire as 'life sciences' and 'medical sciences, health-related sciences, social services'); 'physical sciences and mathematics' ('physical sciences, mathematics, computer sciences'); 'engineering' ('engineering, manufacturing and construction, architecture'); 'humanities and social sciences' ('humanities and arts' and 'social and behavioral sciences'); and 'professions' ('teacher training and education science,' 'business and administration, and economics,' and 'law')

Chapter 6

Academic age stratification

Predictable careers in volatile institutional environments

Introduction

This chapter, in contrast to all the other chapters in this book, uses qualitative empirical material. The material comes from eight European systems—Austria, Croatia, Finland, Germany, Ireland, Poland, Romania, and Switzerland—and consists of 480 semi-structured in-depth interviews, around 60 per country. The interviews were conducted by eight national teams in 2010–2011, transcribed verbatim, and summarized in detailed, standardized interview reports to which this chapter refers. Quantitative methods collect 'numbers'; qualitative methods collect 'words' (Caracelli and Greene 1993: 195). More specifically, we collected and analyzed two independent strands of data in two phases: the survey and the interviews. Then we merged the results of the two strands. We analyzed the survey data quantitatively and the interview data qualitatively, and then merged the two sets of results, seeking 'to obtain different but complementary data on the same topic to best understand the research problem' (Creswell and Plano Clark 2011: 77). In the Polish case, 60 in-depth semi-structured interviews lasting between 40 minutes and 2 hours conducted by Dominik Antonowicz—with whom the first short version of this chapter was written—followed the survey by one year (2010 and 2011, respectively), which made it possible to structure the interviews according to preliminary analyses of the Polish quantitative data. A combination of quantitative and qualitative approaches in this book, with one chapter representing the latter, may lead to less biased results than any of them separately. The two approaches can be complementary or can be used in mixed research designs. In this book, which is predominantly focused on 'numbers,' the qualitative approach focused on 'words' is treated as complementary.

Academic labor markets: the competition within defined timeframes

Academic careers in Europe in their pre-massification period were much more unstructured and much less competitive than today. Currently, as reflected in interviews carried out throughout Europe, 'each step in a career is competitive'

(CH18_MAN), from doctoral and postdoctoral to junior academic and senior academic positions.[1] Competition is the recurrent notion in young academics' descriptions of their work and life. There are significant variations across the European countries studied regarding the level of competition, often different in different places in the academic hierarchy. However, increasing competition has come to the academic profession and is likely to stay: competition for part-time and full-time academic positions, research grants and research funding, and tokens of academic prestige. Young academics interviewed across the eight countries do not seem to be aware of the academic game as a prestige game based on exceptional individual research output funded by highly competitive research funding (as discussed in the Introduction). This awareness probably comes with age—although national reforms in higher education in their countries, and especially newly introduced research evaluation systems and national research council systems, implicitly or explicitly refer to individual-level competition. (See two collections on reforms: Musselin and Teixeira (2014) on designing reform policies and the contrast between expected and actual results, and de Boer et al. (2017) on the processes and outcomes of specifically selected structural reforms.) Poland is perhaps the best case, with powerful cross-generational differences in perceptions of prestige and competition (Kwiek 2017a).

Academic career progression today—as it emerges from the qualitative material—has to be made systematically, in increasingly clearly defined time-frames, and the academic career seems to be sliced into comparable time pe-riods across European systems. Usually, the timeframes are doctoral studies, employment in postdoctoral and junior positions, employment in lower-level senior positions, and, finally, employment in higher-level senior positions (such as traditional chair and/or full professorships, which increasingly are contracts in some systems for financial reasons as professors cost more, which goes against the New Public Management idea of 'doing more with less'). Career steps have to be reached within a certain time period. The competition in academic settings means most often measurable research outputs expected from academics for par-ticular time periods or for particular stages of the academic career. The expecta-tions of academics in the same stages of their careers are becoming largely similar throughout Europe. Croatia, Poland, and Romania are major examples of lower expectations compared with the Western European countries in the sample. There seems to have emerged an interesting combination of career progression requirements linked to age and/or specific timeframes in academic careers. In-creasing competition in all stages of careers is reported, and the competition is related to securing employment (securing a post in the system, or retaining a post in the system, or progressing up the academic ladder in the system) and securing research funding, which is now closely linked to employment.

Today, the link between research funding and employment is viewed as stronger than it was historically. In many cases, generating external funding ac-tually means employment, especially for younger academics. Hiring and funding are therefore increasingly 'two sides of the same coin' (Fumasoli and Goastellec

2015: 76). A growing number of positions in universities are fixed-term, externally funded, and project-based, especially at the doctoral and postdoctoral levels (with postdoctoral periods generally positively impacting research productivity; Horta 2009b). Under the conditions of financial stringency felt in many European systems, the 'market for academics' (Musselin 2010), the 'academic labour market' (Williams et al. 1974), and especially the market for young PhD graduates, has increasingly become a 'winner-take-all market,' in top research universities in particular (Frank and Cook 1995). In such markets, often marginal differences in performance secure the winners a position in the academic system, and marginally lower-performing competitors lose.

In the historically ever-expanding higher education systems, the competition to enter the academic system was traditionally fierce but had less of a 'winner-takes-all' characteristic. With fewer new academic positions in academia today, with considerably higher numbers of potential candidates for academic jobs, and with systems often 'frozen' due to the financial crisis or the aftermath still felt across major European economies, marginal differences in the research performance of prospective entrants and new entrants to the system may count more than ever before, just as social networking abilities may count more. Where small differences matter, 'luck,' 'chance,' 'accident,' and 'opportunity' (historically important in academic careers) are becoming even more important.

Each country has its own 'university configuration' (Musselin 2004), shaping hiring processes, national models of career management, and national academic labor markets. At the same time, the rules of the game for those already in the academic system are much tougher, and the competition vs. collaboration relationship is viewed as differently constructed, with possible unexpected consequences for human relations in the academic workplace, such as distance from one's next-door colleagues. A team of British academics recently commented,

> In this competitive world, an individual academic's biggest rivals may be sitting in the office next door. The need to get a good 'deal' from one's institution in respect of such things as research time allowances, teaching timetables, funding for conference attendance, as well as promotion and any financial rewards on offer, can often result in quiet local distrust and rivalry which may actually be lessened with distance, both institutional and national.
>
> (Brennan, Naidoo, and Franco 2017: 249)

The interviews with European academics clearly show that the role of academic mentors (or academic patrons) has not been diminishing in the last few decades. Early-stage progression in the academic hierarchy is strongly linked to measurable research output and promising research achievements. However, progression is also linked to academic patronage. Academic progression, as a Swiss academic explains, 'has to be based on scientific output, on scientific papers. But also academic networks among peers are important. A good environment for research is needed, however output is the most important criteria' (CH18_MAN). Academic mentors and academic mentorship play a powerful role in the early stages of the academic career, especially in the period of doctoral studies, the completion of which, currently, in most European systems, opens up the possibility of entering the academic profession. A young academic in the Polish context must have a mentor 'who would support him or her in networking and building social capital in his or her research field. Good and supportive mentor is priceless' (PL27_AC).

Academic mentors and early stages of the academic career

The first milestone in the academic career is the decision to stay in the university sector, following, in most European systems, doctoral studies. Many junior academics interviewed explained that their decision to enter doctoral study programs was linked to meeting an intellectual leader. Several channels formalize research activities under the formal umbrella of higher education institutions, which create opportunities to enter the academic profession. Among these channels, the most popular (since the introduction of the Bologna framework of higher education) is conducting research within doctoral study programs. The number of programs and the number of doctoral students have been on the rise in the last decade, however. In many European countries, the current enrollment in doctoral programs is reaching historical records.

Not surprisingly, there is a feeling of increased competition among prospective academics in this new context of expanding doctoral education. Although the pool of doctoral students has been growing substantially, the number of academic posts available has not been keeping up with the pace of the increase in students. Although some programs are specifically designed to produce graduates for the business sector, in most cases in traditional universities doctoral students are inclined to consider an academic career as an important option. Although in most countries the academic profession shows stagnating numbers, the pool of potential candidates seems ever-growing due to the expansion of doctoral studies. Consequently, in massified doctoral education systems, only selected doctorate holders have a chance to enter the academic profession. The 'too many PhDs' question' (Santos, Horta, and Heitor 2016) needs a thoughtful answer—taking into account the needs of changing national academic systems and the career prospects of doctoral holders inside and outside academe. The logic behind the expansion of doctoral education in Europe and in the United States is that 'far more trained researchers than before will seek and will have to seek jobs outside academia and research institutions' (Kehm 2009: 155). Traditional forms of doctoral education and training do not seem to fit new government policy expectations across Europe. Consequently, based on a simple model of supply and demand, the competition for academic appointments has been growing as the number of posts available for doctoral holders outside the university sector has also been falling behind the numbers of new doctorate holders. Part-time, project-based, externally funded and fixed-term appointments seem to be entering the European academic labor market arena for young doctoral holders to a much higher degree than ever before (in a way similar to, although still at a much lower scale, than in the United States; see Kezar and Sam (2010) on a related phenomenon that leads to the new stratification of the academic profession between the new majority of non-tenure-track faculty and the rest).

In the competitive labor market for young potential entrants to the academy, the role of academic mentors, apart from the role of research achievements, emerges as an important issue. Regardless of the legal and institutional status of young researchers, they need an academic mentor who provides them with intellectual support during the entire research process leading to a PhD thesis. And they need mentors beyond doctoral studies, in the transition period potentially leading to university employment: 'regardless of a more rigid or flatter hierarchy, mentoring maintains a central importance in the relationship between senior and junior academics' (Brechelmacher et al. 2015: 35).

The interviews indicate that the cornerstone of an academic career is to be 'discovered' by, and to be 'invited' to work with, the right academic (institutionally, a professor and intellectually, a mentor; there is a 'process of motivated search' between masters and apprentices, as the traditional sociology of science shows, see Zuckerman 1996: 107). In other words, 'meeting the right academic' does not have to be a random incident. For the most able doctoral students, it can be a mutual intellectual discovery based on social interactions in the academic setting, gradually leading to building partnerships in research between senior academics and the most talented, ambitious, and hard-working students or doctoral students with specific knowledge, skills, and attitudes. A good fit in norms, values, and attitudes (or a good fit in Mertonian 'academic ethos') between mentors and their protégées is as important in view of young academics reflecting on their successful paths to university as traditional academic achievements as viewed through the proxy of publications in competitive journals. As reported in Austria and Switzerland, 'after graduation I was invited by my professor to work full-time on a research project as a doctoral candidate' (AT23_AC), and 'for the first contract I was selected from among many, I was doing well, with high marks; it was also a consequence of my good relationships with professors' (CH11_AC).

Employment invitations are also important. A Romanian junior academic reports, 'the coordinating professor of my bachelor degree asked me whether I would like to follow an academic career, and thus, I competed for the university tutor position' (RO55_AC). The Croatian system is reported to be 'very closed in that sense because it rarely (almost never) allows an individual outside the system to enter it' (CR3_AC). Thus, to succeed in competitive academic markets, young doctorate holders need social networking abilities and long-term trustful relationships with academic mentors (which is not entirely different from the past, as reported by Logan Wilson with reference to the best American universities in the post-war period, Wilson 1995, 1979). In most general terms, little has changed since Wilson (1995: 15) wrote in *The Academic Man*:

> entering university work as a life career is very much like entering matrimony: everybody agrees that it is an important event but so many intangibles are involved that nobody knows exactly how it happens. The candidate must choose and be chosen, and despite the indeterministic beliefs of a democratic society, chance and the pressure of circumstances are just as decisive as sentiment and rational choice.

Many academics interviewed across Europe relate their academic careers to what they term 'chance,' 'luck,' 'accident,' or 'opportunity' ('at the foundation of my academic career lie hard work and, last but not least, the opportunity,' RO59_AC; or 'but I also think luck plays an important role since there is a cap of how many academics can be promoted in a given year depending on the money available,' IE55_AC).

The invitation to cooperate in research with the right academic and at the right time of the academic career opens a window of opportunity for young academics. Traditionally, promising students were approached by professors and invited to join their research groups. The criteria of choice, in addition to academic merit, could be trivial but important from the point of view of interpersonal relations. As one of the interviewed academics stressed, the mentoring professor chose her 'because they got along well on an emotional level' (AT55_AC). Nevertheless, the interviewed academics (mostly junior) underscored this particular moment of being an object of intellectual interest in their professional careers as a turning point that sparked their interest in research and made them think seriously about working in higher education in the future: 'A critical point of my academic career was a meeting with the right professor, my mentor who directs me in the right way and also who has helped me to articulate my research plans and ambitions' (PL2_AC).

Professors seem to have the power that enables them to inspire, engage, and guide junior academics through the early stages of their academic careers. Professors can also, especially initially, attune younger academics' minds toward particular problems rather than other problems in research, as well as determine their general ways of thinking within the disciplines they represent. According to interviewees, the influence of mentoring professors cannot be overestimated. Their intellectual imprints are left through mostly informal, indirect, sometimes even intuitively given remarks, advice, or guidelines. Mentoring professors often serve as role models for young academics. These invisible but strong influences have been largely confirmed by junior academics who often declare that their personal successes in research would not be possible without the priceless and often immeasurable, direct and indirect, contribution of their mentors. As reported, in an academic career, 'the most important is the mentor who is taking care of everything. He or she is supervising and mentoring a career of a young academic, paving the way to grants, publications and fellowships' (PL1_MAN).

Meeting a good academic mentor, thus, is the first important milestone in an academic career. Academic mentorship is a difficult task to perform and requires specific personal and professional skills, mutual understanding, and strong willingness to cooperate on both sides of the relationship. Undoubtedly, mentoring is a priceless experience for doctoral candidates who require intellectual inspiration and later on seek, often tacitly, various types of direct or indirect support and intervention in finding good, preferably full-time, employment in the university or public research sectors. There is another side of the coin, too: Mentorship can lead to cloning in academia. Interviewees complained about unfair procedures that carry students further along the academic route by their powerful mentoring professors. Regarding the early stages of an academic career, interviewees underscored that finding a good academic mentor was a turning point in their professional academic careers (it might imply a dead end if the cooperation fails at some point). Apart from serving young academics with their academic expertise, research experience, and academic networks, mentoring professors are often able to secure external funding for the younger academics. In some countries, there is a high dependency of junior academics on senior academics based on the project funding provided by the latter. In addition, mentors can provide access to their scientific networks, and young academics rely on these networks while creating their own networks. These networks will benefit the younger academics in the future, as they report networking is difficult without the support of a well-established scholar. Doctoral students know that to be successful they need to belong to larger research groups. A Romanian young academic emphasizes,

> I need to belong to a consolidated research team because I am aware that this is the only way to achieve performance in research. … To be a member of a sound research team favors publication and has a positive effect on the academic prestige of scientists and on their capacity to train new researchers.
>
> (RO19_AC)

Finally, mentors' expectations are reported to increase after the doctoral dissertation has been completed. The transitional period following the doctoral period verifies the institutional and academic position of mentors and their intentions regarding the professional future of their apprentices, or the employment of junior scholars. The reason is that, by and large, junior academics expect some assistance in getting through the transitional period and in securing employment in the academic sector. A Swiss junior academic pointed out that she became an assistant

> because of [a] good relationship with a professor who offered me to do a master (50 percent) and work at university at 50 percent. I got a lot of support from this professor, with whom I also did my bachelor thesis as well as my specialization year.
>
> (CH7_AC)

In the academic progression path, the initial period of doctoral studies leads to a transition period which for those who wish to stay in academia means seeking part-time or full-time university-paid or project-based employment in any part of the national (or international) system. The international mobility of doctoral students and doctorate holders in Europe has grown substantially. One of the mechanisms used is Marie Curie Actions supported by the European Commission. The vast majority of young doctorate holders seek employment in national systems, however.

Entering the academic profession: growing insecurity and increasing instability

Following meeting the right mentor, the second important milestone in an academic career comes when the decision to stay in academia after defending a doctoral dissertation is made. According to interviewees, young academics are hold in abeyance and have to be highly competitive in their research achievements to be able to enter the academic profession. A mass model of doctoral training leads to a substantial increase in the number of doctoral degree holders, most of whom have no option but to search for employment outside higher education. Doctoral training systems are expanding faster than higher education systems and the employment opportunities the systems provide, however.

In addition, even more than before, in massified systems the traditional rules about selectivity in academia still hold, and traditionally, 'scientific ability is very unevenly distributed' (Ziman 1994: 258–259). Traditionally, most new PhD holders in Europe are inclined to work in the academic sector. Consequently, under competitive pressures, the transformation from the status of a doctoral student to any form of research- or teaching-based employment is a critical moment in career development. A sense of insecurity and instability is prevalent among doctoral students, as reported by young academics throughout Europe: 'Universities in Finland educate such a high number of PhDs at the moment. This, of course, leads to insecurity especially for those who want to stay in academia' (FI72_AC). Uncertainty is also reported among young academics working on part-time contracts (IE1_AC). As Brechelmacher et al. report (2015: 13), '[E]mbarking on an academic career is a risky undertaking. ... What is needed is perseverance, and persistence, not giving up (you need an "absolute need to do it"), steadfastness, ambition, obstinacy, flexibility and a willingness to take risks.'

Despite worsening employment conditions, the academic profession remains an attractive option for young doctoral students (Enders and de Weert 2009b; Enders and Musselin 2008). Despite increasing and differentiated job expectations, often increasing teaching loads (especially for recent entrants to academia in the teaching-focused Type 2 systems analyzed in Chapter 5), relatively decreasing salaries (compared with other professionals), changing employment relations toward less security, less stability, and, more often, a fixed-term, and uncertainty about future developments in the university sector in Europe, higher education still attracts very talented people. Higher education in Europe today is still attractive as a workplace even though it is a long way from what Wilson (1995: 21) described in the mid-1940s as 'reasonably secure tenure, public esteem ... pleasant work and surroundings, sufficient leisure for the pursuit of personal interests, and so on.' Working in higher education can still offer interesting perspectives for professional path development, and job satisfaction levels in European universities are relatively high and consistently so almost throughout the continent (Kwiek and Antonowicz 2013) and globally (Bentley et al. 2013).

There seems to be an oversupply of good candidates for the academic profession and an undersupply of academic positions in stagnating systems. Consequently, there are increasing controversies about academic recruitment processes. For instance, as reported in Austria,

> there is a 'mentality of local emperors' at this university, as heads of departments and professors have the power to decide on tenure-track positions relatively autonomously. The advertisement for an open position is an official act, but the texts are mostly tailored to certain candidates.
>
> (AT44_AC)

Or, as reported in Germany, 'there were several candidates for this position, but through consultation with the professor it was clear that when I am applying for this job, I will get this place' (D208_AC). Some changes that have increased the transparency of hiring processes for young academics have been reported, but change has been slow. In general, the research promise, the research track record, and the notion of 'choosing and being chosen' matter. 'The job market was at one time fairly simple—senior professors were expected to find jobs for their students. This paternalistic arrangement, perhaps practical for small and elite systems, for the most part [has] disappeared' (Altbach 2015: 15).

As strongly as ever before, staying in higher education after completing doctoral dissertations is the ultimate goal for those who think about being full-time academics. The tenure track is a tempting career opportunity, and the transitional period following the period of doctoral studies is decisive about whether the person will stay in academia, and in which part of it. Some interviewees tend to believe (and experience) that the real selection in academia takes place shortly after completing a doctoral dissertation. 'It is most critical to quickly obtain a position immediately after the doctorate, even if it is not a permanent position. It makes it possible to establish networks in the framework of regular employment' (AT50_AC). For some academics, this moment is the most decisive in their careers, a sort of 'do or die' period. Reaching this milestone requires making preparations in advance.

Good publications in internationally respected journals, in the current competitive environment, are believed not to be enough to enter the academic profession. Other personal assets are very useful, including well-developed social skills and social networks built during doctoral studies. A Swiss junior academic declared, 'You need to be "promoted" individually, personally; your work has to be clearly visible' (CH17_AC). Today, most early-stage career opportunities in higher education require external project funding or other external financial contributions. Therefore, young academics believe in getting on well with professors who have access to financial research resources and the power to distribute them. In some countries, social networking and perhaps surprisingly, teaching and pedagogical abilities seem to count more than ever before (FI77_AC).

Social networking, especially international, is believed to matter substantially in successfully generating funding for research. A senior lecturer from Ireland points out,

> there is a huge emphasis now on research and acquiring research funding. But academics in the current climate cannot get funding if they apply on their own or with a couple of colleagues from their department. Instead, you bring in people you know from all over Europe or the world, different disciplines, different countries, and that is how you get funding these days.
>
> (IE7_AC)

Mobility between the higher education sector and the economic sector is often difficult, especially as it is hard to start an academic career after a professional career in the business sector. Entering the academic profession today most often means entering it right after the doctoral or postdoctoral period, without previous experience in the business sector. In some countries (e.g., Poland or Romania), it is very rare to return to academia after early departure to the business world, because the professional career development path is based on cumulative promotion and cumulative research achievements, and lagging behind in measurable research output can be difficult to overcome. In addition, academic achievements are an important criterion in competitive research bids and calls for research proposals and research fellowships. The probability of getting research funding in a competitive environment without accumulated previous research achievements is low. Some higher education systems are more open to interesectoral mobility; other systems (e.g., Polish or Romanian) are almost completely closed to outsiders, and mobility into the higher education sector for latecomers or for practitioners from the business world is of marginal importance for the system as a whole. In European universities with more hierarchical institutional settings, with very limited chances for career progression for junior researchers, or with a limited (and in some countries, decreasing) number of senior academic posts, intersectoral mobility is almost always in one direction: from universities to enterprises. Although full-time returns from the business world to academia seem difficult, some part-time returns (e.g., sharing practical knowledge derived from company experience) still seem possible. In general, they are still reported to be rare. Most European institutions do not consider work experience outside academia important in staff recruitment procedures.

The transformation from being a doctoral student (or a postdoc) to being an academic means passing through a rigorous selection process. The successful passage to academic employment is a turning point, although moving from one postdoc position to another has been reported (see international postdoc work in the United States as academic wage labor and an expression of academic capitalism in Cantwell 2011). Therefore, entering the academic profession in any form becomes the ultimate goal, and the following statement reflects the spirit of this transitional period: 'It was more important to get a foot in the door of the university than anything else' (AT46_AC). One should not be surprised that academics interviewed declared that 'in my personal career, the phase of the dissertation was decisive, not so much as the phase of habilitation' (AT25_AC).

Steps toward full-time employment

Thus, the next critical turning point of an academic career is obtaining full-time secure employment in the higher education or research sector. There are significant differences across the European countries studied because obtaining permanent full-time positions in higher education requires meeting different formal criteria. In a few countries (e.g., Poland), professional stability and secure employment come almost automatically with the habilitation degree. Stability and security have, traditionally, throughout the whole post-war expansion period in European higher education been crucial factors in attracting able individuals to the university; as Bowen and Schuster pointed out long ago, with reference to the US system, 'the excellence of higher education is a function of the kind of people it is able to enlist and retain on its faculties' (Bowen and Schuster 1986: 3). Thus, in this respect, a habilitation degree naturally becomes a milestone in an academic career in those systems where it still exists in theory and in practice. For instance, in Poland 'the existing hierarchy resembles a feudal hierarchy, and everyone knows his or her place in it. In public universities, this hierarchy is overemphasized, and obtaining a habilitation degree implies obtaining a significantly different status at the university' (PL25_AC). Or, as another Polish junior academic remarked,

> the so-called community of scholars is, in fact, comprised of two completely different groups: senior and junior academics. The difference is not only in status in the organization; it is much more than this. Habilitation is a turning point in any academic professional career; it changes working habits, lifestyles, and sometimes also friends.
>
> (PL8_AC)

A young Polish academic comments, 'Feudalism in higher education is a common form of relationship. And taking advantage of junior academics by senior academics is well rooted in some disciplines such as medicine' (PL15_AC).

Nevertheless, European academics still live in what Wilson (1995) termed 'an open-class society: entry into their occupation is more accessible than in most other professions, and advancement in it is closely coupled with individual capability and effort' (206). The higher education work environment may be tough and highly competitive, but it seems to be fair and relatively meritocratic across European systems. In the upper layers of national systems, or in research universities, the role of outstanding research output (and the research funding the output generates) is highly stratifying (as discussed in the Introduction) but also meritocratic, at least to a large extent. The academic profession for most able top research performers may be more meritocratic than other professions as long as the traditional configuration of academic norms rules. New academic rules can certainly destabilize the science system, possibly leading to less meritocracy.

In Poland, which represents in the sample the systems with Habilitation, there is a significant difference in status within the academic community between academics with a habilitation degree and those without it. In this hierarchical community, this degree is a dividing line between two clearly distinguished, and often not interacting, groups of academics. In interviews, academics (particularly junior academics) often refer to this stratification as 'a two class-society,' 'a caste system,' a 'pyramid structure,' or even more often as 'a feudal society': 'The relation can be very feudal—young academics are forced to write [a] doctoral dissertation on a topic that one has neither knowledge nor interest in. But this is the way it should be done, and if one has no knowledge about a given topic, she needs to work harder to get it' (PL7_AC). Or as stressed in another interview, the relation between senior and junior academics is 'underpinned by the old system [the communist system that existed in Poland 1945–1989]. Maybe there is no more "cooking dinners and baking cakes" for professors, but there are still elements of it from the past' (PL29_AC).

Regardless of which description we choose to apply to describe the relation within the academic community in Poland, these descriptions demonstrate the fundamental importance of the habilitation degree in the higher education sector. In a highly stratified community, obtaining a habilitation degree is a milestone in an academic career. The degree guarantees remarkable growth in social and academic status and (almost automatically) provides a permanent full-time university post. For many, the degree is the termination of a long period of professional uncertainty. Traditionally in American universities, the period of uncertainty was short due to '"up or out" policies' (Wilson 1995: 61). However, in other countries (e.g., Finland, Austria, and Switzerland) a habilitation degree or different forms of academic seniority do not guarantee higher academic status and secure employment. The degree creates more opportunities to apply for full-time permanent positions at higher education institutions, but there is little doubt that there is still a long way to go to obtain secure employment in these countries.

The Bologna structure of higher education has made doctoral schools much more accessible for potential future young researchers. The advent of doctoral schools and a mass model of doctoral training largely dismissed the idea of apprenticeship in academia, and selection for faculty positions has been moved up to the postdoc or junior professorial level. A senior Swiss academic explains the internal mechanism of promotion: 'Competitive evaluation and selection are structured processes from the (tenure track) assistant professor onwards: We check for quality according to publications, i.e., research, and teaching quality, too. We ask for four to six references' (CH19_MAN).

The significance of obtaining secure employment as a milestone in an academic career can hardly be questioned in the contemporary academic world. There is strong evidence that a huge gap exists between academics with fixed-term contracts and those with permanent contracts. 'At the university, there is a two-class system of those who are on permanent positions and those who know they have to leave the university eventually,' an Austrian academic explains (AT39_HEP). The process of marketization of higher education also involves the transformation of academic employment relationships.

The direction of the transformation over the last two decades most often implies less stable, less secure, and generally less attractive working conditions in higher education. A Finnish academic summarizes the theme: 'An academic career has previously been very clear, but now it is very uncertain' (FI15_AC). Some academics are employed in externally funded positions for quite a long time, and they apply for university positions many times, as explained in the Austrian context: 'They are not happy. To have to finance yourself on the basis of external funds, it is not easy. The sword of Damocles of not knowing if you will be employed the next year is hanging over them' (AT10_AC). An increasing number of employees work under fixed-term contracts (Aarrevaara, Dobson, and Wikström 2015), and the academics can easily be dismissed if needed without extensive social and financial costs. Egbert de Weert (2002: 78) calls this approach a 'zero-appointments' policy that leads to 'invisible faculties.' Therefore, the transition from fixed-term employment to a full-time permanent position becomes a milestone in academic careers and the ultimate goal for many academics. 'Even in Germany among people with habilitation, the number of limited-term jobs has increased' (DE201_AC). Fixed-time contracts may also effectively limit access to research funding. An Irish junior academic reflects,

> the current academic contracts are of 5-year duration which impacts greatly on an early career academic's ability to apply for research funding because most research funding requires permanency or at least that the academic will remain in that post for the duration of the grant. Moreover, the employment of postdocs is also prevented under the moratorium, so the profession of academia is actually currently suspended. The newer members that are coming in are operating in a much different role (there is a sort of 2-tier system), and I can't call that a profession anymore.

(IE39_AC)

In most countries, the interviewed academics express complaints about recent staff policy changes in higher education that reduced access to permanent posts. As one of the Austrian senior academics stated, the acquisition of well-funded research projects makes 'future fantasies of a permanent position' emerge. A secure position in a higher education institution becomes a personal goal. It is generally expected that the availability of permanent posts in higher education institutions will decrease over time and will become the subject of increasing competition between academics. A Finnish scholar points out, 'There is a huge competition for available posts. More and more is needed in order to get a post' (FI25_AC). Moreover, financial austerity plans introduced in some European countries and major cuts in public spending in higher education in other countries may foster this competitiveness in the academic work environment and make securing full-time employment more difficult to achieve. Policy changes put many academics in a very difficult professional position because at least some of them—like a Finnish senior full-time academic interviewed—'have a permanent position outside university, and he will keep it because university cannot offer him a permanent position. He has achieved what he wanted, although he would like to be a docent one day' (FI14_AC).

New pressures in changing organizations and reforming systems

Academic careers for young academics are becoming more versatile and involve a wide range of different criteria to develop, although scientific recognition, especially through internationally visible publications, is still the core of the academic career that defines academic trajectories. Interviewees report a widespread trend that might imply a departure from a career model based on a limited number of milestones (often associated with various academic 'rites of passage') to a new pattern one interviewee called 'cumulative promotion': 'The criteria for academic careers in the 1970s and the 1980s were "not to fall out of favor with the one or two professor(s) that supported you as a young researcher"; today (over the last five years), measurable scientific qualifications and international experience are required' (AT33_AC). The measurability (or calculability) of national and international research achievements (including mobility) might be more appealing to young academics than 'cumulative promotion'—and certainly more meritocractic.

Job instability in the science sector is growing, causing controversies in academia widely reported in the interviews. A Finnish scholar stresses, 'An academic career is based on quality work and ambition, but an academic career is nowadays very unstable and unforeseen' (FI4_AC). There is a widespread feeling of increasing pressure to produce highly cited publications in peer-reviewed journals and to gain international experience for an academic career to progress. It is also important to publish extensively in international journals. However, it has also been a commonly shared feeling that to produce good publications, academics need to be able to acquire external funding and to build social networks within the academic community. An Irish academic comments,

> There is external pressure to do research, to attract funding, to update the research profile, and to do the student surveys for quality assurance purposes; however, the internal pressure of self-motivation is even greater. [The] main challenge is having many balls to juggle in terms of teaching, research, administration, working for external bodies, and helping in moving the university forward.
>
> (IE53_AC)

According to those who welcome a new system of internationally comparable, increasingly measurable research output used for career progression and research funding opportunities, academics from the old system (for instance, as in this case, Austrian associate professors with permanent civil servant status) still 'do not have to worry about anything' (AT01_AC). Older Polish academics are in the same situation: The new rules of the academic game are not applicable to them (Kwiek 2017a). A new model based on increased professional insecurity is an attempt to make them more active in researching, publishing, and acquiring funding from external sources. There is growing self-motivation in securing research funding. An Irish academic explains, 'The pressure to get external funding comes primarily from within although it also comes from the school, the pressure comes from the university but the support comes [also] from the university' (IE54_AC). A German scholar (DE120_AC) points out that 'university careers used to be more linear than nowadays. Nowadays, a broader positioning is required' (such as foreign languages, interdisciplinary orientation, and external funding). Schuster and Finkelstein (2008: 188) report in the American context, 'the expectations about one's career prospects that an entering academic could have reasonably entertained a generation ago differ strikingly from current realistic expectations. The passageways have become bumpier.' But, at the same time, they do not come as a surprise. European academics' expectations have been evolving for between one and three decades, with the longest experience of reforms perhaps in the case of the United Kingdom system.

Academics report that they undergo regular evaluations that cover various aspects of their work but focus mainly on three areas: research, teaching, and administrative tasks (or service, that is, engagement with the university and its environment). Evaluations are often continuous and built on transparent, quantitative, measurable, and comparable criteria. In the German context, 'the evaluation process becomes an integral part of the academic professional development from the beginning (almost) right to the end, and therefore, the pressure of continued evaluations is increasing' (DE901_AC). The implication is that the evaluation is attached to the academic degree structure and to university positions.

The continuous character of individual evaluation processes carries concrete advantages in the academic setting: the existence of a foreseeable career path with predefined procedures and predefined outcomes. A Finnish academic comments:

> Nowadays, even a lot of publications in A journals is not enough. You have also to be able to raise a lot of project funds. You also have to be able to popularize your scholarly work and have a lot of contacts with your students' future employers. Sometimes, it feels like measuring these academic activities has become more important than activities themselves.
>
> (FI62_AC)

The interviewees also express strong criticism of what they refer to as the 'American model' of academic careers in higher education. The interviewees criticize 'the devastating model of professional development' that is built on fierce competition, uncertainty, instability, and ongoing evaluation of individual research outcomes. However, each discipline can develop its own unique list of milestones. In the linear model of academic professional development, milestones are not centrally defined. Instead, there is a range of opportunities for individuals and translated into milestones in their careers.

In other words, the traditional milestones of academic career development may increasingly be accompanied by a large number of small steps that must be taken regularly and are regularly assessed. The frequency and regularity of evaluations make changes in the academic career a linear, and to a large extent, predictable process. Milestones of professional development are spread over the entire length of the academic career; thus, the small individual steps are critical 'do or die' components. Switzerland provides a good example of this direction of changes: 'Careers are established with points, so that you can plan objectives for the following years' (CH15_AC).

Perhaps the most important element of the academic career is the tenured position. The picture emergent from the interviews indicates that a tenured position gradually becomes nothing more than the final stage in academic professional development, available to some academics only. Obtaining a tenured position (if one exists in the system) is a natural culmination of the research track record and sometimes also previous teaching achievements. Interviews show that there is strong criticism among European academics of taking a too narrow 'research only' perspective of academic promotions, in particular for tenured positions. Finland, for instance, introduced a broader approach to criteria for recruiting professors, taking into account other aspects of academic work (e.g., teaching), but this direction also received some criticism.

The academic profession in most countries studied is becoming increasingly competitive not only for new entrants but also for all academics, at all levels of seniority. The competition for funding and prestige is getting tougher and fiercer. 'Because of the shrinking funding base, the academic profession will become, at least in some disciplines, extremely competitive' (CH29_MAN). In some countries (e.g., Germany), even tenured positions do not take the pressure off academics' shoulders. In the Swiss context,

> the competition is becoming a normal dimension also for the youngest. It is a daily business: By means of transparent procedures, everybody is able to understand where she stands, why she was not appointed, etc. This has to be made explicit. Then there is competition for the third stream of funding, like from the SNF [Swiss National Science Foundation] and from other foundations.
>
> (CH26_MAN)

Even in the countries with the chair system (such as Austria and Germany) in which professorships used to be traditionally well-established positions at universities, radical changes continue. A German professor stresses that 'those who habilitate get under a strong pressure because they need to do their own generation of external funding, and teach on their own, too' (DE118_AC).

New demands and mission overload

The competition to enter the academic profession and to stay in it, especially at lower levels of academic seniority, is accompanied by growing expectations for research output, generation of external funding for research, teaching, and various service missions. (Surprisingly, in the post-communist higher education systems in Poland, Croatia, and Romania, various types of mission activities are rarely mentioned, and the major divide in academics' time allocation is between teaching and research, with a frequent conclusion that the two should ideally be 'in balance,' as a Romanian scholar points out (RO37_AC).)

Universities under conditions of massification across Europe are increasingly expected to be meeting not only the changing needs of the state but also the changing needs of students, employers, the labor market, and industry, as well as the regions in which the universities are located (Pinheiro et al. 2012). The demands on academics increasingly conflict, and universities are caught in 'mission overload.' Globally, for the vast majority of academics, the traditional combination of teaching, research, and service is beyond reach anyway. As a whole, globally, the academic profession is becoming a predominantly teaching profession; gravitation toward more emphasis on teaching is also the case, to varying degrees, in Europe and in the United States (Shin et al. 2014). Among the promotion criteria in most European systems, research output is a critical factor, but there are systems (such as Ireland) in which all three university missions count in moving up the academic ladder and where teaching and service combined may be weighted more than research (for the youngest academics). As reported in the Irish context,

> the criteria for promotion include research, teaching, and contribution (to the department, the faculty, the university, and then to the wider community). For any promotion, you are judged under those three headings. For a

promotion from CL [career lecturer] to SL [senior lecturer], the weighting is 40 (Research), 30 (Teaching), and 30 (Contribution). For a promotion from SL to AP (assistant professor], there is more emphasis on research so the weighting is 60-20-20.

(IE7_AC)

Young academics work under increasing pressure, but at the same time, the pressure seems to be manageable:

Broadly speaking, I do not know if any academic is ever in control of everything. There are always many tasks to carry out, such as setting and marking exam papers. An academic is in control broadly speaking but not on a day-to-day basis. ... An academic firstly feels under pressure from themselves on the research side; to conduct research, get papers published, get grants, be seen to have an active research group. Then there is pressure from the administrative side of the role. The pressure is not present to the extent that I am crumbling under the pressure; I can manage it so far, and it peaks and troughs.

(IE51_AC)

The pressure is manageable because although the professional stability is lower than in previous decades, the requirements for particular steps on the career ladder are more transparent and measurable today. It is perhaps easier to plan a career based on more quantifiable indicators of academic progress that are more similar across academic disciplines and across national higher education systems. Perhaps the new rules of the academic game are tougher than ever, but at least they are known to the academic profession somehow in advance.

There is a clear difference with the past, as reflected by an Irish academic:

in order to get a promotion there are very clear criteria with regards to an academic's teaching, research/publications, and service to the community. [It] was more woolly in the past, how you interpreted those criteria, whereas right now I think the criteria are very much laid down and very clear.

(IE48_AC)

In some countries, the changes are slow but unavoidable. A Polish junior scholar reports:

the academic professional development path is very conservative. It lacks transparency and explicit criteria of academic promotion. Instead, there is a number of informal agreements between senior academics on what is required from junior academics to be awarded habilitation. This is understandable that not all criteria can be explicitly measured and benchmarked, but the existing system does not build trust around the professional academic development path.

(PL31_AC)

Another junior Polish academic reflects that 'informal criteria established by cliques of professors keep the process of awarding academic degrees non-transparent' (PL32_AC). However, the direction of changes in Poland is toward meeting measureable, quantifiable criteria to avoid blocking academic careers through 'informal agreements' for who deserves habilitation and a professorship and based on past (predominantly) research achievements.

Discussion and concluding reflections

Finally, as clear from the qualitative empirical material examined in this chapter, from a longer historical perspective, academics need to be more aware of the processes exogenous to higher education but closely linked to its future, such as changing rationales for public research funding, a revision of the social contract between universities and governments closely linked to the postwar expansion of science in Europe, changing science policies guiding national research priorities, changing demographics, changing social perceptions of the utility of research in the knowledge economy, and a diversified premium for higher education in contemporary economy across different study fields. These factors have a powerful impact on the current, and especially future, academic labor market, and particularly on its expansion in some areas accompanied by contraction in other areas. More volatile, rapidly changing economies and societies certainly mean a less stable and more competitive academic world in the future.

All academic generations are beginning to learn how tough the competition for ever-more concentrated research funding is, but for structural reasons (increased availability of most national research programs in national grant-awarding agencies), the younger generation needs to learn faster. The young generation globally experiences higher levels of part-time or project-based employment (especially in the United States, Cummings and Finkelstein 2012, and in Europe, Brechelmacher et al. 2015). In European universities, junior and senior academics increasingly are worlds apart. However, although senior academics may have higher professional stability, junior academics may have better access to competitive research funding and a more practical approach to top-tier publishing channels. Therefore, junior academics, at least in some systems, tend to be much better prepared for the changing academic world in which a permanent competition for research-driven prestige and resources becomes the dominant feature. Although we agree with Ulrich Teichler's (2014b: 62) general conclusions from his study of German university professors (that junior and senior academics seem to have 'little in common with respect to job security, composition of tasks and influence in academia'), we have to add that junior academics are much better equipped for their professional future in highly volatile academic environments.

Young academics across Europe clearly identify the tensions between insecure, often contract-based employment and mounting publishing pressure (see a collection of case studies from ten countries globally in Yudkevich et al. 2015). The traditional trade-off between higher salaries in more competitive workplaces outside academia and lower salaries combined with more secure and stable academic workplaces does not seem to work anymore (Altbach 2012). Relatively modest academic salaries in most European higher education systems used to be accompanied by working in less stressful working environments (Bentley et al. 2013). As this relative workplace bonus is being globally withdrawn, the attractiveness of the academic profession is at stake (Schuster and Finkelstein 2006; Teichler and Höhle 2013).

The young academic generation see the difference much more clearly today, as a comparator class for them is that of young professionals (their colleagues in generational terms) rather than that of older academics. The contrast is starker than ever. Ulrich Teichler's description links increasing uncertainty to the diminishing attractiveness of an academic career:

> academic careers seem to become more risky in many countries and many sectors. Between the ages of about 30 and 40 years, when those in other careers are settling, there tends to be a high degree of uncertainty and selectivity in academic careers. … Concern is growing that academic careers might lose their attractiveness and that talented individuals might opt out for other careers.
>
> (Teichler 2006: 2)

We have argued in this chapter that the major milestones of the academic career in European universities, despite huge ongoing transformations and reform packages implemented throughout European higher education systems, remain the same. In general, they include the following: entering a doctoral program and completing it with a PhD thesis defense, finding a full- or part-time job in academia, changing academic status from junior to senior academic, and, finally, remaining in the system in a senior academic position.

These traditional milestones are increasingly accompanied by continuous, small-scale steps, almost continuously assessed by peer and administrative bodies. The academic labor market is becoming highly competitive at all levels rather than, as traditional, in lower academic ranks only. Although successive milestones need to be reached, they result more often than ever from a steady accumulation of (predominantly) research achievements. The academic career ladder seems evermore strongly linked to the ability to generate external research funds. Consequently, the role of academic mentors or patrons, willing and able to provide research funding to their protégés during the doctoral and postdoctoral career periods, seems crucial.

Academic careers are much less stable and secure. Lifetime (or even long-term) academic employment can no longer be taken for granted, especially in the case of new entrants to the academic profession. However, academic careers may be becoming more predictable through ever-stronger processes of assessment of quantifiable, comparable (across disciplines and across higher education systems), and internationally measurable research outputs. Through an increasing number of small assessment steps taken in between the major milestones in academic careers, academic progression is somehow less secure but more predictable. In competitive, less stable academic environments, small steps and requirements for moving up the academic ladder may be becoming more uniform across European systems. The interviewees across Europe stress internationally visible research achievements and fund-generating abilities as perhaps the most important components of a successful academic life.

Note

1 The interviews are referred to as follows: The country abbreviation is followed by the interview number (AT-Austria, CH-Switzerland, CR-Croatia, DE-Germany, FI-Finland, IE-Ireland, PL-Poland, and RO-Romania).

Chapter 7

Conclusions and policy implications

Summary of findings

Back to the stratification theme

Rather than positing a single 'academic profession,' this book examines Europe's academic professions from a sociology of science perspective—or, more precisely, sociology of academic careers (Hermanowicz 2012)—based on the most comprehensive cross-national dataset currently available. Key concepts addressed here include social stratification in science, academic career structures, award and recognition systems, patterns of academic behavior and attitudes, and research productivity. Specifically, the six chapters are organized around six variations on the theme of social stratification in science: academic performance stratification, academic salary stratification, academic power stratification, international research stratification, academic role stratification, and academic age stratification. Each of these refers to prototypical figures in higher education and, by extension, in higher education research: *academic top performers, academic top earners, juniors and seniors, internationalists and locals,* and *academics under 40 or young academics*. These categories are the major dividing lines used here to analyze the quantitative empirical material from 17,211 survey respondents across 11 European countries.

In general, the approach to data analysis is structurally similar throughout. With the exception of the qualitative emphasis in Chapter 6, bivariate statistical analysis was followed by logistic regression analysis wherever applicable. The bivariate analyses examined a number of key variables. Academic behavior was captured as distribution of working time (teaching, research, service, administration, and other academic duties); as research productivity (variously defined by different proxy measures); and as research collaboration with international colleagues. Academic attitude was captured as academic role orientation (teaching or research) and primary research orientation. The various dimensions of academic behaviors and academic attitudes were applied to academics across different countries, institutional types, clusters of academic disciplines, age cohorts, academic positions, income brackets, and genders. A modeling approach was used to identify predictors for top research performers (Chapter 1), top earners (Chapter 2), and internationalists (Chapter 4). In our view, the combination of bivariate and logistic regression analyses works better and provides more robust results than either approach alone. Certainly, the survey instrument opens almost endless research directions based on the 400 variables applied across 11 systems. That said, every study has its natural limits, and we firmly believe that the power of research lies in the continuing scholarly conversation to which we hope this book will contribute. Like every intellectual product, this volume looks both forward and back, both theoretically and empirically; as Teichler puts it, 'higher education research has to be forward-looking in order to be socially relevant' (2014c: 147).

Chapter 1 opens the discussion on the increasing intensity of performance stratification within the academic profession. At an individual level, social stratification in science means that the scientific community is not a 'company of equals.' Instead, 'it is sharply stratified; a small number of scientists contribute disproportionately to the advancement of science and receive a disproportionately large share of rewards and the resources needed for research' (Zuckerman 1988: 526). At the relevant levels of analysis, this means that 'individuals, groups, laboratories, institutes, universities, journals, fields and specialties, theories, and methods are incessantly ranked and sharply graded in prestige' (Zuckerman 1988: 526). For academics, recognition of their work is 'the only unambiguous demonstration that what they have done matters to science' (Zuckerman 1988: 526). In science, recognition translates into resources for further research, and the distribution of academic rewards—including research funding—is sharply graded. Stratification of both individuals and institutions seems to have intensified in the last two decades, with evaluations increasingly based on bibliometrics (see Kulczycki 2017). However, the trend noted in Chapter 1 differs little from an account from half a century ago: 'Disciplines, publication in particular journals, types of research, organisations, and rewards are also ranked. Individual scientists can be located in each of these dimensions and their final rank is the sum or product of these evaluations of their research' (Zuckerman 1970: 237).

The pattern of stratification in science—or social inequality in science (Cole and Cole 1973: 15)—is determined by the way rewards are distributed among scientists and by 'the social mechanisms through which the reward system of science operates to identify excellence.' The efficient operation of science depends on 'the way it allocates positions to individuals, divides up the rewards and prizes it offers for outstanding performance, and structures opportunities for those who held extraordinary talent' (Cole and Cole 1973: 15). The underpinning of the stratification system in science is contribution to scientific knowledge— through published research. Prestige, success, and recognition are all inseparable from significant, consequential, high-quality publications.

Sociologists of science have traditionally been interested in the social stratification of science at the micro-level of the individual academic. In the last two decades, however, the focus has shifted to a bird's-eye view, reflecting the greater power of national- and institutional-level data. This book redresses that balance by exploring the views of the individuals at the core of the academic enterprise. The book's renewed theoretical and empirical focus on the academic profession tests the utility of analyzing higher education from the micro-level perspective of the individual academic.

Social stratification in science has been a recurring theme in higher education research for more than half a century. To explore this phenomenon, we have drawn on large-scale comparative quantitative data from across Europe to test the assumption that the increasing tensions in higher education attributed to changes in governance and funding regimes extend to the micro-level of the individual academic. The individuals who collectively constitute the academic profession—or professions, as becomes clear from our findings on stratification— find themselves at the center of these changes and the tensions that ensue. In both elite research-focused institutions and their less prestigious teaching-focused counterparts, systemic and institutional changes filter down into the work and life of academics. The ongoing evolution of governance and funding regimes and academic job requirements mirrors the increasing stratification of institutions and individuals. This book explores how academics operationalize these issues in terms of academia's attractiveness as profession, career, and workplace.

Sharply graded national systems prioritize world-class universities as an enduring ideal type and escalate the obsession with international rankings among university leaders and national governments. This contrasts starkly with the view of higher education in Europe from the 1960s to the 1980s. Science has always been an elite enterprise, and scientists have always been highly stratified, but this reflected the pecking order within the academic profession rather than at institutional or national level. The current stratification in science is driven by the availability of disaggregated individual and institutional data and their novel national and international usage in academic hiring and promotion, national research funding distribution, and measurement of national competitiveness. This effect extends beyond national and institutional levels to individual disciplines and academics within individual institutions. Coupled with data-based national evaluation systems, bibliometrics-based peer review exerts an influence at all levels. As an important component of prestige maximization (described in Chapter 2), increasing access to research resources informs institutional, departmental, and individual strategies. 'Winner takes all' logics predominate, and judgments of excellence extend beyond institutions to individual academics, intensifying their experience of the tensions between teaching and research, economic and social values, and the global scientific (fundamental) and local/regional (applied) goals of research. Big-picture issues of institutional differentiation and mission and the changing character, volume, and structure of national research funding now translate into direct anxieties for individual academics at 'the eye of the storm.'

These issues are routinely analyzed at the macro- and meso-levels of university organization. However, the present research demonstrates that they have far-reaching implications for the academic profession as a whole and can be analyzed using micro-level data. The key issues include competition for research funding and, by implication, for fixed-term project-based employment. How do the ongoing changes in research funding regimes impact on different stakeholders, and especially on academics? Which newcomers are attracted to the profession, and who is lost to the profession in these changing conditions across Europe? What is the impact on the traditional trade-offs between lower academic remuneration and higher professional stability, or between more competitive corporate work and less competitive science work? What are the long-term professional prospects as traditional public service-type academic roles disappear?

In these increasingly stratified systems, both current and prospective academics must now make more considered decisions about where they plan to work in the future—decisions that have important long-term consequences in terms of access to research funding and future career prospects. More international publications in top academic journals increasingly lead to more competitive research funding, and university status increasingly determines academic life chances and how one's working time is distributed. In short, this zero-sum game means that one individual's access to research funding denies another, and a small difference in research output can change the course of one's academic life.

This ideology of excellence pervades European higher education. Its potency is grounded in new bibliometric data and the social stratification of science associated with the revival of traditional competition-based ideas among policymakers across Europe. After decades of comparing nations and institutions, systems of evaluation and assessment now extend to the individual academic. For research funding agencies and evaluation panels as well as university recruitment committees, the ready availability of individual-level data makes the workings of higher education and science systems more visible and more quantifiable in every respect.

In the data-obsessed academy, success in science means winning by the smallest of margins, as the top table is always crowded, rewarding only the few. In science, the logic of winner takes all requires academics to compete with other academics. The same is true at departmental and institutional levels, both nationally and or internationally, as funding depends increasingly on success in the 'quasi-markets' of peer performance evaluation.

Academic performance stratification

Chapter 1 explored academic performance stratification in terms of systematic inequalities in academic knowledge production. The evidence points to an inherent 'undemocracy' (Price 1963; Xie 2014) in relation to individual research performance; the distribution of research productivity is strongly skewed, with a long tail to the right indicating inequality. As a universal academic species across Europe, this tiny 10 percent minority accounts for roughly half of all peer-reviewed academic publications. Top performers produce 53.4 percent of peer-reviewed articles and books chapters, 45.6 percent of publications in

English, and 50.2 percent of internationally co-authored publications. Across the major academic clusters, the mean research productivity of these top performers is 8.56 times higher than that of other academics.

International comparative studies of higher education have not generally explored this unique class. To identify these top performing academics and the factors that increase their chances of entry to this echelon, we investigated whether they share the same patterns of working time distribution and academic role orientation, both of which are traditionally linked to research productivity. Our analysis identified several common features of top performers across the 11 countries studied. They tend to be male, middle-aged (mean age 47), and predominantly full professors. Top performers' research tends to be international in scope or orientation; they collaborate more often both nationally and internationally and publish abroad more often than other academics. They work longer total hours and longer research hours, and they are substantially more research-oriented, with a tendency to focus on basic and theoretical rather than applied research. They sit on national and international committees and boards and are more likely than their lower-performing colleagues to participate in peer review.

These top performers account for the greater part of knowledge production among European academics on three measures: total articles, peer-reviewed articles, and article equivalents (including peer-reviewed articles, book chapters, and authored and edited books). Across the 11 European systems, 45.9 percent of all academic research is produced by the top 10 percent of the most productive academics. In Austria, Finland, Poland, and Portugal, the figure may exceed 50 percent. When measured in terms of peer-reviewed articles, the figure is higher at 53.4 percent. Using the third measure, article equivalents, the figure drops to 37.8 percent. The exception is Poland, where top performers account for 50.1 percent of national research output. These different measures of productivity yield differing results; international differences also vary, depending on which communication channels are used and the extent to which various categories of publication are peer reviewed in a given system.

Working time distribution differs substantially between top performers and other academics. The differential in mean annualized weekly working time is 5.7 hours, ranging from 3.7 hours in Italy to 7.4 hours in Germany and 8 hours in Norway. For example, German top performers work an additional 42.6 days per year when compared with other research-oriented German academics. In Norway, top performers work an additional 46 days. In addition, and in contrast to the expected teaching-research productivity trade-off (Fox 1992; Katz 1973; Dillon and Marsh 1981), top research performers spend more time than their lower-performing colleagues on teaching, service, and administration.

Across all the systems studied, top performers are also more research-oriented than others. Bluntly put, identifying teaching as one's primary interest all but excludes one from the class of research top performers; in Ireland, for example, the maximum level of entry is 1.1 percent. Again, being interested in both but leaning toward teaching all but excludes one from the class of top research performers, with figures ranging from 3 to 8 percent in Finland, Ireland, Italy, the Netherlands, Norway, and the UK. In short, research role orientation is a powerful indicator of top performer status in European countries while teaching orientation virtually excludes one from this class.

Our research indicates a growing discrepancy between self-declared research orientation and actual research productivity. Among European academics, viewing oneself as research-oriented proved less statistically significant as a predictor of top performer status than previous research would suggest. The relative insignificance of institutional predictors provides further support for the 'sacred spark' theory of productivity (Cole and Cole 1973). Regardless of institutional administrative or financial setting, some faculty will always be more innately research-driven than others (Allison and Stewart 1974). To work long productive hours, top performers must have self-discipline and motivation (Sharon and Levin 1992).

These findings confirm that academic knowledge production in Europe hinges on top performers, who are highly homogeneous in terms of working pattern and role orientation. They are similar cross-nationally and differ substantially from other academics intra-nationally. The contribution of non-publishing and low-publishing authors and uncited publications to scientific progress is beyond the scope of this book, and the dependence of eminent scientists on less eminent colleagues (as posited by the Ortega hypothesis) is an interesting direction for future research (see Seglen 1992; Cole and Cole 1973). The belief that all scientists contribute as peers to the collective enterprise of extending knowledge 'serves to integrate the various strata of scientists and legitimates the efforts of rank and file scientists. It provides a degree of stability in a system which is highly competitive and grudging is major rewards to all but a very few' (Zuckerman 1970: 243).

More generally, the system of higher education stratification is stable and is perceived as fair and meritocratic. Scientists seem to accept as legitimate the criteria by which they are judged, and the legitimacy of the system is not in question; the egalitarian ideology that binds scientists together protects the stratified scientific community against polarization. The increasing competition for resources is seen to be informed by the legitimate and widely accepted principle that past success in combination with novel research ideas provide access to resources for research.

Academic salary stratification

A second form of stratification explored here was the relationship between research productivity and academic income. Our research on academic top earners calls into question several common assumptions from traditional studies, which are usually based on single-nation data rather than cross-national comparison. Chapter 2 adopted a cross-national perspective to investigate predictors for entry to the class of top earners, defined as those in the eightieth percentile of gross academic income—that is, the top 20 percent of academics in each of the five major academic clusters and in each country. Interestingly, our results do not support previous findings from single-nation studies, where research time was found to be positively correlated with high academic income, teaching time was negatively correlated with high academic income, and there was a strong correlation between research orientation, gender, and high income (Katz 1973; Dillon and Marsh 1981; Gomez-Mejia and Balkin 1992; Fairweather 1993; McLaughlin et al. 1979). Instead, our findings suggest that the link between higher time investment in research and higher academic income—consistently demonstrated for Anglo-Saxon countries over the last four decades—may be less strong across Continental Europe. While top earners in three European countries were found to work longer total hours, they also worked longer service and/or administrative hours in seven countries.

In terms of individual academic careers, top earners as defined here tend to spend more time on all academic activities *except* teaching and research; specifically, they spend more time on administration and service. The annualized total weekly working time differential between top earners and others ranges from 5.5 hours in Finland to 7.5 hours in Germany and 8.25 hours in Switzerland. For example, when compared with other German academics, top German earners work an additional 43.1 days each year. Of particular interest is the high productivity differential between top earners and other academics, especially in relation to peer-reviewed article equivalents, even though teaching time and research time are not statistically significant differentiating factors. In seven countries (Poland, Germany, Finland, Italy, Norway, Portugal, and the United Kingdom), top earners are 80 to 140 percent more productive than other research-oriented academics over 40 in the university sector. In the case of internationally co-authored article equivalents, the figures rise to 180.49 percent higher in Poland, 178.05 percent higher in the UK and 145.56 percent higher in Germany. In short, the top earners in the majority of these European countries are substantially more productive and publish more internationally co-authored research than other academics from the same (older) age cohort. Surprisingly, while they work longer administrative and service hours—rather than longer research hours and shorter teaching hours, as traditionally assumed in the productivity literature—they are substantially more academically productive.

One of our research questions asked whether high academic income is positively correlated with high research performance, even though it does not seem positively correlated with higher research time investment. We concluded that top earners are disproportionately represented among highly productive academics; for instance, in Germany, an average 43.1 percent of highly productive academics are also highly paid. Across Europe, an average 31.8 percent of national highly productive academics are among the national top earners, ranging from 80 percent in the United Kingdom to about 40 percent in Finland, Germany, and Portugal, and 30 percent in Norway (Poland being the only European exception). This is the first time the prototypical figure of the academic top earner has been identified in the higher education literature.

Academic power stratification

The third type of stratification studied here related to academic power; specifically, we examined the role of collegiality—the role of academic collegial bodies in university governance—in terms of the contrasting power of seniors (professors) and juniors (new entrants). In this regard, we tested the applicability of Olsen's (2007) models of the university as collegial ('rule governed community of scholars') or instrumental ('shifting political agendas'). Using Olsen's ideas to position different higher education systems across Europe in terms of selected variables, we found that the Polish, Swedish, Norwegian, and Dutch systems differ substantially from all other European systems on most items related to Olsen's collegial model, which applies least in Portugal Finland, and the United Kingdom.

Analyzing two aspects of university governance—government influence on academic decisions and academic entrepreneurialism—we assessed the applicability of Olsen's instrumental model using two composite indexes: the Index of Government Influence and the Index of Academic Entrepreneurialism. Poland ranks lowest by far on the former while Switzerland and Austria rank highest. On the latter, Poland and Italy rank lowest while the UK, Netherlands, and Germany rank highest. As compared with other European systems, the Index of Academic Entrepreneurialism is least applicable to the Polish system as perceived by Polish academics. Additionally, using a composite Index of Collegiality, we found collegial bodies such as faculty boards and committees to exert most influence on decision-making in Switzerland and Poland. As defined here and as perceived by academics, collegiality is also higher in the United Kingdom, Portugal, Italy, Ireland, and the Netherlands than in other countries.

As an important aspect of university governance and a recurring theme in studies of academic collegiality, we also explored the distribution of influence and authority across academic career stages. The research question was whether European collegiality is actually a 'collegiality of seniors' and, specifically, how the academic influence of 'professors' might contrast with that of 'new entrants' to the academic profession. In this regard, Chapters 3 and 5 reveal a powerful trend of cross-generation differentiation. Our results reveal a clear pattern of influence and authority across all 11 European countries studied, in that professors are much more influential at all three levels (department, faculty, and institution). In Germany, Austria, and the Netherlands, 70–75 percent of professors are very influential at department level, as compared with only 20–40 percent in all the other countries. While new entrants were reported to be 'very influential' at department level in the Netherlands (24 percent), the very high influence of professors at department level does not translate to faculty and institutional levels. The smallest share of least influential professors was reported in Germany,

Finland, and Portugal; the largest share of least influential new entrants was found in the United Kingdom, Austria, and Germany.

In general, then, there is a strong generational divide in the European academy, with a clear split between professors and new entrants. From this generational perspective, academic collegiality seems confined to a 'collegiality of seniors,' with very limited application to juniors. With few exceptions, this academic power stratification is less in evidence at department level and much more so at institutional level across the systems studied here.

International research stratification

Both institutions and individual academics are stratified by international research collaboration, which tends to be correlated with higher research productivity, as confirmed in Chapters 1 and 4. This form of stratification was examined in terms of 'internationalists' and 'locals' as two prototypical figures that emerged from our study. Across Europe, we found that some systems, institutions, academic clusters, and academics were more internationalized than others in terms of research. This was especially true of two relatively small systems: Ireland and the Netherlands, where more than four in every five academics are collaborating internationally. In Austria, Switzerland, and Finland, about three-quarters of academics collaborate internationally. The least internationalized systems are Poland and Germany (about 48 percent); the remaining European countries in our sample are moderately internationalized in research.

Our study confirms that international research contributes to the increasing stratification of the academic profession, as it is positively correlated with higher publishing and citation rates. European academics who do not collaborate internationally suffer increasing losses in terms of research resources and academic prestige. As research-based competition becomes a constant, local prestige and local publication in a regional language may no longer suffice. Increasingly, internationalists compete with locals for national and institutional prestige and for access to project-based research funding, and mechanisms that enable the rich to get richer while the poor get poorer continue to transform the academic profession. Although beyond the scope of this volume, it seems clear that academic performance stratification is linked to stratification of research resources, and both are linked to the stratification of international research and publishing. To begin, the international stratification of research was explored in terms of two major dimensions—international research collaboration and international research orientation—across countries, disciplines, and generations. Additionally, we examined the correlation between international research collaboration and individual research productivity and systematically compared research productivity and international publication co-authorship among internationalists and locals.

From a cross-generational perspective, the share of internationally collaborating academics was lower for the youngest academics in all 11 countries studied.

There was, however, a striking cross-national differential, as the share of internationally collaborating academics within this cohort ranged from 80 percent (in the Netherlands, Ireland, and the UK) to 40 percent (in Germany, Poland, and Portugal). The predictors for international research collaboration were explored by multivariate modeling. There were substantial cross-disciplinary variations, and being male significantly increased the odds of international research collaboration (by 69 percent). While academics in English-speaking countries were less likely to be internationalists, working in a smaller country substantially increased that likelihood.

We found that research productivity is strongly positively correlated with international research collaboration among European academics. In all academic clusters and in all 11 countries, average productivity was consistently higher for internationalists than for locals. International publication co-authorship is also strongly correlated with international research collaboration; for internationalists, the average rate of international co-authorship is between 4.5 and 7.5 times higher (depending on academic cluster) than for locals. Interestingly, academics who did not collaborate internationally reported no more than 7 percent of publications as internationally co-authored in 'hard' fields and no more than 3 percent in 'soft' fields. Given the more output-oriented incentive and reward systems in European science, it is increasingly important for individual academics to cooperate and co-publish internationally. Multiple-institution papers are more highly cited than single-institution papers, and international co-authors are more highly cited than domestic co-authors (Narin and Whitlow 1990).

We asked whether those who collaborate internationally tend to publish more; the answer was that they do. However, this stratification of the academic profession by international collaboration is not mirrored in domestic collaboration. Across all academic clusters, internationalists publish at least twice as many peer-reviewed articles as locals. However, clusters exhibit considerable differentiation in this regard; in some clusters, internationalists produced over 200 percent more articles during the reference period (222.35 percent in engineering). In the life and medical sciences, physical sciences, mathematics, and professions, the figure ranged between 120 percent and 130 percent. Researchers in the humanities and social sciences produced 106.17 percent more articles.

Academic role stratification

In exploring academic role stratification, we investigated patterns of teaching and research time distribution, teaching and research orientation, and research productivity across academic generations. Specifically, we compared young academics (defined in this book as those under 40) with their older colleagues. Chapter 5 explored intergenerational and cross-national patterns in the teaching–research divide. Young academics were systematically compared with older generations of academics to identify intra-national and cross-national differences. From the sample of 11 countries, the differences were most vivid in Finland, Switzerland,

and the United Kingdom on the one hand, and in Ireland, Poland, and Portugal on the other, and these two clusters were selected for in-depth analysis. With regard to teaching and research, the cross-generational contrast between the two clusters of countries is surprisingly stark in terms of how academics under 40 work (i.e., teaching and research working time distribution) and what they think about their work (i.e., teaching and research orientation).

The results show that in research-focused (Type 1) European systems, represented here by Finland, Switzerland, and the United Kingdom, young academics exhibit behaviors and attitudes that differ fundamentally from those of their older colleagues. In contrast, academics of all generations in teaching-focused (Type 2) European systems, represented here by Ireland, Poland, and Portugal, work and think in largely similar ways. The differences between the two types of higher education system are clear-cut; stratification by academic role (teaching/research) permeates national systems, but, more strikingly, it permeates academic generations within and across systems.

While research-focused Type 1 systems are populated by 'strong young research performers,' teaching-focused Type 2 systems are characterized by 'strong young teaching performers.' Type 1 systems are intergenerational 'research to teaching' systems, and Type 2 systems are intergenerational 'teaching to teaching' systems. Viewed as models (Lave and March 1993), the two types are quite distinct, but national systems within each cluster are strikingly similar with respect to working time distribution and academic role orientation.

In Type 1 systems, young academics exhibited a strong research orientation and allocated three to four times more time to research. For all age groups, decreasing research commitment was accompanied by substantial decline in time spent on research. In contrast, time allocation and academic orientation in Type 2 systems were stable across all academic age groups. Low research orientation among young academics in Type 2 systems was associated with medium to low research hours. For instance, while young academics in Switzerland spend an average 28.5 hours per week on research-related activities and those in Finland an average 26 hours, young academics in Poland and Portugal spend about half that time on research (15.1 and 14.1 hours, respectively). Young Swiss academics spend an average 7.1 hours per week on teaching-related activities, and their Finnish counterparts average 9.9 hours. In contrast, their Polish and Portuguese contemporaries spend about 20 hours on such activities. (Here, 'teaching' refers to teaching-related activities and 'research' indicates research-related activities). In Type 1 systems, there seems to be strong intergenerational division of labor; for academics in their 50s and 60s in Switzerland and Finland, average weekly research time drops dramatically to about 12 hours (8 hours in the UK). In contrast, both young and old academics in Type 2 systems exhibit consistently high teaching performance and stable medium or low research performance.

Our findings indicate that academic attitudes in European systems can be grouped in exactly the same way as academic behaviors. In the six selected countries, research orientation decreases with age: highest for the youngest cohort and lowest for the oldest. In both types of system, high or low research time investment among young academics reflects high or low research orientation. While hard-core research-oriented faculty (interested 'primarily in research') account for 35 percent to 50 percent of young academics in research-focused Type 1 systems, the figure is a modest 7 to 18 percent in teaching-focused Type 2 systems.

Interestingly, in both system types, there was no observed correlation between distribution of research time and research orientation—and productivity across age groups. Our findings indicate that research time and role orientation may matter less than age for research productivity (as shown by comparing the average productivity of academics under 40 with those aged 60 and over). In exploring cross-national and intra-national differences in research productivity by age group and academic cluster, we found no discernible intra-systemic patterns that would differentiate Type 1 and Type 2 systems in terms of research productivity.

Surprisingly, then, radical system differences in average working time distribution and average academic role orientation do not translate into discernible differences in productivity patterns across generations; older academics were consistently found to publish more than younger generations across all (hard) clusters of academic disciplines across all European systems studied. No clear system differences were observed, and, in both system types, research productivity was highest by far among academics in their 50s. In light of previous studies of research productivity, one unexpected finding was that strongly *decreasing* research time investment by academic cohort in Type 1 systems leads to strongly *increasing* research productivity by academic cohort. Academics under 40 were less productive than those in their 50s in all academic clusters and across all countries.

Our findings confirm that the academic profession is hugely stratified in terms of both age and academic role orientation, especially in research-focused Type 1 systems. There is a strong intergenerational divide between highly research-oriented academics under 40 and heavily teaching-involved/low research-oriented academics in their 50s. This intergenerational clash in academic attitudes and behaviors is somehow concealed by the intergenerational distribution of research productivity, which rises consistently with age in all hard academic clusters.

Academic age stratification

Uniquely, Chapter 6 drew on qualitative empirical material from eight European systems, analyzing 480 semi-structured in-depth interviews. The assumption was that the combination of quantitative and qualitative approaches would help to ensure less biased results. The focus on age stratification led us to study academic careers from the perspective of younger academics. The qualitative material shows that academic careers must progress systematically within clearly defined timeframes. Academic careers across Europe are sliced into comparable time periods, with comparable academic requirements—that is, specific measurable research outputs are expected at particular time periods and stages of an academic's career. Employment opportunities are closely linked to research funding; employment often depends on securing external funding, especially for younger academics. At doctoral and postdoctoral levels, an increasing number of positions are fixed-term and funded by research projects.

Aside from measurable research outputs, academic progression can be linked to academic patronage and academic mentors. While the pool of doctoral students grows across Europe, the number of available academic posts has not increased accordingly. Young academics report an increased sense of competition and increasing pressure to produce highly cited publications in prestigious peer-reviewed journals, as well as gaining international experience and securing external funding for research. Academics report undergoing regular evaluations, built increasingly on transparent, quantitative, measurable, and comparable criteria. Individual evaluation processes are continuous in nature, which has the advantage of making one's career more foreseeable, with clearly predefined procedures and outcomes. At the same time, the academic profession is becoming increasingly competitive at all levels of seniority, and more quantifiable indicators of academic progress facilitate better career planning, especially as requirements seem increasingly similar across academic disciplines and systems.

Tensions between younger and older academics differ from country to country but seem more pronounced in systems undergoing large-scale structural changes (as in Poland and Romania in the 2010s). Junior and senior academics in European universities seem worlds apart, as shown in the discussions of power stratification (Chapter 3) and role stratification (Chapter 5). The ongoing invisible intergenerational struggle causes young academics to think that more is required of them than of their older colleagues. At the same time, their understanding of professional instabilities makes them better prepared for a changing academic world in which permanent competition for prestige and research resources is the dominant feature.

Major career milestones in European universities were similar across all systems studied. These include entering and completing a doctoral program, finding a full- or part-time job, moving from junior to senior status, and, finally, remaining in the system in a senior position. These milestones tend to be accompanied by ongoing small steps that are continuously assessed by internal and external bodies, including national and international funding agencies. These successive milestones promote steady accumulation of research achievements and successful generation of external research funding. Our findings identify a paradox; while academic careers are now much less stable and secure, they are also far more predictable. The increasing number of assessment steps makes academic progression less secure for all but more predictable for some. At the core of academic success is internationally visible publication and fund-generating capability.

Policy implications

The multiple dimensions of social stratification in science have several policy implications. Inequalities in academic knowledge production have policy implications at three distinct levels: individual, institutional, and national. The implications differ for those pursuing research-oriented careers funded through competitive research and those interested predominantly in teaching, and for those in research-intensive and teaching-focused institutions. However, the policy implications of highly skewed research performance are especially important for young academics. In particular, it is essential for academics considering a publicly funded research-oriented career to know what to do (and what not to do) at the individual level. Our findings clearly indicate that the chances of success in research are not equal, and indeed that the world of science is utterly unequal. Of the three theories of academic productivity that proved useful in our analyses, the 'sacred spark' theory (Cole and Cole 1973) seems most relevant to high research productivity, and the 'utility-maximizing' theory (Stephan and Levin 1992; Kyvik 1990) seems least important, with the 'cumulative advantage' theory (Merton 1968) falling somewhere between.

To become a top research performer, an academic must invest higher than average amounts of time in research and, surprisingly, in all other academic activities, including teaching, service, and administration. At the individual level, there seems to be a permanent struggle between research time and non-research time, and between research orientation and teaching orientation. Entry to the class of top performers demands long research hours, long working hours, and high research orientation. Deciding what to do or not to do is predominantly an individual matter, but it is also partly institutional; a perfect environment is one in which institutional requirements align with individual expectations.

At institutional and national levels, academic performance stratification means that hiring policies must be carefully planned, with clear national strategies in relation to vertical stratification of the system and associated personnel needs. As national higher education and science systems may be more or less internally competitive and more or less vertically differentiated (Kwiek 2018b), top performers may work alongside low performers (in less internally competitive and less vertically differentiated systems) or in elite universities (in more internally competitive and more vertically differentiated systems). The Italian system is an example of the former type, and the UK system is representative of the latter, with other European systems located somewhere between the two.

In light of the sharp inequality in knowledge production, national higher education policies must be clear about how to proceed in the future. Is knowledge production to be concentrated in a small number of well publicly funded elite institutions, or is it to be maintained and publicly funded across the whole spectrum of institutions, from local and regionally relevant to elite and globally visible? While some European systems (such as Germany; Hüther and Krücken

2018) have traditionally been more equal, others have tended to be more strati-fied (as in the UK, Leišyte and Dee 2012).

Recent excellence-based funding initiatives across Europe point to increas-ing pressure for further concentration of research within systems. In practical terms, the concentration of research in selected institutions (by channeling more funding to them) may translate into concentration of top performers. The policy implications at national level are more important in systems in which research funding depends increasingly on individual research grants, as compared with systems in which research funding is institutionally based. In this regard, Poland can be contrasted with Italy (see Abramo et al. 2011a; Kwiek and Szadkowski 2018). The dilemma is whether to support high performing academics or highly ranked institutions. Beyond theoretical questions of equality versus excellence in publicly funded national systems or 'distributed' versus 'elite' science (Feller 2001), these are practical questions about how to distribute limited research funding fairly and effectively.

At institutional level, the policy implications of inequality in knowledge pro-duction are equally important. As academic science is sharply graded, and ine-qualities in individual productivity are all-pervading, institutions that seek to be research-intensive have three strategy options: try to keep their own top per-formers; try to attract new top performers from other institutions (nationally or internationally); or try to identify potential future top performers through tar-geted, open, and meritocratic hiring policies. Regardless of national and institu-tional policies, however, top performers tend to attract other top performers. At national and institutional levels, less productive research-oriented academics (in the bottom 50 percent) account for a mere 8.5 percent of all peer-reviewed pub-lications across European universities. That means there is significant untapped research and publication potential across all national systems and institutions. At the aggregated national level, the profile of the academic profession is influenced by every hiring decision made at a disaggregated institutional level. In short, individual hiring decisions based on new entrants' background and research po-tential shape national research and publication outputs for years to come.

Academic salary stratification across Europe has multiple policy implications. Perhaps most importantly, academic salaries relate increasingly to research out-put and the availability of competitive research funding. As the quasi-markets of competitive research funding are both national and international, the implica-tions extend to the individual academic. If administrative and service hours (as well as total working hours) are highly correlated with higher earnings, and if top earners are overrepresented among European high performers, then European academics with a taste for research must understand that much of their time will be spent on non-research activities. For individuals considering an academic ca-reer, the core distinction is between research and non-research activities; while research time has traditionally been highly valued, non-research time was tradi-tionally considered less valuable.

The policy implication is that European institutions offering more research time as a proportion of total working time will be more attractive to research-oriented academics than those offering less research time, especially given more or less similar academic salary levels (when adjusted to living costs) across major Western European countries. Systems that offer various forms of merit-based pay may be more attractive to research-oriented academics, and specifically to top performers, than systems that still utilize fixed-level, public service-type salaries. While academic prestige remains central to the academic enterprise, the influence of salary stratification on the academic profession cannot be disregarded. Massification of the academic profession foregrounds both the non-pecuniary advantages of academic work and its pecuniary disadvantages in determining the attractiveness of an academic career.

The policy implications of international research stratification are significant at individual, institutional, and systemic/national levels. At the individual level, the fierce competition for prestige and research resources hinges increasingly on internationalization. Across Europe, internationalists compete directly with locals in sharp contrast to the United States (see Goodwin and Nacht 1991; Finkelstein and Sethi 2014), and in the current policy climate, locals increasingly stand to lose out. As the rules governing academic prestige, incentives, and awards become increasingly homogeneous across the continent, individual evaluations based on prestigious international publications become ever more important for individual academic careers, as elaborated in Chapter 6.

At an aggregated European level, the differences between internationalists and locals are consistent across all clusters and can be summed up in a single statement: 'No international collaboration, no international co-authorship.' There is a powerful relationship between international research cooperation and international co-authorship of peer-reviewed articles. Our findings suggest that only a fraction of nationally isolated science publications (that is, those produced by locals) can be internationally co-authored, and internationally co-authored publications relate directly to collaborative activities with international colleagues. Consequently, national systems seeking to increase the international visibility of their knowledge production need to install international research at the center of national research policies, which requires substantial public investment.

The fundamental divide in science between 'haves' and 'have-nots,' which is another way of understanding the social stratification of science in this book, hinges increasingly on individual involvement in international research—international research collaboration, international research orientation, and international publishing (including international co-authorship). The process of international research stratification includes 'cumulative disadvantage' effects. This means that less productive academics may increasingly be rewarded only marginally or not at all for their research. In particular, the combination of local prestige and local publications that traditionally attracted national funding and employment may no longer suffice.

Across Europe, academic institutions competing nationally and internationally for public funding, high international rankings, and top scientists tend to use the same research-based metrics because their aggregated institutional success hinges on the disaggregated individual research successes of the academics they employ. Broad awareness of the role of international research-based university rankings means that scholarly publishing is more than an individual matter. Publishing (especially international publishing) and competitive research funding linked to publishing channels increasingly determine institutional and/or departmental funding. Employing high-publishing academics generates research funding; conversely, employing low publishing academics attracts little funding.

However, the modalities of international collaboration depend almost entirely on academics themselves. They decide whether and with whom to collaborate, and the decision to internationalize depends on individual choices based on reputation, resources, research interests, and the attractiveness of the potential partner. There is always a trade-off between the time and energy spent on international collaboration and the research and publishing outcomes. External international research collaboration has powerful internal implications, as those who successfully pursue international collaboration become more competitive both institutionally and nationally.

Attractiveness as an international collaboration partner is based on prior international research visibility and output. Academics with no internationally visible research are also invisible for the purposes of international collaboration. This effectively means that the number of potential partners for international collaboration is always limited, both institutionally and nationally. While the decision to collaborate internationally is always made by the individual academic, their institutions are embedded in national settings, and internationalization is funded predominantly from the public purse. For that reason, internationalization policies must reflect the interplay of costs and opportunities at all levels.

While the international academic community serves as the reference group for internationalists, locals publish predominantly for the national academic community. It follows that to be internationally visible, national systems must at least maintain the existing level of internationalists while seeking to internationalize more of their locals. Failure to pursue this goal means that internationalization will remain confined to science elites. Our findings confirm that individual academics are sharply graded by international collaboration; internationalists differ fundamentally in their academic attitudes and behaviors from locals, but both constitute homogeneous groups across European systems. The international visibility of national research hinges on prevailing patterns of collaboration (international, national, none at all) and of publication (international channels, national channels, none at all). These can be changed over time by means of careful policy measures that promote advantageous patterns while discouraging others.

Intergenerational differences in research attitudes and behaviors across European systems have multiple policy implications. First, basic patterns of time distribution at the individual level inform debate about the future attractiveness of the academic profession and workplace. Heavy teaching loads make research involvement and high research productivity more difficult and less probable, with a distinct divide between research-focused Type 1 and teaching-focused Type 2 systems, both in Europe and wherever this typology proves empirically applicable (most probably in Central and Eastern Europe).

Patterns of working time allocation are gender-sensitive; in both Type 1 and Type 2 systems, female academics (all age groups combined) spend more time on teaching than male academics. The starkest gender differential was found in the United Kingdom, where female academics spend 6.4 (58 percent) more weekly hours on teaching and almost 9 hours less (60 percent) on research. This gender differential is not linked to historical differences in employment patterns; in all six countries discussed in Chapter 5, female academics under 40 (that is, recently employed) spent more time on teaching and less time on research. In the UK, young female academics spend 8.1 (92 percent) more hours on teaching each week, and 9.2 fewer hours (a mere 52 percent) on research, all gender differences being statistically significant. An important policy issue is that the processes of cumulative disadvantage combined with the reward system's reinforcement of research mean that early lack of success reduces the likelihood of later scientific success, which is clearly linked to research time investment. The failure to be productive in one's early academic career inevitably leads to failure in later years, disadvantaging female academics as compared to males of the same age.

From an international perspective, future generational shifts are at stake. While overall national research orientation in Type 1 systems may still be growing (as research-focused young academics gradually become mid-career academics), succeeding generations in Type 2 systems should *not* be expected to change the low national research focus. Young academics reaching mid-career should not be expected to adopt a different role orientation as a result of socialization to academia. In Type 2 systems like Poland, Portugal, and Ireland, low research orientation is stable across all age groups, and no fundamental generational shift toward a research orientation can be expected any time soon. One important policy implication of our research is that to increase overall research orientation in such countries (as the only means of increasing national research output and average individual research productivity), natural generational succession will not suffice. Rather, policy measures must be redefined to address the selection, retention, and promotion of academics.

In teaching-focused Type 2 systems, including all new EU member states from Central and Eastern Europe, structural reform of higher education and science systems must focus more on new appointments, with particular attention to academic role orientation (Kwiek 2012). National academic recruitment and promotion policies are increasingly important in systems that are currently underperforming in research terms. In such systems, decisions about who is recruited and who is retained, based in particular on research attitudes and behaviors, may well define the upper limits of future national research output.

At an international level, it seems fundamentally difficult to promote competition between systems that encourage research-oriented attitudes and research-focused academic behaviors (Type 1) and teaching-focused systems with low research orientation (Type 2). Consequently, the intra-European gap in academic knowledge production may be growing ever wider. Reinforced by the replacement of older generations by younger academics, systems of 'young teaching performers' are unable to compete with systems of 'young research performers,' and national prestige and international ranking continues to fall.

Finally, a major policy implication of age stratification in science is the critical question of how to attract and retain top academic talent. As elsewhere in this volume, the attractiveness of an academic career emerges as a key concern for the future of the academic enterprise as a whole. In Chapter 6, interviews with hundreds of European academics confirm the academic profession's continuing attraction. However, given ongoing governance and funding changes across the continent, this appeal cannot be taken for granted. Policy interventions at national and institutional levels must be intergenerationally fair; changes that are perceived to affect the academic lives of juniors more than seniors risk making an academic career less attractive, and social processes that drive the brightest minds away may prove difficult to stop. Institutions cannot thrive without supportive discourses, both internal and external (Kwiek 2017c). External discourses should guarantee stability in relationships between universities and their environment, including public funding and public support; internal discourses should promote a general sense of being part of a socially valuable enterprise. Young professionals will not want to be associated with doomed institutions or declining industries, and the qualitative material in Chapter 6 emphasizes the importance of maintaining the appeal of an academic career for younger generations.

Future research

Toward a comprehensive approach

Two other important points are worth noting here. The first relates to the fundamental role of the survey instrument in understanding the ongoing changes in the academic profession as part of a comprehensive approach to such studies. The second issue concerns European academics' apparent lack of awareness of the wider socioeconomic, demographic, and political contexts in which are inevitably embedded.

The emergence of large-scale bibliometric studies challenges the status of survey-based higher education research in both scholarly and policy terms. In the ongoing contest between these two approaches, the survey appears to be losing. That contest extends well beyond what is more widely read and cited to what is valued in scholarly terms (prestige and status generation) and what is more publicly fundable (research resource generation). Both approaches have clear advantages and limitations. Bibliometrics addresses publication and citation numbers (Rousseau, Egghe, and Guns 2018), which are fundamental to the study of social stratification in science, academic career structures, and award and recognition systems. However, it is important to note that the use of bibliometrics to explore the sociology of academic careers depends almost exclusively on theoretical and analytical frameworks from traditional higher education research. In other words, the transfer of such frameworks has so far been from higher education research to bibliometrics rather than in the other direction. To the extent that bibliometric studies are always informed by theoretical issues, they must be grounded in theory of science (Hjørland 2016), and scholarly research contexts leading to further research are as important as policy contexts that lead to policy decisions (Moed 2005: 14).

One important limitation of bibliometric research on academic careers is the fundamental unit of analysis: the document (i.e., publications and citations). However sophisticated, bibliometric studies are structurally incapable of capturing the individual academic behaviors and attitudes traditionally studied in higher education research. Future studies of the academic profession (and, in particular, academic careers) might usefully combine bibliometric and survey-based tools, data, and methodologies to explore entire populations of academics by combining publication and citation bibliometric data with personal biographical data derived from national and international datasets harmonized with national registries. For instance, one might look at survey data on the behaviors, attitudes, and perceptions of all STEM academics within a national system, possibly accompanied by traditional semi-structured interviews to reduce any quantitative bias. This combination of approaches—bibliometric and survey-based, whole population and sample-based, quantitative and qualitative—seems likely to enhance our understanding of the changes and complexity of academic work and life at individual, institutional, and national levels. This comprehensive approach would require the harmonization of separate datasets and the integration of whole-population and sample-based research. Scholars are rewarded for creating new data but even more so for pursuing topics for which (apparently) no data exist (Borgman 2015: 11).

The comprehensive approach we propose here (already in use in Poland) affords new opportunities at a time when the utility of surveys in the social sciences is being called into question. Similar research has been conducted at national level in Italy (e.g., Abramo et al. 2011a; Abramo et al. 2013) and in Norway (Kyvik and Aksnes 2015; Rørstad and Aksnes 2015). However, these studies do not include all academics and all publications (in all national and international publication channels), nor do they use semi-structured interviews or large-scale surveys of the whole population of scientists. The unwillingness to use performance (and impact) data from large-scale international datasets (such as Web of Science or Scopus) represents a major limitation in research to date on the academic profession.

Existing studies have typically analyzed individual-level independent variables, ranging from age, duration of service, and academic position to more complex variables such as prevailing institutional academic norms, perceived level of academic collegiality, and institutional support for generation of external funding (Fox and Mohapatra 2007). As these variables do not generally emerge in bibliometric studies, the proposed comprehensive approach promises to link the two forms of research, with future benefits for both.

Socioeconomic, demographic, and political contexts

Finally, it is important to note that the future of the academic profession across Europe will ultimately be determined by the wider context in which higher education is embedded. This context has changed significantly in a number of ways.

First, higher education can no longer be regarded as the growth industry of decades ago, when accounts of the social stratification of science first emerged. The growth of academic employment in the long post-war period of expansion can no longer be taken for granted; as John Ziman has argued, since becoming a regular profession in the late nineteenth century, science has been 'a buoyant open-ended enterprise, where talented newcomers were welcome, and where they could look forward to opportunities for personal advancement right through their working lives' (Ziman 1994: 167). The growth of science was linked to the numerical expansion of European universities and available academic posts. The rules for entry and advancement tend to change in times of economic stagnation or contraction of higher education systems, when traditional rules do not apply (see Kwiek 2016b and 2017b).

Second, long-term changes in basic rationales for public funding of research may have had a powerful if delayed impact on academic career opportunities. In Europe, academic careers are linked to public universities and, by extension, to sustained public funding. As the traditional postwar social contract between governments and universities evolves, rationales for public funding of higher education have also changed (Bush 1945; Kwiek 2013b; Szadkowski 2016). Martin and Etzkowitz summarized the situation as follows: 'under the revised social contract there is a clear expectation that, in return for public funds, scientists and universities must address the needs of 'users' in the economy and society' (2000: 7).

Third, the rules of the academic career game increasingly differ across fields of academic research because 'the only arguments that now seem to carry any weight for the expansion of science are those that emphasize its promise of future wealth or other tangible benefits' (Ziman 1994: 85). A knowledge-driven economy means that some forms of university-produced knowledge become 'economically valuable codified knowledge' (Williams 2012: 34), making them much more relevant and more publicly fundable. Expansion in some areas of higher education and university knowledge production may be accompanied by contraction in other areas. The geography of enrolments and areas of study, and consequently the geography of available academic posts across Europe, has evolved systematically. In some countries, that evolution has been guided by new national strategies for higher education and innovation and new 'competitive' research funding regimes, with new science policies targeting specified fields of research (Geuna 1998). Future prospects are likely to differ substantially for academics in nationally defined priority areas (and possibly those defined by the European Union) as against those working in non-priority areas.

The knowledge-driven economy in which our universities operate also influences individual student choices, as wages relate increasingly to academic discipline. It remains unclear how the growing evidence that 'not all graduates are being eagerly sought by employers to contribute to a knowledge economy' (Williams 2012: 33) will impact on future differentiation of the academic profession by discipline. However, the impact of changing national science policies on research funding is already apparent and is commonly seen to threaten funding for arts and humanities, representing large segments of social sciences research. This applies both to research conducted by academics already working in higher education and to the work of new entrants on fixed-term contracts.

Finally, European academics and universities must now adapt constantly to a changing environment. While this effect varies across countries, it can be said to apply to some extent everywhere (de Boer et al. 2017). Changing social, economic, cultural, demographic, and legal settings increasingly impose a state of permanent adaptation on European higher education institutions, affecting both funding and modes of governance (Musselin and Teixeira 2014). However, university reform does not inevitably lead to reformed universities. In general terms, policymakers deploying New Public Management thinking tend to view universities (and other public institutions) as always 'incomplete' and therefore subject to never-ending reform (Brunsson 2009). In this ever-changing external environment, academics must constantly adapt to institutional change. To remain attractive to newcomers with a taste for research, European institutions must continue to promote traditional values, especially academic freedom and institutional autonomy; otherwise, potential academics may opt for industry research, which is less autonomous but better paid.

National policy ultimately determines academics' actual experiences on the ground in fulfilling teaching, research, and service missions. Across Europe, academics work in changing institutions characterized by mission and demand overload. Although often unable to describe these ongoing processes of change, they clearly feel the impacts on their work and life. Social demands on universities have increased significantly as policymakers simultaneously expect 'more education, more research, and more direct interaction with society and the economy' (Bonaccorsi, Daraio, and Geuna 2010: 2). Not surprisingly, then, 'demands on universities outrun their capacities to respond' (Clark 1998: 129). In practical terms, the increasing demands on universities are likely to contribute directly to the declining attractiveness of the academic profession.

The future of European universities hinges on their attractiveness as perceived by their internal constituencies—their 'software,' often neglected at the expense of their 'hardware' or infrastructure (Altbach 2009). Young scientists need to feel welcome on first entering the profession, and they need to be able to see and gladly accept the shape of their long-term personal and professional future. In this regard, the fun of solving scientific puzzles is as important for the academic profession as the prospect of a stable middle-class academic income and predictable career advancement.

Beyond confirming the value of higher education research at the micro-level of the individual academic, this book seeks to demonstrate the importance of the academic profession as the core of the academic enterprise embedded in institutions and national systems. However stratified it becomes in terms of performance, salary, authority, internationalization, academic role, and age, academics still matter and must believe that they can still contribute actively to change across European universities rather than drifting passively in its wake.

Statistical appendices

Table A.I The distribution of the sample population, by country

	All (Large N)	Full-time employed	Employed in the university sector	Full-time employed in the university sector (N)	Involved in both teaching and research	Full-time employed in the university sector involved in both teaching and research	In the selected cohort only*	Valid cases - with income data*	Top Earners (20%)	The Rest (80%)
Austria	1,492	977 65.5%	1,492 100%	977	1,412 94.6%	954 63.9%	459	266	57 22.2%	198 77.8%
Finland	1,374	1,116 81.2%	1,049 76.3%	837	1,193 86.8%	792 57.6%	370	301	60 23.9%	191 76.1%
Germany	1,215	851 70.0%	1,030 84.8%	708	1,098 90.4%	660 54.3%	287	233	53 24.6%	163 75.4%
Ireland	1,126	1,017 90.3%	825 73.3%	742	1,125 99.9%	742 65.9%	373	0	—	—
Italy	1,711	1,651 96.5%	1,711 100.0%	1,651	1,711 100.0%	1,651 96.5%	1,314	1,030	141 13.8%	883 86.2%
Netherlands	1,209	677 56.0%	416 34.4%	298	646 53.4%	266 22.0%	142	120	26 21.8%	93 78.2%
Norway	986	869 88.1%	905 91.8%	809	922 93.5%	766 77.7%	418	395	67 18.3%	300 81.7%
Poland	3,704	3,515 94.9%	1,726 46.6%	1,669	3,659 98.8%	1,643 44.4%	1,061	1,050	160 15.4%	876 84.6%
Portugal	1,513	1,236 81.7%	547 36.2%	468	1,174 77.6%	372 24.6%	164	135	22 18.4%	95 81.6%
Switzerland	1,414	827 58.5%	638 45.1%	372	1,245 88.0%	354 25.0%	147	104	29 28.2%	74 71.8%
United Kingdom	1,467	897 61.1%	438 29.9%	356	840 57.3%	266 18.1%	100	99	35 35.1%	64 64.9%
TOTAL	17,211	13,633 79.2%	10,777 62.6%	8,886	15,025 87.3%	8,466 49.2%	4,835	3,733**	649 18.1%	2,937 81.9%

Note: *Valid cases = those academics who provided income data; excluding observations with '0' salaries, excessively high, and excessively low salaries. Ireland—the income question was not asked. **Some respondents did not provide data on their academic discipline, and the class of top earners was produced using both national and disciplinary scales: hence the total of top earners and the rest is 3,586.

Table A.2 Research productivity (the number article equivalents produced in a 3-year reference period) and high academic income, statistical details. Results of t-tests for the equality of means, top earners (Top) vs. the rest of academics (Rest), in ten countries. Question D4/3: 'How many of the following scholarly contributions have you completed in the past three years?' combined with Question D5: 'Which percentage of your publications in the last three years were—peer-reviewed' (PRAE), 'were—published in a language different from the language of instruction at your current institution' (ENG-PRAE), and 'were—co-authored with colleagues located in other (foreign) countries' (IC-PRAE): 'Articles published in an academic book or journal,' 'Scholarly books you authored or co-authored' and 'Scholarly books you edited or co-edited'. Only full-time academics employed in universities and involved in both teaching and research

Country	Type of articles published	Mean number of articles (3 years)		T	p-value	Group with a significantly larger mean (Top earners or Rest)	% difference	Difference of means	95% confidence interval for the difference of means	
		Top earners	Rest						LB	UB
PL	PRAE	4.49	2.5	4.466	0.000	Top earners	79.60	1.99	1.117	2.868
	IC-PRA	2.3	0.82	4.989	0.000	Top earners	180.49	1.48	0.900	2.067
	ENG-PRAE	4.21	2.22	4.907	0.000	Top earners	89.64	1.99	1.192	2.782
DE	PRAE	11.85	6.1	2.855	0.005	Top earners	94.26	5.75	1.770	9.728
	IC-PRA	4.15	1.69	3.163	0.002	Top earners	145.56	2.46	0.922	3.989
	ENG-PRAE	11.22	5.8	2.758	0.007	Top earners	93.45	5.42	1.536	9.305
AT	PRAE	5.6	3.92	0.871	0.387	—	42.86	1.68	-2.172	5.529
	IC-PRA	2.7	2.17	0.484	0.630	—	24.42	0.53	-1.635	2.688
	ENG-PRAE	7.07	3.92	1.488	0.138	—	80.36	3.15	-1.020	7.302
FI	PRAE	8.73	4.83	2.419	0.017	Top earners	80.75	3.90	0.717	7.076
	IC-PRA	4.16	2.08	2.151	0.033	Top earners	100.00	2.08	0.172	3.985
	ENG-PRAE	9.34	5.1	2.638	0.009	Top earners	83.14	4.24	1.068	7.413
IT	PRAE	8.58	6.02	3.199	0.001	Top earners	42.52	2.56	0.989	4.129
	IC-PRA	2.55	2.01	1.182	0.239	—	26.87	0.54	-0.361	1.439
	ENG-PRAE	9.3	6.23	3.948	0.000	Top earners	49.28	3.07	1.544	4.599
NE	PRAE	8.99	10.91	-0.740	0.462	—	-17.60	-1.92	-7.106	3.271
	IC-PRA	4.69	4.12	0.319	0.751	—	13.83	0.57	-3.030	4.175
	ENG-PRAE	10.23	11.05	-0.297	0.767	—	-7.42	-0.82	-6.336	4.701
NO	PRAE	8.25	4.65	2.984	0.003	Top earners	77.42	3.60	1.224	5.964
	IC-PRA	3.14	1.74	2.202	0.028	Top earners	80.46	1.40	0.149	2.643
	ENG-PRAE	8.57	4.7	3.202	0.002	Top earners	82.34	3.87	1.489	6.241
PT	PRAE	10.55	4.81	2.268	0.026	Top earners	119.33	5.74	0.704	10.773
	IC-PRA	2.88	1.85	0.551	0.587	—	55.68	1.03	-2.824	4.884
	ENG-PRAE	8.71	3.57	2.253	0.027	Top earners	143.98	5.14	0.601	9.675
CH	PRAE	9.52	8.84	0.261	0.796	—	7.69	0.68	-4.615	5.983
	IC-PRA	4.64	4.25	0.200	0.843	—	9.18	0.39	-3.532	4.307
	ENG-PRAE	9.65	8.81	0.331	0.742	—	9.53	0.84	-4.243	5.910
UK	PRAE	11.3	4.63	3.326	0.001	Top earners	144.06	6.67	2.660	10.674
	IC-PRA	3.42	1.23	2.384	0.020	Top earners	178.05	2.19	0.354	4.026
	ENG-PRAE	0.36	0.2	0.742	0.462	—	80.00	0.16	-0.277	0.598

Table A.3 Summary: mean percentage of articles by academics published in an academic book or journal coauthored with colleagues located in other (foreign) countries, by international collaboration and cluster of academic disciplines (in percent). Based on separate analyses of 11 countries. Only academics full-time employed in the university sector and involved in both teaching and research (in percent)

Cluster of academic disciplines	International collaboration	European mean*	PL	DE	AT	FI	IE	IT	NL	NO	PT	CH	UK
Life sciences and medical sciences	Yes	34.67	42.77	30.83	43.12	39.06	24.61	29.05	46.62	38.61	27.99	35.52	20.94
	No	6.69	3.43	8.57	7.70	10.99	2.47	2.87	24.33	7.12	9.91	24.69	5.53
Physical sciences, mathematics	Yes	41.00	44.42	35.66	50.99	37.11	20.17	40.72	47.89	40.14	31.62	63.47	37.97
	No	6.16	11.38	4.38	12.86	1.02	8.18	4.61	5.29	1.39	16.07	31.43	7.07
Engineering	Yes	25.02	66.07	24.15	35.16	15.51	28.63	17.46	26.01	28.20	31.26	47.27	30.07
	No	6.57	3.12	5.62	13.33	7.06	4.05	3.49	4.95	4.42	24.83	-	0.00
Humanities and social sciences	Yes	14.20	13.55	7.29	13.28	14.04	24.38	11.04	21.05	14.82	13.32	11.64	8.43
	No	2.39	1.43	2.75	1.32	0.00	5.18	2.18	8.65	3.37	2.66	10.76	2.22
Professions	Yes	19.14	21.58	15.32	25.90	11.61	26.81	5.93	31.51	28.59	8.07	23.62	15.06
	No	2.54	3.16	2.52	1.32	3.84	3.01	1.41	4.87	1.96	1.95	13.22	2.56
Country mean	Yes	27.76	30.68	26.75	30.73	24.11	24.90	25.67	35.55	30.22	22.70	31.58	22.22
	No	4.76	3.04	5.82	5.75	5.04	4.02	2.84	9.20	4.09	10.46	20.88	3.50

Note: '-' results not statistically significant, p-value>0.05; * all countries combined.

Table A.4 How long do faculty spend on various academic activities (when classes are in session), by age groups. Only academics involved in both teaching and research and employed full-time in the university sector (in hrs per week)

		Finland	Switzerland	United Kingdom	Ireland	Poland	Portugal
Under 40	Teaching	10.5	7.1	11.1	17.7	19.8	20.9
	Research	25.3	28.4	24.1	15.9	15.1	14.4
	Service	1.4	2.9	0.9	1.5	2.8	1.0
	Administration	2.4	3.6	5.6	8.8	4.2	3.2
	Other	1.8	3.0	2.2	3.8	2.8	1.7
	TOTAL working hrs*	41.4	45.1	44.1	47.6	44.7	41.2
40s	Teaching	18.1	10.6	16.9	17.1	19.6	19.6
	Research	15.5	19.9	15.7	14.3	16.5	13.3
	Service	2.4	6.9	0.8	2.6	3.4	1.7
	Administration	6.4	7.5	10.6	10.8	4.3	5.9
	Other	2.9	4.4	3.5	4.1	3.2	2.5
	TOTAL working hrs*	45.3	49.3	47.5	48.9	46.9	42.9
50s	Teaching	21.4	13.3	19.1	17.7	18.0	19.3
	Research	12.5	15.5	12.5	13.9	16.4	12.6
	Service	3.3	9.9	1.8	3.3	3.0	1.8
	Administration	6.7	10.0	13.0	13.8	4.4	5.7
	Other	3.3	4.3	4.6	4.6	3.5	3.3
	TOTAL working hrs*	47.1	53.0	51.0	53.3	45.5	42.8
60s and above	Teaching	22.2	15.4	17.2	16.1	17.4	22.3
	Research	10.8	12.2	7.6	13.9	17.2	9.4
	Service	3.7	7.7	4.2	2.7	2.9	1.8
	Administration	7.8	13.4	12.7	11.3	4.5	7.3
	Other	2.5	4.0	6.1	5.6	3.1	0.9
	TOTAL working hrs*	46.9	52.7	47.7	49.6	45.2	41.8

Note: * Average total working hours is not a sum of means above.

Bibliography

Aarrevaara, T. (2010). Academic freedom in a changing academic world. *European Review*. 18(Suppl 1). 55–69.

Aarrevaara, T., Dobson I., and Wikström, J. (2015). Changing employment and working conditions. In: T. Fumasoli, G. Goastellec, and B. M. Kehm (Eds.), *Academic work and careers in Europe: Trends, challenges, perspectives*. Cham: Springer International Publishing, 95–116.

Abbot, A. (1981). Status and status strain in the professions. *American Journal of Sociology*. 86(4): 819–835.

Abbot, A. (1988). *The system of professions. An essay on the division of expert labor*. Chicago: the University of Chicago Press.

Abrahamson, M. (1965). Cosmopolitanism, dependence-identification, and geographical mobility. *Administrative Science Quarterly*. 10(1): 98–106.

Abramo, G., D'Angelo, C. A., and Caprasecca, A. (2009a). The contribution of star scientists to overall sex differences in research productivity. *Scientometrics*. 81(1): 137–156.

Abramo, G., D'Angelo, C. A., and Di Costa, F. (2009b). Research collaboration and productivity: Is there correlation? *Higher Education*. 57(2): 155–171.

Abramo, G., D'Angelo, C. A., and Solazzi, M. (2011a). Are researchers that collaborate more at the international level top performers? An investigation on the Italian university system. *Journal of Informetrics*. 5(1): 204–213.

Abramo, G., D'Angelo, C. A., and Solazzi, M. (2011b). The relationship between scientists' research performance and the degree of internationalization of their research. *Scientometrics*. 86(3): 629–643.

Abramo, G., D'Angelo, C. A., and Soldatenkova, A. (2017a). An investigation on the skewness patterns and fractal nature of research productivity distributions at field and discipline level. *Journal of Informetrics*. 11(1): 324–335.

Abramo, G., D'Angelo, C. A., and Soldatenkova, A. (2017b). How long do top scientists maintain their stardom? An analysis by region, gender and discipline: Evidence from Italy. *Scientometrics*. 110(2): 867–877.

Abramo, G., Cicero, T., and D'Angelo, C. A. (2013). The impact of unproductive and top researchers on overall university research performance. *Journal of Informetrics*. 7(1): 166–175.

Agarwal, R., and Ohyama, A. (2013). Industry or academia, basic or applied? Career choices and earnings trajectories of scientists. *Management Science*. 59(4): 950–970.

Agrawal, A., McHale, J., and Oettl, A. (2017). How stars matter: Recruiting and peer effects in evolutionary biology. *Research Policy*. 46(4): 853–867.

Aguinis, H., and O'Boyle, E. (2014). Star performers in twenty-first century organizations. *Personnel Psychology.* 67(2): 313–350.

Albarrán, P., Crespo, J. A., Ortuño, I., and Ruiz-Castillo, J. (2011). The skewness of science in 219 sub-fields and a number of aggregates. *Scientometrics.* 88(2): 385–397.

Allan, E. J. (2011). *Women's status in higher education: Equity matters.* San Francisco, CA: Jossey-Bass/Wiley.

Allison, P. D. (1980). Inequality and scientific productivity. *Social Studies of Science.* 10(2): 163–179.

Allison, P. D., and Stewart, J. A. (1974). Productivity differences among scientists: Evidence for accumulative advantage. *American Sociological Review.* 39(4): 596–606.

Allison, P. D., Long, J. S., and Krauze, T. K. (1982). Cumulative advantage and inequality in science. *American Sociological Review.* 47(5): 615–625.

Altbach, P. G. (Ed.). (2000). *The changing academic workplace: Comparative perspectives.* Chestnut Hill, MA: Boston College Center for International Higher Education.

Altbach, P. G. (Ed.). (2003). *The decline of the guru.* New York: Palgrave Macmillan.

Altbach, P. G. (2009). It's the faculty, stupid! The centrality of the academic profession. *International Higher Education.* 55(Spring): 15–17.

Altbach, P. G. (2015). Building an academic career. A twenty-first century challenge. In: M. Yudkevich, P. G. Altbach, and L. E. Rumbley (Eds.), *Young faculty in the twenty-first century. International perspectives,* Albany: SUNY, 5–20.

Altbach, P. G., and Lewis, L. S. (1996). The academic profession in international perspective. In: *The international academic profession. Portraits of fourteen countries.* Princeton: Carnegie, 3–48.

Altbach, P. G., Reisberg, L., and Rumbley, L. E. (2009). *Trends in global higher education: Tracking an academic revolution. A report prepared for the Unesco 2009 world conference on higher education.* Paris: UNESCO.

Altbach, P. G., Reisberg, L., Yudkevich, M., Androushchak, G., and Pacheco, I. F. (Eds.). (2012). *Paying the professoriate: A global comparison of compensation and contracts.* New York: Routledge.

Antonowicz, D. (2016). Digital players in an analogue world: Higher education in Poland in the post-massication era. In: B. Jongbloed and H. Vossensteyn (Eds.), *Access and expansion post-massification: Opportunities and barriers to further growth in higher education participation,* 63–81.

Arimoto, A., Cummings, W. K., Huang, F., and Shin, J. C. (Eds.). (2015). *The changing academic profession in Japan.* Dordrecht: Springer.

Armey, R. K. (1983). Comparing real income: The faculty and the administration. *Change: The Magazine of Higher Learning.* 15(3): 36–40.

Austin, I., and Jones, G. (2016). *Governance of higher education. Global perspectives, theories and practices.* New York and London: Routledge.

Baker, M. (2012). *Academic careers and the gender gap.* Vancouver: UBC Press.

Balkin, D. B., and Gomez-Mejia, L. R. (2002). Explaining the gender effects on faculty pay increases: Do the squeaky wheels get the grease? *Group & Organization Management.* 27(3): 352–373.

Balsmeier, B., and Pellens, M. (2016). How much does it cost to be a scientist? *The Journal of Technology Transfer.* 41(3): 469–505.

Barbezat, D. A., and Donihue, M. R. (1998). Do faculty salaries rise with job seniority? *Economics Letters.* 58(2): 239–244.

Barbezat, D. A., and Hughes, J. W. (2005). Salary structure effects and the gender pay gap in academia. *Research in Higher Education.* 46(6): 621–640.

Becher, T. (1987). The disciplinary shaping of the profession. In: Clark, B. R. (Ed.), *The Academic profession: National, disciplinary, and institutional settings*. Berkeley, CA: University of California Press, 271–303.

Becher, T., and Kogan, M. (1980). *Process and structure in higher education*. New York: Routledge.

Becher, T., and Trowler, P. (2001). *Academic tribes and territories: Intellectual enquiry and the culture of disciplines*. Philadelphia, PA: Open University Press, 2nd ed.

Becker, W. E., and Toutkoushian, R. K. (2003). Measuring gender bias in the salaries of tenured faculty members. *New Directions for Institutional Research*. 117: 5–20.

Bellas, M. L. (1993). Faculty salaries: Still a cost of being female? *Social Science Quarterly*. 74(1): 62–75.

Bentley, P. J. (2015). Cross-country differences in publishing productivity of academics in research universities. *Scientometrics*. 102(1): 865–883.

Bentley, P. J., and Kyvik, S. (2012). Academic work from a comparative perspective: A survey of faculty working time across 13 countries. *Higher Education*. 63(4): 529–547.

Bentley, P. J., and Kyvik, S. (2013). Individual differences in faculty research time allocations across 13 countries. *Research in Higher Education*. 54(3): 329–348.

Bentley, P. J., Coates, H., Dobson, I. R., Goedegebuure, L., and Meek, V. L. (2013). *Job satisfaction around the academic world*. Dordrecht: Springer.

Białecki, I., and Dąbrowa-Szefler, M. (2009). Polish higher education in transition. Between policy making and autonomy. In: Palfreyman, D. and T. Tapper (Eds.), *Structuring mass higher education: The role of elite institutions*. New York: Routledge, 183–197.

Birnbaum, R. (1988). *How colleges work: The cybernetics of academic organization and leadership*. San Francisco, CA: Jossey-Bass.

Blackburn, R. T., and Lawrence, J. H. (1995). *Faculty at work: Motivation, expectation, satisfaction*. Baltimore, MD: Johns Hopkins University Press.

Blackmore, P. (2016). *Prestige in academic life: Excellence and exclusion*. London; New York: Routledge.

Blau, P. M. (1994). *The organization of academic work*. New Brunswick, NJ: Transaction Publishers, 2nd ed.

Bleiklie, I., Enders, J., and Lepori, B. (Eds.) (2017). *Managing universities. Policy and organizational change from a Western European comparative perspective*. New York: Palgrave.

Bonaccorsi, A., and Daraio, C. (2003). Age effects in scientific productivity. *Scientometrics*. 58(1): 49–90.

Bonaccorsi, A., Daraio, C., and Geuna, A. (2010). Universities in the new knowledge landscape: Tensions, challenges, change—an introduction. *Minerva*. 48(1): 1–4.

Borgman, C. L. (2015). *Big data, little data, no data. Scholarship in the networked world*. Cambridge, MA: The MIT Press.

Bornmann, L., and Marx, W. (2012). The Anna Karenina Principle: A way of thinking about success in science. *Journal of the American Society for Information Science and Technology*. 63(10), 2037–2051.

Bornmann, L., Bauer, J., and Schlagberger, E.M. (2017). Characteristics of highly cited researchers 2015 in Germany. *Scientometrics*. 111(1), 543–545.

Bottero, W. (2005). *Stratification: Social division and inequality*. London and New York: Routledge.

Bowen, H. R., and Schuster, J. H. (1986). *American professors: A national resource imperiled*. New York: Oxford University Press.

Boyer, E. L., Altbach, P. G., and Whitelaw, M. J. (1994). *The academic profession. An international perspective*. Princeton, NJ: The Carnegie Foundation.

Bozeman, B., and Boardman, C. (2014). *Research collaboration and team science*. Cham: Springer International Publishing.

Brady, H. E., and Collier, D. (Eds.). (2004). *Rethinking social inquiry: Diverse tools, shared standards*. Lanham, MD: Rowman & Littlefield.

Brechelmacher, A., Park, E., Ates, G., and Campbell, D. F. J. (2015). The rocky road to tenure—career paths in academia. In: Fumasoli, T., G. Goastellec, and B. M. Kehm (Eds.), *Academic work and careers in Europe: Trends, challenges, perspectives*. Cham: Springer International Publishing, 13–40.

Brennan, J., Naidoo, R., and Franco, M. (2017). From academic profession to higher education workforce: Academic careers in the UK. In: *Challenges and options: The academic profession in Europe*. Cham: Springer. 231–252.

Brew, A., and Boud, D. (2009). Understanding academics' engagement with research. In: Brew, A. and D. Boud (Eds.), *Academic research and researchers*. Maidenhead: Open University Press and Society for Research into Higher Education, 189–203.

Brew, A., and Lucas, L. (2009). *Academic research and researchers*. Maidenhead; Blacklick: McGraw-Hill.

Brewer, D. J., Gates, S. M., and Goldman, C. A. (2002). *In pursuit of prestige: strategy and competition in US higher education*. New Brunswick, NJ: Transaction Publishers.

Brunsson, N. (2009). *Reform as routine: Organizational change and stability in the modern world*. Oxford; New York: Oxford University Press.

Brunsson, N., and Olsen, J. P. (1998). Organizational theory: Thirty years of dismantling, and then...? In: J. P. Olsen and N. Brunsson (Eds.), *Organizing organizations*. Bergen-Sandviken: Fagbokförlaget.

Bryman, A. (2012). *Social research methods*. Oxford; New York: Oxford University Press, 4th ed.

Bush, V. (1945). *Science, the endless frontier; A report to the President on a program for postwar scientific research*. Washington: United States Government Printing Office.

Cantwell, B. (2011). Academic in-sourcing: International postdoctoral employment and new modes of academic production. *Journal of Higher Education Policy and Management*. 33(2): 101–114.

Cantwell, B. (2016). The new prudent man: Financial-academic capitalism and inequality in higher education. In S. Slaughter and B. J. Taylor (Eds.), *Higher education, stratification, and workforce development*. Dordrecht: Springer, 173–192.

Cantwell, B., and Kauppinen, I. (Eds.) (2014). *Academic capitalism in the age of globalization*. Baltimore, MD: Johns Hopkins University Press.

Cantwell, B., Marginson, S., and Smolentseva, A. (Eds.). (2018). *High participation systems of higher education*. Oxford: Oxford University Press.

Cantwell, B., Pinheiro, R., and Kwiek, M. (2018). Governance. In: B. Cantwell, S. Marginson, and A. Smolentseva (Eds.), *High participation systems of higher education*. Oxford: Oxford University Press, 1–26.

Caplow, T., and McGee, R. J. (1958). *The academic marketplace*. New York: Basic Books.

Caracelli, V. J., and Greene, J. C. (1993). Data analysis strategies for mixed-method evaluation designs. *Educational Evaluation and Policy Analysis*. 15(2): 195–207.

Carrasco, R., and Ruiz-Castillo, J. (2014). The evolution of the scientific productivity of highly productive economists. *Economic Inquiry*. 52(1): 1–16.

Carvalho, T. (2017). The study of the academic profession—contributions from and to the sociology of professions. In: J. Huisman and M. Tight (Eds.), *Theory and method in higher education research*. Bingley, UK: Emerald Group Publishing, 59–76.

Carvalho, T., and Santiago, R. (Eds.). (2015). *Professionalism, managerialism and reform in higher education and the health service*. New York: Palgrave.

Cavalli, A. and Moscati, R. (2010). Academic systems and professional conditions in five European countries. *European Review*. 18(S1): S35–S53.

Centra, J. A. (1983). Research productivity and teaching effectiveness. *Research in Higher Education*. 18(4): 379–389.

Clark, B. R. (1983). *The higher education system. Academic organization in cross-national perspective*. Berkeley, CA: University of California Press.

Clark, B. R. (1987a). *The academic life. Small worlds, different worlds*. Princeton, NJ: The Carnegie Foundation for the Advancement of Teaching.

Clark, B. R. (Ed.) (1987b). *The academic profession. National, disciplinary & institutional settings*. Berkeley, CA: University of California Press.

Clark, B. R. (1995). *Places of inquiry. Research and advanced education in modern universities*. Berkeley, CA: University of California Press.

Clark, B. R. (1998). *Creating entrepreneurial universities. Organizational pathways of transformation*. New York: Pergamon Press.

Cohen, L., Manion, L., and Morrison, K. (2011). *Research methods in education*. London; New York: Routledge.

Cole, J. R. (1979). *Fair science. Women in the scientific community*. New York: Columbia University Press.

Cole, J. R., and Cole, S. (1973). *Social stratification in science*. Chicago, IL: University of Chicago Press.

Cole, J. R., and Zuckerman, H. (1984). The productivity puzzle: Persistence and changes in patterns of publication of men and women scientists. *Advances in Motivation and Achievements*. 2: 217–258.

Cole, S., and Cole, J. R. (1967). Scientific output and recognition: A study in the operation of the reward system in science. *American Sociological Review*. 32(3): 377–390.

Copes, H., Khey, D. N., and Tewksbury, R. (2012). Criminology and criminal justice hit parade: Measuring academic productivity in the discipline. *Journal of Criminal Justice Education*. 23(4): 423–440.

Cortés, L. M., Mora-Valencia, A., and Perote, J. (2016). The productivity of top researchers: A semi-nonparametric approach. *Scientometrics*. 109(2): 891–915.

Crane, D. (1965). Scientists at major and minor universities: A study of productivity and recognition. *American Sociological Review*. 30(5): 699–714.

Creswell, J. W., and Plano Clark, V. L. (2011). *Designing and conducting mixed methods research*. Los Angeles, CA: SAGE Publications, 2nd ed.

Cummings, J. N., and Kiesler, S. (2007). Coordination costs and project outcomes in multi-university collaborations. *Research Policy*. 36(10): 1620–1634.

Cummings, W., and Bain, O. (2016). Academic advancement and gender: A comparative analysis. In J. F. Galaz-Fontes, A. Arimoto, U. Teichler, and J. Brennan (Eds.), *Biographies and careers throughout academic life*. Dordrecht: Springer, 297–315.

Cummings, W. K., and Finkelstein, M. J. (2012). *Scholars in the changing American academy*. Dordrecht: Springer.

Cummings, W. K., and Teichler, U. (Eds.). (2015). *The relevance of academic work in comparative perspective*. Dordrecht: Springer.

De Boer, H., Enders, J., and Schimank, U. (2007). On the way towards new public management? The governance of university systems in England, the Netherlands, Austria, and Germany. In: D. Jansen (Ed.), *New forms of governance in research organizations.* Dordrecht: Springer Netherlands, 137–152.

De Boer, H., File, J., Huisman, J., Seeber, M., Vukasovic, M., and Westerheijden, D. F. (Eds.). (2017). *Policy analysis of structural reforms in higher education. porcesses and outcomes.* Cham: Palgrave.

De Weert, E. (2009). The organised contradictions of teaching and research: Reshaping the academic profession. In: J. Enders and E. de Weert (Eds.), *The changing face of academic life. analytical and comparative perspectives.* New York: Palgrave, 134–154.

Deardorff, D. K., Wit, H. de, Heyl, J., and Adams, T. (Eds.). (2012). *The SAGE handbook of international higher education.* Thousand Oaks, CA: SAGE Publications.

Dillon, K. E., and Marsh, H. W. (1981). Faculty earnings compared with those of nonacademic professionals. *The Journal of Higher Education.* 52(6): 615.

DiPrete, T. A., and Eirich, G. M. (2006). Cumulative advantage as a mechanism for inequality: A review of theoretical and empirical developments. *Annual Review of Sociology.* 32(1): 271–297.

Dobbins, M. (2011). *Higher education policies in Central and Eastern Europe.* London: Palgrave Macmillan UK.

Dobbins, M. (2015). Exploring the governance of Polish public higher education: Balancing restored historical legacies with Europeanization and market pressures. *European Journal of Higher Education.* 5(1): 18–33.

Dobbins, M., and Knill, C. (2009). Higher education policies in central and Eastern Europe: Convergence toward a common model? *Governance.* 22(3): 397–430.

Dobbins, M., and Knill, C. (2014). *Higher education governance and policy change in Western Europe. international challenges to historical institutions.* New York: Palgrave Macmillan.

Docquier, F., and Rapoport, H. (2012). Globalization, brain drain and development. *Journal of Economic Literature.* 50(3): 681–730.

Drennan, J., Clarke, M., Hyde, A., and Politis, Y. (2013). The research function of the academic profession in Europe. In: U. Teichler and E. A. Höhle (Eds.), *The work situation of the academic profession in Europe: Findings of a survey in twelve countries.* Dordrecht: Springer Netherlands, 109–136.

Dressel, P. P., and Mayhew, L. B. (1974). *Higher education as a field of study. The emergence of a profession.* San Francisco, CA: Jossey-Bass.

Enders, J. (Ed.). (2000). *Employment and working conditions of academic staff in Europe.* Frankfurt: GEW.

Enders, J. (2006). The academic profession. In: J. J. F. Forest and P. G. Altbach (Eds.), *International handbook of higher education.* Dordrecht: Springer Netherlands. 18: 5–21.

Enders, J., and Musselin, C. (2008). Back to the future? The academic professions in the 21st century. In: OECD, *Higher Education to 2030. Volume 1: Demography.* Paris: OECD. 125–150.

Enders, J., and Teichler, U. (1997). A victim of their own success? Employment and working conditions of academic staff in comparative perspective. *Higher Education.* 34(3): 347–372.

Enders, J., and de Weert, E. (Eds.). (2004). *The international attractiveness of the academic workplace in Europe.* Frankfurt am Main.

Enders, J., and De Weert, E. (2009a). *The changing face of academic life: Analytical and comparative perspectives.* New York: Palgrave Macmillan.

Enders, J., and De Weert, E. (2009b). Towards a T-shaped profession: Academic work and career in the knowledge society. In: J. Enders and E. de Weert (Eds.), *The changing face of academic life: Analytical and comparative perspectives.* London: Palgrave Macmillan, 251–272.

Enders, J., Boer, H. F. de, and Leišyte, L. (2009). New public management and the academic profession: The rationalisation of academic work revisited. In: J. Enders and E. de Weert (Eds.), *The changing face of academic life: Analytical and comparative perspectives.* London: Palgrave Macmillan, 36–57.

Enders, J., Boer, H. F. de, and Westerheijden, D. F. (Eds.). (2011). *Reform of higher education in Europe.* Rotterdam: Sense.

Fairweather, J. S. (1993). Faculty reward structures: Toward institutional and professional homogenization. *Research in Higher Education.* 34(5): 603–623.

Fairweather, J. S. (1995). Myths and realities of academic labor markets. *Economics of Education Review.* 14(2): 179–192.

Fairweather, J. S. (2005). Beyond the rhetoric: Trends in the relative value of teaching and research in faculty salaries. *The Journal of Higher Education.* 76(4): 401–422.

Feller, I. (2011). Elite and/or distributed science: An analytical and empirical guide to public policy on the distribution of federal academic R&D Funds. In M. P. Feldman and A. N. Link (Eds.), *Innovation policy in the knowledge-based economy.* Dordrecht: Springer. 189–209.

Ferber, M. A. (1974). Professors, performance, and rewards. *Industrial Relations.* 13(1): 69–77.

Finkelstein, M. J. (1984). *The American academic profession. A synthesis of social scientific inquiry since World War II.* Columbus, OH: Ohio State University Press.

Finkelstein, M. J. (1988). *The American academic profession: A synthesis of social scientific inquiry since World War II.* Columbus; London: Ohio State University Press.

Finkelstein, M. J. (2006). The study of academic careers: Looking back, looking forward. In: J. C. Smart (Ed.), *Higher education: Handbook of theory and research.* Dordrecht: Springer Netherlands, 159–212.

Finkelstein, M. (2010). The balance between teaching and research in the work life of American academics. In: J. C. Shin, A. Arimoto, W. K. Cummings, and U. Teichler (Eds.), *Teaching and research in contemporary higher education.* Dordrecht: Springer Netherlands, 299–318.

Finkelstein, M., and Sethi, W. (2014). Patterns of faculty internationalization: A predictive model. In: F. Huang, M. Finkelstein, and M. Rostan (Eds.), *The internationalization of the academy.* Dordrecht: Springer, 237–257.

Finkelstein, M. J., Conley, V. M., and Schuster, J. H. (2016). *The faculty factor. Reassessing the Amercian academy in a turbulent era.* Baltimore, MD: Johns Hopkins University Press.

Finkelstein, M. J., Seal, R. K., and Schuster, J. H. (1998). *The new academic generation: A profession in transformation.* Baltimore, MD: Johns Hopkins University Press.

Finkelstein, M. J., Walker, E., and Chen, R. (2013). The American faculty in an age of globalization: Predictors of internationalization of research content and professional networks. *Higher Education.* 66(3): 325–340.

Finkenstaedt, T. (2011). Teachers. In: W. Rüegg (Ed.), *A history of the university in Europe. Vol. IV: Universities since 1945.* Cambridge: Cambridge University Press, 162–206.

Fisher, R. L. (2005). *The research productivity of scientists: How gender, organization culture, and the problem choice process influence the productivity of scientists*. Dallas, TX: University Press of America.

Fitzgerald, T. (2013). *Women leaders in higher education: Shattering the myths*. Abingdon; New York: Routledge.

Flanigan, A. E., Kiewra, K. A., and Luo, L. (2018). Conversations with four highly productive german educational psychologists: Frank Fischer, Hans Gruber, Heinz Mandl, and Alexander Renkl. *Educational Psychology Review*. 30(1): 303–330.

Forest, J. J. F. (2002). *I prefer to teach. An international comparison of faculty preference for teaching over research*. New York: RoutledgeFalmer.

Fox, M. F. (1983). Publication productivity among scientists: A critical review. *Social Studies of Science*. 13(2): 285–305.

Fox, M. F. (1985). Location, sex-typing, and salary among academics. *Work and Occupations*. 12(2): 186–205.

Fox, M. F. (1992). Research, teaching, and publication productivity: Mutuality versus competition in academia. *Sociology of Education*. 65(4): 293–305.

Fox, M. F. (2015). Gender and clarity of evaluation among academic scientists in research universities. *Science, Technology, & Human Values*. 40(4): 487–515.

Fox, M. F., and Mohapatra, S. (2007). Social-organizational characteristics of work and publication productivity among academic scientists in doctoral-granting departments. *The Journal of Higher Education*. 78(5): 542–571.

Frank, R. H., Cook, P. J. (1996). *The winner-take-all society: why the few at the top get so much more than the rest of us*. New York: Penguin Books.

Fumasoli, T., and Goastellec, G. (2015). Global models, disciplinary and local patterns in academic recruitment processes. In: T. Fumasoli, G. Goastellec, and B. M. Kehm (Eds.), *Academic work and careers in Europe: Trends, challenges, perspectives*. Cham: Springer International Publishing, 69–94.

Fumasoli, T. and Stensaker, B. (2013). Organizational studies in higher education: A reflection on historial themes and prospective trends. *Higher Education Policy*. 26: 479–496.

Fumasoli, T., Goastellec, G., and Kehm, B. M. (Eds.). (2015). *Academic work and careers in Europe: Trends, challenges, perspectives*. Cham: Springer.

Galaz-Fontes, J. F, Arimoto, A., Teichler, U., and Brennan, J. (Eds.). (2016), *Biographies and careers throughout academic life*. Dordrecht: Springer.

Gaston, J. (1978). *The reward system in British and American science*. New York: Wiley.

Geiger, R. L., and Sá, C. M. (2008). *Tapping the riches of science: Universities and the promise of economic growth*. Cambridge, MA: Harvard University Press.

Georghiou, L. (1998). Global cooperation in research. *Research Policy*. 27(6): 611–626.

Geuna, A. (1998). The internationalisation of European universities: A return to medieval roots. *Minerva*. 6(3): 253–270.

Glaser, B. G. (1963). The local-cosmopolitan scientist. *American Journal of Sociology*. 69(3): 249–259.

Glaser, B. G (1964). Comparative failure in science. *Science*. 143(3610): 1012–1012.

Gläser, J., and Laudel, G. (2016). Governing science. How science policy shapes research content. *European Journal of Sociology*. 57(1): 117–168.

Gläser, J., and Serrano Velarde, K. (2018). Changing funding arrangements and the production of scientific knowledge: Introduction to the Special Issue. *Minerva*. Published on-line 29 January 2018.

Goastellec, G., and Pekari, N. (2013). Gender differences and inequalities in academia: Findings in Europe. In: U. Teichler and E. A. Höhle (Eds.), *The work situation of the academic profession in Europe: findings of a survey in twelve countries.* Dordrecht: Springer Netherlands, 55–78.

Goastellec, G., Park, E., Ates, G., and Toffel, K. (2013). Academic markets, academic careers: Where do we stand? In: B. M. Kehm, and U. Teichler (Eds.), *The academic profession in Europe: New tasks and new challenges.* Dordrecht: Springer, 93–119.

Godin, B., and Gingras, Y. (2000). Impact of collaborative research on academic science. *Science and Public Policy.* 27(1): 65–73.

Gomez-Mejia, L. R., and Balkin, D. B. (1992). Determinants of faculty pay: An agency theory perspective. *Academy of Management Journal.* 35(5): 921–955.

Goode, W. J. (1978). *The celebration of heroes. Prestige as a control system.* Berkeley, CA: University of California Press.

Goodman, P. (1962). *The community of scholars.* New York: Random House.

Goodwin, J. (Ed.). (2012). *SAGE secondary data analysis.* Los Angeles, CA: SAGE.

Goodwin, C. D., and Nacht, M. (1991). *Missing the boat. The failure to internationalize American higher education.* Cambridge: Cambridge University Press.

Gornitzka, Å., and Langfeldt, L. (Eds.). (2008). *Borderless knowledge.* Dordrecht: Springer Netherlands.

Gottlieb, E. E., and Keith, B. (1997). The academic research-teaching nexus in eight advanced-industrialized countries. *Higher Education.* 34(3): 397–419.

Gouldner, A. W. (1957). Cosmopolitans and locals: Toward an analysis of latent social roles. I. *Administrative Science Quarterly.* 2(3): 281.

Greene, J. C. (2007). *Mixed methods in social inquiry.* San Francisco, CA: Jossey-Bass.

Grimes, A. J. (1980). Cosmopolitian-local: A multidimensional construct. *Research in Higher Education.* 13(3): 195–211.

Groves, R. M. (2006). Nonresponse rates and nonresponse bias in household surveys. *The Public Opinion Quarterly.* 70(5): 646–675.

Gulbrandsen, M., and Smeby, J.-C. (2005). Industry funding and university professors' research performance. *Research Policy.* 34(6): 932–950.

Gustavo, M. (2012). E-mail surveys. In: Gideon, L. (Ed.), *Handbook of survey methodology for the social sciences.* New York: Springer, 313–325.

Hagstrom, W. O. (1965). *The scientific community.* New York: Basic Books.

Hagstrom, W. O. (1974). Competition in science. *American Sociological Review.* 39(1): 1.

Hamermesh, D. S., Johnson, G. E., and Weisbrod, B. A. (1982). Scholarship, citations and salaries: Economic rewards in economics. *Southern Economic Journal.* 49(2): 472.

Hansen, W. L. (1992). Salaries and salary determination. In: B. R. Clark and G. Neave (Eds.), *The encyclopedia of higher education. Vol. 2. Analytical perpsectives.* Oxford: Pergamon Press, 1476–1483.

Harman, K. M. (1989). Professional loyalties of university academics: Four ideal types. *The Australian Educational Researcher.* 16(2): 1–11.

Hattie, J., and Marsh, H. W. (1996). The relationship between research and teaching: A meta-analysis. *Review of Educational Research.* 66(4): 507.

Hermanowicz, J. C. (2006). What does it take to be successful? *Science, Technology, & Human Values.* 31(2) 135–152.

Hermanowicz, J. C. (2009). *Lives in science. How institutions affect academic careers.* Chicago, IL: University of Chicago Press.

Hermanowicz, J. (2012). The sociology of academic careers: Problems and prospects. In: J. C. Smart and M. B. Paulsen (Eds.), *Higher education: Handbook of theory and research volume 27*. New York: Springer, 207–248.

Hibberts, M., Burke Johnson, R., and Hudson, K. (2012). Common survey sampling techniques. In: L. Gideon (Ed.), *Handbook of survey methodology for the social sciences*. New York: Springer, 53–74.

Hjørland, B. (2016). Informetrics needs a foundation in the theory of science. In: C.R. Sugimoto (Ed.), *Theories of informetrics and scholarly communication*. Berlin: de Gruyter, 20–47.

Hoekman, J., Frenken, K., and Tijssen, R. J. W. (2010). Research collaboration at a distance: Changing spatial patterns of scientific collaboration within Europe. *Research Policy*. 39(5): 662–673.

Hoffman, D. M., and Horta, H. (2016). The CINHEKS research design: Taking stock and moving forward. In: D. M. Hoffman and J. Välimaa (Eds.), *Re-becoming universities? Higher education institutions in networked knowledge societies*. Dordrecht: Springer, 41–74.

Höhle, E. A. and Teichler, U. (2013). The European academic profession or academic professions in Europe? In: U. Teichler and E. A. Höhle (Eds.), *The work situation of the academic profession in Europe: Findings of a survey in twelve countries*. Dordrecht: Springer: 249–272.

Horta, H. (2009a). Global and national prominent universities: Internationalization, competitiveness and the role of the State. *Higher Education*. 58: 387–405.

Horta, H. (2009b). Holding a post-doctoral position beforme becoming a faculty member: Does it bring benefits for the scholarly enterprise? *Higher Education*. 58: 689–721.

Horta, H., and Santos, J. M. (2016). The impact of publishing during PhD studies on career research publication, visibility, and collaborations. *Research in Higher Education*. 57(1): 28–50.

Horta, H., and Yudkevich, M. (2016). The role of academic inbreeding in developing higher education systems: Challenges and possible solutions. *Technological Forecasting and Social Change*. 113: 363–372.

Huang, F., Finkelstein, M., and Rostan, M. (Eds.). (2014). *The internationalization of the academy. Changes, realities and prospects*. Dordrecht: Springer.

Huisman, J. (1998). Differentiation and diversity in higher education systems. *Higher Education: Handbook of Theory and Research*. XIII: 75–110.

Huisman, J. (2009). Coming to terms with governance in higher education. In: J. Huisman (Ed.), *International perspectives on the governance of higher education: Alternative frameworks for coordination*. London and New York: Routledge, 1–9.

Huisman, J. (2017). Higher education institutions. Landscape designers or contrived organizations? In: P. Scott, J. Gallacher, and G. Perry (Eds.), *New languages and landscapes in higher education*. Oxford: Oxford University Press, 188–203.

Huisman, J., de Weert, E., and Bartelse, J. (2002). Academic careers from a European perspective: The declining desirability of the faculty position. *The Journal of Higher Education*. 73(1): 141–160.

Huisman, J., Maassen, P. A. M., and Neave, G. R. (Eds.). (2001). *Higher education and the nation state: The international dimension of higher education*. Amsterdam; New York: Pergamon.

Huisman, J., de Boer, H., Dill, D. D, and Souto-Otero (Eds.). (2015). *The Palgrave international handbook of higher education policy and governance*. New York: Palgrave.

Hüther, O., and Krücken, G. (2018). *Higher education in Germany—Recent developments in an international perspective*. Dordrecht: Springer.

Janger, J., and Nowotny, K. (2016). Job choice in academia. *Research Policy*. 45(8): 1672–1683.

Jeong, S., Choi, J. Y., and Kim, J.-Y. (2011). The determinants of research collaboration modes: Exploring the effects of research and researcher characteristics on co-authorship. *Scientometrics*. 89: 967–983.

Jeong, S., Choi, J. Y., and Kim, J.-Y. (2014). On the drivers of international collaboration: The impact of informal communication, motivation, and research resources. *Science and Public Policy*. 41(4): 520–531.

Johnson, D. R. (2017). *A fractured profession. Commercialism and conflict in academic science*. Baltimore: Johns Hopkins University Press.

Jones, G. A., Gopaul, B., Weinrib, J., Metcalfe, A. S., Fisher, D., Gingras, Y., and Rubenson, K. (2014). Teaching, research, and the Canadian professoriate. In: J. C. Shin, A. Arimoto, W. K. Cummings, and U. Teichler (Eds.), *Teaching and research in contemporary higher education*. Dordrecht: Springer Netherlands, 335–356.

Jongbloed, B., and Lepori, B. (2015). The funding of research in higher education: Mixed models and mixed results. In: J. Huisman, H. de Boer, D. Dill, and D. Souto-Otero (Eds.), *The Palgrave international handbook of higher education policy and governance*. New York: Palgrave, 439–462.

Jung, J. (2014). Research productivity by career stage among Korean academics. *Tertiary Education and Management*. 20(2): 85–105.

Jung, J. (2015). Gender differences in research scholarship among academics: An international comparative perspective. In: W. K. Cummings and U. Teichler (Eds.), *The relevance of acadmeic work in comparative perspective*. Dordrecht: Springer, 163–178.

Jung, J., Horta, H., and Yonezawa, A. (2018). Introduction: higher education research as a field of study in Asia. In: J. Jung, H. Horta, and A. Yonezawa (Eds.), *Researching higher education in Asia. History, development and future*. Dordrecht: Springer, 1–13.

Jung, J., Kooij, R., and Teichler, U. (2014). Internationalization and the new generation of academics. In: F. Huang, M. Finkelstein, and M. Rostan (Eds.), *The internationalization of the academy*. Dordrecht: Springer, 207–236.

Katz, D. A. (1973). Faculty salaries, promotions, and productivity at a large university. *The American Economic Review*. 63(3): 469–477.

Katz, J. S., and Martin, B. R. (1997). What is research collaboration? *Research Policy*. 26(1): 1–18.

Kehm, B. M. (2009). Doctoral education: Pressures for change and modernisation. In: J. Enders and E. de Weert (Eds.), *The changing face of academic life*. London: Palgrave Macmillan, 155–170.

Kehm, B. M., and Teichler, U. (Eds.). (2013). *The academic profession in Europe: New tasks and new challenges*. Dordrecht: Springer.

Kelchtermans, S., and Veugelers, R. (2013). Top research productivity and its persistence: Gender as a double-edged sword. *Review of Economics and Statistics*. 95(1): 273–285.

Kezar, A. J. (2001). *Understanding and facilitating organizational change in the 21st century: Recent research and conceptualizations*. San Francisco, CA: Jossey-Bass.

Kezar, A. J., and Sam, C. (2010). *Non-tenure-track faculty in higher education: Theories and tensions*. San Francisco, CA: Jossey-Bass.

Kiewra, K. A. (1994). Research news and comment: A slice of advice. *Educational Researcher*. 23(3): 31–33.

Kiewra, K. A., and Creswell, J. W. (2000). Conversations with three highly productive educational psychologists: Richard Anderson, Richard Mayer, and Michael Pressley. *Educational Psychology Review.* 12(1): 135–161.

Knight, J. (2010). Internationalization and the competitiveness agenda. In: L. M. Portnoi, V. D. Rust, and S. S. Bagley (Eds.), *Higher education, policy, and the global competition phenomenon.* New York: Palgrave Macmillan, 205–218.

Knight, J. (2012). Concepts, rationales, and interpretive frameworks in the internationalization of higher education. In: *The SAGE handbook of international higher education.* Thousand Oaks, CA: SAGE Publications, 27–42.

Kogan, M. and Teichler, U. (2007). Key challenges to the academic profession and its interface with management: Some introductory thoughts. In: M. Kogan and U. Teichler (Eds.), *Key challenges to the academic profession.* Paris and Kassel: INCHER, 9–18.

Konrad, A. M., and Pfeffer, J. (1990). Do you get what you deserve? Factors affecting the relationship between productivity and pay. *Administrative Science Quarterly.* 35(2): 258.

Kosmützky, A. (2015). In defence of international comparative studies. On the analytical and explanatory power of the nation state in international comparative higher education research. *European Journal of Higher Education.* 5(4): 354–370.

Kosmützky, A. (2018). A two-sided medal: On the complexity of international comparative and collaborative team research. *Higher Education Quarterly.* 2018: 1–18.

Krücken, G., A. Kosmützky, M., and Torka, M. (Eds.). (2007). *Towards a multiversity? Universities between global trends and national traditions.* Bielefeld: Transcript Verlag.

Kulczycki, E. (2017). Assessing publications through a bibliometric indicator: The case of comprehensive evaluation of scientific units in Poland. *Research Evaluation.* 26(1), 41–52.

Kulczycki, E., Korzeń, M., and Korytkowski, P. (2017). Toward an excellence-based research funding system: Evidence from Poland. *Journal of Informetrics.* 11(1): 282–298.

Kwiek, M. (2006). *The university and the state. A study into global transformations.* Frankfurt and New York: Peter Lang.

Kwiek, M. (2012). Changing higher education policies: From the deinstitutionalization to the reinstitutionalization of the research mission in Polish universities. *Science and Public Policy.* 35(5): 641–654.

Kwiek, M. (2013a). From system expansion to system contraction: Access to higher education in Poland. *Comparative Education Review.* 56(3): 553–576.

Kwiek, M. (2013b). *Knowledge production in European universities. States, markets, and academic entrepreneurialism.* Frankfurt and New York: Peter Lang.

Kwiek, M. (2015a). The internationalization of research in Europe. A quantitative study of 11 national systems from a micro-level perspective. *Journal of Studies in International Education,* 19(2): 341–359.

Kwiek, M. (2015b). The unfading power of collegiality? University governance in Poland in a European comparative and quantitative perspective. *International Journal of Educational Development.* 43: 77–89.

Kwiek, M. (2015c). Academic generations and academic work: Patterns of attitudes, behaviors and research productivity of Polish academics after 1989'. *Studies in Higher Education.* 40(8): 1354–1376.

Kwiek, M. (2016a). The European research elite: A cross-national study of highly productive academics across 11 European systems. *Higher Education,* 71(3): 379–397.

Kwiek, M. (2016b). From privatization (of the expansion era) to de-privatization (of the contraction era). A national counter-trend in a global context. In S. Slaughter and

B. J. Taylor (Eds.), *Higher education, stratification, and workforce development. Competitive advantage in Europe, the US and Canada* (pp. 311–329). Dordrecht: Springer.

Kwiek, M. (2017a). A generational divide in the Polish academic profession. A mixed quantitative and qualitative approach. *European Educational Research Journal.* 17: 1–26.

Kwiek, M. (2017b). International research collaboration and international research orientation: Comparative findings about European academics. *Journal of Studies in International Education.* On-line first. 1–25. http://journals.sagepub.com/doi/10.1177/1028315317747084.

Kwiek, M. (2017c). Higher education, welfare states and austerity: Pressures on competing public institutions. In: J. Nixon (Ed.), *Higher education in austerity Europe.* London: Bloomsbury. 33–45.

Kwiek, M. (2017d). De-privatization in higher education: A conceptual approach. *Higher Education.* 74(2). 259–281.

Kwiek, M. (2018a). Academic top earners. Research productivity, prestige generation and salary patterns in European universities. *Science and Public Policy.* 45(1). 1–13.

Kwiek, M. (2018b). High research productivity in vertically undifferentiated higher education systems: who are the top performers? *Scientometrics.* 115(1). 415–462.

Kwiek, M. (2018c). The robust privateness and publicness of higher education: Expansion through privatization in Poland. In: D. Palfreyman, T. Tapper, and S. Thomas (Eds.), *Towards the private funding of higher education. Ideological and political struggles.* New York: Routledge, 90–111.

Kwiek, M. (2018d). Building a New Society and Economy: High Participation Higher Education in Poland. In: B. Cantwell, S. Marginson, and A. Smolentseva (Eds.), *High Participation Systems of Higher Education.* Oxford: Oxford University Press, 334–357.

Kwiek, M., and Antonowicz, D. (2013). Academic work, working conditions and job satisfaction. In: U. Teichler and E. A. Höhle (Eds.), *The work situation of the academic profession in Europe: Findings of survey in twelve countries.* Dordrecht: Springer, 37–53.

Kwiek, M. and Szadkowski, K. (2018). Higher education systems and institutions, Poland. In J. C. Shin and P. Teixeira (Eds.), *Encyclopedia of international higher education systems and institutions.* 1–9.

Kyvik, S. (1989). Productivity differences fields of learning, and Lotka's law. *Scientometrics.* Vol. 15(3–4). 205–214.

Kyvik, S. (1990). Age and scientific productivity. Differences between fields of learning. *Higher Education.* 19(1). 37–55.

Kyvik, S., and Aksnes, D. W. (2015). Explaining the increase in publication productivity among academic staff: A generational perspective. *Studies in Higher Education.* 40(8). 1438–1453.

Kyvik, S., and Larsen, I. M. (1997). The exchange of knowledge: A small country in the international research community. *Science Communication.* 18(3). 238–264.

Kyvik, S., and Olsen, T. B. (2008). Does the aging of tenured academic staff affect the research performance of universities? *Scientometrics.* 76(3). 439–455.

Landry, R., and Amara, N. (1998). The impact of transaction costs on the institutional structuration of collaborative academic research. *Research Policy.* 27(9). 901–913.

Laudel, G. (2002). What do we measure by co-authorships? *Research Evaluation.* 11(1). 3–15.

Lave, C. A., and March, J. G. (1993). *An introduction to models in the social sciences.* Lanham, MD: University Press of America.

Lazarsfeld, P. F., and Thielens, W. (1958). *The academic mind. Social scientists in a time of crisis.* Glencoe, IL: The Free Press of Glencoe, Illinois.

Leathwood, C., and Read, B. (2009). *Gender and the changing face of higher education: A feminized future?* Maidenhead, UK: Open University Press.

Lee, S., and Bozeman, B. (2005). The impact of research collaboration on scientific productivity. *Social Studies of Science.* 35(5). 673–702.

Leišyte, L., and Dee, J. R. (2012). Understanding academic work in a changing institutional environment. In: J. C. Smart and M. B. Paulsen (Eds.), *Higher education: Handbook of theory and research.* Dordrecht: Springer Netherlands, vol. 27, 123–206.

Leišyte, L., and Hosch-Dayican, B. (2017). Gender and academic work at a Dutch University. In: H. Eggins (Ed.), *The changing role of women in higher education. Academic and leadership issues.* Dordrecht: Springer, 95–117.

Levin, S. G., and Stephan, P. E. (1989). Age and research productivity of academic scientists. *Research in Higher Education.* 30(5). 531–549.

Levin, S. G., and Stephan, P. E. (1991). Research productivity over the life cycle: Evidence for academic scientists. *The American Economic Review.* 81(1). 114–132.

Levy, D. C. (2018). Global private higher education: an empirical profile of its size and geographical shape. *Higher Education.* On-line first: 30 January 2018, https://link.springer.com/article/10.1007/s10734-018-0233-6.

Lewis, J. M. (2013). *Academic governance: Disciplines and policy.* New York: Routledge.

Lewis, J. M., Ross, S., and Holden, T. (2012). The how and why of academic collaboration: Disciplinary differences and policy implications. *Higher Education.* 64(5). 693–708.

Leydesdorff, L. (2001). *The challenge of scientometrics: The development, measurement, and self-organization of scientific communications.* Parkland, IL: Universal Publ, 2nd ed.

Locke, W., Cummings, W. K., and Fisher, D. (Eds.). (2011). *Changing governance and management in higher education. the perspectives of the academy.* Dordrecht: Springer.

Lotka, A. J. (1926). The frequency distribution of scientific productivity. *Journal of the Washington Academy of Sciences.* 16(12). 317–323.

Luukkonen, T., Persson, O., and Sivertsen, G. (1992). Understanding patterns of international scientific collaboration. *Science, Technology, & Human Values.* 17(1). 101–126.

Maassen, P. A. M., and Olsen, J. P. (2007). *University dynamics and European integration.* Dordrecht: Springer.

Machado-Taylor, M. de L., Soares, V. M., and Teichler, U. (Eds.). (2017). *Challenges and options: The academic profession in Europe.* Dordrecht: Springer.

Magalhães, A. M., and Amaral, A. (2009). Mapping out discourses on higher education governance. In: J. Huisman (Ed.), *International perspectives on the governance of higher education: Alternative frameworks for coordination.* New York: Routledge, 182–197.

Manning, K. (2013). *Organizational theory in higher education.* London: Routledge.

March, J. G., and Olsen, J. P. (1989). *Rediscovering institutions: The organizational basis of politics.* New York: The Free Press.

Marginson, S. (1991). Academic salaries: Will award restructuring make a difference? *Journal of Tertiary Education Administration.* 13(1): 19–44.

Marginson, S. (2009). The academic professions in the global era. In: J. Enders and E. de Weert (Eds.), *The changing face of academic life. Analytical and comparative perspectives.* New York: Palgrave Macmillan, 96–115.

Marginson, S. (2014). University research: The social contribution of university research. In: J. C. Shin and U. Teichler (Eds.), *The future of the post-massified university at the crossroads*. Cham: Springer International Publishing, 101–118.

Marginson, S. (2016a). The worldwide trend to high participation higher education: Dynamics of social stratification in inclusive systems. *Higher Education*. 72: 413–434.

Marginson, S. (2016b). High participation systems of higher education. *The Journal of Higher Education*. 87(2): 243–271.

Marginson, S. (2016c). Global stratification in higher education. In S. Slaughter and B. J. Taylor (Eds.), *Higher education, stratification, and workforce development*. Dordrecht: Springer, 13–34.

Marini, G., and Reale, E. (2016). How does collegiality survive managerially led universities? Evidence from a European survey. *European Journal of Higher Education*. 6(2): 111–127.

Marquina, M., and Ferreiro, M. (2015). The academic profession: The dynamics of emerging countries. In: W. K. Cummings and U. Teichler (Eds.), *The relevance of academic work in comparative perspective*. Cham: Springer International Publishing, 179–192.

Marquina, M., and Jones, G. A. (2015). Generational change and academic work: an introduction. *Studies in Higher Education*. 40(8). 1349–1353.

Marquina, M., Yuni, J., and Ferreiro, M. (2015). Generational change in the Argentine academic profession through the analysis of 'life courses.' *Studies in Higher Education*. 40(8): 1392–1405.

Marsh, H. W., and Hattie, J. (2002). The relation between research productivity and teaching effectiveness: Complementary, antagonistic, or independent constructs? *The Journal of Higher Education*. 73(5): 603–641.

Martin, B., and Etzkowitz, H. (2000). The origin and evolution of the university species. *Organisation of Mode*. (2).

Martínez, R. S., Floyd, R. G., and Erichsen, L. W. (2011). Strategies and attributes of highly productive scholars and contributors to the school psychology literature: Recommendations for increasing scholarly productivity. *Journal of School Psychology*. 49(6). 691–720.

Mayrath, M. C. (2008) Attributions of productive authors in educational psychology journals. *Educational Psychology Review*. 20(1): 41–56.

McLaughlin, G. W., Montgomery, J. R., and Mahan, B. T. (1979). Pay, rank, and growing old with more of each. *Research in Higher Education*. 11(1): 23–35.

McNay, I. (1995). From the collegial academy to corporate enterprise: The changing cultures of universities. In: T. Schuller (Ed.), *The changing university?* Buckingham: SRHE/Open University Press, 105–115.

Melguizo, T., and Strober, M. H. (2007). Faculty salaries and the maximization of prestige. *Research in Higher Education*. 48(6): 633–668.

Melin, G. (2000). Pragmatism and self-organization. *Research Policy*. 29(1): 31–40.

Melin, G., and Persson, O. (1996). Studying research collaboration using co-authorships. *Scientometrics*. 36(3). 363–377.

Merton, R. K. (1968). The Matthew Effect in science: The reward and communication systems of science are considered. *Science*. 159(3810): 56–63.

Merton, R. K. (1973). *The sociology of science: Theoretical and empirical investigations*. Chicago, IL: University of Chicago Press.

Mesch, G. (2012). E-mail surveys. In: L. Gideon (Ed.), *Handbook of Survey Methodology for the Social Sciences*. Dordrecht: Springer. 313–326.

Millett, J. D. (1962). *The academic community. An essay on organization*. New York: McGraw-Hill.

Moed, H. F. (2005). *Citation analysis in research evaluation*. Dordrecht: Springer.

Moore, W. J., Newman, R. J, and Turnbull, G. K. (2011). Reputational capital and academic pay. *Economic Inquiry*. 39(4): 663–671.

Morgan, G. (1986). *Images of organization*. New York: SAGE Publications.

Musselin, C. (2004). *The long march of French universities*. New York: RoutledgeFalmer.

Musselin, C. (2010). *The market for academics*. New York: Routledge.

Musselin, C., and Enders, J. (2008). Back to the future? The academic professions in the 21st century. In: OECD, *Higher Education to 2030, Volume 1, Demography*. OECD Publishing, 125–150.

Musselin, C., and Teixeira, P. N. (Eds.). (2014). *Reforming higher education*. Dordrecht: Springer.

Nanbu, H., and Amano, T. (2015). Labor conditions. In: A. Arimoto, W. K. Cummings, F. Huang, and J. C. Shin (Eds.), *The changing academic profession in Japan*. Cham: Springer International Publishing, 119–133.

Narin, F., and Whitlow, E. S. (1990). *Measurement of scientific cooperation and coauthorship in CEC-related areas of science*. Luxembourg: Office for Official Publications of the EC.

Neave, G., and Rhoades, G. (1987). The academic estate in Western Europe. In: B. R. Clark (Ed.), *The academic profession: National, disciplinary, and institutional settings*. Berkeley, CA: University of California Press, 211–270.

Neave, G. R., and Vught, F. van, (Eds.). (1991). *Prometheus bound: The changing relationship between government and higher education in Western Europe*. Oxford: New York: Pergamon Press.

Neave, G. R., and Vught, F. van, (Eds.). (1994). *Government and higher education relationships across three continents: The winds of change*. Oxford; Tarrytown, NY: Published for the IAU Press, Pergamon.

Nixon, J. (Ed.). (2017), *Higher education in austerity Europe*. London: Bloomsbury.

O'Boyle Jr., E., and Aguinis, H. (2012). The best and the rest: Revisiting the norm of normality of individual performance. *Personnel Psychology*. 65(1): 79–119.

OECD (2016). *Education at a glance. OECD indicators*. Paris: OECD.

OECD (2017). *Main science and technology indicators*. Paris: OECD.

Olsen, J. P. (2007). The institutional dynamics of the European university. In: P. Maassen and J. P. Olsen (Eds.), *University dynamics and European integration*. Dordrecht: Springer, 25–54.

Ortega y Gasset, J. (1993). *The revolt of the masses*. New York: W.W. Norton.

Paradeise, C., Reale, E., and Goastellec, G. (2009). A comparative approach to higher education reforms in Western European countries. In: C. Paradeise, E. Reale, I. Bleiklie, and E. Ferlie, (Eds.), *University governance. Western European comparative perspectives*. Dordrecht: Springer. 197–225.

Paradeise, C., Reale, E., Bleiklie, I., and Ferlie, E. (Eds.). (2009). *University governance. Western European comparative perspectives*. Dordrecht: Springer.

Patterson-Hazley, M., and Kiewra, K. A. (2013). Conversations with four highly productive educational psychologists: Patricia Alexander, Richard Mayer, Dale Schunk, and Barry Zimmerman. *Educational Psychology Review*. 25(1): 19–45.

Perianes-Rodriguez, A., and Ruiz-Castillo, J. (2015). Within- and between-department variability in individual productivity: The case of economics. *Scientometrics*. 102(2): 1497–1520.

Perkin, H. (1969). *Key profession. The history of the association of university teachers.* London: Routledge & Kegan Paul.

Pinheiro, R., and Antonowicz, D. (2015). Opening the gates or coping with the flow? Governing access to higher education in Northern and Central Europe. *Higher Education.* 70(3): 299–313.

Pinheiro, R., Benneworth, P., and Jones, G. A. (Eds.). (2012). *Universities and regional development: a critical assessment of tensions and contradictions.* London: New York: Routledge.

Piro, F. N., Rørstad, K., and Aksnes, D. W. (2016). How does prolific professors influence on the citation impact of their university departments? *Scientometrics.* 107(3): 941–961.

Porter, S. R., and Umbach, P. D. (2001). Analyzing faculty workload data using multilevel modeling. *Research in Higher Education.* 42(2): 171–196.

Porter, C. O. L. H., Itir Gogus, C., and Yu, R. C- F. (2010). When does teamwork translate into improved team performance? A resource allocation perspective. *Small Group Research.* 41(2): 221–248.

Postiglione, G. A., and Jung, J. (2013). World-class university and Asia's top tier researchers. In: Q. Wang, Y. Cheng, and N. C. Liu (Eds.), *Building world-class universities.* Rotterdam: SensePublishers, 161–179.

Postiglione, G. A., and Jung, J. (Eds.). (2017). *The changing academic profession in Hong Kong.* Dordrecht: Springer.

Price, D. J. de S. (1963). *Little science, big science.* New York: Columbia University Press.

Print, M., and Hattie, J. (1997). Measuring quality in universities: An approach to weighting research productivity. *Higher Education.* 33(4): 453–469.

Prpić, K. (1996). Characteristics and determinants of eminent scientists' productivity. *Scientometrics.* 36(2): 185–206.

Ramsden, P. (1994). Describing and explaining research productivity. *Higher Education.* 28(2): 207–226.

Ramsden, P., and Moses, I. (1994). Associations between research and teaching in Australian higher education. *Higher Education.* 23(3): 273–295.

Rhoades, G. (1992). 'Governance' Models. In: B. R. Clark and G. Neave (Eds.), *The encyclopedia of higher education. Vol. 2 analytical perspectives.* Oxford. Pergamon, 1376–1384.

Rhoades, G., Kiyama, J. M., McCormick, R., and Quiroz, M. (2008). Local cosmopolitans and cosmopolitan locals: New models of professionals in the academy. *The Review of Higher Education.* 31(2): 209–235.

RIHE (2008). *The changing academic profession over 1992–2007: International, comparative, and quantitative perspective.* Hiroshima: RIHE.

Rigney, D. (2010). *The Matthew Effect. How advantage begets further advantage.* New York: Columbia University Press.

Roach, M., and Sauermann, H. (2010). A taste for science? PhD scientists' academic orientation and self-selection into research careers in industry. *Research Policy.* 39(3): 422–434.

Rørstad, K., and Aksnes, D. W. (2015). Publication rate expressed by age, gender and academic position—A large-scale analysis of Norwegian academic staff. *Journal of Informetrics.* 9(2): 317–333.

Rosen, S. (1981). The economics of superstars. *The American Economic Review.* 71(5): 845–858.

Rostan, M. (2012). Beyond physical mobility. In: M. Vukasović, P. Maassen, M. Nerland, B. Stensaker, R. Pinheiro, and A. Vabø (Eds.), *Effects of higher education reforms*. Rotterdam: SensePublishers, 239–258.

Rostan, M., and Ceravolo, F. A. (2015). The internationalisation of the academy: Convergence and divergence across disciplines. *European Review*. 23(S1): 38–54.

Rostan, M., Ceravolo, F. A., and Metcalfe, A. S. (2014). The internationalization of research. In: F. Huang, M. Finkelstein, and M. Rostan (Eds.), *The internationalization of the academy*. Dordrecht: Springer Netherlands, 119–143.

Rostan, M., Finkelstein, M., and Huang, F. (2014). Concepts and methods. In: F. Huang, M. Finkelstein, and M. Rostan (Eds.), *The internationalization of the academy*. Dordrecht: Springer Netherlands, 23–36.

Rousseau, R., Egghe, L., and Guns, R. (2018). *Becoming metric-wise. A bibliometric guide for researchers*. Cambridge: Chandos Publishing.

Rüegg, W. (Ed.). (2004). *Universities in the nineteenth and early twentieth centuries (1800–1945)*. Cambridge; New York: Cambridge University Press.

Ruiz-Castillo, J., and Costas, R. (2014). The skewness of scientific productivity. *Journal of Informetrics*. 8(4): 917–934.

Rumbley, L. E., Pacheco, I. F., and Altbach, P. G. (2008). *International comparison of academic Salaries: An exploratory study*. Boston, MA: Center for International Higher Education.

Ryder, N. B. (1965). The cohort as a concept in the study of social change. *American Sociological Review*. 30: 843–861.

Sandström, U., and van den Besselaar, P. (2016). Quantity and/or quality? The importance of publishing many papers. *PLOS ONE*. 11(11): 1–16.

Santiago, R., Carvalho, T., and Cardoso, S. (2015). Portuguese academics' perceptions of higher education institutions' governance and management: A generational perspective. *Studies in Higher Education*. 40(8): 1471–1484.

Santos, J. M., Horta, H., and Heitor, M. (2016). Too many PhDs? An invalid argument for countries developing their scientific and academic systems: The case of Portugal. *Technological Forecasting and Social Change*. 113: 352–362.

Schimank, U., and Winnes, M. (2000). Beyond Humboldt? The relationship between teaching and research in European university systems, *Science and Public Policy*. 27(6): 397–408.

Schuster, J. (1992). Academic Labor Markets. In: B. R. Clark and G. Neave (Eds.), *The encyclopedia of higher education. Vol. 3. Analytical perspectives*. Oxford: Pergamon Press, 1537–1547.

Schuster, J. H., and Finkelstein, M. J. (2008). *The American faculty: The restructuring of academic work and careers*. Baltimore, MD: Johns Hopkins University Press.

Seglen, P. O. (1992). The skewness of science. *Journal of the American Society for Information Science*. 43(9): 628–638.

Serenko, A., Cox, R. A. K., Bontis, N., and Booker, L. D. (2011). The superstar phenomenon in the knowledge management and intellectual capital academic discipline. *Journal of Informetrics*. 5(3): 333–345.

Shattock, M. (2006). *Managing good governance in higher education*. Maidenhead, UK: Open University Press.

Shen, H., and Xiong, J. (2015). An empirical study on impact factors of faculty remuneration across 18 higher education systems. In: U. Teichler and W. K. Cummings (Eds.), *Forming, recruiting and managing the academic profession*. Cham: Springer International Publishing, 163–185.

Shin, J. C. (2014). The university as an institution of higher learning: Evolution or devolution? In: J. C. Shin and U. Teichler (Eds.), *The future of the post-massified university at the crossroads*. Cham: Springer International Publishing, 13–27.

Shin, J. C., and Cummings, W. K. (2010). Multilevel analysis of academic publishing across disciplines: Research preference, collaboration, and time on research. *Scientometrics*. 85(2): 581–594.

Shin, J. C., and Teichler, U. (Eds.). (2014). *The future of the post-massified university at the crossroads. Restructuring systems and functions*. Dordrecht: Springer.

Shin, J. C., Jung, J., and Kim, Y. (2014a). Teaching and research of korean academics across career stages. In: J. C. Shin, A. Arimoto, W. K. Cummings, and U. Teichler (Eds.), *Teaching and research in contemporary higher education*. Dordrecht: Springer Netherlands, 177–196.

Shin, J. C., Arimoto, A., Cummings, W. K., and Teichler, U. (Eds.). (2014b). *Teaching and research in contemporary higher education. Systems, activities and rewards*. Dordrecht: Springer.

Shin, J. C., Kim, Y., Lim, H., Shim, B., and Choi, Y. (2015). The 'sandwich generation' in Korean academe: Between traditional academic authority and meritocratic culture. *Studies in Higher Education*. 40(8): 1406–1422.

Sidiropoulos, A., Gogoglou, A., Katsaros, D., and Manolopoulos, Y. (2016). Gazing at the skyline for star scientists. *Journal of Informetrics*. 10(3): 789–813.

Slaughter, S., and Cantwell, B. (2012). Transatlantic moves to the market: the United States and the European Union. *Higher Education*. 63: 583–606.

Slaughter, S., and Leslie, L. L. (1997). *Academic capitalism: Politics. policies, and the entrepreneurial university*. Baltimore, MD: Johns Hopkins University Press.

Slaughter, S., and Rhoades, G. (2004). *Academic capitalism and the new economy. Markets, state, and higher education*. Baltimore, MD: Johns Hopkins University Press.

Slaughter, S., and Taylor, B. R. (Eds.). (2016). *Higher education, stratification, and workforce development. Competitive advantage in Europe, the US and Canada*. Dordrecht: Springer, 311–329.

Smeby, J.-C., and Gornitzka, Å. (2008). All cosmopolitans now? In: Å. Gornitzka and L. Langfeldt (Eds.), *Borderless knowledge*. Dordrecht: Springer Netherlands, 22: 37–50.

Smeby, J.-C., and Trondal, J. (2005). Globalisation or Europeanisation? International contact among university staff. *Higher Education*. 49(4): 449–466.

Smeby, J.-C., and Try, S. (2005). Departmental contexts and faculty research activity in Norway. *Research in Higher Education*. 46(6): 593–619.

Spector, P. E. (1981). *Research designs*. Beverly Hills, CA: Sage Publications.

Stephan, P. E. (1996). The economics of science. *Journal of Economic Literature*. 34(3): 1199–1235.

Stephan, P. E. (2010). The economics of science. Funding for research. *SSRN Electronic Journal*.

Stephan, P. E. (2012). Pay inequality makes for better science. *Scientific American*. 307(4).

Stephan, P. E. (2015). *How economics shapes science*. Boston, MA: Harvard University Press.

Stephan, P. E., and Levin, S. G. (1991). Inequality in scientific performance: Adjustment for attribution and journal impact. *Social Studies of Science*. 21(2): 351–368.

Stephan, P. E., and Levin, S. G. (1992). *Striking the mother lode in science: The importance of age, place, and time*. New York: Oxford University Press.

Stern, S. (2004). Do scientists pay to be scientists? *Management Science*. 50(6): 835–853.

Stoop, I. (2012). Unit non-response due to refusal. In: L. Gideon (Ed.), *Handbook of survey methodology for the social sciences*. New York: Springer, 121–147.

Szadkowski, K. (2016). The university of the common: Beyond the contradictions of higher education subsumed under capital. In: M. Izak, M. Kostera, and M. Zawadzki (Eds.), *The future of university education*, Basingstoke, UK: Palgrave, 39–62.

Teichler, U. (1996). Comparative higher education: Potentials and limits. *Higher Education*. 32(4): 431–465.

Teichler, U. (2006). *The formative years of scholars*. London: Portland Press.

Teichler, U. (2014a). Opportunities and problems of comparative higher education research: The daily life of research. *Higher Education*. 67(4): 393–408.

Teichler, U. (2014b). Teaching and research in Germany: The notions of university professors. In: J. C. Shin, A. Arimoto, W. K. Cummings, and U. Teichler (Eds.), *Teaching and research in contemporary higher education*. Dordrecht: Springer Netherlands, 61–87.

Teichler, U. (2014c). Possible futures for higher education: Challenges for higher education research. In: J. C. Shin and U. Teichler (Eds.), *The future of the post-massified university at the crossroads. Restructuring systems and functions*. Dordrecht: Springer, 145–166.

Teichler, U., and Cummings, W. K. (Eds.). (2015). *Forming, recruiting and managing the academic profession*. Dordrecht: Springer.

Teichler, U., and Höhle, E. A. (Eds.). (2013). *The work situation of the academic profession in Europe: Findings of a survey in twelve countries*. Dordrecht: Springer.

Teichler, U., and Kogan, M. (2007). Key challenges to the academic profession and its interface with management: Some introductory thoughts. In: M. Kogan and U. Teichler (Eds.), *Key challenges to the academic profession*. Kassel: Jenior, 9–18.

Teichler, U., Arimoto, A., and Cummings, W. K. (2013). *The changing academic profession. Major findings of a comparative survey*. Dordrecht: Springer.

Teixeira, P. N. (2011). The changing public–private mix in higher education: Analysing Portugal's apparent exceptionalism. In: G. Neave and A. Amaral (Eds.), *Higher education in Portugal 1974–2009*. Dordrecht: Springer Netherlands, 307–328.

Teixeira, P. N. (2017). A bastion of elitism or an emerging knowledge proletariat? Some reflections about academic careers with an economic slant. In: M. L. Machado-Taylor, V. M. Soares, and U. Teichler (Eds.), *Challenges and options: The academic profession in Europe*. Cham: Springer, 29–47.

Teodorescu, D. (2000). Correlates of faculty publication productivity: A cross-national analysis. *Higher Education*. 39(2): 201–222.

Thursby, M., Thursby, J., and Gupta-Mukherjee, S. (2007). Are there real effects of licensing on academic research? A life cycle view. *Journal of Economic Behavior & Organization*. 63(4): 577–598.

Tight, M. (2012). *Researching higher education*. Maidenhead, Berkshire: Society for Research into Higher Education and Open University Press, McGraw Hill, 2nd. ed.

Toutkoushian, R. K., and Paulsen, M. B. (2016). *Economics of higher education*. Dordrecht: Springer Netherlands.

Toutkoushian, R. K., Porter, S. R., Danielson, C., and Hollis, P. R. (2003). Using publications counts to measure an institution's research productivity. *Research in Higher Education*. 44(2): 121–148.

Vabø, A., Padilla-González, L. E., Waagene, E., and Næss, T. (2014). Gender and faculty internationalization. In: F. Huang, M. Finkelstein, and M. Rostan (Eds.), *The internationalization of the academy*. Dordrecht: Springer Netherlands, 183–205.

Vught, F. van, and Maassen, P. A. M. (1996). *Inside academia: New challenges for the academic profession.* Utrecht : De Tijdstroom.

Wagner, C. S. (2006). International collaboration in science and technology: Promises and pitfalls. In: L. Box and R. Engelhard (Eds.), *Science and technology policy for development: Dialogues at the interface [based on the rewarding exchanges that took place in a workshop entitled 'Providing Demand' held in Leiden in 2004].* London: Anthem Press, 165–176.

Wagner, C. S., and Leydesdorff, L. (2005). Network structure, self-organization, and the growth of international collaboration in science. *Research Policy.* 34(10): 1608–1618.

Wanner, R. A., Lewis, L. S., and Gregorio, D. I. (1981). Research productivity in academia: A comparative study of the sciences, social sciences and humanities. *Sociology of Education.* 54(4): 238.

Ward, M. E. (2001). The gender salary gap in British academia. *Applied Economics.* 33(13): 1669–1681.

Ward, M. E., and Sloane, P. J. (2000). Non-pecuniary advantages versus pecuniary disadvantages; Job satisfaction among male and female academics in Scottish universities. *Scottish Journal of Political Economy.* 47(3): 273–303.

Welch, A. R. (1997). The peripatetic professor: The internationalisation of the academic profession. *Higher Education.* 34(3): 323–345.

Whitley, R. (2000). *The intellectual and social organization of the sciences.* Oxford; New York: Oxford University Press, 2nd ed.

Williams, G. (2012). Some wicked questions from the dismal science. In: P. Temple (Ed.), *Universities in the knowledge economy: Higher education organisation and global change.* London and New York: Routledge.

Williams, G. L., Blackstone, T., and Metcalf, D. H. (1974). *The academic labour market: Economic and social aspects of a profession.* Amsterdam; New York: Elsevier.

Wilson, L. (1979). *American academics: Then and now.* New York: Oxford University Press.

Wilson, L. (1995). *The academic man: A study in the sociology of a profession.* New Brunswick, NJ: Transaction.

Wit, H. de. (2002). *Internationalization of higher education in the United States of America and Europe: A historical, comparative, and conceptual analysis.* Westport, CN: Greenwood Press.

Wolszczak-Derlacz, J., and Parteka, A. (2010). *Scientific productivity of public higher education institutions in Poland: A comperative bibliometric analysis.* Warsaw: Ernst & Young.

Xie, Y. (2014). 'Undemocracy': Inequalities in science. *Science.* 344(6186): 809–810.

Xie, Y., and Shauman, K. A. (2003). *Women in science: Career processes and outcomes.* Cambridge, MA: Harvard University Press.

Yair, G., Gueta, N., and Davidovitch, N. (2017). The law of limited excellence: Publication productivity of Israel Prize laureates in the life and exact sciences. *Scientometrics.* 113(1): 299–311.

Yin, Z., and Zhi, Q. (2017). Dancing with the academic elite: A promotion or hindrance of research production? *Scientometrics.* 110(1): 17–41.

Yudkevich, M. (2016). Academics and higher education expansion. In: J. C. Shin and P. Teixeira (Eds.), *Encyclopedia of international higher education systems and institutions.* Dordrecht: Springer. 1–3 (on-line first).

Yudkevich, M., Altbach, P. G., and Rumbley, L. (2015). *Young faculty in the twenty-first century: International perspectives.* Albany, NY: State University of New York.

Ziman, J. M. (1994). *Prometheus bound: Science in a dynamic steady state*. Cambridge; New York: Cambridge University Press.

Zuckerman, H. (1970). Stratification in American science. *Sociological Inquiry*. 40(2): 235–257.

Zuckerman, H. (1988). The sociology of science. In: N. J. Smelser (Ed.), *Handbook of sociology*. Newbury Park: Sage, 511–574.

Zuckerman, H. (1991). The careers of men and women scientists: A review of current research. In: H. Zuckerman, J. R. Cole, and J. T. Bruer (Eds.), *The outer circle: Women in the scientific community*. New York: W.W. Norton and Company.

Zuckerman, H. (1996). *Scientific elite: Nobel laureates in the United States*. New Brunswick, NJ: Transaction Publishers.

Index